ARABIC ASTRONOMY BEE-KEEPING BIOLOGY
ANISATION CALCULUS C ISTRY
COMMERCIAL CORRESPONDENC TO
OKING CRICKET DRAWING ON
ELECTRICITY IN THE HOUSE ELOCUTI ERY
ENGLISH RENASCENCE TO THE ROMANTIC REVIVAL ROMANTIC
EVERYDAY FRENCH TO EXPRESS YOURSELF FISHING TO FLY
SE BOOK GARDENING GAS IN THE HOUSE GEOGRAPHY OF
ONARY GERMAN GRAMMAR GERMAN PHRASE BOOK GOLF
GOOD FARM ACCOUNTING GOOD FARM CROPS GOOD FARMING
IT FARMING GOOD GRASSLAND GOOD AND HEALTHY ANIMALS
GOOD POULTRY KEEPING GOOD SHEEP FARMING GOOD SOIL
LE HINDUSTANI HISTORY ABRAHAM LINCOLN ALEXANDER THE
AU CONSTANTINE COOK CRANMER ERASMUS GLADSTONE AND
MILTON PERICLES PETER THE GREAT PUSHKIN RALEIGH RICHELIEU
ODROW EMENT
LIAN LETTER
ENGIN ANICS
ODERN ORING

. . . AND HE WILL BE YET WISER *Proverbs 9 9*

HILOSO HYSICS
PLUMBI UBLIC
RECKO SSIAN
ITS AND PURPOSE SOCCER SPANISH SPE AND
SW SWEDISH TEACHING THINKING TRIG METRY
BRI H RAILWAYS FOR BOYS CAMPING FOR BOYS AND GIRLS
FOR GIRLS MODELMAKING FOR BOYS NEEDLEWORK FOR GIRLS
OYS AND GIRLS SAILING AND SMALL BOATS FOR BOYS AND GIRLS
ORK FOR BOYS ADVERTISING & PUBLICITY ALGEBRA AMATEUR
NG BIOLOGY BOOK-KEEPING BRICKWORK BRINGING UP
TRY CHEMISTRY CHESS CHINESE COMMERCIAL ARITHMETIC
RAVELLING TO COMPOSE MUSIC CONSTRUCTIONAL DETAILS
G DUTCH DUTTON SPEEDWORDS ECONOMIC GEOGRAPHY
T EMBROIDERY ENGLISH GRAMMAR LITERARY APPRECIATION
VAL ROMANTIC REVIVAL VICTORIAN AGE CONTEMPORARY
FISHING TO FLY FREELANCE WRITING FRENCH FRENCH
USE GEOGRAPHY OF LIVING THINGS GEOLOGY GEOMETRY
SE BOOK GOLF GOOD CONTROL OF INSECT PESTS GOOD
ARM CROPS GOOD FARMING GOOD FARMING BY MACHINE
GOOD AND HEALTHY ANIMALS GOOD MARKET GARDENING
GOOD SHEEP FARMING GOOD SOIL GOOD ENGLISH GREEK
RY ABRAHAM LINCOLN ALEXANDER THE GREAT BOLIVAR BOTHA
RANMER ERASMUS GLADSTONE AND LIBERALISM HENRY V JOAN OF
T PUSHKIN RALEIGH RICHELIEU ROBESPIERRE THOMAS JEFFERSON
HOME NURSING HORSE MANAGEMENT HOUSEHOLD DOCTOR
RNALISM LATIN LAWN TENNIS LETTER WRITER MALAY
ONENTS WORKSHOP PRACTICE MECHANICS MECHANICAL
MORE GERMAN MOTHERCRAFT MOTORING MOTOR CYCLING
PHY PHYSICAL GEOGRAPHY PHYSICS PHYSIOLOGY PITMAN'S
ESE PSYCHOLOGY PUBLIC ADMINISTRATION PUBLIC SPEAKING

3/-

THE TEACH YOURSELF BOOKS
EDITED BY LEONARD CUTTS

BOOK-KEEPING

Uniform with this
Volume and in the same
Series

Teach Yourself Advertising and Publicity
Teach Yourself Banking
Teach Yourself Book-Keeping
Teach Yourself Business Organisation
Teach Yourself Commercial Art
Teach Yourself Commercial Correspondence
Teach Yourself Commercial Travelling
Teach Yourself Dutton Speedwords
Teach Yourself Economics
Teach Yourself Gregg Shorthand
The Teach Yourself Letter Writer
Teach Yourself Management
Teach Yourself Money
Teach Yourself Personal Efficiency
Teach Yourself Pitman's Shorthand
Teach Yourself Public Administration
The E.U.P. Ready Reckoner
Teach Yourself Salesmanship
Teach Yourself Secretarial Practice
Teach Yourself Typewriting

TEACH YOURSELF BOOK-KEEPING

An Introduction to Book-keeping and Business Methods

By
DONALD COUSINS
Chartered Accountant

ENGLISH UNIVERSITIES PRESS LTD.
LONDON

TO

H. C.

Originally published as "Elements of Book-keeping and Business Methods" 1938
First printed in this edition 1941
Reprinted 1950, 1951, 1954

Printed in Great Britain for the English Universities Press, Limited, by Richard Clay and Company, Ltd., Bungay, Suffolk

INTRODUCTION

I BELIEVE I am justified in offering this book in the " Teach Yourself " series, if only in an effort to correct the view, so widely and so mistakenly held, that the subject of Book-keeping is dull, and that its teaching must needs be unimaginative.

My aim has been to offer a guide to the beginner in the Business and Professional world which shall :

(*a*) Be readable and interesting ;

(*b*) Carefully avoid the error of treating the subject as though it were altogether unrelated to the ordinary routine of business life ;

(*c*) Adequately cover the usual examination syllabuses.

There are few walks of life wherein an understanding of the first principles of Book-keeping and Accounts can fail to be of some practical use.

To those beginning their studies in the Accountancy profession this volume will, I hope, give real inspiration and help, and provide a sound basis for the more advanced work that comes later.

To the business executive who may have little taste for the counting-house and records generally I hope it will give an insight into an indispensable business function.

Very largely, the Accountant, as such, is concerned with interpreting the Book-keeper's work and " pointing the moral," but it is from the Book-keeper's hands that he derives the necessary raw material.

In equal measure, the executive must be able to make full use of all the information which his book-keeping system provides, and it will be conceded that none can criticise who is totally unfamiliar with the way in which that system operates.

Doubts may be resolved, unspoken questions answered and weak points in an existing system shown up when a fresh pair of eyes is brought to bear ; the writer has on more than one occasion been asked by a business man :

"I wish you would tell me why both sides of a Balance Sheet add up to the same figure," or, "why does the stock in my Trading Account differ from the stock in the Balance Sheet?"

Many carefully graded exercises, for self-examination and the class-room alike, follow the individual chapters, and as an appendix there is a reprint of the Stage I papers of the Royal Society of Arts for the past seven years.

In conclusion, the writer has not been unmindful of the needs of the teacher, and has endeavoured to deal with each stage of the subject so as to facilitate class-room exposition.

DONALD COUSINS.

NOTE TO FOURTH EDITION

HAVING regard to the change in 1953 in the syllabus of the Stage 1—Elementary—examinations of the Royal Society of Arts I have, with their kind permission, substituted in this edition more recent papers of theirs, and these are followed by the fully worked paper of the July (1953) examination as held under the new regulations.

DONALD COUSINS.

CONTENTS

CHAP.		PAGE
I.	What is Book-keeping?	9
II.	The Business Transaction, Purchases and Sales	13
III.	Purchase and Sales Transactions, and the Ledger Accounts . . .	31
IV.	Cash Transactions	59
V.	The Bank Reconciliation . . .	79
VI.	Petty Cash, Etc.	89
VII.	The Debit and Credit Journal . .	95
VIII.	Writing Up the Books . . .	105
IX.	The Trial Balance	122
X.	Four-Column Trial Balance . .	128
XI.	What is Profit or Loss? . . .	134
XII.	The Revenue Account. . . . The Trading Account. The Profit and Loss Account. The Appropriation Account.	137
XIII.	The Balance Sheet	147
XIV.	Adjustments in the Final Accounts .	162
XV.	Depreciation	172
XVI.	Partnership	182
XVII.	The Criticism and Interpretation of Accounts	196

CHAP.		PAGE
XVIII.	Limited Companies, and the Companies Act, 1948	207
	Answers	222
	Appendix. Examination Papers—Royal Society of Arts	226
	Completely Worked R.S.A. Paper	259
	Index	265

CHAPTER I

WHAT IS BOOK-KEEPING?

Question. What is Book-keeping?

Answer. The process of correctly recording in Books of Account transactions in money, or money's worth.

Question. What are Books of Account?

Answer. The Ledger is the only Book of Account, so called because all the transactions, after being first recorded in subsidiary books, are afterwards grouped or summarised in **Accounts** in the Ledger.

Question. What is the difference between "money" and "money's worth" transactions?

Answer. If £5 is paid in cash as wages to a workman, this is a transaction in **money**; if I buy goods on credit from Smith value £100, it is a transaction in **money's worth.**

Question. Why should goods be bought on "credit"?

Answer. Almost all business dealings are conducted on a credit basis, that is, the supplier of goods, like Smith, is content to accept payment at some future date; the only exception is in the case of "ready money" transactions in the retail trade, like those of a private individual, who buys goods over the counter.

Question. How does the necessity for recording these transactions arise?

Answer. Even in the smallest business the proprietor or manager will want to have accurate and up-to-date information about how much he has bought and sold, how much money he has received and paid away in respect of his purchases and sales, and so on. In respect of their cash receipts and payments, even private individuals often find it convenient to have the same information.

You can imagine that with a very large business, chaos would quickly result without this information.

Question. So Book-keeping really involves analysing in some way or another these various transactions?

Answer. You should rather say, recording these transactions so as to permit of analysis, but in a systematic fashion, in some way that can be applied to all businesses, of whatever kind, and which is intelligible not only now, but at any future time.

Question. Do you mean by this "the Double Entry System of Book-keeping"?

Answer. Yes.

Question. What is its real meaning?

Answer. That just as every transaction involves at least two parties, so the record of the transaction should be made in the light of its twofold aspect.

Question. So it does not mean recording the same transaction twice?

Answer. No, not at all. Let me put it in this way. If I have bought goods value £100 from Smith on credit, the first part of the twofold aspect is that my business has received goods for the disposal of which my storekeeper, or some other person, is accountable; the second part of the twofold aspect is that Smith, my supplier, has become my creditor, and has a claim on me for £100.

Question. Would it be the same if you had bought the goods and paid for them at once, instead of getting credit?

Answer. Yes, that would be in this case a cash purchase. But instead of Smith, my banker or cashier would be my creditor, having paid money away for me. They then would have the claim on me for £100.

Question. I do not quite see how your cashier or your banker could be your creditor. The cashier would be a servant, dependent on a weekly or monthly salary.

Answer. What you say about the position of the cashier is very true, but in the first place, when you began business, you would entrust a sufficient sum of money to these people for which you would at the outset consider them as accountable or indebted to you. They would be your debtors. So if later they paid money away for you, such payments reduce their indebtedness which after all is just the same thing as saying they are your creditors to that extent, the position of the creditor being the reverse of that of debtor.

Question. What is the real advantage of the Double Entry System?

Answer. For the reason that every transaction can be looked at from its twofold aspect, the record made is complete instead of being partial only.

The practical advantage is that you put the whole of the facts on record. These are :—

(*a*) Your storekeeper is answerable for £100 worth of goods.
(*b*) Somebody, Smith or your banker, has a claim on you for £100.

Obviously, to know both these facts is of first importance in any business.

Question. Well, does this hold good with other than just buying transactions? Would the same state of affairs exist with the selling of goods?

Answer. In exactly the same way. The first aspect in the selling transaction is that your storekeeper has issued £100 worth of goods as an ordinary sale. The second is that the person who has received them has become your debtor, *i.e.*, he is indebted to you, on the assumption that you, in this case, are giving him credit, because **you** are the supplier.

Question. Does the Double Entry System stop at this?

Answer. No. It goes much further. Because of this twofold aspect I have been talking about, it enables you to compare the proceeds of the sales you have made with the cost to you of the goods you have bought, and so obtain your profit or loss on trading.

Similarly, as it shows the claims other people have on you (your creditors), and the claims you have on other people (your debtors) you can tell very quickly what is the position of affairs of your business at any particular date so far as these people are concerned.

Question. Is the latter point important?

Answer. Yes. If the creditors of the business exceed in amount its debtors, any stock in its warehouse which it hopes to sell, and the ready money it has available, it may be insolvent, that is to say, it cannot pay its debts as they become due.

Question. When we began talking, you said the Ledger was the only Book of Account, and that all transactions were first recorded in what you called "subsidiary books."

What are these Subsidiary Books, and why are they kept in addition to the Ledger?

Answer. The Subsidiary Books are termed Journals or

Day Books because, very much like a journal or diary, they are entered up daily.

They are designed to relieve the various accounts in the Ledger of a great amount of detail which, while indispensable to the business, can better be given in a subsidiary book than in the Ledger itself.

If you take, for example, the purchasing side of a business, a very great amount of detail may have to be recorded as to the supplier, the quantity, quality and price per unit of the goods, total amount payable and so on.

But, so far as the Double Entry or twofold aspect of all the buying transactions is concerned, they are all in the first place purchases or goods for which the storekeeper is responsible. In the second place, credit must be given to all the various suppliers from whom the purchases have been made. Thus there will be one account in the Ledger for incoming goods, or purchases, and other accounts, also in the Ledger, for the individual suppliers.

Question. So the Journals or Day Books do not form part of the Double Entry System at all?

Answer. That is so. These Subsidiary Books are outside the Double Entry System altogether. Their function is to provide, in the first instance, the material from which the Ledger Accounts are entered up subsequently.

That is why they are so often referred to as books of **prime** or **first entry**. With very few exceptions indeed, it is a well-recognised rule in Book-keeping that no transaction shall be recorded in a Ledger Account that has not first been made the subject of record in a subsidiary book, or Book of First Entry.

Question. Now that you have given me this introduction, can we proceed to take a typical business transaction, and record it first in the subsidiary books, and then in the Ledger?

Answer. Yes, that is what we are now going to do. But first of all we will consider the various kinds of business transactions.

CHAPTER II

THE BUSINESS TRANSACTION, PURCHASES AND SALES

The Business Transaction

We are familiar in our daily life with buying articles we want and paying cash for them. But unless we are in business the idea of selling goods is not so familiar, nor is the process of receiving payment for what we have sold. And yet every business is concerned with buying and selling goods as has been seen, usually on a credit basis, so that at some later date it pays for what it has bought and is in turn paid for what it has sold.

These are clearly recurrent transactions in particular goods which the business merchants or manufactures.

Merchanted Goods are those which it resells in the same condition as when purchased. **Manufactured Goods** are the finished article which, with the assistance of work-people, are worked up from the raw material.

Thus from the purely trading standpoint a kind of trade cycle can be recognised. Goods are bought first of all in sufficient quantity to meet customers' requirements, either as the finished article or as raw material. They are what is called the **Stock** or **Stock in Trade** of the business.

When the goods are sold in the finished state to customers at selling price, and on credit terms, these customers become the **debtors** of the business, *i.e.*, they are indebted to it, and when they in turn make payment the **Cash in Hand** or **Cash at Bank** of the business is replenished.

From these increased cash resources moneys once again become available for the business to buy more goods, and so the cycle repeats itself.

We should remember that not only is this the case, but that at any given time a business will necessarily possess :

(*a*) Stock in Trade ;
(*b*) Claims on customers, which may shortly be described as Debtors, or Book Debts ;
(*c*) Cash in Hand and/or Cash at Bank.

These forms of property, property of very different kinds, represent the trading resources of the business, and in total form part of its **Capital.**

It is very important for us to understand correctly the meaning of **Capital** in the book-keeping sense.

Supposing we bought goods from Jones, value £100, for payment a month after they had been delivered, Jones would be our creditor, and during that month we might sell the goods at a profit and so obtain the cash to pay him when the time came.

That would be an ideal case, because then the business apparently need have no cash resources **of its own**; it could rely on Jones, and other suppliers, to finance its operations. The capital invested in the business, represented by the stock of goods value £100 supplied by Jones, would be in effect **Jones's Capital,** and not the proprietor's Capital at all.

In practice we find, however, that such an ideal state of affairs can seldom, if ever, arise.

First of all, we may not be able to sell all the goods we purchased from Jones in the credit period of one month.

Secondly, we shall in all probability be obliged to extend credit to our customers, just as Jones did to us.

Thirdly, we shall be obliged to possess certain (cash) resources to pay our staff and workpeople week by week, and

Fourthly, if ours is a new business, Jones or any other supplier may be unwilling to supply us with goods on credit until they have experience of what may be called our " credit-worthiness."

There is also to be remembered that an important part of every business's resources will be a factory, or warehouse, or office, or the right to occupy these, for which a rent will be paid. Such property does not, and cannot form part of the trading resources, because it would clearly never occur to us to sell our business premises in which all the work was carried on.

Enough has been said for us to realise that a certain minimum amount of property, or of **Capital**, must be possessed by the business from the time it was commenced, and we can realise also how varied are the forms which this Capital may take.

Our task will always be rendered easier if we think of

Capital as the resources or the property of a business. Indeed, the term "**Capital**" has no meaning to the business man unless it is represented by property of some kind or another, property to which he refers as the business **Assets.** In future, therefore, we will use the term "**Assets**" alone.

While we are going to examine Capital more fully at a later stage, let us now remember that there are such forms of property as **Fixed Assets,** *i.e.*, the factory or warehouse mentioned above, and other forms which we call **Current Assets,** which correspond to our trading assets, such as stock in trade, claims on customers, and money in the bank.

The distinction between these two kinds of property is of the utmost importance, because our **Fixed Assets** have been bought to be retained, while our **Current Assets,** as we have seen, are an essential result of the business's everyday transactions. Indeed, they enter into and form part of these transactions.

There are just two more points, and the first is for us to grasp the business man's definition of **Capital** as representing not merely the **Assets,** but

The Excess of the Assets over the Liabilities of a Business.

An example will help to make this clear :—

Example. Brown begins business on January 1, 1938, with £1,000 in cash. He buys for cash factory premises at a cost of £500, and goods on credit from Smith costing £200.

The total assets of his business are :—

Factory, cost	£500	
Stock of goods, cost . . .	200	
Cash in Bank	500	
		£1,200

but this is **not** the amount of **Brown's Capital** invested in the business because £200 of these assets have been supplied on credit by Smith, for which the business is liable to him. What is owing to Smith is, therefore, a liability of the business and because we define Capital above as corresponding to "the excess of the Assets over the

Liabilities of a business," Brown's Capital = **Total Assets** £1,200, less **Liabilities** £200 = £1,000, or put in another way, Brown's Capital of £1,000 is represented by

Fixed Assets		£500
Current Assets	£700	
Less Liabilities . . .	200	
		500
		£1,000

We are justified in deducting the liability to Smith from the total of the **Current** Assets, since it is out of them that we intend to pay him.

The other point which we ought now to be in a position to appreciate is that

Capital is a Liability of the Business to its proprietor.

At first sight this appears to be rather different from what we should expect.

We have seen that from its commencement the business must be provided with a certain minimum amount of property, or Capital and for the sake of convenience we defined Capital in the first place as the equivalent of property, or Assets, and more fully in the second place as representing " the excess of the Assets over the Liabilities of a business."

Let us now see if we can reconcile what appears to be a contradiction in terms.

If the proprietor, instead of investing a part of his Capital in setting up the business, had lent £1,000 to a friend in consideration of the payment of interest at 6% per annum, the loan would clearly be an investment yielding an annual income of £60, and the amount of the loan, looked at from the standpoint of the borrower, would as clearly be a liability.

The borrower's financial position could be stated thus :—

" **Liability** £1,000, represented by **Cash** £1,000."

In exactly the same way, when the proprietor invests Capital in a business, he is just as truly entitled to regard it as an investment, answerable to him for interest, or in this case **Profit,** period by period.

From the standpoint of the business, looked at as distinct from its proprietorship, there is a **Liability** to account for the amount of the proprietor's Capital put at its disposal for the purpose of profit earning.

At any time, therefore, the business should be able to prepare a statement of its position, and of how it has dealt with such Capital, that is to say, by what kinds of property that Capital is represented.

The financial position of the business would similarly be :—

Liability to proprietor £1,000, represented by, in the first instance, **Cash** £1,000.

The only difference between the two examples is that, in the first case, the borrower would sooner or later have to repay the loan, while in the second the repayment of the proprietor's Capital would involve shutting down the business.

For this reason, in the latter case, the Capital invested is usually regarded as a **permanent** or **fixed liability,** or indeed, as it is in law, a postponed or deferred liability.

The Place of the Purchase and Sales Journals in the Book-keeping System

Most of us are familiar with the practice of making a daily note of matters in which we are interested. For this purpose we use our diary, as a kind of daily record, entering in it brief but sufficient details of what has taken place.

Such entries may be made by the private individual, and they form very often a useful reference for the future.

In the early stages of business development it is not difficult for us to imagine the proprietor of the business making a similar record of his transactions with people who had become his suppliers and customers, narrating what he had bought, and from whom; what he had sold, and to whom. Just as a diary is a daily record, so also is a **Journal.** It is written up as soon as possible after the transaction has taken place. It is essentially a **primary** record, and hence we derive the meaning of the term "Journal" in book-keeping as a book of "**first entry.**" No matter what subsequent use we make of the particulars recorded in it, the desirability of a primary record is obvious.

To the extent that the transactions of the business are recurrent, even in the smallest undertaking we should expect to see a record of :—

(*a*) Purchases ;
(*b*) Sales ;
(*c*) Payments to suppliers ;
(*d*) Receipts from customers.

As soon as the transactions entered into became more numerous, some kind of analysis of the Journal would be imperative if the proprietor at any time wished to know :—

(*a*) How much he had purchased ;
(*b*) How much he had sold ;
(*c*) What was the total of his cash payments, and of
(*d*) His cash receipts.

With numerous daily transactions, putting on record the fact that £100 worth of goods had been purchased on credit from Jones, and £100 worth of goods had been sold on credit to Smith, the Journal entries might take the following form :—

(*a*) Warehouseman chargeable with incoming goods **at cost** £100. Jones to be credited with £100.
(*b*) Smith chargeable with goods £100. Warehouseman to be credited with issue of goods at selling price £100.

If, however, we took matters a step further, and used the Symbols **Dr.** (debtor) instead of "chargeable with" and **Cr.** (creditor) instead of "to be credited," the entries could easily be stated in the following way :—

(*a*) Warehouseman	Dr.	£100
Jones	Cr.	100

and

(*b*) Smith	Dr.	£100
Warehouseman	Cr.	100

This would be a much simpler and more concise way of putting the transaction on record, but the repetition of the recurrent entries over a period of time would make detailed analysis always essential to arrive at, for example :

(*a*) Our total purchases, and
(*b*) Our total sales for that period, quite apart from the need for similar analysis as regards cash paid and cash received.

For that reason, the first form of Journal was modified to accord with these requirements of the proprietor, and in one section of it were recorded **purchases,** in another **sales** and in yet another **cash,** either in total, or as in many cases to-day :—

(*a*) **Cash received,** and
(*b*) **Cash paid.**

To the first of these subsections of the Journal was given the title :

Purchase Journal,

to the second :

Sales Journal,

and to the third :

Cash Book or Cash Journal,

with the result that in them we now find—

(*a*) Our total purchases ;
(*b*) Our total sales ; and
(*c*) Our purely cash transactions, in as great a detail as we desire, or the requirements of the business demand.

If it be said that certain transactions take place which do not permit of entry in the above three subdivisions of the Journal, the answer is that the early form of Journal is still retained for such (comparatively infrequent) transactions, and is dealt with in Chapter VII.

Supposing we begin with the **Purchase Journal,** or **Day Book :—**

Example. Enter the following purchases in the Purchase Day Book of H. Yates, a cycle dealer, total the Day Book, but do not post the entries to the Ledger.

1937

Feb. 2. Received invoice from the Speedy Cycle Co., Ltd., for :—

2 Gent.'s Roadsters, model A625 at £6 10*s*. less 20% trade discount.

2 Ladies' Roadsters, model A725 at £6 12*s*.6*d*. less 20% trade discount.

2 crates at 10*s*. each.

„ 15. The Drake Cycle Co., Ltd., invoiced :—

3 Gent.'s Special Club models B21 at £5 5*s*. less 15% trade discount.

2 Ladies' Special Club models B20 at £5 10*s*. less 15% trade discount.

2 crates at 12*s*. 6*d*. each.

„ 27. Received invoice from the Victoria Manufacturing Co., Ltd.:—

2 Racing models A16 at £7, less 15% trade discount.

1 crate at 10*s*.

(Union of Educational Institutions.)

In these three purchase transactions, we notice :—

(*a*) That the goods purchased are exclusively for resale, *i.e.*, they are goods in which Mr. Yates is dealing.

(*b*) That a deduction is made on account of **trade discount.** This is a usual allowance made by a supplier to a retailer with whom he has regular dealings, and may represent :—

1. A margin of profit for the retailer, who sells the goods at the advertised list price.
2. An inducement to the retailer to continue to trade with the supplier.

Prior to entry in the last four columns of the Day Book, it is seen that the trade discount has been deducted in the " details " column, and we must always be careful to follow this procedure.

All that concerns Mr. Yates is the **net cost** to him of the cycles he has bought.

H. YATES.

PURCHASE DAY BOOK.

FEBRUARY, 1937.

Date.	Supplier.	Description.	Details. £ s. d.	Total. £ s. d.	Gent's Models. £ s. d.	Ladies' Models. £ s. d.	Crates and Packing. £ s. d.
1937 Feb. 2	Speedy Cycle Co., Ltd.	2 Gent's Roadsters, Model A625, at £6 10*s*.	13 0 0				
		2 Ladies' Roadsters, Model A725, at £6 12*s*. 6*d*.	13 5 0				
			26 5 0				
		Less 20% Trade Discount	5 5 0				
			21 0 0				
		2 Crates at 10*s*.	1 0 0	22 0 0	10 8 0	10 12 0	1 0 0
" 15	Drake Cycle Co., Ltd.	3 Gent's Special Club models, B21, at £5 5*s*.	15 15 0				
		2 Ladies' Special Club models, B20, at £5 10*s*.	11 0 0				
			26 15 0				
		Less 15% Trade Discount	4 0 3				
			22 14 9				
		2 Crates at 12*s*. 6*d*.	1 5 0	23 19 9	13 7 9	9 7 0	1 5 0
" 27	Victoria Manufacturing Co., Ltd.	2 Racing models, A16, at £7	14 0 0				
		Less 15% Trade Discount	2 2 0				
			11 18 0				
		1 Crate at 10*s*.	10 0	12 8 0	11 18 0		10 0
				£58 7 9	£35 13 9	£19 19 0	£2 15 0

(*c*) That the suppliers have in each case included in their invoice price the cost of crates. These clearly do not refer to the cost of the goods dealt in, and are therefore entered in a separate column. Moreover, it is usual for the suppliers to issue **credit notes** as and when the crates are later returned to them in good condition. There may in consequence be a recovery of all or the greater part of the total purchase cost under this heading.

The solution to the example, as shown, enables Mr. Yates to see at a glance :—

(*a*) From whom he has purchased.
(*b*) What has been purchased.
(*c*) The total cost of the purchases, suitably analysed, including
(*d*) The cost of crates, packing, etc.

Example. From the following particulars compile the Sales Day Book, Purchase Day Book, and Returns Book of D. Morris.

Full details must be shown in the Day Books. No posting to the Ledger is required.

Mar. 10. Sold to W. Humphrey, Lincoln, 200 yards black cloth at 3*s*. 6*d*. per yard ; 100 yards of best brown cloth at 3*s*. 9*d*. per yard. Whole invoice less 10% trade discount.

„ 12. Received invoice from R. Ridgewell, Bolton, for 50 pairs of blankets at 11*s*. per pair ; 3 dozen woollen shawls 12*s*. each.

„ 15. Sent a debit note to W. Hunt for £12, being an overcharge on goods supplied on February 5.

„ 18. Sent an invoice to S. Boham, Coventry, for 100 yards of velvet at 2*s*. 6*d*. per yard, less 5% trade discount ; 300 yards of black cloth at 3*s*. 6*d*. per yard ; trimmings £7 5*s*. 4*d*.

„ 20. Bought goods from B. Davis, Ely, 500 yards of black cloth at 1*s*. 3*d*. per yard ; 400 shawls at 9*s*. each ; sundry remnants £15.

„ 22. W. Humphrey, Lincoln, returned 50 yards of the black cloth supplied on March 10, as being of inferior quality.

Mar. 23. Received a debit note from A. Jenkinson, Wolverhampton, for 20 yards of velvet returned at 3*s*. 2*d*. per yard less 20% trade discount.

„ 24. Sent an invoice to T. Butterworth, Norwich, for 300 yards of velvet at 2*s*. 9*d*. per yard less 5% trade discount; 150 yards of best brown cloth at 3*s*. 9*d*. per yard less 10% trade discount; 12 gross of buttons at 2*d*. per dozen.

„ 27. Received a credit note from V. Luxton, for 30 yards of white cloth returned at 1*s*. 3*d*. per yard.

„ 29. Bought from General Supplies, Ltd., London, showcases and fittings £57 10*s*. net.

Note.—Great care must be exercised in setting out the Day Books.

(Union of Educational Institutions.)

Before beginning to record these transactions in the Purchase and Sales Journals, it is essential for us to realise that they are being stated from the point of view of the business of which D. Morris is the proprietor.

Indeed, we may first proceed to classify each of them as being :—

(*a*) A purchase transaction.
(*b*) A sales transaction.
(*c*) The return of goods to a **supplier,** or the obtaining of an allowance *from* him.
(*d*) The return of goods by a **customer,** or the granting of an allowance *to* him.

In the two latter cases the result will be, as we shall expect, that the amount of the original purchases and sales will be reduced accordingly, but **instead of altering** the entries in the Purchases and Sales Journals, we shall make use of **Purchase Returns Journals** and **Sales Returns Journals.** (See pages 24–27.)

Let us now summarise the points arising in this and the first example.

In the first place, the **analysis columns** which under each ruling follow the total column, enable us to dissect as fully as we may wish the details of our purchases and sales.

D. Morris.

Fo. 1.

PURCHASE DAY BOOK.

March, 1937.

Date.	Supplier.	Description.	Invoice No.	Details.	Total.	Cloth.	Blankets.	Shawls.	Sundries.	Special Items.
1937				£ s. d.	£ s. d.	£ s. d.	£ s. d.	£ s. d.	£ s. d.	£ s. d.
Mar. 12	R. Ridgwell, Bolton.	50 pairs Blankets at 11*s*. pair .	—	27 10 0						
		3 dozen Woollen Shawls at 12*s*. each . .	1	21 12 0	49 2 0		27 10 0	21 12 0		
„ 20	B. Davis, Ely.	500 yards Black Cloth at 1*s*. 3*d*. per yard . .		31 5 0						
		400 Shawls at 9*s*. each . .		180 0 0						
		Remnants . .	2	15 0 0	226 5 0	31 5 0		180 0 0	15 0 0	
„ 29	General Supplies, Ltd., London.	Showcases and Fittings . .	3		57 10 0					57 10 0
					£332 17 0	£31 5 0	£27 10 0	£201 12 0	£15 0 0	£57 10 0

D. MORRIS.

SALES DAY BOOK.

MARCH, 1937.

Date.	Customer.	Description.	Invoice No.	Details.	Total.	Cloth.	Velvet.	Sundries.
				£ s. d.	£ s. d.	£ s. d.	£ s. d.	£ s. d.
1937 Mar. 10	W. Humphrey, Lincoln.	200 yards Black Cloth at 3*s.* 6*d.* per yard .		35 0 0				
		100 yards best Brown Cloth at 3*s.* 9*d.* per yard		18 15 0				
				53 15 0				
		Less 10% Trade Discount . . .	4	5 7 6	48 7 6	48 7 6		
„ 18	S. Boham, Coventry.	100 yards Velvet at 2*s.* 6*d.* per yard . .		12 10 0				
		Less 5% Trade Discount . . .		12 6				
				11 17 6				
		300 yards Black Cloth at 3*s.* 6*d.* per yard		52 10 0				
		Trimmings	5	7 5 4	71 12 10	52 10 0	11 17 6	7 5 4
„ 24	T. Butterworth, Norwich.	300 yards Velvet at 2*s.* 9*d.* per yard . .		41 5 0				
		Less 5% Trade Discount . . .		2 1 3				
				39 3 9				
		150 yards best Brown Cloth at 3*s.* 9*d.* per yard		28 2 6				
		Less 10% Trade Discount . . .		2 16 3				
				25 6 3				
		12 gross Buttons at 2*d.* per dozen . .	6	1 4 0	65 14 0	25 6 3	39 3 9	1 4 0
					£185 14 4	£126 3 9	£51 1 3	£8 9 4

D. MORRIS.

PURCHASES RETURNS AND ALLOWANCES BOOK.

MARCH, 1937.

Date.	Supplier.	Description.	Debit Note No.	Details.	Total.	Cloth.	Blankets.	Shawls.	Sundries.
				£ s. d.	£ s. d.	£ s. d.	£ s. d.	£ s. d.	£ s. d.
1937 Mar. 15	W. Hunt.	Overcharge goods supplied Feb. 5	7		12 0 0				12 0 0
„ 27	V. Luxton.	30 yards White Cloth returned at 1*s*. 3*d*. per yard . .	Their credit note 8		1 17 6	1 17 6			
					£13 17 6	£1 17 6			£12 0 0

D. MORRIS.

SALES RETURNS AND ALLOWANCES BOOK.

MARCH, 1937.

Date.	Customer.	Description.	Credit Note No.	Details.	Total	Cloth.	Velvet.	Sundries.
				£ s. d.	£ s. d.	£ s. d.	£ s. d.	£ s. d.
1937 Mar. 22	W. Humphrey, Lincoln.	50 yards Black Cloth, invoice Mar. 10, inferior, at 3*s.* 6*d.* per yard.		8 15 0				
		Less 10% Trade Discount . .	9	17 6	7 17 6	7 17 6		
„ 23	A. Jenkinson, Wolverhampton.	20 yards Velvet at 3*s.* 2*d.* per yard .		3 3 4				
		Less 20% Trade Discount . .	Their debit note 10	12 8	2 10 8		2 10 8	
					£10 8 2	£7 17 6	£2 10 8	

Secondly, we see that an **Invoice No.** column is provided. In this is entered the No. **given by the business** to its suppliers' invoices, as well as to its own invoices to customers. If for any reason the original purchase invoice or copy sales invoice has to be consulted, it can quickly be referred to on the purchase or sales invoice files.

Thirdly, Returns and Allowances Books, whether for purchases or sales, are ruled in almost exactly the same way as the Purchase and Sales Journals themselves, the difference being that the heading **" Invoice No."** is replaced by **" Debit Note No.,"** and **" Credit Note No."** respectively, thus facilitating reference to these documents.

Fourthly, it is apparent that a check can be placed on the arithmetical accuracy of the book-keeping work by agreeing periodically, say at the end of each month, the " cross " cast or " cross addition " of the **Analysis Columns** with the cast or addition of the **Total Column** in each of the subsidiary books.

Finally, in the second example we have an instance of the purchase by the business of capital goods, or **fixed assets,** in the shape of the showcases and fittings.

As these have been bought for retention and not for resale, it is essential to provide an additional analysis column, in this case headed **" Special Items."** Alternative headings might be " Capital Items," or " Capital Additions."

The provision of this column enables us to see at a glance the total value of such special or capital purchases during the period.

Tests and Questions

1. Explain briefly the theory of " Double Entry," and of " Debit and Credit." (University of Birmingham.)

2. What do you understand by the term Double Entry, as applied to a system of account keeping? Give examples to illustrate. (University of Birmingham.)

3. " Book-keeping by double entry means recording the same transaction twice." Criticise this assertion briefly. (Royal Society of Arts.)

4. State the advantages to be derived from keeping a set of books on the Double Entry System and contrast this method with any other system you know of. (University of Manchester.)

5. In arranging the work of the counting house of a manufacturing company, enumerate your recommendations for dealing with inward invoices and give the ruling of the book in which you suggest they should be entered. (University of Manchester.)

6. Explain fully the functions of the Purchase Analysis Journal. Give a specimen ruling thereof and insert six entries therein, showing totals, and explain how these should be dealt with.
(University of Manchester.)

7. Goods purchased by a business may comprise either goods for resale at a profit, or goods for retention and use. Give **two** examples of each, and explain how such purchases are recorded in the books of account. (University of Birmingham.)

8. " The books of prime entry are developments from the ordinary Journal." Comment on this statement, and give draft rulings for a Purchase Day-Book and a Sales Day Book in a business having three main departments. (University of Birmingham.)

9. Explain clearly the nature of the following documents: invoice, debit note, statement.
(East Midland Educational Union.)

10. What is the columnar method of recording credit purchases and sales? Illustrate your answer by examples.
(East Midland Educational Union.)

11. P.Q. & Co., Merchants, have three departments, A, B, and C. It is desired to keep separate trading accounts for each. With this end in view, give the ruling of the Sales Day Book, making therein six specimen entries, and explain how the book would function. (University of Manchester.)

12. A trader wishes to ascertain separately the gross profit earned by each of the two departments which comprise his business.

Show how the columnar system of book-keeping would allow him to do this without opening any additional books or accounts. Give any necessary rulings and explain how the system works.
(Royal Society of Arts.)

13. What are Returns Inwards and Outwards? Where should these items be entered in the books of a trader? What effect has each upon the profits of a business?
(Union of Educational Institutions.)

14. On February 1 B. Grey owed A. White £6 5*s*. for goods supplied.

On February 13 he bought from White on credit three shirts at 8*s*. 11*d*. each, six pairs of socks for 13*s*. 6*d*., and a pair of flannel trousers for 17*s*. 11*d*. The following day he sent a cheque for £5 on account, and on February 20 he bought a dressing gown for £1 7*s*. 6*d*.

Set out in full the invoice made out by White relating to the purchases on February 13, and the statement at the end of the month. (Royal Society of Arts.)

15. XY is a manufacturer of electrical appliances. Give the ruling for a Purchase Book which you would recommend he should keep, entering therein the undermentioned items, representing invoices received, and explain how the book would function in the system of Double Entry book-keeping.

Feb. 2. AB, £25 for goods.
„ 4. PQ, £12 for repairs to machinery.
„ 5. CD, £10 for advertising.
„ 6. AB, £75 for goods.
„ 8. X Corporation, £40 for general rates.
P.O. telephones, £14.
„ 12. GH, £100 for goods.
„ 14. Y Railway Company, £10 for carriage.
„ 15. AB, £250 for new plant.

(University of Manchester.)

16. On February 1, 1932, you supplied to T. Thomas, 20 doz. grey pullovers at 4*s.* 9*d.* each, less a trade discount of 7½%. Thomas returned 4 doz. pullovers as not up to sample and you agreed to credit him with their value.

Enter the item in the Returns Book concerned and draw up the credit note to Thomas. How would you deal with this transaction in the Ledger? (East Midland Educational Union.)

17. On January 1, 1937, R. Rich sold G. Jones goods to the amount of £50 5*s.*; on February 13, Jones paid Rich £25 on account; on February 27, Rich sold Jones £48 10*s.* of goods; on March 3, Jones returned to Rich £7 15*s.* goods (not being up to sample); on March 13, Jones paid Rich £24 and was allowed £1 5*s.* discount to clear the January account. As on March 31, Rich sent a quarterly statement to Jones. Set out the statement so sent in proper form. (Union of Lancashire and Cheshire Institutes.)

18. Enter the following transactions of Milner & Co., Ltd., in the appropriate books of prime entry; rule off at February 28, 1938, and post as necessary to the Impersonal and Private Ledgers.

Note.—Special care should be taken in drafting the form of the books of prime entry.

1938.

Feb. 4. Bought of T. Lloyd, Lincoln, 500 yards of baize at 1*s.* per yard, 2,000 yards of satin at 4*s.* 6*d.* per yard, less 10% trade discount in each case.
„ 10. Sold to T. Williams, York, 400 yards curtain material at 2*s.* 8*d.* per yard, and sundry fittings £8. Box charged £1.
„ 11. Bought showcase and counter for showroom from Universal Supplies, Ltd., London, £37 10*s.*
„ 12. Returned to T. Lloyd, Lincoln, 200 yards of satin as invoiced on February 4.
„ 18. Bought of J. Grey, Taunton, 300 yards velvet at 3*s.* 6*d.* per yard, less 5% trade discount and 250 yards baize at 1*s.* per yard net.
„ 20. Received debit note from T. Williams, York, for box invoiced on February 10.
„ 24. Sold to D. Wilson, Coventry, 300 yards baize at 1*s.* 4*d.* per yard net, and 600 yards satin at 5*s.* 6*d.* per yard less 10% trade discount.

(Birmingham Commercial College.)

CHAPTER III

PURCHASE AND SALES TRANSACTIONS, AND THE LEDGER ACCOUNTS

Question. As I see it, the Purchase and Sales Day Books are written up from the original purchase invoices, and the copies of the sales invoices to customers?

Answer. Yes, that is so, but it is of the utmost importance that every purchase invoice, whether for goods or services, shall be certified by the responsible officials of the business as to its correctness before being entered in the Purchase Journal. With regard to sales invoices, these may be issued on the basis of the warehouseman's record of deliveries.

Question. The final column in the first example's Purchase Journal was headed "Crates and Packing," but there was no similar column in the second case. Why is this?

Answer. Suppliers may or may not charge for crates and packing material. If they do so, a record must clearly be made of the expense. Under this head, it is, however, a cost which we should record separately because it may be recoverable if and when such items as crates are returned to the suppliers; otherwise the cost must be borne by the business.

Question. With both the Purchase and the Sales Journals there is then no one particular form of ruling?

Answer. No. There cannot be. The system of book-keeping must be such as will give the information in each particular case in the form in which it is required, or can be of the greatest use. For this reason care must be exercised in the choice of the analysis columns. These may represent the principal materials dealt in, or the departments responsible for their production and sale, and so on.

Question. If goods are bought and sold on credit, I should have thought it was also very important to know :—

(*a*) How much the business has purchased **from any one supplier,** and
(*b*) How much it has sold **to any one customer.**

But as there are numerous transactions with different suppliers and customers, how could this be done from the Journals alone?

Answer. By means of the **Ledger,** or principal book of account, we are able to discover very quickly not only what has been purchased from or sold to any particular person, but **how that person stands in relation to the business at any particular time,** that is, whether he is its creditor or debtor. Put in another way, we want to know how much we have sold to each customer period by period because if possible we hope to increase our sales to him, and we also want to know how much that customer owes us for goods delivered, since his payments to us provide the monies out of which we have to pay our suppliers.

Question. So the Ledger Account records not only the trading aspect of our transactions, **but also** the **cash aspect**?

Answer. Yes. Both aspects must be recorded as affecting suppliers and customers, but at the moment we are only concerned with the **trading aspect.**

The Ledger

(*a*) Personal Accounts

We have spoken of Ledger Accounts as playing an essential part in summarising the transactions of the business so far as they concern those with whom it deals.

It is now necessary to describe the Ledger Account rather more precisely, and to consider its other functions.

Its usual **form** is as follows :—

JONES.

DR. CR.

Date.	Details.	Amount.	Date.	Details.	Amount.
		£ s. d.			£ s. d.

In the form, we notice :—

(*a*) **Name of Account.** This may be the name of the person, in this case Jones, who is either a supplier or a customer of the business. It may represent, on the other hand, the impersonal subject-matter with which the account deals. For the moment, we will take it to be the former only.

(*b*) The vertical double line in the centre divides the account into two equal parts. That on the left we term the **Debit** or debtor side, denoted by the symbol **Dr.,** and that on the right the **Credit,** or creditor side, with the symbol **Cr. On both sides** of the account, it will be observed, there are three columns, headed respectively :—

Date,
Details, and
Amount.

In the ordinary way, a separate page, or folio of the Ledger, is used for each account opened, and the Ledger itself may be a bound book, a loose-leaf book, or in the form of cards, with a separate card for each account.

If we assume that Jones is a **supplier of goods** to the business, the structure of the account enables us to put to his credit, *i.e.*, on the right-hand, or **credit** side, the value of the goods supplied by him. The right-hand side may also be regarded generally as that on which we enter benefits received **by the business.** The supply of goods on credit is clearly such a benefit and Jones may be said to have performed, to this extent, a " credit-worthy " action.

Furthermore, his account is said to be " in credit," in that he is a **creditor** of the business. Let us suppose Jones has supplied goods to the value of £10. This being an ordinary purchase transaction, the first record will be made in the Purchase Journal, as we have seen. It will ultimately be put (or " posted," as we must accustom ourselves to saying) to the credit of **Jones's account,** as follows :—

JONES.

DR. CR.

Date.	Details.	P.R.J. Fo.	Amount.	Date.	Details.	P.J. Fo.	Amount.
				1938 Jan. 1	By Goods .	2	£ s. d. 10 0 0

At this point we must remember :—

(*a*) That it is altogether unnecessary to repeat here the full description of the goods. By inserting a column for the Purchase Journal folio (P.J. Fo.) we can readily turn back to the initial entry in the Purchase Journal and, if we wish, to the original document, on which it was based, *i.e.*, the supplier's invoice.

(*b*) The purpose of our Ledger Account with Jones is to summarise or assemble within it **all our transactions** with him ; otherwise it would be impossible to determine the position of the business in relation to him.

Because we are now thinking of Jones as a **supplier,** it is logical to assume, in the first instance, that any items on the left-hand or **debit** side will be in respect of payments made to him : offsetting the amounts standing to his credit.

If, however, the business has had occasion to return goods to him owing to unsatisfactory quality, or error in price, and a **credit note** is received signifying his acceptance of them, this also is a matter which must be recorded on the **debit** side. The effect of the return of the goods is **to reduce the liability of the business** to Jones as its creditor. In this case, the initial entry will have been made in the **Purchase Returns or Allowances Book,** and from that we shall post to the **debit** of Jones's Ledger Account, as under :—

JONES.

DR. CR.

Date.	Details.	P.R.J. Fo.	Amount.	Date.	Details.	P.J. Fo.	Amount.
1938 Jan. 6	To Returns or Allowances	3	£ s. d. 1 10 0	1938 Jan. 1	By Goods .	2	£ s. d. 10 0 0

Should Jones, on the other hand, be a **customer of the business** a Ledger Account will be opened in identical **form,** but if goods to the value of £10 are **sold to him,** his account will be **debited,** that is the entry will be made on the **left-hand** side :—

JONES.

DR. CR.

Date.	Details.	S.J. Fo.	Amount.	Date.	Details.	S.R.J. Fo.	Amount.
1938 Jan. 1	To Goods .	2	£ s. d. 10 0 0				

He now appears as a **debtor** to the business, as indeed he is, the details of the original sale being found on Folio 2 of the **Sales Journal.**

The business in this case has performed the " creditworthy " action, and as such is entitled to regard Jones as **chargeable** with it. He is **indebted** to the business, and therefore the entry appears on the debit side.

Finally, should goods be returned by him, or the business make him any kind of allowance, the amount, as posted from the **Sales Returns and Allowances** Book, will be put to his credit.

The result will be, as we should expect :—

(*a*) To offset to that extent his original indebtedness of £10.

(*b*) To indicate that the business, having delivered defective goods, or made an overcharge, now proceeds to give Jones **the necessary credit.**

The Ledger Account would then appear :—

JONES.

DR. CR.

Date.	Details.	S.J. Fo.	Amount.	Date.	Details.	S.R.J. Fo.	Amount.
1938 Jan. 1	To Goods .	2	£ s. d. 10 0 0	1938 Jan. 6	By Returns or Allowances	3	£ s. d. 1 10 0

When the **cash** as well as the **trading** aspect of these transactions has been dealt with, we shall be in a position to determine, at any time and irrespective of the number of items, the **balance of indebtedness** due either **to** or **by** the business.

So far as we have been dealing with **persons external to the business,** the **personal** aspect of the sales and purchase transactions has now been recorded.

By that we mean **the effect upon the persons** with whom the transactions have been entered into, resulting in their becoming, until the question of **payment** arises, the creditors or debtors of the business.

If we have carefully followed the construction of the Ledger Account as shown, it is apparent that the entries are postings from the various books of first entry—from the Journals. That is to say, the Journals provide the basis for the writing up of all Ledger Accounts.

We may even lay it down as a rule with very few exceptions that :—

> " No entry shall be made in a Ledger Account, unless it has first appeared in the Journal."

(*b*) Impersonal Accounts.

It was stated on page 33 that the name of the account might be that of the person with whom the business dealt, or of the impersonal subject-matter referred to in it.

The former we may now term a **Personal Account,** and the latter an **Impersonal,** or **Nominal** Account.

Jones's account, whether he be a supplier or a customer, is a **Personal Account.** His position, as someone external to the business, has been looked at from the **personal aspect.**

There is, however, **another aspect** to be considered, and that is :—

> **The effect upon the business** as an impersonal unit, of the transactions with Jones and any other suppliers and customers.

When in the first place we regarded him as a **supplier** his account was credited with £10, but at the same time we must remember that the business then came into possession of £10 worth of **goods.** It is therefore natural to regard the stores or warehouse as **chargeable** in this amount. As a department of the business it may further be regarded **impersonally,** and the necessary charge made to it in an **impersonal account,** headed

Warehouse, or,
Goods purchased, or, more usually,
Purchases.

Thus the heading refers to the **subject-matter** of the account and not to the name of the warehouseman, or storekeeper, which is immaterial because he represents the **business.** If at first sight it seems strange that the charge to the warehouse for goods purchased should call for record in such an account we may find an explanation in the following :—

(*a*) The essence of the double-entry system is to record the dual aspect of each transaction **within the Ledger,** or book of account.

In the event of no " Warehouse " or " Purchases " Account being opened we should have recorded in the Ledger **one aspect of the transaction only**—the personal aspect.

(*b*) The business, or its proprietor, desires to know, period by period, how much has been **purchased** of the various kinds of goods dealt in.

The opening of the Ledger Account for **" purchases "** permits the periodic totals of the Purchase Journal to be posted to it on the chargeable, or debit side.

Sometimes it is contended, and with truth, that the total cost of purchases, suitably analysed, can be seen at a glance in the Purchase Journal.

This, however, is no reason for eliminating the Ledger Account for " purchases," because, as stated above, we desire to complete the **double entry within the Ledger,** and also obtain, **in the summarised form which the Ledger Account gives**, the total charge to the warehouse for goods received by it month by month during the trading year.

As in practice the various subdivisions of the Journal are ruled off at monthly intervals, a note of the monthly totals in summarised form is clearly very helpful.

The following illustrates in another way what has been described above :—

PURCHASE JOURNAL.

(Book of First Entry.)

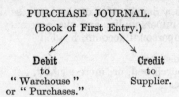

Debit to "Warehouse" or "Purchases."

Credit to Supplier.

or, in account form :—

IMPERSONAL LEDGER ACCOUNT.

PURCHASES.

DR. CR.

Date.	Details.	P.J. Fo.	Amount.	Date.	Details.	Fo.	Amount.
1938			£ *s.* *d.*				
Jan. 31	To Total Purchases for Month .	2	10 0 0				

We may also add that, from the point of view of the business, the charge or **debit** to the "Purchases" Account may be made by taking the **total** only of the appropriate column in the Purchase Journal.

This is in striking contrast to the necessity for giving **credit** to each separate supplier in **his own personal account.** We cannot avoid this latter step because we must know at any time **how the business stands in relation to each supplier.**

Purchase Returns and Allowances

It was seen on page 34 that Jones, as a supplier, was charged or **debited** with the goods returned to him, or the allowance claimed from him. As the result in either case is to **reduce the initial debit** to "Purchases" Account, the double entry will be completed by **crediting** that account, as follows :—

PURCHASE RETURNS AND ALLOWANCES BOOK.

(Book of First Entry.)

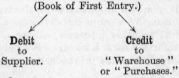

Debit to Supplier.

Credit to "Warehouse" or "Purchases."

or, in account form :—

IMPERSONAL LEDGER ACCOUNT.

PURCHASES.

DR. CR.

Date.	Details.	P.J. Fo.	Amount.	Date.	Details.	P.R.J. Fo.	Amount.
1938			£ s. d.	1938			£ s. d.
Jan. 31	To Total Purchases for Month .	2	10 0 0		By Total Returns and Allowances for Month.	3	1 10 0

Purchases of a Capital Nature

In the second example we saw that the purchase by D. Morris of showcases and fittings was recorded, together with his other purchases, in the Purchase Journal kept by him.

The personal aspect of this transaction is a credit to the suppliers in the Ledger Account opened in their name, *i.e.*, a **personal account.**

But, as with the receipt of goods by the warehouse on behalf of the business, we have similarly to put on record somewhere the purchase of these capital goods, or **fixed assets.**

There can be no question of charging them to the warehouse, since they are not goods in which the business is dealing.

But, nevertheless, an account must be opened for them in the Ledger, having regard to the necessity for completing the double entry **in the Ledger,** and so we may decide to open an account under the general heading of :—

"Fixtures and Fittings."

In this case the business has acquired property for the use or value of which it is liable to account to its proprietor, even though such property is not intended for resale, and it is right that it should be charged or, as we say, **debited** with the purchase cost of £57 10*s*.

The question now arises : **"In which section of Ledger** shall the account be opened ? "

What we have already done is to describe :—

(*a*) **Personal Accounts,** as with Jones.
(*b*) **Impersonal Accounts,** *e.g.*, Purchases,

the latter being the counterpart, in summarised form, of the former, so far as concerns **the effect upon the business.**

It is customary, in practice, having regard to the existence of these two types of account, to utilise **two entirely separate Ledgers,** known respectively as the **Personal Ledger** and the **Impersonal Ledger.**

As in the ordinary trading business of even quite moderate size the number of customers may be very large, we often find that the Personal Ledger is divided into two parts. The first part we call the **Sales Ledger,** as it is restricted to accounts with customers, and the latter the **Purchase Ledger,** as in it all the suppliers' accounts are opened.

By contrast, the accounts in the **Impersonal Ledger** will not be very numerous, and in the main they relate to those matters which affect the business in its **ordinary trading activities,** such as purchases, sales, wages, etc.

We could, of course, from the standpoint of the effect upon the business, open the "**Fixtures and Fittings**" **Account** in the Impersonal Ledger, and in that account record all dealings in that particular class of property.

But because the fixtures and fittings have no direct relation to the day-to-day trading activities, a **further section of the Ledger** is provided for the accounts of this and similar types of **fixed asset.**

This further section is termed the **Private Ledger,** and represents the third and final division of the Ledger as a book of account.

Once again, we post the **total** of the " special items " or " capital items " column in the Purchase Journal, so that the Fixtures and Fittings Account appears as follows :—

FIXTURES AND FITTINGS.

DR. CR.

Date.	Details.	P.J. Fo.	Amount.	Date.	Details.	Fo.	Amount.
1938			£ s. d.				
Jan. 31	To Showcases and Fittings .	2	57 10 0				

or in diagram form :—

PURCHASE JOURNAL.
(Book of First Entry.)

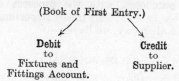

Debit to Fixtures and Fittings Account.	Credit to Supplier.

Sales.

Much of what we have said in regard to the completion of the double entry under the heading of purchases will apply in the case of **Sales,** although in the **reverse direction.**

We are still dealing with the **impersonal aspect, or the effect upon the business** of the delivery of goods from the warehouse to the customer.

What we must realise is that if goods are sold to Brown, for example, in his capacity as a **customer,** the warehouse having delivered the goods, is entitled to take credit to itself, as representing the business, for the goods that have passed out of its possession.

From the **personal aspect,** the customer Brown must, of course, be charged or **debited** with what he has received at **selling price.**

Impersonally the business is thus entitled to **credit** in an impersonal account, which may be headed :—

Warehouse, or
Goods sold, or more usually,
Sales.

Our reasons for so doing are :—

(*a*) As in the case of purchases, the double entry must be completed **within the Ledgers.**

(*b*) The business, or its proprietor, desires to know, period by period, how much has been **sold** of the various kinds of goods dealt in.

Therefore, if we open an account in the Impersonal Ledger, headed "**Sales,**" the periodic totals of the Sales Journal will be posted to it on the **credit** side, and, as with purchases, the Sales Journal will usually be ruled off at monthly intervals.

At any time, therefore, we may obtain a comparison of the **cost of purchases,** with the **proceeds of sales,** by examining these two accounts in the **Impersonal Ledger.**

Stated in another way, we have :—

SALES JOURNAL.

(Book of First Entry.)

↙ ↘

Debit to Customer.

Credit to "Warehouse" or "Sales."

or, in account form, assuming the sales value for the period to be £20 :—

SALES.

DR. CR.

Date.	Details.	Fo.	Amount.	Date.	Details.	S.J. Fo.	Amount.
				1938			£ s. d.
				Jan. 31	By Total Sales for Month	4	20 0 0

It will be noted from the "Details" column in the account, that we need concern ourselves only with the **total sales** as shown in the Sales Journal.

This is because, irrespective of the **kind** of goods sold, they may all be regarded as **sales,** and dealt with in the Ledger as one item.

In recording the **personal aspect,** however, a separate **debit** to each customer **in his own personal account** is essential if we are to know precisely :—

(*a*) How much has been sold to him.

(*b*) The amount of his indebtedness to the business at any particular time.

Sales Returns and Allowances

Should Brown, to whom £20 worth of goods have been sold, return any part of the goods, or make a claim on the business for an allowance in respect of the invoice price to him, the effect upon the business will be to reduce the initial **credit** to "Sales" Account. In other words, the latter account will be **debited** :—

SALES RETURNS AND ALLOWANCES BOOK.

(Book of First Entry.)

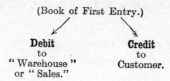

Debit to "Warehouse" or "Sales."	**Credit** to Customer.

or, in account form, assuming the amount of the allowance to be £5 :—

IMPERSONAL LEDGER ACCOUNT.

SALES.

DR. CR.

Date.	Details.	S.R.J. Fo.	Amount.	Date.	Details.	S.J. Fo.	Amount.
1938			£ *s.* *d.*	1938			£ *s.* *d.*
Jan. 31	To Total Returns and Allowances for Month.	5	5 0 0	Jan. 31	By Total Sales for Month	4	20 0 0

Sales of a Capital Nature.

These are far less frequently encountered than purchases of this class of goods.

It is possible to record such sales by inserting a "special items" column in the Sales Journal, but in practice use is almost always made of the earliest form of Journal, or the ordinary Debtor and Creditor Journal (without analysis columns) as illustrated in Chapter 7.

Examples that may be cited are the sale of a motor lorry, traveller's motor-car, or machine tool.

The Journal entry in such a case provides the basic narrative of the transaction for entry in the Ledgers, these being the personal (Sales) Ledger so far as the person to whom they are sold is concerned, and the account of the particular asset in the Private Ledger so far as concerns the effect on the business.

For the sake of completeness we may take the following :—

Example. On January 1, 1938, D. Morris had in his factory machinery of a book value of £500. On January 15 a stitching machine was sold to a dealer, realising £15.

PRIVATE LEDGER ACCOUNT.

MACHINERY.

DR. CR.

Date.	Details.	Fo.	Amount.	Date.	Details.	Fo.	Amount.
1938			£ *s.* *d.*	1938			£ *s.* *d.*
Jan. 1	To Balance .		500 0 0	Jan. 15	By A. Dealer, Stitching Machine.		15 0 0

An important point in connection with this transaction would be the loss on sale, *i.e.*, the proceeds of sale of £15 would have to be compared with that proportion of the commencing balance of £500 which represented the actual machine sold.

In this respect, no such difficulty would, of course, arise with **purchases** of capital goods. Here we are concerned with the purchase cost alone.

Once again, we may state the transaction in diagram form :—

SALES JOURNAL

or

ORDINARY JOURNAL.

(Book of First Entry.)

Debit to Customer. — **Credit** to Machinery Account.

While the **Personal Ledger** is restricted to the accounts of suppliers and customers in its purchase and sales sections respectively, the following examples are typical of the accounts appearing in the **Impersonal Ledger** and the **Private Ledger** :—

Impersonal Ledger (sometimes also called the **Nominal Ledger**).	**Private Ledger.**
Purchases.	Capital (of Proprietor).
Sales.	Factory, Warehouse or Office Premises.
Purchase Returns.	Machinery.
Sales Returns.	Tools.
Wages.	Fixtures and Fittings.
Carriage.	Motor Vehicles.
Salaries.	Patents.
Cash Discounts Allowed.	Trade Marks.
Cash Discounts Received.	Stock.
Bad Debts.	Bills of Exchange (Payable and Receivable).
Travelling Expenses.	Investments.
Packing Expenses.	Loans.
Repairs.	
Interest Paid.	and so on.
Interest Received.	
Rent.	
Rates.	
Commission.	

It might be added that in a general way, of the items appearing above, those under the heading of the "**Impersonal Ledger**" relate to accounts in which we find details of the **profit and loss,** or **revenue position of the business.**

Those, on the other hand, under the heading of the "**Private Ledger**" relate to the **assets and liabilities of the business.**

Now that we have become acquainted with the general application of Double Entry principles to the recording of Purchases and Sales transactions **within the Ledgers,** let us carry the Example on page 22 a stage further, and imagine we have been instructed to **post to the Ledger Accounts** from the various books of Prime Entry which we have already written up.

(*a*) **Purchases.**

In the Purchase Day Book of D. Morris we see it is necessary to give **credit** to each one of the three suppliers whose names appear therein. Such credit will clearly be given in the **Personal** (**Purchase**) **Ledger,** and the three accounts required will be opened as follows :—

D. Morris.

PURCHASE LEDGER.

R. RIDGWELL, BOLTON.

Dr. Cr.

Date.	Details.	Fo.	Amount.	Date.	Details.	P.J. Fo.	Amount.
				1937 Mar. 12	By Goods .	1	£ s. d. 49 2 0

B. DAVIS, ELY.

Dr. Cr.

Date.	Details.	Fo.	Amount.	Date.	Details.	P.J. Fo.	Amount.
				1937 Mar. 20	By Goods .	1	£ s. d. 226 5 0

GENERAL SUPPLIES, LTD., LONDON.

Dr. Cr.

Date.	Details.	Fo.	Amount.	Date.	Details.	P.J. Fo.	Amount.
				1937 Mar. 29	By Goods .	1	£ s. d. 57 10 0

In each case the entries appear on the **credit side** since, until payment is made to them, the suppliers are creditors of the business.

The use of the word " Goods " in the " Details " column is all that is necessary, as full particulars of the goods can quickly be found on Folio 1 of the Purchase Journal itself.

We must now consider the **impersonal aspect,** which is the charge to the warehouse for " Goods Purchased," or **" Purchases."** It is necessary, too, for us to remember that by this is meant **" goods purchased for resale,"** so that we must in any event exclude the item of Showcases and Fittings.

Our Impersonal Ledger Account for Purchases will then be :—

PURCHASES.

Dr. Date.	Details.	P.J. Fo.	Amount.	Date.	Details.	Fo.	Amount. Cr.
1937			£ s. d.				
Mar. 31	To Total for **Month :**						
	Cloth .		31 5 0				
	Blankets		27 10 0				
	Shawls .		201 12 0				
	Sundries.		15 0 0				
		1	£275 7 0				

But it is scarcely likely that we shall rest content with the *form* of this account, because month by month new totals will appear in it, and the subsequent addition of the " Amount " column will be somewhat complicated.

For this reason, it may be preferred to open a separate Purchases Account **for each class of goods,** or to enter them in one account, but in **columnar** form.

Let us assume the former method is selected. We shall then have :—

IMPERSONAL LEDGER.

PURCHASES—CLOTH.

Dr. Date.	Details.	P.J. Fo.	Amount.	Date.	Details.	Fo.	Amount. Cr.
1937			£ s. d.				
Mar. 31	To Total for Month .	1	31 5 0				

PURCHASES—BLANKETS.

Dr. Date.	Details.	P.J. Fo.	Amount.	Date.	Details.	Fo.	Amount. Cr.
1937			£ s. d.				
Mar. 31	To Total for Month .	1	27 10 0				

PURCHASES—SHAWLS.

DR. CR.

Date.	Details.	P.J. Fo.	Amount.	Date.	Details.	Fo.	Amount.
1937			£ s. d.				
Mar. 31	To Total for Month .	1	201 12 0				

PURCHASES—SUNDRIES.

DR. CR.

Date.	Details.	P.J. Fo.	Amount.	Date.	Details.	Fo.	Amount.
1937			£ s. d.				
Mar. 31	To Total for Month .	1	15 0 0				

In regard to the showcases and fittings purchased, an account in the **Private Ledger** will be opened, as under :—

FIXTURES AND FITTINGS.

DR. CR.

Date.	Details.	P.J. Fo.	Amount.	Date.	Details.	Fo.	Amount.
1937			£ s. d.				
Mar. 31	To Total for Month .	1	57 10 0				

It must be noted that the charge to the business for **purchases** and **fixtures and fittings** is made on the **debit** side, the amount in each case being the **total** of the appropriate analysis column in the Purchase Journal.

We thus see that :—

(*a*) The Purchase Journal as a Book of Prime Entry provides a basis for the Double Entry.

(*b*) The dual aspect of the transactions has been recorded **within the Ledgers.**

(*c*) Arithmetical agreement has been obtained, in that the sum of the **credit** entries or postings in the Purchase Ledger is equal to the sum of the **debit** postings in the **Impersonal** and **Private Ledgers.**

(*d*) While the postings to the Impersonal and Private Ledger Accounts are made on March 31 and in **total** only, those to the Personal Ledger are made as soon as possible after the initial record in the Journal. It is essential to have our Ledger Account with each supplier "up to date."

(*b*) Purchase Returns and Allowances

In the Purchase Returns Book we see there are two entries relating, in the first case, to an overcharge, and in the second, to the return of goods by the business to one of its suppliers.

In recording the **personal aspect** we must therefore remember that the suppliers' accounts in the Purchase Ledger will be **debited,** resulting in a reduction of any amounts hitherto standing to their **credit.**

This is a logical step to take because, had the overcharge not been detected, we should have **debited** Hunt with a payment **greater** than was actually due to him. The issue of a Debit Note now clearly reduces the amount of any subsequent payment to him by the business.

Further, the **receipt of a Credit Note** from Luxton enables the business to debit him with the cost of the goods returned for which, when purchased, it had originally given him credit.

The Purchase Ledger Accounts of the two suppliers will then appear as follows :—

PURCHASE LEDGER.

W. HUNT.

DR. CR.

Date.	Details.	P.R.J. Fo.	Amount.	Date.	Details.	P.J. Fo.	Amount.
			£ s. d.				
1937 Mar. 15	To Overcharge	1	12 0 0				

V. LUXTON.

DR. CR.

Date.	Details.	P.R.J. Fo.	Amount.	Date.	Details.	P.J. Fo.	Amount.
			£ s. d.				
1937 Mar. 27	To Returns .	2	1 17 6				

As this is the only information we have concerning these suppliers the result is that they are shown as **debtors** to the business to this extent, it being assumed that they have received payment in full in some previous period.

In practice, however, it is almost certain that in the first case at least, payment would not be made until the overcharge in question had been corrected.

With regard to the **impersonal** aspect, we can now appreciate that the warehouse will be **credited.** The reason for giving it credit now, is that it was originally charged or **debited** with the goods purchased at the invoice or cost price to the business. The credit thus given to it puts on record the fact that its responsibility is lessened by the amount, in total, of £13 17*s.* 6*d.*

The Purchase Returns, or Returns Outwards Accounts, will then be credited on March 31 with the **total of** the appropriate analysis columns in the Purchase Returns Journal as under :—

PURCHASE RETURNS—CLOTH.

DR. CR.

Date.	Details.	Fo.	Amount.	Date.	Details.	P.R.J. Fo.	Amount.
							£ *s.* *d.*
				1937 Mar. 31	By Total for Month .	1	1 17 6

PURCHASE RETURNS—SUNDRIES.

DR. CR.

Date.	Details.	Fo.	Amount.	Date.	Details.	P.R.J. Fo.	Amount.
							£ *s.* *d.*
				1937 Mar. 31	By Total for Month .	2	12 0 0

Once more, it is seen that :—

(*a*) The Double Entry is completed within the Ledgers, Personal and Impersonal.

(*b*) Arithmetical agreement is maintained, the sum of the **debit** items being equal to the sum of the **credits,** and

(*c*) While the postings to the accounts of Hunt and Luxton are made on the dates of the transactions with them, those to the Purchase Returns Accounts are made in total on March 31.

(*c*) **Sales.**

The Sales Journal gives us full particulars of the sales to the three customers for whom we shall open separate accounts in the **Sales Ledger.**

To record the personal aspect, we must show that they are debtors to the business, and therefore their accounts will be in **debit,** taking the following form :—

W. HUMPHREY, LINCOLN.

DR. CR.

Date.	Details.	S.J. Fo.	Amount.	Date.	Details.	Fo.	Amount.
1937 Mar. 10	To Goods .		£ *s.* *d.* 48 7 6				

S. BOHAM, COVENTRY.

DR. CR.

Date.	Details.	S.J. Fo.	Amount.	Date.	Details.	Fo.	Amount.
1937 Mar. 18	To Goods .		£ *s.* *d.* 71 12 10				

T. BUTTERWORTH, NORWICH.

DR. CR.

Date.	Details.	S.J. Fo.	Amount.	Date.	Details.	Fo.	Amount.
1937 Mar. 24	To Goods .		£ *s.* *d.* 65 14 0				

We should now be able to understand the meaning of what has been done in our book-keeping work. If in the case of **personal** accounts, like those set out above, the entries appear on the debit side, or there is an excess in value of debit entries over credit entries, the person whose name appears at the head of the account is always a debtor to the business. He is chargeable to the extent of paying the business for the goods it has sold to him.

If a similar state of affairs is found to exist in an **impersonal** account, such as " Purchases," it indicates that the official of the business under whose control the goods have come is chargeable to account for them until the time of their ultimate sale.

But as we are here dealing with **sales,** it is necessary to give **credit** to the warehouse which has parted with goods on the instructions of the Sales Department, and has therefore reduced its responsibility to account in the proper way.

Thus, an account will be opened in the **Impersonal** Ledger for " Goods Sold " or " Sales," as follows :—

SALES.

DR. CR.

Date.	Details.	Fo.	Amount.	Date.	Details.	S.J. Fo.	Amount.
				1937			£ s. d.
				Mar. 31	By Total for Month:		
					Cloth .		126 3 9
					Velvet .		51 1 3
					Sundries.		8 9 4
							£185 14 4

As explained on page 47, in connection with the analysis of purchases, we shall, however, almost certainly prefer to open separate Sales Accounts for the various kinds of goods to correspond with the columns in the Sales Journal.

The result will then be :—

SALES—CLOTH.

DR. CR.

Date.	Details.	Fo.	Amount.	Date.	Details.	S.J. Fo.	Amount.
				1937			£ s. d.
				Mar. 31	By Total for Month .		126 3 9

SALES—VELVET.

DR. CR.

Date.	Details.	Fo.	Amount.	Date.	Details.	S.J. Fo.	Amount.
				1937			£ s. d.
				Mar. 31	By Total for Month .		51 1 3

SALES—SUNDRIES.

DR. CR.

Date.	Details.	Fo.	Amount.	Date.	Details.	S.J. Fo.	Amount.
				1937			£ s. d.
				Mar. 31	By Total for Month .		8 9 4

By means of these analysed Impersonal Accounts it is now possible for the proprietor of the business to compare, month by month, the **purchase cost** with the **proceeds of sale** of the various articles in which he is dealing.

(*d*) **Sales Returns and Allowances.**

As with Purchases, we find in this book two entries which must be posted to the Ledger, involving the completion of the **personal aspect** at once and as a separate posting to the account of each customer, and of the **impersonal aspect** at the end of the month, and in total only.

We find, however, this difference from Purchases : The goods returned by Humphrey are part of those sold to him during the month under review; while both items come under the head of " Returns," there being no question of an overcharge.

Let us try to visualise what these two entries mean. If we are in any doubt, it may be simpler to deal first with the Impersonal aspect.

The warehouse has received the goods, increasing its stock, for which it is accountable. It is, therefore, logical that we should charge or **debit** it with the **total** value of the returned goods.

At the same time, the customers have performed a " credit-worthy " action, to this extent offsetting the original charge or debit made to them individually. It is equally reasonable, therefore, to **credit** them with the returned goods. This credit, in the case of Humphrey, will cause his account to appear as under :

W. HUMPHREY, LINCOLN.

DR. CR.

Date.	Details.	S.J. Fo.	Amount.	Date.	Details.	S.R.J. Fo.	Amount.
1937			£ s. d.	1937			£ s. d.
Mar. 10	To Goods .		48 7 6	Mar. 22	By Returns .		7 17 6

and from it we can see that his original indebtedness is now reduced, **which is in line with the facts.**

As regards Jenkinson, he too will receive **credit,** as follows :—

A. JENKINSON, WOLVERHAMPTON.

DR. CR.

Date.	Details.	Fo.	Amount.	Date.	Details.	S.R.J. Fo.	Amount.
				1937 Mar. 23	By Returns .		£ s. d. 2 10 8

But, since we know nothing of his original indebtedness to the business, the position is that he appears as a creditor for the amount shown above. Payment may either be made to him in settlement, or more probably, the credit will be taken into account by him when he next pays for any further goods supplied.

Finally, to complete the double entry, we shall post the totals of the appropriate columns in the Sales Returns Journals to the **Debit** of the Impersonal Ledger Accounts for "**Sales Returns—Cloth**" and "**Sales Returns—Velvet,**" just as we did with **Purchases.**

In both cases, the warehouse has received goods, either from a supplier, or from a customer.

SALES RETURNS—CLOTH.

DR. CR.

Date.	Details.	S.R.J. Fo.	Amount.	Date.	Details.	Fo.	Amount.
1937 Mar. 31	To Total for Month .		£ s. d. 7 17 6				

SALES RETURNS—VELVET.

DR. CR.

Date.	Details.	S.R.J. Fo.	Amount.	Date.	Details.	Fo.	Amount.
1937 Mar. 31	To Total for Month .		£ s. d. 2 10 8				

Summary.

With each of the Journals we have been careful to regard them as providing the basis for the completion of the double entry **within the Ledgers.** They have, therefore, served their purpose in enabling us to look at each one of the **purchasing** and **selling transactions** from their **dual aspect,** or the Personal and Impersonal aspect.

Irrespective of the **Number** of these transactions during any particular period, we are now in a position to tabulate the information contained in the Ledger Accounts in the form of the **balances** thereon. These balances will be obtained by a scrutiny of each account, so that the amount of one item or of the total items on the debit side will be termed a **debit balance,** or if on the credit side, a **credit balance.** Where entries appear on both debit and credit sides, the excess of the one side over the other will also be termed the balance, according to its nature, but this we shall appreciate more readily after dealing with Cash Receipts and Cash Payments.

In the meantime, we will extract and state the balances as they now appear in the various Ledger Accounts :—

Page.	Ledger.	Name of Account.	Dr. £	s.	d.	Cr. £	s.	d.
46	Purchase	R. Ridgwell				49	2	0
"	"	B. Davis				226	5	0
"	"	General Supplies, Ltd.				57	10	0
49	"	W. Hunt	12	0	0			
"	"	V. Luxton	1	17	6			
53	Sales	W. Humphrey	40	10	0			
51	"	S. Boham	71	12	10			
"	"	T. Butterworth	65	14	0			
54	"	A. Jenkinson				2	10	8
47	Impersonal	Purchases—Cloth	31	5	0			
"	"	" Blankets	27	10	0			
48	"	" Shawls	201	12	0			
"	"	" Sundries	15	0	0			
50	"	Purchase Returns—Cloth				1	17	6
"	"	" " Sundries				12	0	0
52	"	Sales—Cloth				126	3	9
"	"	" Velvet				51	1	3
53	"	" Sundries				8	9	4
54	"	Sales Returns—Cloth	7	17	6			
"	"	" " Velvet	2	10	8			
48	Private	Fixtures and Fittings	57	10	0			
			£534	19	6	£534	19	6

It should be mentioned that in the average business by far the greater number of accounts will be found in the **Personal Ledgers,** and especially in that section of those Ledgers containing the accounts of customers, or **Sales** Ledger. So large may this become as a result of the business enlarging its sales connection that its division on an alphabetical or territorial basis may be essential if the Accounting Department is to do its work with speed and efficiency.

Tests and Questions

1. Name the different Ledgers employed in the ordinary trading concern, and mention the classes of account you would expect to find in each.

(University of Birmingham.)

2. Explain carefully :—

(*a*) Nominal Accounts.
(*b*) Real Accounts.
(*c*) Personal Accounts.

(East Midland Educational Union.)

3. On which side of the following Ledger Accounts would you expect to find the balance? Give reasons for your answer in each case :—

Bad Debts Account.
Plant and Machinery Account.
Sales Account.
Discount Account.
Returns Outwards Account.

(Union of Educational Institutions.)

4. W. Green has the following transactions with J. Black :—

1936			£
July	10.	Goods sold to W. Green	420
„	15.	Goods returned by W. Green	20
Sept.	30.	Interest charged	2
Oct.	10.	Cheque received from W. Green	392
„	10.	Discount deducted	10
„	11.	W. Green charged with discount deducted in error	10

You are required to show how each of the foregoing items would be recorded in the books of J. Black.

(University of Manchester.)

5. Brown and Smith are two merchants. At January 1, 1932, Smith owes Brown £146 3*s*. 9*d*., and during the month of January the following transactions took place between them :—

1932			£	s.	d.
Jan.	5.	Brown purchased goods of Smith	126	4	3
,,	12.	Smith sends goods to Brown	50	1	9
,,	15.	Brown pays cash to Smith	95	0	0
		Smith allows discount	5	0	0
,,	20.	Smith allows Brown's claim for damaged goods	10	0	0
,,	24.	Smith sells to Brown goods	131	6	8
,,	30.	Brown borrows from Smith for temporary accommodation	50	0	0

You are required :—

(*a*) To give the account of Brown in the Ledger of Smith, and

(*b*) To bring down the balance at the end of January, 1932, and

(*c*) To state which party is indebted to the other.

(Institute of Bankers.)

6. From the following particulars, draw up the Capital Account of J. Owen as it would appear in his books for the year 1933. Balance it off as on December 31, 1933, and bring down the balance :—

	£	s.	d.
Capital as January 1, 1933	416	5	1
Profit for the year 1933 was	314	5	6
On October 15 J. Owen paid in additional capital	500	0	0
During the year J. Owen drew out of the business for private expenses	250	0	0
On December 31, 1933, interest on capital was allowed	22	0	0

(Union of Educational Institutions.)

7. (*a*) Make entries to record the following :—

1935
Jan. 5. Purchase of goods from B. & Co., £300.
Feb. 5. Payment by cheque to B. & Co., *less* 5% cash discount.

(*b*) On February 20, 1935, it was discovered that bank charges under date of December 31, 1934, amounting to £5 5*s*., had not been recorded. Adjust.

(*c*) On December 31, 1934, the balance on Motor Vans Account was £100, representing an Élite lorry. A new Élite lorry was purchased for cash on March 31, 1935, for £275, and £75 was allowed in part exchange for the old lorry, the cash passing being £200. Make the appropriate entries to record and dispose of the matter.

(University of Birmingham.)

8. In what Ledger or other accounts, and upon which side of such accounts, would you expect to find the following :—

(*a*) £500 paid for new machinery.
(*b*) £170 received from J. Robinson in full settlement of his account of £172 12*s*. 6*d*.
(*c*) £600 received from an Insurance Company in settlement of a claim for damages to premises by fire.
(*d*) £75 received for the sale of old motor van.
(*e*) £250 paid to J. Fitter in full settlement of an account due to him three months hence of £260 15*s*.

(Royal Society of Arts.)

CHAPTER IV

CASH TRANSACTIONS

Question. From what you have been saying about the accounts in the various Ledgers, am I correct in thinking that all they show at the moment are balances in respect of Trading Transactions?

Answer. Yes, in respect of Purchases and Sales on Credit Terms. What we now have to do is to consider the Receipt and Payment of **Cash** by the business, usually at the end of the period of credit allowed to or by it.

Question. You said at an earlier stage that some portion of the Capital with which the business was begun must necessarily be in the form of Cash. That would be in order to pay its running expenses?

Answer. Not only such expenses as Wages and Salaries, but also to pay suppliers who might at the outset be unwilling to give credit to a new business.

Question. Would it be right to describe such Cash as the **Working Capital** employed?

Answer. It forms a part, but by no means the whole, of the Working Capital, as we shall see later. A better definition would be that it is a **Liquid Asset,** and its subsequent use for the purposes of the business may result in its becoming a **Current Asset,** as when goods are bought for stock, or a **Fixed Asset**, when Plant, Fittings, etc., are purchased.

Question. In the case of goods in which the business dealt, you said these were entrusted to the warehouse manager, who was responsible for their receipt and issue. Is the cashier similarly responsible for the Cash Assets?

Answer. No, only for what is termed **Cash in Hand**; this, however, is negligible in amount as compared with the moneys lying in the Bank Account of the business, or **Cash at Bank.** Between the two, there is this difference: the **Cashier,** as a servant of the business, will always be, on balance, accountable to it for cash held by him. The **Bank,** on the other hand, may sometimes be the creditor of the business, as where moneys are advanced on loan or by way of overdraft.

Procedure in Office on Receipt of Cash.

On the opening of each day's incoming mail, all remittances from customers will be passed on to the cashier. They will usually be accompanied by the statements of account which the business has issued at monthly intervals to its customers.

The cashier will :—

(*a*) Compare the amount remitted with the total of the statement and, at the same time, check the **Cash Discount** which the customer may have deducted.

(*b*) **Cash Discount** is the inducement offered by the business to its customers to pay within the recognised period of credit. As such it is an expense to the business, which must always be taken into account with the accompanying remittance. If the terms upon which business is done are " $2\frac{1}{2}$% monthly account," and the customer's debt is £100, then **if he pays on or before the end of the month following delivery of the goods to him,** he need remit £97 10*s*. only. On the other hand, if he pays after the expiry of the credit period, the discount will not ordinarily be allowed.

To the extent that Cash Discount refers to the customers of the business, it is termed **Discount Allowed,** and it differs from **Trade Discount,** which we discussed on page 20, in that it always relates to the cash or financial aspect of each transaction. Looked at in another way, it assists the business in collecting what is due to it from its customers, and in maintaining a minimum of **Cash** or **Liquid Assets.**

The cashier will also :—

(*c*) So far as **cheques** are received, cross these, if they are uncrossed, or if already crossed, insert the name of the bankers of the business who are, of course, the collecting bankers.

(*d*) Enter the remittances in detail in either a rough cash diary or Journal, as a preliminary to entry in the Cash Book proper, or enter them at once in the Cash Book. Whichever alternative is adopted, such initial entry is a **Prime** or **First** entry, and therefore corresponds to the record of Purchases or Sales in the Purchase and Sales Journals.

(*e*) List the remittances on the counterfoil of the bank paying-in book, so that the total thereof is in agreement with the total of the entries for the particular business day appearing in the Cash Book of the business. Thus, the amount actually banked will agree with the business records.

(*f*) Make out, in the name of each customer, formal receipts, which may be attached to the statements of account and then issued to the customers for retention by them.

The Cash Book or Cash Journal will then be available for the ledger clerks, whose duty it will be to post the amount of each remittance **to the credit of the Ledger Account of the customer from whom it was received.**

Book-keeping Entries.

We can best approach these by considering the cashier as being very much in the same position as the warehouseman, with the difference that he is responsible for **cash** instead of **goods.**

If, therefore, we apply the same reasoning to his responsibility as a servant of the business we shall charge him with **all incoming cash.** It is logical to do this, so that he may at any time be accountable for its safe custody and disposal.

Using a term with which we have now become familiar, the cashier will be **debited** with all moneys received and, as was indicated above, each of the customers will be **credited,** the latter having performed a " credit-worthy " action in paying to the business what is due by them.

We may, therefore, if we so desire, as is often done in practice, commence our records by opening a **Cash Received Journal** in which all moneys received from customers, whether in the form of cheques, notes, coin, etc., will be entered. Bearing in mind the fact that in many cases Cash Discount has been allowed to the customers, it will be helpful to show the amount of the discount **by the side of** the item to which it relates, as follows :—

CASH RECEIVED JOURNAL.

Date.	Customer.	Total.			Discount.			Cash.		
1938		£	*s.*	*d.*	£	*s.*	*d.*	£	*s.*	*d.*
Feb. 20	G. Green	100	0	0	2	10	0	97	10	0

From this it is apparent that G. Green has now settled his debt of £100, and in collecting its due from him, the business has been obliged to incur an **expense** of £2 10*s.* which, clearly, must reduce the figure of **profit** it expects to make.

Like the Purchase and Sales Journals, the Cash Book will probably be ruled off and totalled at the end of each month, with the result that, as with our Purchase and Sales transactions, we shall find it desirable :—

(*a*) To give **credit** to **each customer** immediately on receipt of his separate remittance.

(*b*) To **debit** or charge the **cashier** in total with the cash receipts, irrespective of the individual details making up the total.

The Cash Received Journal enables us to do this, and at the same time to comply with **double entry principles,** as the following diagram shows :—

CASH RECEIVED JOURNAL.
(Book of First Entry.)

↙ ↘

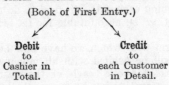

Debit to Cashier in Total. — **Credit** to each Customer in Detail.

or in account form :—

Fo. 1.

CASH RECEIVED JOURNAL.

Date.	Customer.	Total.			Discount.			Cash.		
1938		£	*s.*	*d.*	£	*s.*	*d.*	£	*s.*	*d.*
Feb. 20	G. Green	100	0	0	2	10	0	97	10	0
" 22	B. Brown	50	0	0	–	–	–	50	0	0
		£150	0	0	£2	10	0	£147	10	0

SALES LEDGER.

G. GREEN.

DR. CR.

Date.	Details.	Fo.	Amount.	Date.	Details.	C.R.J. Fo.	Amount.
				1938			£ s. d.
				Feb. 20	By Cash .	1	97 10 0
					" Discount	1	2 10 0
							£100 0 0

B. BROWN.

DR. CR.

Date.	Details.	Fo.	Amount.	Date.	Details.	C.R.J. Fo.	Amount.
				1938			£ s. d.
				Feb. 22	By Cash .	1	50 0 0

PRIVATE LEDGER.

CASH.

DR. CR.

Date.	Details.	C.R.J. Fo.	Amount.	Date.	Details.	Fo.	Amount.
1938			£ s. d.				
Feb. 28	To Total Cash .	1	147 10 0				

In the above, we note **firstly** that the **Cash Account** appears in the **Private Ledger.** This is as we should expect because the Private Ledger is concerned with **Assets** and **Liabilities,** and Cash Received is manifestly an **Asset.**

Secondly, we note that, while our aim is to complete the Double Entry **within the Ledgers,** the sum of the two credit balances on the accounts of Green and Brown is £150, whereas we have a debit balance on Cash Account of £147 10*s*. only.

That is to say, so far as **discount allowed** is concerned, we have given credit to G. Green personally **in the Ledger** for that amount, but we have not impersonally noted its effect upon the business. The business must be charged with that amount as an expense or loss resulting from its dealings with Green, and it is therefore necessary to open in the Impersonal Ledger an account for **Discounts Allowed.**

DISCOUNT ALLOWED.

DR. CR.

Date.	Details.	C.R.J. Fo.	Amount.	Date.	Details.	Fo.	Amount.
1938			£ s. d.				
Feb. 28	To Total Discount .	1	2 10 0				

Arising from this we see that—

(*a*) The double entry is completed **within the Ledgers.**

(*b*) A Debit Balance in an **Impersonal** Ledger Account, *e.g.* Discount, is a business **expense,** and a debit balance on a **Private** Ledger Account is for our present purpose an **Asset** of the business.

(*c*) Any Debit Balances formerly appearing on the accounts of Green and Brown in the **Sales Ledger** will have been extinguished by the posting to their credit of the cash now received.

Procedure in Office on Payment of Cash

Periodically, say at monthly intervals, the business will pay its **suppliers** for what has been purchased from them. At the end of each month a statement of account may have been received from them setting out the balance in their favour. This will be compared with the total standing to their credit in the various **Purchase Ledger** Accounts. Care will be taken to deduct, if omitted in the statement, the value of any goods returned to them by the business, and similarly a deduction will be made for Cash Discount, discount which in this instance we may rightly term **discount received,** or **receivable,** considering it, that is, from the standpoint of the business.

Thus on or before the end of the month following delivery of the goods a list will be prepared of all **accounts payable,** setting out :—

(*a*) The folio of the supplier's account in the Purchase Ledger,

(*b*) The name of the supplier,

(*c*) The total amount due,

(*d*) The amount of the discount, and

(*e*) The sum now payable.

This list, together with the Statement of Account received from the suppliers, will be submitted to the proprietor, or to some responsible official of the business, by whom the cheques issued in settlement will be signed.

Book-keeping Entries

When the warehouseman issued goods to customers, it was seen at an earlier stage that he would be given credit for their value at **selling price,** the credit being given in "Goods Sold" or **Sales** Account.

With the **payment** of cash, we have likewise to give **credit** to the cashier, which is only logical, having charged or **debited** him with cash **received.**

We shall, at the same time, **debit** the cash payment to each of the suppliers, thus offsetting the amounts for which they appear as **creditors,** and indicating that the liability of the business to them is now discharged.

For this purpose, a **Cash Paid Journal,** or Cash Paid Book, may be opened, as a Book of First Entry, ruled with columns for discount earned and the actual cash paid.

CASH PAID JOURNAL.

Date.	Supplier.	Total.			Discount.			Cash.		
		£	s.	d.	£	s.	d.	£	s.	d.
1938 Feb. 23	L. Lindsay	30	0	0		15	0	29	5	0

The record shown above indicates that a liability to L. Lindsay of £30 has been satisfied by a cash payment of £29 5*s*. and that a **profit** of 15*s*. has been earned.

The Cash Paid Journal enables us to :—

(*a*) Charge or **debit each supplier** immediately on payment of money to him.

(*b*) **Credit** the **cashier** in total with the total cash payments, irrespective of the individual details.

This may be put in another way :—

CASH PAID JOURNAL.
(Book of First Entry.)

↙ ↘

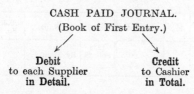

Debit to each Supplier **in Detail.**

Credit to Cashier **in Total.**

or in account form :—

Fo. 2.

CASH PAID JOURNAL.

Date.	Supplier.	Total.			Discount.			Cash.		
1938		£	s.	d.	£	s.	d.	£	s.	d.
Feb. 23	L. Lindsay	30	0	0		15	0	29	5	0
„ 26	M. Morris	75	0	0	1	17	6	73	2	6
		£105	0	0	£2	12	6	£102	7	6

PURCHASE LEDGER.

L. LINDSAY.

DR. CR.

Date.	Details.	C.P.J. Fo.	Amount.			Date.	Details.	Fo.	Amount.
1938			£	s.	d.				
Feb. 23	To Cash .	2	29	5	0				
	„ Discount.	2		15	0				
			£30	0	0				

M. MORRIS.

DR. CR.

Date.	Details.	C.P.J. Fo.	Amount.			Date.	Details.	Fo.	Amount.
1938			£	s.	d.				
Feb. 26	To Cash .	2	73	2	6				
	„ Discount.	2	1	17	6				
			£75	0	0				

PRIVATE LEDGER.

CASH.

DR. CR.

Date.	Details.	Fo.	Amount.	Date.	Details.	C.P.J. Fo.	Amount.		
				1938			£	s.	d.
				Feb. 28	By Total Cash .	2	102	7	6

As the counterpart of cash received, but in the reverse direction, the Cash Account in the Private Ledger has a credit balance, which here denotes a **liability.** This will be clearer to us if we think of the banker of the business instead of its cashier. If he has paid money away on behalf of the business to its suppliers, the banker will have a claim upon it to that extent, and this claim is, of course, a liability of the business.

So far as the balances on the Ledger Accounts are concerned, the sum of the **debits** in the Purchase Ledger is seen to be £105, while the **credit** on Cash Account is £102 7*s*. 6*d*.

The impersonal aspect of discount received, or discount earned, is that a profit of £2 12*s*. 6*d*. has been made for which credit may be taken. We may therefore open, again in the Impersonal Ledger, the following account :—

DISCOUNT RECEIVED.

DR. CR.

Date.	Details.	Fo.	Amount.	Date.	Details.	C.P.J. Fo.	Amount.
							£ *s*. *d*.
				1938 Feb. 28	By Total Discount .	2	2 12 6

Once more, the double entry is completed **within the Ledgers,** and we see that a credit balance on an Impersonal Ledger Account is a business **profit,** a similar balance on a Private Ledger Account being a **liability** of the business.

Goods and Cash Compared

(*a*) When **goods** are bought, **Purchases** Account is debited and the individual suppliers credited ; when **goods** are sold, the individual customers are debited, and **Sales** Account is credited.

In the Impersonal Ledger there are thus two accounts in respect of the trading transactions, purchases and sales.

But in our **cash** dealings, recorded in total in the Private Ledger, **we have only one cash account,** debited as regards cash received and credited with cash paid.

(*b*) Goods purchased will be valued at **cost price** per unit, but goods sold at **selling price.** Moreover, in a manufacturing business at least, goods purchased may largely consist of raw materials, while goods sold will be the finished product—an essentially different article. With cash, however, whether it be cash received or cash paid, the value per unit is the same in a country having a stable currency.

For these reasons, we are able to **merge** our cash received and our cash paid **in one account** only, or by using the figures already given above :—

CASH.

DR. DR.

Date.	Details.	C.R.J. Fo.	Amount.	Date.	Details.	C.P.J. Fo.	Amount.
1938			£ s. d.	1938			£ s. d.
Feb. 28	To Total Cash .	1	147 10 0	Feb. 28	By Total Cash .	2	102 7 6

It is clear that the excess of the debit side, or £45 2*s*. 6*d*., represents an **asset** of the business, while if the larger amount appeared on the credit side, it would be a **liability.**

From this we may draw three conclusions :—

(*a*) That instead of having two Books of First Entry, a Cash Received Journal and a Cash Paid Journal, **one book will suffice,** and we may call it the Cash Journal, or as is more usual the **Cash Book.**

(*b*) That if such is the case the Ledger Account for cash can be dispensed with, and because it contains all our cash receipts and payments, **the Cash Book is not only a Book of Prime Entry, but is also a Ledger Account,** in that,

(*c*) Whether the cashier or the banker is entrusted with the cash resources, **the position of the business in relation to either** can quickly be seen from a perusal of the Cash Book.

Proceeding on the basis that incoming cash remittances are banked intact on the day of receipt, and all payments are made by cheque, writing up the Cash Book daily as a

Book of First Entry is equivalent to writing up the Ledger Account with the bank.

If, however, a minimum amount of cash must be retained by the business in order to pay petty expenses, and if, also, wages and salaries have to be paid in cash and not by cheque, it is necessary to provide **additional columns** in the Cash Book to record purely cash, as distinct from banking transactions.

We may now take an example to make this clear :—

Example. From the following particulars, draw up the three-column Cash Book of V. Treat. No posting to the Ledger is required and no money is to be paid into the bank unless and until instructions are given.

Jan. 1. Commenced business with cash in hand £21 and cash at bank £175.
,, 2. Paid into bank out of office cash £17.
,, 3. Cash sales £36.
,, 4. Drew cheque £10 for private use ; paid Wages by cash £6.
,, 5. Paid Rent by cheque £22.
,, 6. Paid into bank additional capital £110.
,, 8. Received a cheque from Light Bros. £22 in settlement of their account of £22 15*s*.
,, 9. Paid Brown & Sons cheque for £48, receiving discount £2 11*s*.
,, 10. Received a cheque from Bilton, Ltd., value £14, in settlement of their account of £14 10*s*.
,, 11. Drew cheque £28 for office use.
,, 12. Paid into bank the two cheques received from Light Bros. and Bilton, Ltd., respectively.
,, 13. Paid Jennens, Ltd., cheque £95, having deducted discount 5% from their account.
,, 16. Light Bros. cheque was returned by the bank marked R/D.
,, 31. Interest and bank charges for the month £1 8*s*.

Balance off the Cash Book and bring down the balances as on January 31.

(Union of Educational Institutions.)

If we look more closely at this example, we shall see that provision is made in the columns headed " Cash "

V. TREAT.

CASH BOOK.

DR.

Date.		Discount. £ s. d.	Cash. £ s. d.	Bank. £ s. d.
1938				
Jan. 1	To Capital A/c		21 0 0	175 0 0
„ 2	„ Cash			17 0 0
„ 3	„ Cash Sales		36 0 0	
„ 6	„ Capital A/c			110 0 0
„ 8	„ Light Bros.	15 0	22 0 0	
„ 10	„ Bilton, Ltd.	10 0	14 0 0	
„ 11	„ Bank		28 0 0	
„ 12	„ Cash, cheques per contra			36 0 0
		£1 5 0	£121 0 0	£338 0 0
Feb. 1	To Balances b/d		62 0 0	111 12 0

CR.

Date.		Discount. £ s. d.	Cash. £ s. d.	Bank. £ s. d.
1938				
Jan. 2	By Bank		17 0 0	
„ 4	„ Drawings			10 0 0
„ 4	„ Wages		6 0 0	
„ 5	„ Rent			22 0 0
„ 9	„ Brown & Sons	2 11 0		48 0 0
„ 11	„ Cash			28 0 0
„ 12	„ Bank, cheques from Light Bros. and Bilton, Ltd.		36 0 0	
„ 13	„ Jennens, Ltd.	5 0 0		95 0 0
„ 16	„ Light Bros., cheque returned	15 0		22 0 0
„ 31	„ Interest and Bank Charges			1 8 0
„ 31	„ Balances c/d		62 0 0	111 12 0
		£8 6 0	£121 0 0	£338 0 0

and " Bank " respectively for a statement at any time of the position of the business as regards :—

(*a*) Its cashier, and
(*b*) Its banker.

At the beginning of the month the proprietor introduced as Cash Capital £196, divided as shown, and the description of the item " To Capital A/c " indicates that that is the Account in the Ledger which is to be credited.

In addition, during the month, as we should expect, cheques are drawn on the Bank Account in order to replenish the moneys in the hands of the cashier. It should not be difficult for us to realise what happens in this case. Firstly, the bank pays out money, and thereby reduces its accountability to the proprietor of the business. For this it must be **credited,** but, simultaneously, the accountability of the **cashier** is increased, and so, on the left hand, or debit side of the Cash Book we enter the amount of £28 in the **cash** column.

Secondly, in our wording of the items in the Cash Book, we must be careful to choose words which will indicate at once **where the corresponding (debit or credit) entry is to be found.** For example, on January 2, when money is paid **from cash** into the bank, we say on the **credit side,** " By Bank," indicating that the bank column is to be charged with the amount.

Thirdly, when a cheque received from a customer is returned by the bank marked R/D (refer to drawer, or Light Bros.) we must bring the Cash Book into line with the bank's own view of the position, and having **charged** the bank with £22 on January 12 now give them credit on January 16. We thus cancel the original charge to the bank and, **to complete the double entry within the Ledgers,** post the amount to the **debit** of Light Bros.' Account, thereby reviving the original debt due from them. Their position is thus what it was before the worthless cheque was received.

Fourthly, we see that columns are provided in which to record cash discount **allowed** and **received.** When the cheque from Light Bros. was first received on January 8, 15*s.* was allowed to them as discount, the **total** due by them being £22 15*s.* But as their cheque is returned on January 16 it is not enough merely to credit the bank with the amount of the **cheque**; we must in addition write back to Light Bros. the discount which was, of course, only allowed by the business in the belief that the cheque was good.

And lastly, credit is given to the bank for interest and charges made by them for the month. They will, **in their own books,** have debited the business with this sum, and in order that the two sets of records shall be in agreement, this entry must be made.

In the result, and on January 31, balances can be inserted on the **credit side** of the Cash Book (representing the amount by which the debit side exceeds the credit side) and **brought down** on February 1, as the **opening balances** for the new period. The balances, it will be noted, are in both cases **debit balances,** indicating the existence of an Asset in the form of :—

(*a*) Cash in hand £62, and
(*b*) Cash at bank £111 12*s*.

Before we pass from this example let us look at the **Discount Allowed** and **Discount Received** Accounts in the Impersonal Ledger.

DISCOUNT ALLOWED.

DR. CR.

Date.	Details.	Fo.	Amount.	Date.	Details.	Fo.	Amount.
193– Jan. 31	To Total for Month .		£ *s.* *d.* 1 5 0				

DISCOUNT RECEIVED.

DR. CR.

Date.	Details.	Fo.	Amount.	Date.	Details.	Fo.	Amount.
				193– Jan. 31	By Total for Month .		£ *s.* *d.* 8 6 0

To deal with the former, we notice that while both the cheques received from, **and** the discount allowed to Light Bros. and Bilton, Ltd., appear on the **debit** side of the Cash Book these customers will each receive **credit** for the **total** in their respective Ledger Accounts. But only the amount of the **actual money** they pay is debited in the cash and bank columns. Accordingly, to complete the double entry, we must have in the Impersonal Ledger an account for **discounts allowed,** in which the further debit required will be shown.

Let us take one other

Example. John Smith, a merchant, does not pay all cash received into his bank. He desires to record all cash received and paid and all his bank transactions in one Cash Book. His transactions during the first few days of January, 1935, were as under :—

1935			£
Jan.	1.	Cash in hand	150
		Bank overdraft	72
		Received cash from A. B. (after allowing him discount £1)	15
,,	2.	Paid into bank	145
,,	3.	Drew cheque for C. D. (after deducting discount £3)	27
,,	4.	Received cheque from E. F. (after allowing him discount £30) and paid it into bank	270
,,	5.	Drew from bank in cash	20
		Paid wages (on presentation of an open cheque at bank)	30
,,	7.	E. F.'s cheque returned by bank, dishonoured.	
,,	8.	Received cash from G. H. (after allowing discount £2)	48
,,	9.	Paid into bank	25
,,	10.	Paid cash to J. K. (after deducting discount £4)	36
,,	11.	Cheque book received from bank . .	1

You are required (*a*) to record these transactions in a suitable form of Cash Book; (*b*) to rule off and balance the book; (*c*) to state clearly how the discounts are dealt with in the Ledger.

(Institute of Bankers.)

JOHN SMITH.

CASH BOOK.

JANUARY, 1935.

DR. | CR.

Date.	Receipts.	Discount. £ s. d.	Cash. £ s. d.	Bank. £ s. d.	Date.	Payments.	Discount. £ s. d.	Cash. £ s. d.	Bank. £ s. d.
1935					1935				
Jan. 1	To Balance b/d		150 0 0		Jan. 1	By Balance b/d			72 0 0
„ 1	„ A. B.	1 0 0	15 0 0		„ 2	„ Bank		145 0 0	
„ 2	„ Cash			145 0 0	„ 3	„ C. D.	3 0 0		27 0 0
„ 4	„ E. F.	30 0 0		270 0 0	„ 5	„ Cash			20 0 0
„ 5	„ Bank		20 0 0		„ 5	„ Wages			30 0 0
„ 8	„ G. H.	2 0 0	48 0 0		„ 7	„ E. F., cheque returned	30 0 0		270 0 0
„ 9	„ Cash			25 0 0	„ 9	„ Bank		25 0 0	
					„ 10	„ J. K.	4 0 0	36 0 0	
					„ 11	„ Bank charges, Cheque Book			1 0 0
					„ 11	„ Balances c/d		27 0 0	20 0 0
		£33 0 0	£233 0 0	£440 0 0			£37 0 0	£233 0 0	£440 0 0
Jan. 12	To Balances b/d		27 0 0	20 0 0					

Debited to "Discount Allowed" Account. (↓ from Discount column, Dr. side)

Credited to "Discount Received" Account (↓ from Discount column, Cr. side)

Cash Book Postings to Ledger Accounts

CASH BOOK, being

(*a*) Book of First Entry, and
(*b*) Ledger Account with the Cashier and Banker.

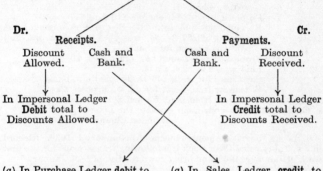

Dr.			**Cr.**
Receipts.		**Payments.**	
Discount Allowed.	Cash and Bank.	Cash and Bank.	Discount Received.
In Impersonal Ledger **Debit** total to Discounts Allowed.			In Impersonal Ledger **Credit** total to Discounts Received.

(*a*) In Purchase Ledger **debit** to individual suppliers.
(*b*) In Impersonal Ledger **debit** to Wages, Cash Purchases or other Expense Accounts.
(*c*) In Private Ledger **debit** to Asset Accounts (if purchased) or Liability Accounts if paid off or reduced.

(*a*) In Sales Ledger **credit** to individual customers.
(*b*) In Impersonal Ledger **credit** to Bank Interest Received, Cash Sales, or other Income Accounts.
(*c*) In Private Ledger **credit** to Asset Accounts (if sold) or Liability Accounts if, *e.g.*, money borrowed, or new capital introduced.

Tests and Questions

1. Say what benefits a trader will derive from his having an account at a bank, and explain how he would open the account.
(University of Birmingham.)

2. Define trade discount and cash discount. State clearly how these are treated in books of account.
(East Midland Educational Union.)

3. What is a cheque? What is the effect of crossing it? How many parties are there to a cheque?
(Union of Lancashire and Cheshire Institutes.)

4. A trader receives an account from X. Y., his landlord, for £75 in respect of one quarter's rent, which he pays on the date of receipt.

Explain the different ways which might be adopted to record this item in books kept on the Double Entry System.
(University of Manchester.)

5. From the following particulars write up A. Bondman's Cash Book for the week commencing July 5, 1937, and balance the Cash Book as at July 10, 1937 :—

July 5. Cash in hand £15 10*s*., and in bank £176 3*s*. 9*d*.
,, 5. Paid by cheque to F. Abbot his account of £46 10*s*. 6*d*., less 5% cash discount.
,, 6. Paid in cash, postage stamps £1 10*s*. 6*d*., new typewriter ribbon 3*s*.
,, 7. Purchased goods for cheque £10 9*s*. 2*d*.
Received cheque from R. Beal in payment of his account of £37 3*s*. 5*d*., less $2\frac{1}{2}$% cash discount, and paid the cheque into bank.
,, 8. Purchased for cheque new office desk £9 10*s*.
,, 10. Paid wages in cash £3 1*s*.
Cash sales for week £56 7*s*. 2*d*. paid into bank.
Withdrew from bank for office purposes £5.
Withdrew from bank for self £6.

Post the items in your Cash Book to the Ledger.
(London Chamber of Commerce.)

6. Leslie Morris commences business on January 1, 1936. Record in a suitably ruled Cash Book the following transactions for the first week of January, 1936, and bring down the balances on January 7 :—

1936			£	s.	d.
Jan. 1.	L. Morris paid into bank on account of Capital		700	0	0
,, 2.	Received and paid into bank direct the following :—				
	Jones (after allowing discount £5) .		45	0	0
	Wilson (after allowing discount 10*s*.) .		12	10	0
	Graham (after allowing discount 7*s*. 6*d*.)		15	0	0
,, 2.	Drew cheque for office cash . . .		20	0	0
,, 4.	Wilson's cheque returned by bank unpaid.				
,, 5.	Drew cheque for		115	0	0
	Covering Wages	£100			
	Salaries	15			
,, 5.	Bought goods for cash		5	0	0
,, 6.	Received the following :—				
	Peters, covering goods . . .	£25			
	Rent receivable	2			
	Sanders, in notes (after allowing discount £1)	39			
			66	0	0
,, 6.	Paid cash into bank		35	0	0
,, 7.	Paid by cheque :—				
	Lister (after deducting discount 10*s*.) .		19	10	0
	White (after deducting discount £1 10*s*.) .		58	10	0

How would you deal with the totals of the columns Discounts Allowed, and Discounts Received, when the Cash Book is ruled off on January 7, 1936 ? (Birmingham Commercial College.)

7. On June 20, 1936, H. Rivers received from S. Wells an invoice

for £514. Of this amount £510 represented the cost of goods purchased and £4 the carriage thereon.

On June 30, 1936, H. Rivers returned to S. Wells goods to the value of £60.

After the invoice had been entered in the books, it was discovered that a trade discount of 20% had not been deducted from the cost or from the item relating to goods returned and an adjusting entry was made to correct these mistakes.

The account was paid by cheque on July 31, 1936, less $2\frac{1}{2}$% discount.

You are required to show the entries in the respective books of account of H. Rivers to record the foregoing transactions.

(University of Manchester.)

8. From the following particulars write up the Cash Book of Thomas Mixture for the month of January, 1932, and bring down the balances at the end of the month. It is not Mr. Mixture's rule to bank all cash and make all payments by cheque.

1932			£	s.	d.
Jan.	1.	Cash in hand	17	9	1
,,	1.	Balance overdrawn at bank	36	8	3
,,	2.	Received cash sales	42	9	2
,,	4.	Banked cash	15	0	0
,,	4.	Paid Jackson & Co. by cheque	14	2	1
,,	5.	Received Jones' cheque (direct to bank)	81	6	4
,,	6.	Paid salaries in cash	24	10	0
,,	7.	Bought goods for cash (paid from office cash)	11	0	0
,,	8.	Drew office cash from bank	16	0	0
,,	9.	Received cash sales	2	3	9
,,	13.	Paid salaries in cash	24	10	0
,,	16.	Received Smith's cheque at bank	36	2	3
,,	20.	Paid Brown by cheque	16	11	1
,,	20.	Received from Jones in coin	26	9	2
,,	20.	Paid salaries in cash	24	10	0
,,	23.	Drew office cash from bank	35	0	0
,,	26.	Received Jones' cheque (direct to bank)	17	3	8
,,	27.	Paid salaries in cash	24	10	0
,,	27.	Paid office cash into bank	10	0	0
,,	28.	Jones' cheque returned by bank unpaid	17	3	8

(Institute of Bankers.)

9. The Cash Book of Thomas Jones for the first week of January, 1937, is as follows :—

1937			Discount. £	Bank. £	1937			Discount. £	Bank. £
Jan.	1.	To Balance		752	Jan.	3.	By Wages		59
,,	2.	,, Sundry Customers :			,,	5.	,, Sundry Suppliers :		
		L. Smith	1	39			G. Green	3	57
		V. Latham	4	76			T. Robson	2	78
,,	4.	,, Rents Receivable		17	,,	5.	,, V. Latham, cheque returned	4	76
	6.	,, Plant A/c (machine tool sold)		26	,,	6.	,, Cash Purchases		18
			£5	£910				£9	£288

You are required :—

(*a*) To indicate to which Ledger each entry in the above Cash Book would be posted.

(*b*) To make the Cash postings in such Ledger Accounts, including the Discount Account.

(Birmingham Commercial College.)

10. From the following particulars you are required to write up the three-column Cash Book of K. Walker. No posting to the Ledger is required :—

1933

Mar. 1. Cash in hand £36 10*s*. 4*d*.
,, 1. Overdrawn at bank £185 4*s*. 7*d*.
,, 2. Paid into bank £25.
,, 3. Paid wages by cash £11 0*s*. 3*d*.
,, 4. Received cheque from R. Francis value £35 10*s*. 8*d*. in settlement of an amount owing £36 9*s*. 3*d*.
,, 4. Cash sales £53 11*s*. 6*d*.
,, 4. Received a cheque from M. Scott £23 17*s*. 11*d*., and allowed him discount 12*s*. 6*d*.
,, 5. Paid S. Marsh by cheque the balance of his account £24 15*s*., less 5% discount.
,, 5. Cash purchases £23.
,, 6. Paid cheques from R. Francis and M. Scott into the bank.
,, 8. K. Walker paid into the bank additional capital £140.
,, 9. Drew cheque £16 for office use.
,, 10. Paid L. Hopecraft cheque £18 16*s*. 3*d*., being allowed discount 9*s*. 5*d*.
,, 10. M. Scott's cheque was returned by the bank marked R/D.
,, 11. Drew cheque £5 for private use.
,, 11. Bought plant and machinery £170 and paid the amount by cheque.
,, 12. Paid sundry small expenses by cash £3 5*s*. 8*d*.
,, 31. Bank charges £4 6*s*. 5*d*.

Balance the Cash Book as on March 31 and bring down the balances. (Union of Educational Institutions.)

CHAPTER V

THE BANK RECONCILIATION

It is the practice of banks to render periodically to their customers, whether they are business houses or private individuals, a statement of their position in relation to the bank. This statement is a copy of the customer's account in the bank's Ledger, and usually will be rendered from the bank's standpoint. That is to say, moneys paid in, or **lodgments** by the customer will be put to his credit, and moneys withdrawn by cheque will be debited to him. Thus, at any time, there will be a balance either in favour of or against the customer.

Before the use of book-keeping machines became general, **Bank Pass Books** were issued to all new customers, the items in which were written up by the bank for the customer to compare with the bank columns in his own Cash Book. He could thus satisfy himself that :—

(*a*) The bank had given him credit for all moneys which he had debited to it in his Cash Book.

(*b*) Similarly, when the bank **debited him** with paid cheques, he could see that the name of the payee and the amount for which the cheque had been drawn were also in agreement with the **credit** side of his Cash Book.

At intervals it was, of course, necessary for the Pass Book to be returned to the bank in order to be written up to date.

In many cases to-day, however, the bank's statement is rendered in the form of **loose sheets,** which the customer can insert in a suitable cover or binder, so that he has a continuous record of the bank's version of the position between them.

We have seen elsewhere that it is the custom for suppliers of goods to the business to render statements of account which are valuable corroborative evidence of the accuracy of the Purchase Ledger Accounts.

This being the case, the importance of a similar statement as regards cash itself—the most liquid asset of the business—can readily be appreciated, more particularly if the bank is the **creditor** of the business, as on loan or overdraft account to which a limit has been set.

The occasions on which a bank makes a mistake in writing up the Pass Book or loose sheets are rare indeed, but we do not infrequently find that at times mistakes are made by the cashier in the **Cash Book,** and also in **omitting to record** some particular receipt or payment.

Many banks, to prevent lack of agreement between their own records and the Cash Books of their customers, print at the bottom of each Pass Book sheet :—

> "The items and balance shown on this statement should be verified and the bank notified promptly of any discrepancy."

In ordinary business practice, it is the custom to rule off and balance the Cash Book at monthly intervals, bringing down the ascertained balance to the beginning of the new period. To the extent that it refers to the bank columns in the Cash Book, this balance represents :—

either (*a*) Cash at bank (Dr.)
or (*b*) Bank overdraft (Cr.)

and as such will certainly be required for the information of the proprietor of the business, or of the Board of Directors in a Limited Company.

It will, therefore, be the cashier's duty to prepare at the end of each month what is termed a **bank reconciliation,** or **bank agreement,** attesting the accuracy and completeness of his Cash Book records.

In the affairs of a private individual, this reconciliation may be easily and quickly prepared ; it may be the work of a few minutes only, but with a business house, where lodgments are being made daily throughout the month, and the number of cheques drawn by the business is very large, the labour involved may be much greater.

We must now consider the nature of the work to be done, bearing in mind that the **Pass Book** shows the position of the business **in the light of the information in the bank's possession.**

Supposing the reconciliation is to be prepared on January 31, we may commence with the **Pass Book balance** at that date, using a sheet of cash-ruled paper which we can later file away for future reference. Our task is then to **reconcile** or **agree** this balance with the balance appearing in the **Cash Book.**

If, as is usually the case, there is a difference between the two balances, it may be due to :—

(*a*) **Cheques drawn and issued by the business to its suppliers** and entered in the proper way on the credit side of the Cash Book, **but not yet presented** by the collecting banker for payment.

As the cheques so drawn have to be sent to suppliers, banked by them, and subsequently passed through the clearing, several days may elapse before they reach the paying bank. We must thus **deduct** from the Pass Book balance if favourable to the business, the amount of the unpresented cheques, or **add** if an overdraft exists. On the other hand, if we have begun by taking the **Cash Book figure,** we should add the amount to a debit balance, or deduct it from a credit balance.

(*b*) **Cheques paid in by the business** which on presentation to the paying bank are refused because of, *e.g.* :—

1. Lack of funds to meet them.
2. Countermand of instructions to pay by the Drawer.
3. Death of the Drawer.
4. Some irregularity on the face of the cheque, such as absence of Drawer's signature, inacceptable endorsement, etc.

In these cases, the collecting banker, having given credit when the cheque was lodged, will now **debit the account,** returning the unpaid cheque to the business. The latter will at once take up the matter with its own customer, and endeavour to obtain satisfaction.

In any event, as we saw on page 71, the cashier should credit the bank with the amount involved, *i.e.*, enter it as though it were a payment on the credit side of the Cash Book. Should he have omitted to do this, for purposes of the reconciliation he must, if beginning with a favourable **Pass Book** balance, add the amount, or deduct it if unfavourable.

In beginning with the **Cash Book,** the reverse steps would of course be taken.

(*c*) 1. **Bank interest allowed.**

2. **Bank interest and commission charged.**

We have already explained these items as representing, so far as the business is concerned, either a **profit** or an **expense.**

The bank will enter them in its own account with the customer at half-yearly intervals, as on June 30 and December 31, but does not usually give the customer a separate advice that it has done so. Accordingly, the latter may be altogether unaware of the items until he receives his Pass Book. The proper course is then to **debit** the Bank Column in the Cash Book with the interest allowed by the bank, or **credit** it with the interest and commission charged.

If this has not been done, we shall proceed as follows in preparing the Bank Reconciliation :—

Interest allowed.

(*a*) **Commencing with Pass Book balance.**
If " in favour," deduct.
If overdrawn, add.

(*b*) **Commencing with Cash Book balance.**
If a debit balance, add.
If overdrawn, deduct.

The reverse, of course, applies with interest and commission charged, *i.e.* :—

(*a*) **Commencing with Pass Book balance.**
If " in favour," add.
If overdrawn, deduct.

(*b*) **Commencing with Cash Book balance.**
If a debit balance, deduct.
If overdrawn, add.

In making these adjustments, we must always remember

the aim in view, which is to link the Pass Book balance with the Cash Book balance, or vice-versa. Whether we begin with the Pass Book or the Cash Book does not affect the result, but the former may give the more reliable commencing figure, as it is so much less subject to the risk of error.

Example. The balance shown by the Bank Statement on March 31, 1937, indicates an overdraft of £20 17*s*. 6*d*., whilst, on the same date, the Bank Column in the Cash Book shows a credit balance of £41 17*s*.

Comparing the two records, you find that two cheques drawn on March 31, one for £20 8*s*. and the other for £7 15*s*. 3*d*., had not been presented for payment, whilst one of £7 3*s*. 9*d*. paid into the bank on the same date had not yet been credited.

Prepare a Reconciliation Statement.

(East Midland Educational Union.)

	£	*s*.	*d*.	£	*s*.	*d*.
Overdrawn per Pass Book . .				20	17	6
Add cheques drawn but unpresented :						
March 31	20	8	0			
,, 31	7	15	3			
				28	3	3
				49	0	9
Less cheque paid in but not yet credited .				7	3	9
Credit balance as per Cash Book . . .				£41	17	0

In this second illustration, we will begin instead with the balance according to the **Cash Book.**

Example. On March 30, 1935, your Cash Book shows that you have in the bank the sum of £817 4*s*. 9*d*.

On checking your Cash Book with the Bank Pass Book you find that cheques drawn by you amounting to £214 3*s*. 6*d*. have not passed through the bank, that a cheque for £84 2*s*. 8*d*. has not yet been credited to you, and that the bank has credited you with interest £22 1*s*. 6*d*., and debited you with discount and other charges £14 7*s*. 3*d*.

Draw up a reconciliation statement, showing adjustments between your Cash Book and Bank Pass Book.

(College of Preceptors.)

	£	s.	d.
Balance in hand per Cash Book . . .	817	4	9
Add cheques drawn but unpresented .	214	3	6
	1031	8	3
Less cheque paid in but not credited .	84	2	8
	947	5	7
Add interest credited by bank . .	22	1	6
	969	7	1
Less discount and other charges made by bank	14	7	3
Balance per Pass Book	£954	19	10

Here we see that only the balance per Cash Book is given, and that we have to calculate the Pass Book figure.

Our third illustration introduces other kinds of error in the Cash Book :—

Example. From the undernamed particulars, prepare a reconciliation of the Bank Pass Book balance with the Cash Book balance.

	£
Balance per Pass Book in favour	60
Balance per Cash Book overdrawn	80
Unpresented cheques	144
Uncleared cheques inwards	26

Further,

(*a*) A cheque for £20 paid to J. Jones has been entered in error in the Cash Column of the Cash Book.

(*b*) The debit side of the Cash Book (Bank Column) has been undercast by £50.

(*c*) The cashier has omitted to record bank commission of £8.

If we decide to begin with the **Pass Book** figure :—

	£
Balance per Pass Book (in favour) . . .	60
Adjust unpresented cheques . . .	144
i.e., when presented there will be an **overdraft** of .	84
Less uncleared cheques	26
(Paid in but not credited by bank)	
	58
Less cheque to J. Jones	20
(As this has been paid by the bank and will appear in the Pass Book)	38
Less Commission	8
(Charged by the bank and appearing in the Pass Book)	30
Add undercast in Bank Column of Cash Book .	50
Overdrawn per Cash Book	£80

If we preferred, we could begin instead with the **Cash Book** :—

	£
Overdrawn per Cash Book	80
Adjust unpresented cheques	144
(Drawn and entered in Cash Book but not in Pass Book)	
Favourable balance of	64
Less uncleared cheques	26
(Paid in but not credited in Pass Book)	
	38
Less cheque to J. Jones	20
(Paid by bank and therefore appearing in Pass Book)	18
Less commission charged by bank . . .	8
	10
Add undercast in Bank Column of Cash Book .	50
Balance per Pass Book (in favour) . . .	£60

Tests and Questions

1. Upon a cashier obtaining the Pass Book from the bank, he finds that the amount of the overdraft appearing therein differs from that shown by his Cash Book.

Give the possible explanations of this difference and, using your own figures, prepare a statement showing how the two amounts would be reconciled. (University of Manchester.)

2. On January 1, 1934, a trader obtained his Pass Book and on comparing it with his Cash Book discovered that all items agreed except the following :—

(*a*) Cheques drawn and entered in the Cash Book, totalling £317 5*s*. 9*d*., had not been presented at the bank.
(*b*) A country cheque for £17 10*s*., lodged the previous day, did not appear in the Pass Book.
(*c*) The Pass Book showed an item of interest on overdraft amounting to £7 3*s*. 3*d*. not entered in the Cash Book.
(*d*) The trader had, in December, discounted with the bank bills of exchange for £1,200 and entered this amount in his Cash Book. The proceeds credited, as shown by the Pass Book, amounted to £1,193 1*s*. 5*d*.

The trader's Cash Book showed a balance, on December 31, 1933, of £219 17*s*. 6*d*. overdrawn.

State (*a*) what balance the Pass Book showed on the same day, and (*b*) what would be the balance of the trader's Cash Book after making the necessary additional entries.

(Royal Society of Arts.)

3. On June 30, 1936, a trader's Cash Book showed his bank balance to be £71 3*s*. 7*d*. overdrawn.

On procuring his Pass Book from the bank he found that a country cheque for £19 10*s*. lodged by him on June 29 had not yet been credited by the bank, four cheques drawn on June 30, amounting in total to £181 6*s*. 10*d*., had not yet been presented for payment, and the bank on June 30 had entered a charge of £10 5*s*. 3*d*. for commission and interest.

Draw up a statement showing the balance as shown by the Pass Book. (Royal Society of Arts.)

4. From the following particulars prepare a statement showing how the difference between the Cash Book balance and the Pass Book balance is reconciled :—

	£	*s*.	*d*.
Pass Book balance—June 30, 1931 . . .	1,401	12	6
Cash Book balance—June 30, 1931 . . .	557	10	1

Cheques drawn prior to June 30, 1931, but not presented until after that date :—

	£	*s*.	*d*.
P.	29	4	1
Q.	801	3	6
R.	5	14	9
S.	132	6	3

	£	s.	d.
Country cheques paid into the bank on June 30, 1931, not collected until July 2, 1931	116	3	11
Bank charges and interest to June 30, 1931, not entered in the Cash Book	8	2	3

(Royal Society of Arts.)

5. On November 30, 1932, the Cash Book of E. Simpson disclosed a debit balance of £212, and his Bank Pass Book at the same date a balance in his favour of £261.

Prepare a bank reconciliation at November 30, taking into account that a cheque payable to E. Simpson in respect of a 4% dividend (less tax at 5*s.* in the £) on his holding of 1,000 ordinary shares of £1 each in Greystones Foundry, Ltd., was entered in the Cash Book on November 30, but not credited in the Pass Book until December 1, and that cheques drawn by E. Simpson on November 28, as follows, were not presented at the bank by the payees until December 3.

	£	s.	d.
H. Simpson, salary	8	6	8
Corporation electric supply	35	13	4
Trade Supplies, Ltd. (a creditor)	35	0	0

(University of Birmingham.)

6. On December 31, 1929, John Smith found that his Bank Pass Book showed a balance in the bank of £88 12*s.* 6*d.*, whereas according to his Ledger his Bank Account was overdrawn by £57 13*s.* 9*d.* On checking over the figures he discovered that the following cheques had not been presented :—

	£	s.	d.
Wilkins & Co.	96	3	4
Turnbull & Snow	63	0	0
Samuel & Son	85	10	0

while a payment in of £90 on December 31 had not yet been credited by the bank, and the bank's charges for the half-year amounting to £8 7*s.* 1*d.* had not been entered in his Ledger.

How would John Smith reconcile his Ledger with the Pass Book, and how would this affect his accounts ?

(University of Birmingham.)

7. A. Shiner's Cash Book for July, 1936, is as follows :—

DR.						CR.				
1936		£	s.	d.	1936			£	s.	d.
June 30.	To Balance . .	817	4	3	July 3.	By Lomas & Co. .		151	4	7
July 4.	" J. Bell . .	15	15	0	" 8.	" Smith, Ltd. .		32	0	0
" 9.	" Salt & Son .	92	10	8	" 10.	" C. Jervis .		1	16	10
" 18.	" Williams, Ltd.	1	4	6	" 20.	" Evans & Co. .		10	18	2
" 29.	" E. Harris .	81	3	3	" 27.	" P.M.G. Telephones .		5	6	3
" 31.	" James & Co. .	14	16	2	" 29.	" D. Greene .		1	15	11
					" 30.	" J. Johnson .		84	17	9
					" 31.	" Kenrick, Ltd. .		25	14	6

His Bank Pass Book shows for August, 1936, the following :—

1936			£ s. d.	1936			£ s. d.
July 31.	To Balance .	.	806 11 10	Aug. 3.	By Kenrick, Ltd. .		25 14 6
Aug. 2.	„ James & Co.	.	14 16 2	„ 6.	„ F. David	.	10 10 6
„ 3.	„ Saul & Co.	.	100 15 8	„ 7.	„ D. Greene	.	1 15 11
				„ 7.	„ J. Johnson	.	84 17 9

Prepare a Bank Agreement as at July 31, 1936.

(University of Birmingham.)

8. At January 31, 1938, the Cash Book of Hugh Gibson showed a balance overdrawn of £117, while according to his Bank Pass Book at that date there was a balance in his favour of £72. A comparison of the two records revealed the following :—

(*a*) A cheque for £25 sent to B. Murray had been entered in the cash column of the Cash Book.
(*b*) Bank charges of £17 at December 31, 1937, were not entered at all in the Cash Book.
(*c*) The Bank had debited Gibson's Account with a cheque for £11 received from D. Carter, which had been returned dishonoured. The fact of dishonour was not shown in the Cash Book.
(*d*) The Bank Column on the Receipts side of the Cash Book was found to be undercast £10.
(*e*) Unpresented cheques amounted to £232.

You are required to prepare the Bank Reconciliation at January 31, 1938, in proper form, setting out your adjustments clearly.

(Birmingham Commercial College.)

9. A cash book which you are examining shows a balance at the bank on May 31, 1944, of £1,531 2*s*. 1*d*. The bank pass book at the same date shows a different balance. Your investigations reveal:—

A cheque drawn for £12 3*s*. 1*d*. was entered in the cash book as £13 2*s*. 1*d*.

An item for goods sold £125 9*s*. 6*d*. which had been settled on April 30 had been entered in full whereas the customer had deducted £5 3*s*. 1*d*. discount.

On page 70 of the cash book the receipts side was short cast £100.

A lodgment amounting to £7 8*s*. 10*d*. in respect of cash sales was not entered in the cash book.

A cheque amounting to £159 5*s*. 8*d*. received from a customer, who subsequently went bankrupt, had been returned by the bank but no entry of the return had been made in the cash book.

Cheques amounting in all to £394 12*s*. 6*d*. issued to creditors and entered in the cash book had not been presented for payment at May 31, 1944.

Cheques paid into the bank on June 2 amounting to £954 16*s*. 2*d*. were entered in the cash book on May 31.

Make the appropriate adjustments to the cash book balance and prepare a statement reconciling it with the balance in the pass book.

CHAPTER VI

PETTY CASH, ETC.

We have seen that the general rule in cash transactions is to pay all cash received into bank on the day of receipt, and to make all payments by cheque.

We have also seen that as regards wages and salaries payable by the business to its workpeople and staff, some departure from this rule is inevitable, although in the first instance a cheque is issued to the Cashier in order that he may obtain the necessary notes and coin from the bank.

It is, however, necessary in all businesses, irrespective of their type or size, to make provision for the payment in notes or coin of a great variety of *small amounts* which may be regarded as sundry or incidental expenses. They are usually termed **Petty Cash payments,** and must receive our attention because :—

(*a*) They recur at regular intervals.
(*b*) It is usually impracticable to issue a cheque in payment of any one of them.
(*c*) The person receiving payment may be an employee of the business.
(*d*) In total they may amount, period by period, to a not inconsiderable sum.

From the standpoint of the business it is most desirable to separate the records of Petty Cash payments from the main Cash Book records. It would clearly be inconvenient to have the latter cumbered with a large number of miscellaneous small payments and for this reason, **as a separate book of prime entry,** it is usual to keep a Petty Cash Book, the responsibility for the entries in which, and for the **Petty Cash balance,** may be entrusted to the Cashier or, in the case of a large business, to one of his assistants.

Weekly or monthly, the latter may be handed a sum in cash thought sufficient to meet all demands for the selected period. He will then submit a list of his payments to the

Cashier and receive a sum to replenish his reduced cash balance.

It is often made a rule that the Petty Cashier shall take a receipt for each payment, and frequently specially printed forms bearing the name of the business are provided for this to be done. These receipt forms, when completed with the name of the recipient, and details of the amount and nature of the expense, are preserved by the Petty Cashier as independent evidence of payment.

To permit of a suitable classification of expense items, the Petty Cash Book may be ruled with **analysis columns** into which the total paid can be extended. This facilitates the subsequent posting of the analysis columns to the Impersonal and other Ledger Accounts.

Example. On March 1, a cheque for £20 was handed to the Petty Cashier to pay Petty Cash expenses for the month, which were as follows :—

			£	s.	d.
Mar.	1.	Postage stamps	2	0	0
,,	3.	Carriage		4	9
,,	4.	Tram fares			9
,,	5.	Shorthand note books		10	6
,,	6.	Postage stamps	1	0	0
,,	8.	Fare to London	1	5	0
,,	9.	Sundry trade expenses		10	3
,,	11.	Pencils		2	6
,,	14.	Trunk call		1	3
,,	16.	Envelopes		5	0
,,	18.	Stationery		17	6
,,	31.	Carriage		5	4

Rule a Petty Cash Book in analysis form, with five analysis columns, headed Postages and Telephone, Carriage, Travelling Expenses, Stationery and Sundry Trade Expenses respectively. Enter the foregoing items and close the books as on March 31, showing clearly the balance of cash in hand.

(Union of Educational Institutions.)

As regards the above, it should be noted that in certain cases, *e.g.*, Rail Fares, the nature of the payment does not permit of a receipt being obtained from an outside source.

PETTY CASH BOOK.

Dr. Cr.

Cash Received.	Date.	Details.	Receipt No.	Total.	Postages and Telephone.	Carriage.	Travelling Expenses.	Stationery.	Sundry Trade Expenses.
£ s. d.	193–			£ s. d.	£ s. d.	£ s. d.	£ s. d.	£ s. d.	£ s. d.
20 0 0	Mar. 1	Per Cashier							
	„ 1	Brown, Stamps	1	2 0 0	2 0 0				
	„ 3	L.M.S., Carriage	2	4 9		4 9			
	„ 4	Hunt, Fares	3	9			9		
	„ 5	White, Notebooks	4	10 6				10 6	
	„ 6	Brown, Stamps	5	1 0 0	1 0 0				
	„ 8	Lyle, Rail fare, London	6	1 5 0			1 5 0		
	„ 9	Sundry expenses	7	10 3					10 3
	„ 11	White, Pencils	8	2 6				2 6	
	„ 14	Hunt, Trunk Call	9	1 3	1 3				
	„ 16	White, Envelopes	10	5 0				5 0	
	„ 18	White, Stationery	11	17 6				17 6	
	„ 31	G.W.R., Carriage	12	5 4		5 4			
				7 2 10	3 1 3	10 1	1 5 9	1 15 6	10 3
	„ 31	Balance	c/d	12 17 2					
£20 0 0				£20 0 0					
12 17 2	Apr. 1	Balance	b/d						

For this reason, the employee receiving the money should be required to fill up a Voucher Form giving the required details, but wherever possible an independent receipt should always be procured and filed with the firm's voucher.

Further, **like the main Cash Book,** the Petty Cash Book is not only a book of First Entry; it is also a Ledger Account with the **Petty Cashier.** In other words, he is debited with what he receives, and given credit for what he pays away on behalf of the business. The balance of £12 17*s.* 2*d.* is therefore the sum for which he is accountable at the end of the month. Since credit is given to him personally for his payments, it remains to consider **their effect upon the business.** Impersonally, the business must be debited with the **totals** of the expenses set out in the analysis columns, for each one of which an account will be opened in the **Impersonal Ledger.** With Postages and Telephones we should have, for example :—

POSTAGES AND TELEPHONES.

DR. CR.

Date.	Details.	P.C.B. Fo.	Amount.	Date.	Details.	Fo.	Amount.
193–			£ *s.* *d.*				
Mar. 31	To Petty Cash Total .	1	3 1 3				

Imprest System.

As applied to Petty Cash, this means that a definite sum of money, say £20, is handed to the Petty Cashier and at the end of the week or month he is reimbursed the **amount expended,** *e.g.*, £7 2*s.* 10*d.* in the above example. His Petty Cash balance is thus restored to its original figure.

The merits of the system are that :—

(*a*) At any time actual cash, or vouchers and receipts should be available for the imprest of £20.

(*b*) As the periodic reimbursements are the actual expenses paid, and not mere advances on account only, they are as such brought prominently to the notice of the Chief Cashier or other responsible official of the business.

Postage Book

It will be observed that in the last example an analysis column headed " Postages " was provided in the Petty Cash Book.

This is a typical Petty Cash payment, recurring at regular intervals. The employee of the business having the custody of the stamp money may or may not be the Petty Cashier, but in any case it is desirable to have a record of the outgoing mail.

For this purpose it is customary to use a **Stamp Book** or **Postage Book,** of which the following is a suitable ruling :—

Date.	Cash Received.	Name of Addressee.	Town.	Stamps Used.
	£ *s.* *d.*			£ *s.* *d.*

The Postage Book may properly be described as a **Memorandum Book** whose purpose is to amplify and serve as a check upon the payments appearing in the " Stamps " column. It does not form a part of the Double Entry System.

The Petty Cashier, when making each payment, should himself enter the **date** and **amount** in the first two columns, and it should be expected that the difference between the " **Cash Received** " column and the " **Stamps Used** " column represents either the value of stamps in hand and unused or, alternatively, the balance of cash in hand available for their purchase.

It is desirable that when further advances are made for buying stamps, the Postage Book should be produced to the Petty Cashier and initialled by him after seeing that it is written up to date and verifying the balance shown.

Tests and Questions

1. Assuming that you are handing over to a junior your duties as Petty Cashier, write short and concise instructions as to his duties, and how they are to be performed.

(Union of Lancashire and Cheshire Institutes.)

2. Give a ruling for a Petty Cash Book with separate analysis columns for wages, national insurance, postage and stationery, and office expenses.

Insert sufficient entries to illustrate fully the method of using a book of this description and briefly explain its advantages.

(Royal Society of Arts.)

3. Give a ruling for an analysed form of Petty Cash Book; insert specimen entries for a short period and show what postings are made.

How would you deal with any exceptional payments not falling under one of the columnar headings provided for?

(Royal Society of Arts.)

4. What is the Imprest System of dealing with Petty Cash?

Rule a columnar Petty Cash Book illustrating the principle, and insert *three* entries therein.

(Union of Lancashire and Cheshire Institutes.)

CHAPTER VII

THE DEBIT AND CREDIT JOURNAL

Question. You said on page 19 that the Journal in its earliest form was still used for certain purposes, and that it would be referred to at a later stage?

Answer. Yes, and for the reason that while the majority of the transactions carried out relate to purchasing, selling and the receipt and payment of cash, there are nevertheless others which do not fall under these headings.

Question. So that in the absence of a Book of Prime Entry, like this earliest form of the Journal, you cannot set out the dual aspect of these particular transactions prior to entry in the Ledger?

Answer. As was stated earlier, **it is desirable that no entry shall be made in a Ledger Account unless it has first been recorded in a Book of Prime Entry.** Thus in certain cases the use of the Journal, or Debit and Credit Journal as it is sometimes termed, is essential. Moreover, while the information that can be given in the ordinary form of Ledger Account is limited, as much information as may be required including reference to documents, correspondence, etc., may be shown in the Journal proper. This we describe as the "**Narration.**"

Question. Can you give me examples of such entries?

Answer. It will help you to consider them as representing business transactions which are not capable of entry in the ordinary Purchase, Sales and Cash Journals. For example, if Brown, a customer, owes the business £20 which he cannot pay, a Bad Debt of £20 has been made. Brown will be **credited** with £20 in his Personal Account in the Sales Ledger, and **Bad Debts** Account (an expense to the business) will be **debited** with that amount in the Impersonal Ledger. Supposing also that Smith both buys goods from and sells goods to the business, in the Purchase Ledger there will be an account with him as a supplier, and in the Sales Ledger as a customer. If on balance he is indebted to the business he will only remit the difference in full settlement, therefore the balance on his Purchase Ledger Account must be transferred or posted to the credit of his Sales Ledger Account.

Question. In effect then, for these and other similar transactions the Debit and Credit Journal is the only book in which the prime or first entry can be made?

Answer. Yes, but it is also appropriate, as we shall see shortly, for recording what are termed **opening** and **closing** entries. The former relate to the introduction into the business of **Capital** in one form or another; the latter refer either to the construction of the periodic **Profit and Loss Account** and the **Balance Sheet,** or to the realisation of the business property by sale or otherwise, and so on.

Question. And in all these cases it is important to give adequate **narration**?

Answer. If this were not done, the exact meaning of each Journal entry might be difficult to explain at some later date. Further, the making of the entry enables us conveniently to summarise the position for subsequent posting to the **Ledger Accounts.** Let us now proceed to work through some definite examples.

Example. Give the necessary Journal entries to record the following :—

(*a*) Having deducted 5% cash discount when paying the account of Lakeside, Ltd., a letter is received from them notifying us that only $2\frac{1}{2}$% can be allowed.

The difference (£2 15*s*. 6*d*.) is being carried forward in their books.

(*b*) Goods to the value of £51 10*s*. have been purchased from C. Ridley and goods value £30 sold to him. Both accounts are subject to a cash discount of 5%, and a cheque for the net balance is forwarded to him. Close the account.

(East Midland Educational Union.)

		Dr. £ s. d.	Cr. £ s. d.
(*A*) 1938			
Feb. 1	Discounts Received . . . . . . Dr.	2 15 6	
	To Lakeside, Ltd.		2 15 6
	Being discount not allowed as per their letter January 29, 1938.		
(*B*)			
Feb. 4	Sundries . . . . Dr.		
	C. Ridley (B.L. A/c)	28 10 0	
	Discounts Allowed	1 10 0	
	To C. Ridley (S.L. A/c)		30 0 0
	Being transfer of Sales Ledger Balance and Discount Allowed to Bought Ledger on settlement.		

Should it happen, as in (*B*) above, that **either** the **debit** or **credit** aspect affects more than one Ledger Account, it is usual to prefix the word "**Sundries**" to the entries, in this case to the debits.

C. Ridley's account in the **Bought Ledger** will then be as follows :—

C. RIDLEY.

DR. CR.

Date.	Details.	J.O. Fo.	Amount.	Date.	Details.	Fo.	Amount.
1938			£ s. d.	1938			£ s. d.
Feb. 4	To Sundries .	1	28 10 0	Feb. 1	By Balance .	b/d	51 10 0
" 4	" Bank .	C.B.2	20 8 6				
	" Discount .	2	2 11 6				
			£51 10 0				£51 10 0

In posting from the Debit and Credit Journal to the Ledger Accounts, the word "Sundries" again appears in the "Details" Column. It is unnecessary, and would indeed be a waste of time, to repeat the whole of the information in the Ledger Account, when all that is required can be found on Fo. 1 of the Journal.

The two entries for the cheque £20 8*s*. 6*d*., and discount £2 11*s*. 6*d*., will, of course, be posted from the Cash Book in the ordinary way.

With both (*A*) and (*B*) we must observe that adequate narration is always an essential feature of Journal entries.

Example. A. B. purchased from C. D. a motor delivery van for cash £180 in April, 1935, and in October he bought another for £210, giving the one bought in April in part payment, and paying the balance of £60 in cash. Show these entries in A. B.'s books of entry, and give the relevant Ledger Accounts.

(The College of Preceptors.)

Fo. 6.

PURCHASE JOURNAL.

Date.	Supplier.	Description.	Inv. No.	Ledger Fo.	Total.	Goods.	Special Items.
					£ s. d.	£ s. d.	£ s. d.
1935 Apr.	C. D.	Motor Van	1	2	180 0 0		180 0 0
					Motors A/c Private Ledger Fo. 8 £180		
Fo. 34. 1935 Oct.	C. D.	Motor Van	40	2	210 0 0		210 0 0
					Motors A/c Private Ledger F. 8 £210		

Fo. 10.

CASH BOOK.

DR. CR.

Date.	Details.	Fo.	Amount.	Date.	Details.	Fo.	Amount.
				1935			£ s. d.
				Apr.	C. D. . .	2	180 0 0
Fo. 25				Oct.	C. D. . .	2	60 0 0

Fo. 19.

JOURNAL.

		Fo.	Dr. £	Cr. £
1935 Oct.	Sundries : Dr.			
	To Motors A/c	P.L.8		180
	C. D.	B.L.2	150	
	Loss on Sale of Assets A/c . . .	I.L.9	30	
	Being Sale in part exchange of Ajax Van per C. D.'s invoice No. 40, September 29, 1935.			

Fo. 2.

PURCHASE LEDGER.

C. D.

DR. CR.

Date.	Details.	Fo.	Amount.	Date.	Details.	Fo.	Amount.
1935			£ s. d.	1935			£ s. d.
Apr.	To Bank .	C.B.10	180 0 0	Apr.	By Goods .	P.J.6	180 0 0
Oct.	" Sundries.	J.19	150 0 0	Oct.	" Goods .	34	210 0 0
"	" Bank .	C.B.25	60 0 0				
			£210 0 0				£210 0 0

Fo. 8.

PRIVATE LEDGER.

MOTORS.

DR. CR.

Date.	Details.	Fo.	Amount.	Date.	Details.	Fo.	Amount.
1935			£ s. d.	1935			£ s. d.
Apr.	To Goods .	P.J.6	180 0 0	Oct.	By Sundries .	19	180 0 0
Oct.	" Goods .	34	210 0 0				

In looking at this illustration, we see that the cost of the van purchased in April is extended in the Purchase Journal into the "**Special Items**" Column. It would be wrong to analyse it as **Goods,** because it is apparently a **Capital** Asset. As such, it is debited to Motors A/c in the Private Ledger of A. B. When the second van is bought in October, exactly the same procedure is followed. At this point, however, a record has to be made of the disposal of the first van in part payment.

Having charged the business with two vans, we must, in effect, give it credit in **Motors Account** for :—

(*a*) The part exchange value of £150.
(*b*) Loss on Sale of £30.

We may only charge the former to C. D. as we have done in his personal account. The latter is a special kind of expense remaining to be borne by the business and will be shown separately in the Impersonal Ledger :—

LOSS ON SALE OF ASSETS. Fo. 9.

DR. CR.

Date.	Details.	Fo.	Amount.	Date.	Details.	Fo.	Amount.
1935 Oct.	To Sundries .	J.19	£ s. d. 30 0 0				

It is desirable that we should notice from now on the utility for reference purposes of the Folio Column in each Ledger Account. The insertion of the folio numbers prefixed by the initial letter of the book of prime entry makes immediate reference a simple matter.

Example. Journalise the following transactions in the books of L. Denton :—

Jan. 1. L. Denton commenced business with stock valued at £93, cash at bank £78, and fixtures value £55. £40 was owing to M. Robinson.

Mar. 10. Plant and machinery bought on credit from Langham Bros., value £123.

Apr. 11. K. Atkins, a debtor for £23, is known to be insolvent and the debt is written off as bad.

June 23. Goods valued £18 2*s.* 6*d.* bought from Blake Bros. entered in the Purchase Day Book and posted in error to the debit of Blake Bros. Account in the Bought Ledger.

June 28. Cheque £15 2*s.* 5*d.* posted to the debit of Jones Bros. instead of to the debit of Jones, Ltd.

(Union of Educational Institutions.)

The entries on *January* 1 are an instance of the use of the Journal for **opening** the books of a business. It is also apparent that the amount of L. Denton's Capital at this date is £186.

The Cash Book balance will be debited in the bank column of the **Cash Book,** and the £40 owing to M. Robinson credited to his personal account in the **Bought Ledger** The other items will be posted to accounts in the **Private Ledger.**

JOURNAL.

		Dr. £	s.	d.	Cr. £	s.	d.
Jan. 1	Sundries: Dr.						
	To Sundries						
	Cash at Bank	78	0	0			
	Stock	93	0	0			
	Fixtures	55	0	0			
	M. Robinson				40	0	0
	Capital				186	0	0
	Being Assets and Liabilities introduced this day.						
Mar. 10	Plant and Machinery Dr.	123	0	0			
	To Langham Bros.				123	0	0
	Being purchase on credit of drilling machinery and lathe for tool shop.						
Apr. 11	Bad Debts Dr.	23	0	0			
	To K. Atkins				23	0	0
	Being amount written off per collector's report dated April 1.						
June 23	To Blake Bros.				36	5	0
	Being goods purchased £18 2*s*. 6*d*. posted in error to the debit of A/c and now adjusted.						
June 28	Jones, Ltd. Dr.	15	2	5			
	To Jones Bros.				15	2	5
	Being cheque posted in error to debit of Jones Bros.						

The purchase of machinery on March 10 could quite well be shown in the "special items" column of the Purchase Journal, and the present record is only an **alternative** to this.

The entry on June 23 is interesting as showing the correction of an error in **one Ledger Account,** that of Blake Bros.

Purchases Account in the Impersonal Ledger will have been **debited** on June 30 with the total of the Purchase Day Book for the month, which includes the item of £18 2*s*. 6*d*.

At the same time, because of the error, there is also a **debit** on a personal account in the Purchase Ledger of £18 2*s*. 6*d*. Clearly Blake Bros. should have been **credited** originally with £18 2*s*. 6*d*., and to adjust the position, it will now be necessary to journalise a credit to them of double the amount, or £36 5*s*. In so doing, we shall cancel the debit error and record their position as creditors for £18 2*s*. 6*d*.

The point cannot be too strongly emphasised that ability

to journalise successfully presupposes a thorough understanding of double entry principles. Transactions of the kind dealt with in the foregoing examples, while not so common as purchasing, selling and cash transactions, will inevitably arise in all businesses at some time or another, and call for initial record in the Debit and Credit Journal, in the manner illustrated.

Tests and Questions

1. Explain the uses of the Journal in the system of double entry book-keeping. (University of Manchester.)

2. Explain the use of the Journal proper. What entries, other than the opening entry, would you expect to find in this book? (Union of Educational Institutions.)

3. The following errors are discovered in the books of a business concern :—

(*a*) £47 10*s*. paid for new office furniture has been charged to office expenses.

(*b*) £39 3*s*. 6*d*., representing a monthly total of discounts allowed to debtors, has been posted from the debit side of the Cash Book to the *credit* of Discount Account.

(*c*) An entry of £10, representing the retail value of goods returned to X & Co., wholesalers, has been made in the Returns Outwards Book and posted. The amount should have been £7, the invoiced value of the goods in question.

Show the entries necessary to correct these errors. The original wrong entries are not to be deleted. Subject to this restriction, make the corrections in whatever form you consider most appropriate. (Royal Society of Arts.)

4. You are required to give the Journal entries necessary to correct the undermentioned errors in the books of a Limited Company :—

(*a*) Cost of advertising the Prospectus, £200, charged to Advertising Account.

(*b*) Allowance of £50 made by a supplier of machinery entered in the Returns Outward Book and included in the total posted to Purchases Account.

(*c*) £500 received from a customer for goods yet to be delivered posted to the credit of Sales Account.

(*d*) Imprest of £20 handed to the Petty Cashier debited to General Expenses Account. (University of Manchester.)

5. Give the Journal entries necessary to record the following facts in the books of I. Markham, a manufacturer :—

1934

Jan. 1. I. Markham commenced business with cash in hand, £36; cash at bank, £141; plant and machinery, £180; and stock value £200.

„ 28. Bought plant and machinery on credit from Speed & Co., Ltd., value £130.

Mar. 3. A debt for £25 owing by B. Sykes proves worthless.

„ 10. The plant and machinery purchased on credit from Speed & Co. was returned as not being according to specification.

„ 31. £25 interest on capital to be allowed.

(Union of Educational Institutions.)

6. Record by way of Journal entry the following in the books of A., a merchant :—

(*a*) X. is both a supplier and a customer. The debit on his Sales Ledger Account is £40, and the credit on his account in the Bought Ledger is £60.

On February 29, 1936, a cheque in full settlement is sent to him, less 2½% cash discount.

(*b*) Purchase of office fixtures £100, and stationery, etc., £10, from Office Supplies, Ltd.

(*c*) Provision on March 31, 1936 (the date when A. closes his books) for interest at 5% per annum for six months in respect of a loan of £500 by Mrs. A.

(*d*) Sale of delivery van of book value of £100, in part exchange at the price of £80, against a new van costing £135.

(Birmingham Commercial College.)

7. Give Journal entries to record or correct the following :—

1936

Jan. 6. £25 cheque received credited to John White, instead of James White, both being customers.

„ 14. Cuthbert agreed to accept 15*s*. in £ in full settlement of the balance of £180 appearing on his account in the Bought Ledger at December 31, 1935.

„ 17. Matthews, a customer, owed the business £200 on December 31, 1935. It is agreed to allow him £5 for window display expenses, and 5% gross for special trade discount.

„ 19. Arnold, a customer, to be charged by agreement £4 interest on his overdue account.

„ 24. Wilkins, a supplier, takes over plant and tools valued at £20 as part payment of the balance due to him of £32. (Birmingham Commercial College.)

8. The book-keeper employed by John Horton handed you a Trial Balance which included on the debit side an item " Suspense Account, £97 8*s*. 2*d*." He stated that this was the difference between the two sides of the Trial Balance which he could not trace. On investigation you find that the difference is caused by the following errors :—

(*a*) The Sales Day Book has been over-cast on page 87 by £100.

(*b*) The Returns Outwards for November, amounting to £30 11*s*. 8*d*., have been posted to personal accounts only.

(*c*) A cheque for £70 6*s*. 4*d*. received from Barton Bros. has been posted to their Sales Ledger account as £76 4*s*.

(*d*) A first and final dividend amounting to £2 7*s*. 6*d*. received from the trustee in bankruptcy of Hubert Wilkins has not been posted to the Sales Ledger account. The full amount of the debt (£19) has been written off as bad during the year.

(*e*) A cheque for £12 4*s*. 10*d*. paid to J. Smithson for goods supplied has been posted to his credit in the Sales Ledger.

Show the entries (Journal *or* Ledger) which are necessary to correct the above errors. (Royal Society of Arts.)

CHAPTER VIII

WRITING UP THE BOOKS

We have now become acquainted with the various books of prime entry and the Ledgers to which they serve as a basis, and we have realised in particular that the **double entry is completed within the Ledger.**

The examples that have been taken up to this point have largely dealt with the ordinary purchasing, selling and cash transactions of the business, and have been selected to illustrate the true meaning of double entry.

We ought now, therefore, to be in a position to look at other examples which include all these transactions and aim at the preparation of the Final Accounts, as they are termed, or the **Revenue Account** and **Balance Sheet.**

It is of the utmost importance that in working through them we try to put ourselves in the position of the Bookkeeper, and consider **every transaction** from the standpoint of its effect on :—

(*a*) The Profit or Loss result of the business, and
(*b*) Its Asset and Liability, or Capital position.

Example. On February 1, 1937, R. Ready had the following Assets and Liabilities : Cash in hand £10 ; Cash at bank £200 ; Creditors : B. Bright £75 and C. Clowes £95 ; Debtors : R. Wright £60, and S. Tune £70 ; Furniture and fittings £180 ; Stock on hand £340.

Open the books by Journal entry, find and credit his capital, and then enter the following transactions in the proper subsidiary books, post to the Ledger and extract a Trial Balance at February 27, 1937. The Cash Book and Personal Accounts should be balanced, and the balances brought down.

1937			£
Feb.	1.	Received cash from R. Wright . .	30
,,	2.	Sold on credit to M. Moses goods . .	50
,,	4.	Bought on credit from C. Clowes goods .	120

1937				£
Feb.	5.	Paid wages, cash		12
,,	6.	Drew cheque for personal use . .		25
		Cash sales for week		150
,,	9.	Paid cash to bank		140
,,	12.	Received cash from S. Tune	£67	
		Allowed him discount .	3	
			—	70
		Paid wages, cash.		15
,,	13.	Paid C. Clowes by cheque .	£90	
		Discount allowed . .	5	
			—	95
		Cash sales for week		87
,,	17.	Sold on credit to R. Wright, goods .		52
,,	19.	R. Wright returned goods . . .		10
		Paid wages, cash.		16
,,	20.	Cash sales for week		96
,,	22.	Paid cash to bank		190
,,	27.	Paid rent, cash		20
		Cash sales for week		82

(Union of Lancashire and Cheshire Institutes.)

Before we begin the work of opening the books for the month, it will be helpful to consider first the transactions and the business practice concerning them.

(*a*) The amount of the proprietor's capital is not stated, but as we know it to be the excess of the Assets over the Liabilities we can easily discover it, **and record it together with the other opening balances.**

(*b*) It is apparent that in the Cash Book there must be columns for " Cash " as well as for " Bank." Cash Discounts also have to be provided for.

(*c*) Both Cash and Credit Sales are made. Only the **Credit Sales** will be recorded in the Sales Journal, *i.e.*, in order to put on record the position of the customer as a debtor to the business, pending payment by him.

(*d*) There is no need to open columnar or analysis Purchase and Sales Journals. The one word " goods " is the only indication we have of the purchases and sales as a whole.

(*e*) Columns for " £'s " only need be given.

R. Ready.

JOURNAL.

Fo. 1.

			Fo.	Dr.	Cr.
1937					
Feb. 1	Sundries	Dr.		£	£
	To Sundries				
	Cash in Hand		C.B.2	10	
	Cash at Bank		2	200	
	R. Wright		S.L.20	60	
	S. Tune		25	70	
	Furniture and Fittings		P.L.65	180	
	Stock on Hand		70	340	
	To B. Bright		B.L.15		75
	„ C. Clowes		10		95
	„ Capital		P.L.75		690
	Being Assets, Liabilities and Capital at this date.			£860	£860

The Journal entries as set out above enable us to post to the various Ledgers the balances outstanding on February 1.

Thus, the cash items will appear on the **debit** side of the Cash Book; accounts will be opened in the Sales Ledger for Wright and Tune, again as **debits**; and in the Purchase Ledger for Bright and Clowes, but on the **credit** side.

Similarly, **debit** balances will appear in the Private Ledger for Furniture and Stock, while R. Ready's Capital Account will be **credited** with £690.

Fo. 3.

PURCHASE JOURNAL.

Date.	Supplier.	Fo.	Total.
1937			£
Feb. 4	C. Clowes	B.L.10	120
			I.L. Fo. 30

Note.

	Abbreviation.
Cash Book	C.B.
Purchase Journal	P.J.
Sales Journal	S.J.
Sales Returns Journal	S.R.J.
Journal	J.
Bought Ledger	B.L.
Sales Ledger	S.L.
Impersonal Ledger	I.L.
Private Ledger	P.L.

CASH BOOK.

Fo. 2.

Date.		Fo.	Dis-count.	Cash.	Bank.	Date.		Fo.	Dis-count.	Cash.	Bank.
1937			£	£	£	1937			£	£	£
Feb. 1	To Balances . .	J.1		10	200	Feb. 5	By Wages . .	I.L.55		12	
,, 1	,, R. Wright . .	S.L.20		30		,, 6	,, Drawings . .	P.L.80			25
,, 6	,, Cash Sales . .	I.L.40		150		,, 9	,, Bank . .	C		140	
,, 9	,, Cash . . .	C			140	,, 12	,, Wages . .	I.L.55		15	
,, 12	,, S. Tune . .	S.L.25	3	67		,, 13	,, C. Clowes . .	B.L.10	5		90
,, 13	,, Cash Sales . .	I.L.40		87		,, 19	,, Wages . .	I.L.55		16	
,, 20	,, Cash Sales . .	,,		96		,, 22	,, Bank . .	C		190	
,, 22	,, Cash . . .	C			190	,, 27	,, Rent . . .	I.L.60		20	
,, 27	,, Cash Sales . .	I.L.40		82		,, 28	,, Balance . .	c/d		129	415
			£3	£522	£530				£5	£522	£530
			I.L.46						I.L.50		
Mar. 1	To Balances . .	b/d		129	415						

Fo. 4.

SALES JOURNAL.

Date.	Customer.	Fo.	Total.
1937			£
Feb. 2	M. Moses		50
„ 17	R. Wright		52
			£102
			I.L. Fo. 35

Fo. 5.

SALES RETURNS JOURNAL.

(Returns Inwards).

Date.	Customer.	Fo.	Total.
1937			£
Feb. 19	R. Wright		10
			I.L. Fo. 45

Having first written up the Books of Prime Entry **in respect of the transactions during the month,** and brought down the Cash and Bank Balances as instructed, we are able to post as we should in practice, from the Journals to the appropriate Ledger Accounts.

Let us begin with the **Personal** Ledgers, dealing first with that section relating to the Accounts of Suppliers, or **Bought Ledger.**

Fo. 10.

BOUGHT LEDGER.

C. CLOWES.

Dr. Cr.

Date.	Details.	Fo.	Amount.	Date.	Details.	Fo.	Amount.
1937			£ s. d.	1937			£ s. d.
Feb. 13	To Bank .	C.B.2	90 0 0	Feb. 1	By Balance .	J.1	95 0 0
	„ Discount.	„	5 0 0	„ 4	„ Goods .	P.J.3	120 0 0
„ 28	„ Balance .	c/d	120 0 0				
			£215 0 0				£215 0 0
				Mar. 1	By Balance .	b/d	120 0 0

Fo. 15.

B. BRIGHT.

DR. CR.

Date.	Details.	Fo.	Amount.	Date	Details.	Fo.	Amount.
				1937			£ s. d.
				Feb. 1	By Balance .	J.1	75 0 0

As no transactions have taken place on Bright's account, the opening balance on February 1 remains unchanged on February 28.

Next we may turn to the **Sales Ledger** :—

Fo. 20.

R. WRIGHT.

DR. CR.

Date.	Details.	Fo.	Amount.	Date.	Details.	Fo.	Amount.
1937			£ s. d.	1937			£ s. d.
Feb. 1	To Balance .	J.1.	60 0 0	Feb. 1	By Cash .	C.B.	30 0 0
„ 17	„ Goods .	S.J.4	52 0 0	„ 19	„ Returns	S.J.R.5	10 0 0
				„ 28	„ Balance	c/d	72 0 0
			£112 0 0				£112 0 0
Mar. 1	To Balance .	b/d	72 0 0				

Fo. 23.

M. MOSES.

DR. CR.

Date.	Details.	Fo.	Amount.	Date.	Details.	Fo.	Amount.
1937			£ s. d.				
Feb. 2	To Goods .	S.J.4	50 0 0				

Fo. 25.

S. TUNE.

DR. CR.

Date.	Details.	Fo.	Amount.	Date.	Details.	Fo.	Amount.
1937			£ s. d.	1937			£ s. d.
Feb. 1	To Balance .	J.1	70 0 0	Feb. 12	By Cash .	C.B.2	67 0 0
					„ Discount		3 0 0
			£70 0 0				£70 0 0

The **Impersonal,** or as it is sometimes termed, the **Nominal Ledger,** may now receive attention.

Within this, as we know, we shall expect to find the accounts dealing **with the effect upon the business** of the transactions entered into.

Fo. 30.

PURCHASES.

DR. CR.

Date.	Details.	Fo.	Amount.	Date.	Details.	Fo.	Amount.
1937			£ *s.* *d.*				
Feb. 28	To Total for Month .	P.J.3	120 0 0				

Fo. 35.

CREDIT SALES.

DR. CR.

Date.	Details.	Fo.	Amount.	Date.	Details.	Fo.	Amount.
				1937			£ *s.* *d.*
				Feb. 28	By Total for Month .	S.J.4	102 0 0

Fo. 40.

CASH SALES.

DR. CR.

Date.	Details.	Fo.	Amount.	Date.	Details.	Fo.	Amount.
				1937			£ *s.* *d.*
				Feb. 6	By Cash .	C.B.2	150 0 0
				„ 13	„ Cash .	„	87 0 0
				„ 20	„ Cash .	„	96 0 0
				„ 27	„ Cash .	„	82 0 0
							£415 0 0

Fo. 45.

SALES RETURNS.

DR. CR.

Date.	Details.	Fo.	Amount.	Date.	Details.	Fo.	Amount.
1937			£ *s.* *d.*				
Feb. 28	To Total for Month .	S.R.J.5	10 0 0				

Fo. 46.

DISCOUNTS ALLOWED.

DR. CR.

Date.	Details.	Fo.	Amount.	Date.	Details.	Fo.	Amount.
1937			£ s. d.				
Feb. 28	To Total for Month .	C.B.2	3 0 0				

Fo. 50.

DISCOUNTS RECEIVED.

DR. CR.

Date.	Details.	Fo.	Amount.	Date.	Details.	Fo.	Amount.
				1937			£ s. d.
				Feb. 28	By Total for Month .	C.B.2	5 0 0

Fo. 55.

WAGES.

DR. CR.

Date.	Details.	Fo.	Amount.	Date.	Details.	Fo.	Amount.
1937			£ s. d.				
Feb. 5	To Cash .	C.B.2	12 0 0				
„ 12	„ Cash .	„	15 0 0				
„ 19	„ Cash .	„	16 0 0				
			£43 0 0				

Fo. 60.

RENT.

DR. CR.

Date.	Details.	Fo.	Amount.	Date.	Details.	Fo.	Amount.
1937			£ s. d.				
Feb. 27	To Cash	C.B.2	20 0 0				

Lastly, there is the **Private Ledger** to be considered.

Here we shall have first of all two **Asset** Accounts, for Furniture and Stock respectively, and one **Liability** Account, for Capital.

Fo. 65.

FURNITURE AND FITTINGS.

Dr. Cr.

Date.	Details.	Fo.	Amount.	Date.	Details.	Fo.	Amount.
1937 Feb. 1	To Balance .	J.1	£ s. d. 180 0 0				

Fo. 70.

STOCK.

Dr. Cr.

Date.	Details.	Fo.	Amount.	Date.	Details.	Fo.	Amount.
1937 Feb. 1	To Balance .	J.1	£ s. d. 340 0 0				

Fo. 75.

CAPITAL.

Dr. Cr.

Date.	Details.	Fo.	Amount.	Date.	Details.	Fo.	Amount.
				1937 Feb. 1	By Balance .	J.1	£ s. d. 690 0 0

If, however, we look at the Cash Book, we see that on February 6 **R. Ready,** the proprietor, drew a cheque £25 for his personal use. This is a withdrawal from the business of :—

(*a*) A part of the amount now standing to his credit on Capital Account, or

(*b*) The profit which he estimates is being earned.

In either event, it must be debited in the Ledger in the Capital Account above, or in a " Drawings " Account opened for the purpose :—

Fo. 80.

DRAWINGS.

Dr. Cr.

Date.	Details.	Fo.	Amount.	Date.	Details.	Fo.	Amount.
1937 Feb. 6	To Bank .	C.B.2	£ s. d. 25 0 0				

Having now posted all the transactions to the Ledgers, and recorded **their dual aspect,** it is to be expected that arithmetical agreement has been obtained, in that the sum of the **Debit** Balances should equal the sum of the **Credit Balances on February 28.**

Let us therefore extract the Balances on the Accounts and list them as Debits or Credits, according to their nature :—

Ledger.	Account.	Fo.	Dr.	Cr.
			£	£
Cash Book	Cash	2	129	
" "	Bank	"	415	
Bought	C. Clowes	10		120
"	B. Bright	15		75
Sales	R. Wright	20	72	
"	M. Moses	23	50	
Impersonal	Purchases	30	120	
"	Credit Sales	35		102
"	Cash Sales	40		415
"	Sales Returns	45	10	
"	Discounts Allowed	46	3	
"	" Received	50		5
"	Wages	55	43	
"	Rent	60	20	
Private	Furniture and Fittings	65	180	
"	Stock, February 1	70	340	
"	Capital	75		690
"	Drawings	80	25	
			£1,407	£1,407

In total the Double Entry is seen to be completed **within the Ledger Accounts,** regarding the Cash Book as a Ledger for this purpose.

This list, or summary of **Ledger Balances,** we call a **Trial Balance.** Its extraction at any time enables us :—

(*a*) To satisfy ourselves of the arithmetical accuracy with which the routine work of writing up the Books of Prime Entry, and posting to the Ledgers, has been carried out.

(*b*) To provide a basis for the preparation of the Final Accounts, or **Revenue Account** and **Balance Sheet.**

Because of its importance, we must consider it at greater length.

Tests and Questions

1. N. Bell was in business as a wholesale merchant and on January 1, 1937, he had the following assets and liabilities: Cash in hand, £25; Bank overdraft, £675; Stock of goods, £1,400; Motor vans, £175; Fixtures and fittings, £225. Sundry Debtors: J. Betts, £160; E. Evans, £150. Sundry Creditors: T. Brown, £210; F. Shaw, £150.

Enter the above and the following transactions into the proper subsidiary books, post to the Ledger and extract a Trial Balance. The Cash Book and, where necessary, the Ledger Accounts should be balanced and the balances brought down.

Jan. 4. Received from J. Betts cheque for £158 in full settlement of his account for £160. Paid cheque to bank.
,, 6. Sold goods on credit to E. Evans, £300.
,, 9. Paid wages in cash, £15.
,, 11. Sold goods for cash, £35.
E. Evans returned goods. Sent him credit note for £12.
,, 15. Sold a motor van for cash, £45.
,, 18. Paid cash into the bank, £50.
,, 23. Paid wages in cash, £15.
Purchased on credit new motor van from the Albion Motor Co., Ltd., for £100.
,, 25. Received cheque from E. Evans for £435 in full settlement of the amount due from him. Paid cheque to bank.
Purchased goods on credit from F. Shaw, £200.
,, 27. Paid T. Brown cheque for £205 in full settlement of the amount due to him on January 1.

N.B.—No Trading and Profit and Loss Accounts or Balance Sheet are required. (Union of Educational Institutions.)

2. On March 1, 1934, A. Walker commences business with £5,000 in cash of which he pays £4,500 into the bank. Enter the following transactions in the books of original entry, post to Ledger Accounts and extract a Trial Balance.

Mar. 2. Bought premises and paid £1,500 by cheque.
,, 4. Purchased on credit from J. Raleigh :—
30 gent's cycles at £5 1*s*. 6*d*. each.
45 ladies' cycles as £4 16*s*. each.
20 children's cycles at £3 11*s*. 6*d*. each.
,, 5. Bought at an auction sale sundry goods for £53 17*s*. 10*d*. and paid for them by cash.
,, 6. Sold to S. Taylor :—
1 gent's cycle at £6 17*s*. 6*d*.
1 ladies' cycle at £5 12*s*. 6*d*.
1 tandem at £8 8*s*.
,, 8. Returned to J. Raleigh :—
10 children's cycles invoiced on the 4th and received a credit note.
,, 10. Paid J. Raleigh by cheque the amount due, less 5% cash discount.

Mar. 12. Bought office furniture for cash £25 10*s.* 6*d.*
„ 16. S. Taylor paid by cheque the amount due.
„ 18. Paid by cheque rent £15 10*s.*
Paid by cash wages £7 6*s.* 9*d.*
Paid by cash insurance £1 15*s.* 6*d.*
Cash sales for the period £119 17*s.* 6*d.*
„ 20. Paid all cash into the bank except £10 13*s.* 4*d.*

(East Midland Educational Union.)

3. R. Simpson was in business as a wholesale cutler and jeweller. On January 1, 1936, his financial position was as follows : Cash in hand, £40; Cash at bank, £350; Stock, £1,000; Fixtures and fittings, £160. Sundry Creditors: M. Marsh, £150; D. Steele, £200. Sundry Debtors: H. Robins, £275; J. Long, £175.

Enter the above and the following transactions into the proper subsidiary books, post to the Ledger, and extract a Trial Balance. The Cash Book and, where necessary, the Ledger Accounts should be balanced and the balances brought down.

Jan. 2. Received from H. Robins on account, cheque for £200, which was paid to bank.
„ 3. Sold to D. Dennis & Co., Ltd. :—
1 gross table knives at 30*s.* a dozen,
1 gross table forks at 35*s.* a dozen;
the whole subject to a trade discount of 10%.
„ 4. Paid wages in cash £15.
„ 6. Cash sales paid to bank, £97.
„ 7. Bought from Silversmiths, Ltd. :—
2 electro-plated coffee services at £10 10*s.* each,
2 electro-plated tea services at £8 8*s.* each;
the whole subject to a trade discount of 15%.
„ 8. Paid M. Marsh by cheque £147 10*s.* in settlement of his account of £150.
„ 11. Paid wages in cash £15.
„ 13. Cash sales paid to bank £85.
„ 15. Withdrew from bank for office cash £45.
„ 17. Sold to J. Long :—
2 dozen pairs scissors at 1*s.* 6*d.* per pair,
2 dozen pocket knives at 1*s.* 3*d.* each;
the whole subject to a trade discount of 15%.
„ 18. Paid wages in cash £15.
R. Simpson withdrew £10 for private purposes by cheque.
„ 18. Cash sales paid to bank £76.
„ 20. Received from J. Long in full settlement of the amount due from him on January 1, cheque for £173. Paid cheque to bank.

N.B.—No Trading and Profit and Loss Account or Balance Sheet is required. (Union of Educational Institutions.)

4. On January 1, 1936, the financial position of R. Mason, gentlemen's outfitter, is as follows: Cash in hand, £9 16*s.* 6*d.*; Stock, £750; H. Atherton (Dr.), £6 10*s.* 9*d.*; Fixtures and fittings, £150; A. Baker (Cr.), £76 19*s.* 3*d.*; Bank overdraft, £35 6*s.* Find and credit his capital.

During the month his transactions were as follows :—

Jan.	4.	Bought goods from G. Henry & Co., to the value of £162 10*s*., less 12½% trade discount.
,,	6.	Paid A. Baker the amount owing, less 5% cash discount.
,,	7.	Returned to G. Henry & Co. goods to the gross value of £20 15*s*.
,,	9.	Sold goods to H. Atherton, £13 13*s*.
,,	9.	Received from G. Henry & Co. credit note for the net amount of goods returned.
,,	10.	H. Atherton settled his account of January 1, less 2½% cash discount.
,,	14.	Bought new showcase £15 15*s*. from W. Dixon.
,,	19.	Sold goods to N. Dobbin £14 10*s*.
,,	20.	Bank realised £50 securities to reduce the overdraft.
,,	23.	Sold shop fittings for cash £5 10*s*. 6*d*.
,,	26.	Cash sales for the period £62 17*s*. 10*d*.
,,	28.	Paid all cash into bank except £9 16*s*. 6*d*.

Enter the transactions in the appropriate subsidiary books—post to the Ledger Accounts and extract a Trial Balance.

N.B.—Trading Account, Profit and Loss Account and Balance Sheet are not required. (East Midland Educational Union.)

5. In the form of Cash Book provided, after properly heading each column, enter all the money transactions below and balance the Book.

Journalise the opening balances and remaining transactions. (*Note :* Purchases and Sales Books may be used, if preferred.)

Post the entries to the Ledger. Extract a Trial Balance.

Close and balance the Ledger.

On October 1, 1936, S. Strong reopened his books with the following balances in addition to his Capital Account :—

	£	*s*.	*d*.
Cash	47	9	2
K. Knight & Co. (Cr.)	176	19	2
D. Day (Dr.)	225	14	7
Bank (overdraft)	217	8	4
Rent accrued	20	0	0
Stock of goods	741	3	9

During the month his transactions were :—

			£	*s*.	*d*.
Oct.	3.	Received cheque from D. Day to settle account	220	0	0
,,	5.	Paid same into bank	220	0	0
,,	8.	Sold to D. Day :—			
		150 boxes (12) tennis balls at 10*s*. per box	75	0	0
		3 doz. rackets at 30*s*. each	54	0	0
,,	10.	D. Day returned 3 rackets damaged	4	10	0
,,	13.	Sundry cash sales	83	14	9
,,	14.	Paid into bank	100	0	0

			£	s.	d.
Oct.	16.	Bought of K. Knight & Co. :—			
		Job lot tennis balls	37	14	9
		2 doz. croquet sets at 45s. each . .	54	0	0
,,	19.	Paid landlord by cheque	20	0	0
,,	21.	Paid K. Knight & Co. on account . .	150	0	0
,,	22.	Sold to D. Day sundry sports fittings and received cheque (banked) . . .	43	17	6
,,	26.	D. Day's cheque returned dishonoured .	43	17	6
,,	27.	Cash purchases to date	7	6	10
,,	28.	Drew cheque for self	25	0	0
,,	30.	Wages and expenses for month paid by cheque	30	8	2
		and in cash	11	2	9
,,	31.	Rent accrued	20	0	0
		Bank charges		14	6
		Interest on capital at 4% per annum .		—	
		Stock of goods on hand valued at . .	668	3	1

(College of Preceptors.)

6. On November 1, 1932, John Maynard commenced business on his own account, trading under the style of The Bon Marché.

He paid £1,000 into the bank account of the business on that date, and also borrowed £500 from his father, Robert Maynard, to assist him in the venture.

The following transactions were entered into during the month of November :—

1932			£	s.	d.
Nov.	1.	Paid rent by cheque three months to January 31, 1933	37	10	0
,,	2.	Obtained cheque book from bank . .		8	4
,,	2.	Bought material on credit :—			
		Forrester & Co.	126	10	0
		Arnold & Sons	39	15	0
		H. Meyrick, Ltd.	112	18	6
,,	3.	Bought office fittings for cash . . .	7	10	0
,,	3.	Drew cheque for cash	25	0	0
,,	4.	Sold goods on credit :—			
		E. Walker	21	3	9
		J. Roberts	12	0	10
		L. Morley	26	5	0
		H. Longden		17	8
,,	4.	Paid wages in cash	2	5	0
,,	11.	Sent cheque to Forrester & Co. . . .	125	0	0
		and obtained discount	1	10	0
,,	16.	Received cheque from Roberts . . .	12	0	0
		and allowed discount			10
,,	19.	Received cheque from Morley	25	0	0
		and allowed discount	1	5	0
,,	24.	Paid wages in cash	2	5	0
,,	27.	Sent cheque to Arnold & Sons . . .	39	0	0
		and obtained discount		15	0
,,	30.	Returned defective goods to H. Meyrick, Ltd.	9	7	6

Enter the above transactions in the proper books of prime entry, post to the Ledger, and extract a Trial Balance at November 30.

(University of Birmingham.)

7. W. Allen is in business as a wholesale and retail stationer. The balances in his books on March 1 were :—

	£	s.	d.	£	s.	d.
Cash in hand	19	8	7			
Cash at bank	88	7	9			
Stock	985	3	4			
A. Reid (Dr.)	91	7	8			
Capital				1,184	7	4
	£1,184	7	4	£1,184	7	4

Open the books by means of Journal entry. Enter the following transactions in the books of original entry, post to Ledger Accounts, and extract a Trial Balance :—

Mar. 2. Bought of Barking & Co. :—
100,000 envelopes at 8*s.* 6*d.* per 1,000.
250 reams of writing paper at 5*s.* 6*d.* per ream.
60 doz. bottles blue-black ink at 3*s.* 9*d.* per doz. bottles.
Less 10% trade discount.
,, 4. Paid carriage in cash, £6 2*s.* 6*d.*
,, 4. Sold to L. Lyons :—
200 calendars at 1*s.* 10*d.* each.
5,000 foolscap envelopes at 9*s.* 3*d.* per 1,000.
25 reams of blotting paper at 6*s.* 6*d.* per ream.
,, 5. A. Reid paid his account by cheque which was paid to the bank.
,, 8. L. Lyons returned 3,000 envelopes invoiced on the 4th, and sent him credit note.
,, 9. The bank returned Reid's cheque dishonoured.
,, 11. Paid Barking & Co. by cheque less 5% cash discount.
,, 15. Sold to H. Cooper :—
50 packets quarto paper at 1*s.* 3*d.* per packet.
8 doz. stencils at 6½*d.* each.
12 doz. envelopes 8 in. by 6 in. at 3 for 5*d.*
,, 18. Cash sales for the period, £96 16*s.* 3*d.*
,, 18. Paid in cash, wages £15 10*s.* 9*d.*, rent £6 16*s.* 9*d.*, insurance £2 2*s.*
,, 18. Paid all cash into bank except £2 6*s.* 8*d.*

N.B.—No Trading Account, Profit and Loss Account, or Balance Sheet is to be prepared. (East Midland Educational Union.)

8. On January 1, 1934, R. Baxter commenced business as a coal merchant with £550 in cash. On the same date he opened a current account at the bank and paid in £500. His transactions during the month follow :—

Jan. 1. Bought a second-hand motor lorry by cheque, £85 10*s.*
Bought from the Victory Colliery Co., Ltd. :—
50 tons, 15 cwt. best coal at 22*s.* 6*d.* per ton.
35 tons, 10 cwt. nuts at 15*s.* 6*d.* per ton.
„ 4. Cash sales £8 9*s.* 7*d.*
„ 4. Sold to J. Yates, 3 tons, 10 cwt. 2 qr. best coal at 37*s.* 6*d.* per ton.
„ 6. Paid Victory Colliery Co. £50 on account by cheque.
„ 8. Bought from The Agecroft Coal Co. 43 tons house coal at 23*s.* 3*d.* per ton.
„ 10. J. Yates settled his account by cheque and allowed him 5% cash discount.
„ 12. Sold to W. Jones 10 tons, 15 cwt. house coal at 32*s.* 9*d.* per ton.
„ 12. Paid carriage in cash £5 2*s.* 10*d.*
„ 15. Settled the account of the Victory Colliery Co. by cheque and was allowed 5% cash discount on the original account.
„ 16. Cash sales £32 15*s.* 7*d.*
„ 16. Paid sundry expenses in cash £13 4*s.* 6*d.*
„ 16. Paid all cash into the bank except £6 9*s.* 3*d.*

You are required to enter the above transactions in the books of original entry, to post to Ledger Accounts, and to extract a Trial Balance.

No Trading Account, Profit and Loss Account, or Balance Sheet is required. (East Midland Educational Union.)

9. Robert Salmon, a wholesale grocer, was, on January 1, 1937, in the following financial position : Premises, £1,300; Fixtures and fittings, £100; Cash in hand, £44 2*s.* 3*d.*; Stock, £620; Cash at bank, £51 7*s.* 3*d.* Debtors : A. Hardy, £14 10*s.*; G. White, £8 8*s.* Creditors : Grocery Supplies, Ltd., £54 17*s.* 8*d.*; Mills Brothers, £33 9*s.* 10*d.*

Open the Accounts necessary to record this position in the Ledger, and post, through correct books of original entry, the following transactions :—

1937
Jan. 2. Paid, by cheque, wages £15 13*s.* 8*d.*
„ 3. Sold, on credit, to A. Hardy 2 dozen tinned fruits at 11*s.* 6*d.* per dozen, and 20 tins biscuits at 4*s.* 6*d.* per tin.
„ 5. Purchased, for cash, biscuits £13 12*s.* 6*d.*
„ 6. Paid, by cheque, the amount due to Grocery Supplies, Ltd., less 2½% cash discount.
Cash sales to date £24 5*s.* 3*d.*
„ 9. Purchased, on credit, from Grocery Supplies, Ltd., 10 gross tins condensed milk at 5*s.* 6*d.* per dozen net, and 1½ cwt. cheese at £6 per cwt., less 20% trade discount.
„ 11. Received cheque, which was paid into the bank, from A. Hardy, for the amount of his account to date less 5% cash discount.
Purchased for cash, new showcase £15.

Jan. 14. Returned to Grocery Supplies, Ltd., ½ cwt. cheese supplied on the 9th inst.

„ 16. Paid, by cheque, wages £14 17*s*. 3*d*., insurance £2 3*s*. 8*d*.
Sold, on credit, to B. Ruston, 4 dozen tins biscuits at 6*s*. per tin, less 15% trade discount.

„ 17. Purchased, on credit, from Loxley & Co., 1 chest tea £10 10*s*.
Cash sales to date £20 15*s*. 1*d*.

„ 19. Paid into bank from office cash £50.

„ 21. Agree to allow G. White £1 8*s*. in consequence of defects in goods previously supplied to him.

„ 22. Paid, by cheque, to Mills Brothers, £20 on account.

„ 25. Robert Salmon pays into the bank, as additional capital, £200.

Balance the accounts as on January 25, 1937, and extract a Trial Balance. (East Midland Educational Union.)

CHAPTER IX

THE TRIAL BALANCE

Two advantages have just been claimed for the Trial Balance. The first, that it is evidence of the arithmetical accuracy of the book-keeping work, clearly has reference to the dual aspect from which every transaction may be regarded, each transaction having been looked at from the twofold aspect upon which the double entry system relies.

Are we therefore justified in assuming that the routine work underlying the Trial Balance calls for no further comment? Is arithmetical accuracy alone all with which we need be concerned?

The answer to these two questions is **"no."**

Apparent proof of accuracy is not the same as conclusive proof, and we have to realise that errors may exist in the underlying work which the Trial Balance will not reveal.

If, for example, a **transaction has been altogether omitted** from the books, neither its **debit** nor its **credit** aspect can have been recorded.

Goods may have been purchased from Brown, a supplier, and an invoice duly received. But if, in course of checking prior to entry in the Purchase Journal, the invoice is lost or mislaid, nothing will ultimately appear to the **credit** of the **Supplier's Account** in respect of it. Similarly as it has never been entered in the Purchase Journal, it cannot form part of the Total Purchases for the month which are posted to the **debit** of Purchases Account.

Such an **error of omission** would be discovered only when the supplier's **Statement of Account** comes to hand.

Another example would be neglect to record in the Cash Book any discount deducted by a customer.

The customer would be credited with too little in his Personal Account, causing an Asset in the form of a Book Debt to be **overstated,** and **Discounts Allowed** Account would be under debited, resulting in the **understatement** of an expense to the business.

There are also errors which we may describe as **compensating errors.** In this sense, an error in one direction is counterbalanced by an error in another direction of equal amount. Hence, again the lack of agreement is not disclosed by the Trial Balance.

The following are examples of **compensating errors** :—

(*a*) The total of **Sales Account** on one page of the Impersonal Ledger is inadvertently carried forward £10 less than it should be, *i.e.*, there is **short credit** of £10.

At the same time, the addition of Wages Account is made £10 too little, so that there is a **short debit** of £10.

(*b*) In extracting the balances on the Sales Ledger Accounts, an item of £110 is entered on the list of balances as £100, causing a **short debit** of £10, while a cheque for £10 from Jones, a customer, has been debited in the Cash Book but never posted to the credit of his account in the Sales Ledger. The **total book debts** are correctly shown in the List of Balances, **although the detail items are incorrect.**

We may also have to deal with **errors of principle.** Supposing £5 is paid by way of deposit in connection with the supply of Electricity to the business. This deposit is refundable if and when the business closes down, and therefore is an **Asset.** If the amount is debited to Heat, Light, and Power Account in the Impersonal Ledger it will in all probability be written off as an **expense** for the particular period, resulting in an **overstatement of working expenses,** and an **understatement of Assets.**

Secondly, should a part of the Fixtures and Fittings be sold to a dealer when the offices are being modernised, and entered as a sale in the Sales Journal, Sales Account will be improperly inflated, **because the goods are not those in**

which the business is dealing. Further, the Fixtures and Fittings Account will not record the reduction in value.

Here also the Trial Balance is of no help in the detection of the errors.

We must not, however, assume that its value as a basis for the preparation of the Final Accounts is seriously lessened. So far as accounts in the Impersonal and Private Ledger are concerned, these are not usually numerous, neither are the entries appearing therein, and great care is taken in practice to record the true facts.

Similarly when the Sales and Purchase Ledger Balances are extracted and totalled, it is usual for the work to be checked before the figures are finally accepted.

Errors which the Trial Balance will Show

If there is a " difference " on the Trial Balance, search must be made for the probable cause.

We can compare the names of the accounts appearing in it with those in some previous Trial Balance, and note any omission. We can also scrutinise each item in the light of its description and the definition that :—

(*a*) **A Debit Balance** is either an **Asset** or an **Expense,** and
(*b*) **A Credit Balance** is either a **Liability** or a **Profit.**

Thus if we regard **Sales** as a **Profit,** Sales Returns, or **Returns Inwards** should be considered as an **Expense,** or Debit Balance. If the returned goods remain in the warehouse unsold we could alternatively look on them as an **Asset,** but they would still be a Debit Balance.

It will not take long to go through the accounts in the **Impersonal** and **Private Ledgers,** if need be, to satisfy ourselves that they are apparently in order, and we should probably do this before re-examining the Sales and Purchase Ledger Accounts. Because they are so rarely met with, **Credit** Balances on the **Sales Ledger** and **Debit** Balances on the **Purchase Ledger** should also be considered as a likely source of error.

If nothing is thus brought to light, and assuming the (monthly) totals of the Books of Prime Entry have been checked to the Impersonal Ledger, the following steps can be taken :—

(*a*) Check the additions (or casts) of the Books of Prime Entry.
(*b*) Check the postings in detail from the Books of Prime Entry to the Sales and Purchase Ledgers.

The two latter checks involve a great deal of time and labour, but should result in locating the error, and obtaining agreement in the Trial Balance.

Example. The following Trial Balance was extracted from the books of F. Briers on December 31, 1936. Do you think that it is correct? If not, rewrite it in its correct form.

	Dr.	*Cr.*
	£	£
Capital Account		1,000
Stock at January 1, 1936 . . .	825	
Purchases and Sales	1,275	1,590
Returns Inwards		80
Returns Outwards	70	
Discounts Received	80	
Discounts Allowed		70
Motor Vans		175
Wages and Salaries	250	
Carriage		70
Rent and Rates	185	
Sundry Debtors	760	
Sundry Creditors		725
Cash in Hand	20	
Bank Overdraft	245	
	£3,710	£3,710

(Union of Educational Institutions.)

Although the total debits equal the total credits, the Trial Balance is very far from being correct.

It should instead appear as under :—

	Dr.	Cr.
	£	£
Capital Account		1,000
Stock at January 1, 1936	825	
Purchases	1,275	
Sales		1,590
Returns Inwards	80	
Returns Outwards		70
Discounts Received		80
Discounts Allowed	70	
Motor Vans	175	
Wages and Salaries	250	
Carriage	70	
Rent and Rates	185	
Sundry Debtors	760	
Sundry Creditors		725
Cash in Hand	20	
Bank Overdraft		245
	£3,710	£3,710

The adjustments made, and the reasons for them are :—

(*a*) **Returns Inwards.** As an expense or Asset (of which we spoke on page 124) this is a Debit Balance.

(*b*) **Returns Outwards,** *i.e.*, to **suppliers.** These are sometimes called Purchase Returns, and are a Credit Balance.

(*c*) **Discounts Received.** As a profit to the business, the amount represents a Credit Balance.

(*d*) **Discounts Allowed.** Clearly an expense, and so a Debit.

(*e*) **Motor Vans** are an Asset of the business and will be a Debit Balance in the Private Ledger.

(*f*) **Carriage.** The cost of carriage is a business expense, and a Debit in the Impersonal Ledger.

(*g*) **Bank Overdraft.** As a liability due to the bank this must be a Credit Balance in the Cash Book.

EXERCISE.

On February 1, 1946, X. started a business of a 2*d*. Library with a Capital of £100, borrowed from his father.

He opened a Bank Account in his own name with the £100.

As from February 1, he rented a small shop for £1 per week, payable in advance.

His preliminary expenditure came to £10, divisible as to Advertising and Circulars £6, Cleaning and Repairs £3, and Postage and Sundries £1. All these amounts were paid in cash.

From a firm of Publishers called A., Ltd., he ordered a stock of 1,000 Books, for which he paid £50.

His weekly expenses for the business, starting with the week commencing February 8, came to £1 10*s*. (Advertising 10*s*., Cleaning 10*s*., and Sundries 10*s*.).

His Cash Takings and his Drawings for the eight weeks ended March 27 were as follows :—

Week ending.	Cash Takings.			Drawings.		
	£	*s*.	*d*.	£	*s*.	*d*.
February 8th . . .	Nil			1	0	0
,, 15th . . .	3	0	0	1	0	0
,, 22nd . .	5	0	0	1	10	0
,, 29th . . .	7	0	0	2	0	0
March 6th	8	0	0	2	0	0
,, 13th	10	0	0	2	10	0
,, 20th	9	0	0	2	0	0
,, 27th	10	0	0	2	0	0

Takings were banked weekly intact, and a Petty Cash Float of £5 was maintained to meet the rent, all weekly expenses, and X.'s personal drawings.

On February 8 he took out a Comprehensive Insurance Policy, covering all risks, and paid a premium of £8.

Other transactions were as follows :—

During the week ended March 6, X. decided to make some changes in his Stock. He held a sale of old and unpopular books, and disposed of 200 copies at 6*d*. each. He reckoned that they had cost him 1*s*. each to buy.

On March 8 he ordered another 500 Books from A., Ltd., which were invoiced to him at £40. One hundred of these were found to be unsuitable, and he returned them to A., Ltd., receiving a Credit Note in exchange for their cost (£8), less £1 for carriage and packing.

On March 15 he changed a cheque for a customer, A. Smith. Smith owed him 10*s*. for two books which he had lost, and gave him a cheque for £1. X. gave Smith 10*s*. change in cash. The cheque was paid into Bank at the end of the week with the rest of the money, but was returned.

On March 20, X. received a prize of £20 in a competition, and decided to pay off £20 of the loan he had received from his father.

On March 24 his shop window was smashed by the window cleaners in an accident. X. had to pay £2 for immediate repairs, but entered a claim for this amount with the Insurance Company.

You are required to write up the Books of X. recording the above transactions, and to prepare a Trial Balance as at March 27, 1946.

(University of Birmingham.)

CHAPTER X

FOUR-COLUMN TRIAL BALANCE

THE purpose of this form of Trial Balance is to assist us further in the preparation of the Profit and Loss Account and Balance Sheet. It demonstrates in a manner which is not apparent in the ordinary form of Trial Balance with which we have dealt, the fact that :—

(*a*) A **Debit** Balance is either an **Asset** or an **Expense,** and
(*b*) A **Credit** Balance is either a **Liability** or a **Profit.**

Let us redraft the Trial Balance of R. Ready shown on page 114, in **four-column form** :—

Account.	Ledger.	Fo.	Revenue.		Capital.	
			Dr.	Cr.	Dr.	Cr.
			£	£	£	£
Cash	Cash Book	2			129	
Bank	,, ,,	,,			415	
C. Clowes . . .	Bought	10				120
B. Bright . . .	,,	15				75
R. Wright . . .	Sales	20			72	
M. Moses . . .	,,	23			50	
Purchases . . .	Impersonal	30	120			
Credit Sales . . .	,,	35		102		
Cash Sales . . .	,,	40		415		
Sales Returns . . .	,,	45	10			
Discounts Allowed . .	,,	46	3			
,, Received . .	,,	50		5		
Wages	,,	55	43			
Rent	,,	60	20			
Furniture and Fittings .	Private	65			180	
Stock	,,	70	340			
Capital	,,	75				690
Drawings . . .	,,	80			25	
			£536	£522	£871	£885

Commencing Stock, although an Asset, is entered in the **Revenue** column, because it represents goods in which the business is dealing. The Stock on hand at February 27, 1937, will be recorded in :—

(*a*) The Revenue column (Credit), and
(*b*) The Capital column (Debit),

thus enabling us to record :—

(*a*) The true Profit, and
(*b*) The existence of the Asset of Stock at this date.

SUMMARY.

	Dr.	*Cr.*
	£	£
Revenue	536	522
Capital	871	885
	£1,407	£1,407

What we have now done is to show in the **first two columns** all those items which are of a Revenue character, and which alone will concern us in ascertaining Profit or Loss.

In the **third and fourth columns** are found the accounts which relate to Assets except closing Stock, and Liabilities, and as such compose the Balance Sheet of the business.

Tests and Questions

1. Can the arithmetical agreement on the Debit and Credit Columns in a Trial Balance be considered conclusive proof of the accuracy of the book-keeping work?

Illustrate your answer with at least three suitable examples.

(University of Birmingham.)

2. Write short notes on :—

(*a*) Errors of omission,
(*b*) Errors of commission,
(*c*) Compensating errors,

giving two examples of each. (Royal Society of Arts.)

3. On taking out a Trial Balance from a set of books, a book-keeper found that the Dr. side exceeded the Cr. by £9.

Assuming that this "difference" was due to a single mistake, mention as many types of error as you can think of, each different in principle, any one of which could have caused it.

(Royal Society of Arts.)

4. On preparing a Trial Balance from a set of books the sides are found not to agree, the Dr. total being £25,305 1*s.* 11*d.* and the Cr. £25,080 12*s.* 9*d.* You are convinced that nothing has been omitted and that all the figures are arithmetically correct, all postings, additions, etc., having been independently checked.

What is the probable nature of the error made and what will be the correct totals of the Trial Balance?

(Royal Society of Arts.)

5. The following errors were discovered in a set of books kept by Double Entry :—

(*a*) An item of £52 in the Sales Day Book posted to the customer's account as £50 2*s*.
(*b*) Bank interest amounting to £60 charged by the bank on an overdraft, entered on the debit side of the Cash Book in the bank column.
(*c*) An item of £15 for goods returned by a customer entered in the Returns Outwards Book and omitted to be posted.
(*d*) A payment by cheque of £10 to X. Y., entered in the Cash Book on the credit side in the cash column.

State by what amount the totals of the Trial Balance disagreed.
(University of Manchester.)

6. The Assets Balances in a Trial Balance amount to £8,500, the Capital (less Drawings) to £4,000, and the Gross Income or Profits to £6,000. The Total Debit Balances amount to £12,000. The only adjustment not appearing in the Ledger is Closing Stock valued at £1,000. What is the profit for the year, and what is the amount of the liabilities? Show your workings.
(University of Birmingham.)

7. (*a*) Explain shortly the value of preparing at any given date a Trial Balance from the books of a business.

(*b*) Amend the following Trial Balance as you think necessary to correct same.

TRIAL BALANCE.

November 30, 1932.

	Dr. £	Cr. £
J. Livingstone, Capital		1,000
Wages	268	
Purchases	1,249	
Sales		3,108
Rent Paid		50
Discount Received		12
Electricity		16
Salaries	52	
Carriage	5	
Plant and Machinery	1,201	
Leamington Bank, Ltd., Overdraft	47	
Cash in hand	6	
L. Pawson (supplier)		61
F. Thomas (supplier)		19
V. Wyles (customer)	33	
S. Watson (customer)	105	
P. Robbins (customer)	11	
Stock, December 1, 1931		926
Furniture and Fixtures, December 1, 1931		325
	£2,977	£5,517

(University of Birmingham.)

8. State what "difference" would be caused in the books of a business by each of the following errors :—

(*a*) The omission from the list of debtors' balances, compiled for the purpose of the Trial Balance, of a debt of £12 5*s*. due from P. & Co.
(*b*) Omission to post from the Cash Book to the Discount Account the sum of £5 7*s*. 6*d*., representing discounts allowed to debtors during July.
(*c*) Omission to make any entry in respect of an allowance of £8 10*s*. due to Q. & Co. in respect of damaged goods.
(*d*) Posting an item of wages paid, correctly entered as £31 15*s*. in the Cash Book, as £31 5*s*. in the Ledger Account.
(*e*) Posting £2, being cash received from the sale of an old office typewriter, to the debit side of "Office Equipment" Account.

Note.—These errors are to be taken as affecting different sets of books having no relation one to another.

(Royal Society of Arts.)

9. (*a*) Define the term "Trial Balance."

(*b*) If the Debit and Credit sides of a Trial Balance agree in amount is this conclusive evidence that the whole of the Book-keeping has been correctly done? If not, why not?

(*c*) From the following list of balances extracted from the books of M. Brake prepare a Trial Balance as on March 31, 1931 :—

BALANCES, MARCH 31, 1931.

	£	*s*.	*d*.
Capital, M. Brake	13,000	0	0
Drawings, M. Brake	1,200	0	0
Purchases	11,564	9	2
Sales	23,914	12	1
Stock, April 1, 1930	7,624	9	0
Sundry Creditors	2,715	11	6
Bills Payable	3,000	0	0
Furniture and Fittings	250	0	0
Carriage on Purchases	115	9	6
General Expenses	1,246	8	7
Wages	6,351	12	0
Salaries	1,286	10	6
Bank Loan (secured by a Mortgage on the Premises)	3,500	0	0
Freehold Premises	6,000	0	0
Sundry Debtors	6,214	2	3
Returns Inwards	321	3	4
Bank Charges and Interest	261	9	6
Postage and Stationery	114	6	9
Carriage on Sales	384	10	6
Discounts Allowed	633	4	5
Discounts Received	16	8	6
Cash at Bank	245	4	4
Cash in hand	23	12	3
Bills Receivable	2,310	0	0

(Royal Society of Arts.)

10. The following Trial Balance contains certain errors. You are required to discover them and draw up a correct Trial Balance.

	Dr. £	Cr. £
H. Jones, Capital Account		6,000
,, Current Account (Cr.)		1,091
S. Brown, Capital Account		4,000
,, Current Account (Dr.)		57
Salaries and Wages	3,140	
Rent and Rates	520	
Sales, less Returns		22,556
Purchases, less Returns	17,245	
Stock	5,472	
Trade Debtors	10,314	
Trade Creditors		3,591
Fixtures and Fittings	550	
Manufacturing Expenses	926	
,, ,, (unpaid)	102	
Office Expenses	341	
Carriage Inwards	559	
Carriage Outwards		253
Bank Overdraft		1,956
Interest on Overdraft		42
Bad Debts written off	112	
,, Reserve	250	
Cash in hand	15	
	£39,546	£39,546

(Royal Society of Arts.)

11. The following is the "Trial Balance" of Diminishing Returns owned by X. Y. at December 31, 1934:—

	Dr. £	Cr. £
Capital		650
Bank	126	
Machinery	452	
Fixtures	78	
Stock, January 1, 1934		340
Purchases	2,242	
Wages	1,135	
Salaries	312	
Rent	100	
Sales		4,612
Repairs	57	
Bad Debts	24	
Heat and Light	48	
Bills Receivable	118	
Debtors	852	
Creditors		475
	£5,544	£6,077

Amend the Trial Balance, taking the following into account :—

(*a*) No entry had been made in the ledger in respect of a bill for £24 discounted with the bank on December 20, 1934. Discounting charges (£1) had, however, been debited to the customer's account.

(*b*) The Sales Day Book had been undercast £89.

(*c*) The bank confirmed the overdraft at the sum shown on December 31, 1934.

(*d*) X. Y.'s private drawings of £208 had not been posted to the Ledger.

(*e*) A sale of £10 had not been posted to the account of I. Jones, a customer.

(Birmingham Commercial College.)

12. At December 31, 1935, the accountant of A.B.C., Ltd., has failed to balance his books of account. The difference has been carried to the debit of a Suspense Account.

Subsequently, the following errors are discovered :—

(*a*) The total of the Sales Day Book for June has been posted to Sales Account in the Impersonal Ledger as £2,784 1*s.* 3*d.* The Day Book total is £2,748 1*s.* 3*d.*

(*b*) Cash discounts allowed for the month of November, £37 2*s.*, and Discounts received, £19 16*s.* 1*d.*, have been posted to the wrong sides of the Ledger Account.

(*c*) An allowance to a customer of £1 18*s.* 6*d.* has been posted to the debit of his account in the Sales Ledger.

(*d*) A book debt of £14 10*s.* 8*d.*, due by L., a customer, has been omitted from the list of Sales Ledger balances.

(*e*) Cash drawings of the proprietor, amounting to £20, have not been posted to the Ledger.

(*f*) Goods purchased costing £21 2*s.* were posted to the credit of the Supplier's Ledger Account, and also to the credit of "Sundry Purchases" Account in the Bought Ledger.

After the discovery and correction of the errors mentioned, the books balanced. You are required :—

1. To show the Suspense Account as it originally appeared.
2. To make the requisite corrective entries.

(Royal Society of Arts.)

CHAPTER XI

WHAT IS PROFIT OR LOSS?

Question. The profit made seems to be represented by an increase in the Assets of the business during the period. Is this always the case?

Answer. Yes. The word "Profit" has no meaning except in the sense of an increase of Net Assets. You could just as truly say that Profit represents an increase in Capital. Put in another way, if the Capital invested at the commencement is a liability of the business, the liability is greater at the end of the period to the extent of the Profit earned.

Question. What, then, is a Loss?

Answer. A shrinkage in the Net Assets, or the extent to which they fall short of the initial Capital. If the latter had at one time comprised £100 worth of stock which owing to a general drop in prices had to be sold for £90 cash, an Asset of £90 would replace one of £100 and a Loss of £10 would have been incurred.

Such a loss would be described as a **Revenue Loss**, because stock is a part of the **Current Assets** of the business, or its Trading property. But if **Fixed Assets,** like Plant and Machinery, are sold at a figure below their book value, a **Capital Loss** is said to have been sustained.

Question. Referring again to the last example, the proprietor had withdrawn £25 from the business for his personal use, and yet you put the item in the third, or **Asset** column of the Trial Balance.

Should it not have been entered in the first or **Expense** column?

Answer. No, and for this reason. In the majority of businesses the owners will withdraw periodically either cash or goods (sometimes both) for their private use. These withdrawals are probably made to cover their living expenses, and have no relation whatever to the **expenses of**

the business. We may regard them as withdrawals **on account of accruing profits.**

Therefore they properly appear elsewhere than in the Revenue columns of the Trial Balance. To enter them in the third or **Asset** column is the only alternative and is justified in point of fact if we look upon the initial Capital as a **Liability.** In withdrawing money or goods from the business, the proprietor has really reduced the Capital invested in the first place, assuming no Profits, or insufficient Profits, have been earned to cover the withdrawals.

Question. Should drawings then be set against **Profits,** rather than against Capital?

Answer. Often it is found convenient to proceed in this way. The Capital Account, as we have seen, is credited with whatever the proprietor first introduces. Any periodic drawings are then debited to a separate, or **Drawings Account.** This is sometimes called a **Current Account.** Subsequently when the figure of profit is ascertained it is put to the credit of Drawings Account, and any resultant balance probably represents the proprietor's under or over estimate of the profits. Of course, withdrawals may be made on account of Capital, and would be debited to Capital Account, but these are somewhat exceptional.

Question. Am I right in thinking that the Trial Balance, whether in the ordinary or in the Four-Column Form, gives the whole of the information needed for preparing the Final Accounts?

Answer. No. Even in the simple case of R. Ready, in the last example, certain **adjustments** may have to be made. It is true, however, to say, as we did, that it provides a **basis** for their preparation.

Question. What are these adjustments?

Answer. It will be better for us to consider them after we have become familiar with the ordinary form of **Revenue Account and Balance Sheet,** because they affect both.

The main additional factor we have to take into account is, however, that of **Stock in Trade.**

In ascertaining our profit figure, it is not enough to compare the cost of goods purchased with the proceeds of goods sold. Since a minimum amount of stock has always to be held by the business this will in any event be part of the cost of purchases, but clearly it cannot appear in the sales **until it is sold.** Thus, at any particular date, *e.g.*, the date to which the business makes up its accounts, allowance must be made for the existence of the stock **then on hand,** and its proper value.

In the case of a new business, if we thought in terms of **quantities** only, we might say **purchases** equal **sales** plus **stock on hand at the end** of the period. Therefore closing stock **must** be included in the second column of the Trial Balance, and as it is a part of the property of the business at the same date, it **appears also** in the third or **Asset** column, *i.e.*, in the former as a credit, and in the latter as a debit.

CHAPTER XII

THE REVENUE ACCOUNT

The Trading Account—the Profit and Loss Account—the Appropriation Account

WHAT has just been discussed enables us to proceed to this first section of the Final Accounts.

Our task is to determine, in a suitable way, the Profit or Loss which has resulted from the carrying on of the ordinary transactions of the business.

We have always to remember with regard to the Final Accounts that they must be clear and informative, and free from unnecessary detail.

The period in respect of which they are drawn up will vary according to the requirements of the proprietor. In many cases it is customary to prepare them at yearly intervals, or at the date of the business's financial year end. This may be December 31, March 31, the end of the busy season, or some other date when perhaps there is least pressure of work on the office staff.

The **Revenue Account** is usually divided into three sections :—

(*a*) The Trading Account.
(*b*) The Profit and Loss Account.
(*c*) The Appropriation Account.

For our present purpose it is the first two sections which are important.

In all three sections, however, we find that the **form** adopted is that of the **ordinary Ledger Account,** using the **Dr.** and **Cr.** symbols which are a feature of the latter.

Trading Account

The purpose of this account is to determine what is called the **gross profit or loss.**

In it, after making due allowance for stocks carried at

the beginning and the end of the period, we compare in a merchanting business the proceeds of sales with the cost of goods sold.

Example. On January 1, 1937, A. Graham had a stock of goods value £1,216. His purchases for the year amounted to £10,340, and his sales to £15,000. Transport charges on incoming goods amounted to £208. He valued his stock on December 31, 1937, at £1,764. Show his Trading Account.

TRADING ACCOUNT.

Year ended December 31, 1937.

Dr.		£ s. d.		Cr. £ s. d.
To Stock, January 1, 1937		1,216 0 0	By Sales . . .	15,000 0 0
„ Purchases .	£10,340		„ Stock, December 31, 1937 . . .	1,764 0 0
„ Carriage Inward .	208	10,548 0 0		
„ **Gross Profit** . .		5,000 0 0		
		£16,764 0 0		£16,764 0 0

It is important we should notice the following points :—

(*a*) The account is headed " Year ended December 31, 1937," implying that it is a survey of the transactions throughout the year.

(*b*) The cost of purchases is increased by the transport charges paid, and represents **delivered cost** to the business. Apart from this no other kind of expense whatever is included.

(*c*) **Gross Profit** is seen to be the excess of sales over the purchased cost of the goods sold. It is the first stage in the determination of the final, or net, profit.

Stock in Trade.

Sometimes a difficulty may arise as to the measurement of the quantity and value of the **Stock** at **December 31, 1937,** which is shown above at £1,764.

We saw on page 135 how necessary it was to take it into account by means of an actual stocktaking.

In this process the goods on hand will be counted,

weighed, measured, etc., listed on stock sheets, and priced at purchased cost. They cannot be valued at the higher selling price because they are not yet sold, and may never be sold. It is reasonable to value them at cost price, because in doing so we are merely carrying forward **from one period into another** a part of the Cost of Purchases.

It may be that at the date of stocktaking the market price (or present buying price) is less than the cost price. Provided, however, that there is no selling deficiency, *i.e.*, the cost price, together with any selling expenses yet to be incurred, does not exceed the selling price, no adjustment is required. The business is not to be penalised only because it failed to buy at the bottom of the market.

A final point to note is that in the Trading Account the ratio of **gross profit** to **sales** or **turnover** is an important one in all businesses. Expressed as a percentage it amounts in this case to $33\frac{1}{3}\%$ of the Sales.

Let us now consider the **closing entries** in the Ledger Accounts concerned.

PRIVATE LEDGER.

STOCK.

DR. CR.

Date.	Details.	Fo.	Amount.	Date.	Details.	Fo.	Amount.
			£ s. d.				£ s. d.
1937 Jan. 1	To Balance .	b/d	1,216 0 0	1937 Dec. 31	By Transfer to Trading A/c .		1,216 0 0
Dec. 31	To Transfer to Trading A/c .		1,764 0 0	Dec. 31	By Balance .	c/d	1,764 0 0
1938 Jan. 1	To Balance .	b/d	1,764 0 0				

(*a*) On January 1, 1937, **stock then on hand** of course appears as a Debit Balance and is transferred on December 31 to the **debit** of the Trading Account.

(*b*) At the same time the closing stock figure of £1,764 is debited above and posted to the **credit** of Trading Account.

(*c*) The debit of £1,764 is then brought down on January 1, 1938.

As in making these entries in the **Stock Account** we are transgressing the rule that no first entry shall be made in any Ledger Account, it may be preferred to use the **Debit and Credit Journal** as the proper Book of Prime Entry. Its use for this purpose was referred to on p. 96. The record in this Journal would then be :—

			Dr. £	Cr. £
1937 Dec. 31	Trading A/c, 1937	Dr.	1,216	
	To Stock			1,216
	Being Transfer of Stock at January 1, 1937.			
1937 Dec. 31	Stock	Dr.	1,764	
	To Trading A/c, 1937			1,764
	Being Stock at this date transferred.			

We could also journalise the transfers from the other Accounts which will be found in the Impersonal Ledger. Unless we do so, the closing entries will appear as follows :—

PURCHASES.

Dr. Cr.

Date.	Details.	Fo.	Amount.	Date.	Details.	Fo.	Amount.
1937			£ s. d.	1937			£ s. d.
Dec. 31	To Total Purchases for Year .		10,340 0 0	Dec. 31	By Transfer to Trading A/c . .		10,340 0 0

CARRIAGE INWARDS.

Dr. Cr.

Date.	Details.	Fo.	Amount.	Date.	Details.	Fo.	Amount.
1937			£ s. d.	1937			£ s. d.
Dec. 31	To Total Expenses for Year .		208 0 0	Dec. 31	By Transfer to Trading A/c		208 0 0

As regards **Sales** the transfer will be made from the **debit** of Sales Account to the credit of Trading Account.

SALES.

Dr. Cr.

Date.	Details.	Fo.	Amount.	Date.	Details.	Fo.	Amount.
1937			£ s. d.	1937			£ s. d.
Dec. 31	To Transfer to Trading A/c .		15,000 0 0	Dec. 31	By Total Sales for Year .		15,000 0 0

In a **manufacturing** business, on the other hand, the Trading Account will be in somewhat different form. In addition to purchases, **wages** paid to workpeople employed in the actual production of the goods will be debited.

Purchases here will include in the main **raw materials** and component parts.

As **gross profit** in a **merchanting** business is ascertained after comparing the proceeds of sales with the cost of goods sold, similarly in a **manufacturing** business the proceeds of sales are compared with the **Direct Cost,** or Prime Cost, of production, which covers **both purchases and workpeople's wages.**

Our justification for dealing with it in this way may be stated as follows :—

(*a*) **Merchanting business.** Every sales order booked involves a direct and proportionate increase in Purchases.

(*b*) **Manufacturing business.** Every sales order calls for not only a direct increase in purchases, but also a direct increase in workpeople's wages.

In (*b*) apart from these direct expenses or production, there are also the general factory expenses to be considered. These include rates on the factory premises, repairs to plant and machinery, power costs for operating the plant, and so on. It would be incorrect for us to include these in the Trading Account unless we are instructed to do so, because their inclusion would convert the Account into a Manufacturing, or Working Account.

Profit and Loss Account

This follows immediately after the Trading Account, of which it is really a continuation.

It commences with the balance brought down from the Trading Account, which as we have seen is a **gross profit** if a **credit** balance, or a **gross loss** if a **debit** balance.

Its purpose is to ascertain the final or **net profit** of the business for the period by including :—

(*a*) The remaining **expenses,** other than those already dealt with in the Trading Account.

(*b*) The **incidental sources** of **income,** such as
Cash Discounts received,
Bank Interest received, etc.

In form it is precisely similar to the Trading Account, the expenses or debits appearing on the left-hand side, and the incidental sources of income or credits on the right-hand side.

As regards both debits and credits in the Profit and Loss Account, care must be taken that :—

(*a*) The expenses are those **of the business only** (*excluding* such items as Proprietor's drawings, or private payments made on his behalf).
(*b*) **The whole of the expenses** relating to the period under review are properly brought in.

We shall see at a later stage the importance of the latter point, but meanwhile let us look at the form and construction of the Profit and Loss Account.

Example. From the items set out below select those which should appear in the Trading (or Goods) and Profit and Loss Account, prepare those accounts (only) showing the Gross Profit and the Net Profit or Loss.

	£
Capital	2,400
Freehold Premises	1,350
Stock at January 1, 1929	650
Debtors	360
Creditors	512
Purchases	3,500
Sales	5,000
Returns Inwards	20
Discounts Allowed	52
Salaries	220
Trade Expenses	153
Rates and Taxes	90
Fixtures and Fittings	62
Cash at Bank	450

The stock on hand at December 31, 1929, was £215.

(National Union of Teachers.)

TRADING AND PROFIT AND LOSS ACCOUNT.

Year ended December 31, 1929.

DR. CR.

	£ s. d.		£ s. d.
To Stock, January 1, 1929	650 0 0	By Sales . . £5,000	
,, Purchases . . .	3,500 0 0	*Less* Returns 20	4,980 0 0
,, *Gross Profit*, c/d . .	1,045 0 0	,, Stock, December 31, 1929 . . .	215 0 0
	£5,195 0 0		£5,195 0 0
To Salaries . . .	220 0 0	By Gross Profit b/d . .	1,045 0 0
,, Trade Expenses . .	153 0 0		
,, Rates and Taxes .	90 0 0		
,, Discounts Allowed .	52 0 0		
,, *Net Profit* . . .	530 0 0		
	£1,045 0 0		£1,045 0 0

The remaining items in the list, with which we have not dealt, are of a Capital nature, and will appear in the Statement of Assets and Liabilities, or Balance Sheet of the business.

The information below the "Gross Profit Line" comprises the **Profit and Loss Account** proper.

The transfers from the Accounts in the **Impersonal** Ledger will be made as follows :—

SALARIES.

DR. CR.

Date.	Details.	Fo.	Amount.	Date.	Details.	Fo.	Amount.
1929			£ s. d.	1929			£ s. d.
Dec. 31	To Total Salaries for Year .		220 0 0	Dec. 31	By Transfer to Profit and Loss A/c .		220 0 0

TRADE EXPENSES.

DR. CR.

Date.	Details.	Fo.	Amount.	Date.	Details.	Fo.	Amount.
1929			£ s. d.	1929			£ s. d.
Dec. 31	To Total for Year .		153 0 0	Dec. 31	By Transfer to Profit and Loss A/c .		153 0 0

RATES AND TAXES.

DR. CR.

Date.	Details.	Fo.	Amount.	Date.	Details.	Fo.	Amount.
1929			£ *s.* *d.*	1929			£ *s.* *d.*
Dec. 31	To Total for Year .		90 0 0	Dec. 31	By Transfer to Profit and Loss A/c .		90 0 0

DISCOUNTS ALLOWED.

DR. CR.

Date.	Details.	Fo.	Amount.	Date.	Details.	Fo.	Amount.
1929			£ *s.* *d.*	1929			£ *s.* *d.*
Dec. 31	To Total for Year .		52 0 0	Dec. 31	By Transfer to Profit and Loss A/c .		52 0 0

Alternatively, instead of making the transfers direct to the Profit and Loss Account, we may use the **Debit and Credit Journal,** with the result that the following Journal entries will appear as **closing entries** :—

		Dr. £	Cr. £
1929 Dec. 31	**Sundries**		
	Profit and Loss A/c . . . . . . Dr.	515	
	To Sundries		
	Salaries		220
	Trade Expenses		153
	Rates and Taxes		90
	Discounts allowed		52
	Being transfer of Expense Account balances to Profit and Loss Account as above.		

If the latter method be adopted the words "By Sundries" will describe the credit entries in each of the Ledger Accounts, in place of "By Transfer to Profit and Loss Account."

Appropriation, or Net Profit and Loss Account

As its name implies, this third section deals with the ascertained Net Profit or Loss, and its distribution among the proprietors of the business.

Thus in a partnership firm the Net Profit figure will here be divided in the ratio in which the partners share profits and losses.

In the case of a Limited Company, the appropriation account shows how the Net Profits are divided in dividend to the shareholders according to their respective rights and interests.

The necessity for such an account rarely, if ever, arises where the position of a sole trader is under consideration, the Net Profit being carried direct to the Capital or Current Account of the proprietor, as already explained.

Tests and Questions

1. What do you understand by (*a*) Capital Expenditure, (*b*) Revenue Expenditure?

State some items coming under each of these headings in the case of a Company carrying on business as manufacturers of aeroplanes. (University of Manchester.)

2. What is the object in preparing a Trading Account as distinct from a Profit and Loss Account? Explain what information may be obtained from the former and its importance to a trader. (University of Manchester.)

3. What do you understand by a "Nominal Account"?

State some exceptions to the general rule that such accounts are closed when the Profit and Loss Account has been prepared, indicating the reasons for any balances which may remain. (University of Manchester.)

4. What are the reasons for dividing the ordinary revenue account of a business into two sections, the Trading Account and the Profit and Loss Account? (Royal Society of Arts.)

5. What is the object of calculating gross profit and net profit? Does gross profit measure the prosperity of a business? (East Midland Educational Union.)

6. (*a*) What may be the advantages to a business of having: (i) a Cash Received Book, (ii) a Cash Paid Book, (iii) a Private Cash Book, instead of a Single Cash Book only?

(*b*) The stock of goods held by Edward Newman on January 1, 1936, consisted of 1,000 units valued at 10*s*. each.

At December 31, 1936, 800 units were held in stock, of which the cost price was 10*s*. per unit, and the then market value 8*s*. per unit.

Show how the Stock Account would appear in Newman's Ledger for the year 1936. (University of Birmingham.)

7. A fire occurred on the premises of a merchant on June 15, 1932, and a considerable part of the stock was destroyed. The value of the stock salved was £450.

The books disclosed that on April 1, 1932, the stock was valued at £3,675, the purchases to the date of the fire amounted to £10,494 and the sales to £15,650.

On investigation it is found that during the past five years the average gross profit on the sales was 36%.

You are required to prepare a statement showing the amount the merchant should claim from the Insurance Company in respect of stock destroyed or damaged by the fire.

(Royal Society of Arts.)

8. On January 5, 1937, Ambrose sold goods to Applejohn.

The goods had cost Ambrose £100, and the selling price was 50% on cost, payment being due on monthly account less $2\frac{1}{2}$% for cash.

On January 28, 1937, Applejohn returned a part of the goods, and Ambrose sent him a credit note for £40.

The amount due was paid by cheque on February 28, 1937, but three days later the cheque was returned by the bank unpaid, and ultimately 15*s*. in the £ was received from Applejohn and accepted in full settlement.

Show :—

(*a*) Applejohn's Account in the books of Ambrose;
(*b*) What profit or loss Ambrose made on the whole transaction.

(University of Birmingham.)

9. A business has three departments, A, B, and C. You are asked to calculate the working profit in each department, by reference to the following :—

	£
Opening Stocks, B	1,280
,, ,, C	640
Closing Stocks, B	1,320
,, ,, C	650
Purchases	6,000
Wages	1,800
General Expenses	1,250
Sales, B	6,800
,, C	3,200

All purchases are made for A department in the first instance. A department (which has no sales) processes the goods and then re-issues them to B and C departments at fixed prices.

The issues to B were valued at £5,000 and to C at £2,400.

25% of the wages are charged to B, 20% to C, 10% to general expenses, and the balance to A.

The general expenses are recharged as follows :—

Department A, 7% on output value,
,, B, 10% on sales value,
,, C, 7% on sales value,

any difference being carried to the Profit and Loss Account.

(University of Birmingham.)

10. PQ carries on business as a merchant, but, although he has taken stock regularly at the end of December in each year, he has not kept proper books of account. He keeps a Cash Book, Petty Cash Book and Personal Ledgers.

If requested by him to ascertain the result of his trading for the past year, explain briefly how you would proceed.

(University of Manchester).

CHAPTER XIII

THE BALANCE SHEET

TOGETHER with the Revenue Account, we have described this as a part of the Final Accounts of the business. It has been not inaptly defined as "a flashlight photograph of the position of affairs of the business at a particular date."

More precisely we can speak of it as a Statement of Assets and Liabilities, including the balance of the Revenue Account made up to the date at which the Balance Sheet is prepared.

That it is a Statement of Assets and Liabilities justifies us in confining our attention to the "Capital" columns of the four-column Trial Balance, the **debit balances** in which were seen to represent **Assets,** and the **credit balances, Liabilities.**

The fact that it includes the ascertained balance on the Revenue Account implies that this balance, if a Credit, will be shown as a Liability and if a Debit, as an Asset.

In other words, the business having an **initial liability** to its proprietor for the amount of Capital invested by him, has now a **further liability** in respect of the profit earned. Had a loss been sustained, it would be a Conventional Asset, or Asset in name only, *i.e.*, it would appear on the Assets side of the Balance Sheet as representing the extent to which **the Assets as a whole were deficient in relation to the Capital.**

It is important for us to remember that the Balance Sheet is the complement to the Revenue Account and is indeed an essential part of the Final Accounts, for this reason. When the business was begun Capital was invested in it, perhaps in the first place in the form of cash. Almost at once this cash would be spent in the acquisition of various forms of property, of the kind we have defined as Fixed Assets, or Current Assets.

The former represented property which the business must

possess as part of its equipment; the latter consisted of property in which the business was dealing.

If the Current Assets were therefore so dealt in by the proprietor or his manager as to produce a Profit, ascertained by the preparation of a Revenue Account, it would clearly be very desirable to draw up a further Balance Sheet at **the end of each trading period,** showing just what Assets existed in the hands of the business at that date. Provided no additions to or withdrawals from Capital had taken place, and each Asset held was reasonably and properly valued in each succeeding Balance Sheet, any increase in the Total Assets would represent a **profit,** and conversely any decrease a **loss.**

In the latter case, as the loss appeared in the Balance Sheet as an " Asset," it could quite well be deducted from the **liability** of the business to its proprietor on **Capital** Account, disclosing at that point a **loss of Capital,** which, of course, is in line with the facts.

The Form of the Balance Sheet

We have seen that the Revenue Account is prepared very much in the form of the ordinary Ledger Account.

In form, it is a summarised Ledger Account to which all the balances appearing in the " Revenue " columns of the Trial Balance are transferred at the end of the financial year of the business. By so doing, an ultimate balance (either of Profit or Loss) is struck.

But we still have to deal with the balances appearing in the " Capital " columns. It is these latter remaining balances, **and the balance of the Revenue Account,** which are entered in a " sheet of balances " or **Balance Sheet.**

We could, if we wished, show this Balance Sheet in the form of an ordinary Ledger Account, debiting to it the Assets, and putting the Liabilities on the credit side.

The opposite, however, is the almost universal practice in this country, the Debit and Credit sides being reversed. Thus, Liabilities are shown on the left hand or " Debit " side of the Balance Sheet, and Assets on the right hand or " Credit " side, and this is true whether the business be owned by a sole trader, a partnership firm, or a Limited Company.

As a result, in reading the Balance Sheet in the ordinary way, from left to right, we begin with the Liabilities, and then turn to a study of the Assets out of which they are to be met.

We can also regard the Balance Sheet as a "**classified summary**" of the Ledger Balances remaining on the books after the preparation of the Revenue Account, and including the balance of this latter Account.

The Balance Sheet and the Trial Balance Contrasted

While both are drawn up at a particular date, the former includes only those balances which are, or have become **Assets** and **Liabilities**; the latter includes as well the various Impersonal Ledger balances relating to **expenses** and **gains.**

The Balance Sheet is a properly marshalled statement of the Assets and Liabilities, setting them out in their order of Realisability or Priority. The Trial Balance merely lists the whole of the balances in the order in which they happen to appear in the Ledgers.

Further, the purpose of the Balance Sheet is to give information to the proprietor of the business as to its financial position, whereas the Trial Balance is extracted primarily to prove the arithmetical accuracy of the book-keeping work.

Finally, the Balance Sheet always includes the value of the Stock on Hand at the end of the period; the Trial Balance, unless in four-column form (and not necessarily then) does not show this Asset.

Let us now take two illustrations involving some of the points we have been discussing :—

Example. From the following items construct the Balance Sheet of L. Redfern as on December 31, 1933.

	£
Capital as at January 1, 1933	200
Motor vans as at December 31, 1933	220
Cash at bank as at December 31, 1933	70
Profit for the year	300
Land and buildings as at December 31, 1933	410
Drawings for the year	150
Stock of Goods, December 31, 1933	230
Loan from A. Herbert	400
Debtors as at December 31, 1933	200
Sundry Creditors as at December 31, 1933	380

(Union of Educational Institutions.)

In this first case, it may be helpful if we list the items as **Assets** (Debits) or **Liabilities** (Credits), *i.e.* :—

	Dr.	*Cr.*
	£	£
Capital, January 1, 1933 . . .		200
Motor vans, December 31, 1933 . .	220	
Cash at bank, December 31, 1933 . .	70	
Profit for the year		300
Land and Buildings, December 31, 1933 .	410	
Drawings	150	
Stock of Goods, December 31, 1933 .	230	
Loan from A. Herbert		400
Debtors as at December 31, 1933 . .	200	
Sundry Creditors as at December 31, 1933		380
	£1,280	£1,280

We may then proceed as follows, remembering :—

(*a*) That a Balance Sheet is always prepared at some definite date.

(*b*) That the balances on the various Accounts of which it is made up are **not** transferred to it as is the case with the Revenue Account.

L. Redfern.

BALANCE SHEET AS AT DECEMBER 31, 1933.

Liabilities.	£	£	*Assets.*	£	£
Loan from A. Herbert .	400		Cash at Bank . .		70
Sundry Creditors . .	380		Debtors . . .		200
		780	Stock of Goods . .		230
Current Account :			Motor Vans . .		220
Profit for year . .	300		Land and Buildings .		410
Less Drawings . .	150				
	150				
Capital Account :					
As at January 1, 1933 .	200				
		350			
		£1,130			£1,130

It should be noted that :—

(*a*) The Assets are stated in their order of realisability, beginning with the liquid asset of "Cash at Bank."

(*b*) Cash, Debtors and Stock represent **Current Assets,** while Motor Vans and Land and Buildings are **Fixed Assets.**

(*c*) Although **Profit** and **Drawings** have been shown in a Current Account they might equally well have been recorded in Capital Account only.

Example. From the following particulars construct the Balance Sheet of T. Tomlinson as on March 31, 1935 :—

Capital April 1, 1934, was £500. The loss for the year to March 31, 1935, was £120 and his drawings were £22. On March 31, 1935, the Stock was £248, the Bank Overdraft £132, the Debtors £326, the Loan from F. Weston £220, the Fixtures and Fittings £148, Creditors £290, Cash in Hand £5, Machinery £273.

(Union of Educational Institutions.)

If we have studied the first illustration carefully, it should not be necessary to list the balances again before constructing the Balance Sheet.

Looking at the information given, we see, however, that a **trading loss** of £120 has been sustained, and in addition there are drawings of £22. The initial Capital has thus **decreased** by £142.

T. Tomlinson.

BALANCE SHEET AS AT MARCH 31, 1935.

Liabilities.		£	£	*Assets.*	£	
Bank Overdraft		132		Cash in Hand		5
Loan from F. Weston		220		Debtors		326
Creditors		290		Stock		248
			642	Fixtures and Fittings		148
Capital Account:				Machinery		273
April 1, 1934		500				
Less Loss, year to March 31, 1935	£120					
Drawings	22					
		142				
			358			
			£1,000			£1,000

As regards the Liabilities, we may note here that the first two relate to **cash advances,** the item " Creditors " referring to the Purchase Ledger Accounts of suppliers for **goods** or **services.**

Having considered separately the Trading and Profit and Loss Accounts, and the Balance Sheet, we may now, as in a practical case, prepare each of them from an ordinary two-column Trial Balance.

Example. From the following balances prepare the Trading Account, Profit and Loss Account, and Balance Sheet of J. Farmer, a retailer, for half year ended June 30, 1937 :—

	£	*s.*	*d.*	£	*s.*	*d.*
Petty Cash . . .	5	0	0			
Sundry Creditors . . .				49	7	10
Cash at Bank . . .	99	18	11			
Furniture, Fixtures and Equipment . . .	40	0	0			
Purchases . . .	841	13	6			
Sales				1,161	16	2
Stock . . .	111	3	0			
Office Expenses . . .	4	9	3			
Rent, Rates and Taxes .	99	15	6			
Lighting and Heating .	18	3	1			
Advertising . .	7	10	8			
Delivery Expenses . .	6	6	0			
Capital . .				200	0	0
Drawings . . .	156	0	0			
Carriage on Purchases. .	21	4	1			
	£1,411	4	0	£1,411	4	0

Stock on June 30, 1937, £108 5*s*.

(London Chamber of Commerce.)

J. Farmer.

PROFIT AND LOSS ACCOUNT.

Six Months ended June 30, 1937.

Dr.	£ s. d.	£ s. d.		£ s. d.	Cr. £ s. d.
To Stock, Jan. 1, 1937		111 3 0	By Sales		1,161 16 2
„ Purchases	841 13 6		„ Stock, June 30, 1937		108 5 0
„ Carriage on Purchases	21 4 1				
		862 17 7			
„ Gross Profit, c/d		296 0 7			
		1,270 1 2			1,270 1 2
To Rent, Rates and Taxes		99 15 6	By Gross Profit, b/d		296 0 7
„ Lighting and Heating		18 3 1			
„ Advertising		7 10 8			
„ Delivery Expenses		6 6 0			
„ Office Expenses		4 9 3			
„ Net Profit, carried to Capital A/c		159 16 1			
		£296 0 7			£296 0 7

J. Farmer.

BALANCE SHEET AS AT JUNE 30, 1937.

	£ s. d.	£ s. d.		£ s. d.	£ s. d.
Sundry Creditors		49 7 10	Petty Cash	5 0 0	
Capital Account	200 0 0		Cash at Bank	99 18 11	
Add Net Profit for half year to date	159 16 1				104 18 11
			Stock		108 5 0
	359 16 1		Furniture, Fixtures and Equipment		40 0 0
Less Drawings	156 0 0				
		203 16 1			
		£253 3 11			£253 3 11

We should note that as the Trading Account and the Profit and Loss Account are only divisions of the Revenue Account, they may conveniently be shown together, as above, in one statement.

Tests and Questions

1. What effect would the following errors made by a book-keeper have upon (*a*) the Trial Balance, (*b*) the annual accounts of a business :—

(i) An item of £50 for goods sold to C. D. posted from the Sales Journal to the credit of C. D.'s Ledger Account.

(ii) An item of £12, representing the purchase of a desk, placed in the general expenses column of the Purchase Journal.

(iii) A sum of £15, representing interest allowed by the banker, entered in the correct column on the credit side of the Cash Book. (University of Manchester.)

2. Enumerate the assets you would expect to find on the Balance Sheet of A. B., a motor-car manufacturer, grouping them into the different classes.

Why is the distinction between different types of asset important ? (University of Manchester.)

3. At December 31, 1937, the Cash Book of Simmonds, a sole trader, shows an overdraft of £98. The following cheques had been drawn and entered in the Cash Book on December 30, but were not presented for payment until January 4, 1938.

	£
Grey	61
Maddox	34
Wilson	10

Bank charges of £8 for the half-year ended December 31, 1937, were entered in the Cash Book in the first week of January only.

A cheque for £35, received from Foxton, a customer, and duly banked, was returned dishonoured on December 24, but Simmonds had omitted to make the appropriate entry in the Cash Book.

Prepare a Reconciliation, showing the Bank Pass Book balance at December 31, 1937. (University of Birmingham.)

4. From the following particulars draw up the Balance Sheet of B. Wilton as on December 31, 1936 : Land and buildings, £1,000; Machinery, £325; Motor vans, £120; Fixtures and fittings, £70; Stock on hand at December 31, 1936, £950; Sundry debtors, £856; Cash in hand, £29; Sundry creditors, £1,820; Bank overdraft, £1,200; Loan from A. Mather, £200; Capital as at January 1, 1936, £230; Loss for the year, £100.

State briefly your opinion of the financial position of B. Wilton. (Union of Educational Institutions.)

5. A. B., an engineer, decides to erect a new machine in his works. He dismantles an old machine and uses material therefrom

to the value of £50 in the erection of the new machine. Additional materials are purchased from outside sources at a cost of £150, and the wages amount to £200.

Explain how the foregoing items would be dealt with in his books.

(University of Manchester.)

6. In the form of Cash Book provided, after properly heading each column, enter all the money transactions below and balance the book.

Journalise the opening balances and remaining transactions. (Note: Purchases and Sales Books may be used, if preferred.)

Post the entries to the Ledger. Extract a Trial Balance.

Draw up a Profit and Loss Account and Balance Sheet.

On May 1, 1937, D. Robinson, nurseryman, reopened his books with the following balances in addition to his Capital Account: Cash, £43 14*s.* 8*d.*; Rent outstanding, £40; Bank overdraft, £185 16*s.* 2*d.*; M. Merritt (Cr.), £182 12*s.* 4*d.*; S. Service (Dr.), £281 17*s.* 4*d.*; Stock, £482 16*s.* 6*d.*

During the month his transactions were :—

			£	*s.*	*d.*
May	3.	Received cheque from S. Service	250	0	0
,,	5.	Sold to S. Service :—			
		7 doz. rose bushes 5*s.* 6*d.* each	23	2	0
		5 doz. rose standards 6*s.* each	18	0	0
		Misc. plants	17	7	3
,,	7.	S. Service's cheque returned dishonoured	250	0	0
,,	10.	S. Service paid in cash (banked)	175	0	0
,,	14.	Bought of M. Merritt :—			
		6 doz. fruit trees 4*s.* 3*d.* each	15	6	0
		10 doz. shrubs 3*s.* 6*d.* each	21	0	0
,,	18.	Paid M. Merritt by cheque to settle account to 1st inst.	180	0	0
,,	21.	Returned to M. Merritt 9 shrubs damaged	1	11	6
,,	25.	Cash sales	23	15	2
,,	26.	Bought for cash sundry plants at auction	8	14	3
,,	27.	Paid rent outstanding by cheque	40	0	0
,,	29.	Drew cheque for self	20	0	0
,,	31.	Wages and expenses for month :			
		paid by cheque	39	12	9
		and in cash	9	7	4
		Bank charges	2	5	7
		Rent accrued	40	0	0
		Interest on capital at 4% p.a.			
		Stock on hand valued at	475	0	10

(College of Preceptors.)

7. The following balances were extracted from the books of D. Wright on December 31, 1933. You are required to prepare a Trading Account, Profit and Loss Account and Balance Sheet as on that date.

	Dr. £	s.	d.	Cr. £	s.	d.
Cash in Hand	16	9	2			
Bank Overdraft				118	6	9
Stock, January 1, 1933	679	14	0			
Purchases and Sales	1,497	6	0	2,649	17	6
Wages	371	19	3			
Insurance	15	15	0			
Bank Charges	11	16	6			
Furniture and Fittings	115	13	0			
Returns Inwards and Outwards	30	19	8	23	17	5
Sundry Drs. and Crs.	175	13	9	66	15	4
Land and Buildings	2,000	0	0			
Discount				15	4	6
Capital						

Stock at end £116 9*s.* 7*d.*

(East Midland Educational Union.)

8. From the following Trial Balance of J. Lowe, prepare Trading and Profit and Loss Accounts for the year ended March 31, 1934, and a Balance Sheet as on that date.

The stock on hand at March 31, 1934, was valued at £550.

	£	£
Purchases	2,130	
Carriage Inwards	35	
Sales		2,960
Stock, April 1, 1933	400	
Trade Expenses	85	
Fixtures and Fittings	200	
Discounts Allowed	90	
J. Lowe: Capital		600
Returns Inwards	75	
Cash in Hand	15	
Sundry Debtors	240	
Salaries	120	
J. Lowe: Drawings	250	
Discounts Received		40
Sundry Creditors		400
Cash at Bank	270	
Rent	50	
Rates	40	
	£4,000	£4,000

(East Midland Educational Union.)

9. The following Trial Balance was extracted from the books of R. Parr on December 31, 1935 :—

	Dr.	Cr.
	£	£
Capital		3,500
Drawings	145	
Stock at January 1, 1935	2,600	
Purchases and Sales	4,500	6,500
Returns Outwards		60
Returns Inwards	100	
Salaries	475	
Trade Expenses	205	
Bad Debts	23	
Discount Account (balance)		35
Sundry Debtors	3,575	
Sundry Creditors		1,960
Insurance	22	
Fixtures and Fittings	185	
Motor Vans	265	
Rent, Rates and Taxes	355	
Bank Overdraft		395
	£12,450	£12,450

The value of the stock on hand was £1,795.

You are required to prepare Trading and Profit and Loss Accounts for the year ended December 31, 1935, and a Balance Sheet as on that date. (Union of Educational Institutions.)

10. The following balances were extracted at April 30, 1934, from the books of C. D. :—

(*a*) Prepare therefrom a Trading and Profit and Loss Account for the year ended on that date, and also a Balance Sheet.

(*b*) Do the results of the business for the year justify the drawings of £350 by C. D. ?

	£
Office Salaries	628
Insurance	61
Discounts Received	33
Sales	7,350
Bad Debts	69
Plant and Machinery	430
Commission	127
Investment Interest Received	30
Stock, May 1, 1933	1,110
Repairs	98
Sundries	46
Goods Returned by Customers	100
Discounts Allowed	115
Rent and Rates	322

	£
Purchases	4,290
Sundry Debtors	143
Travelling Expenses	263
Wages and National Insurance . .	3,004
General Insurance	34
Carriage Inwards	87
Sundry Creditors	1,426
C.D. : Capital, May 1, 1933 . . .	3,250
Cash at Bank	109
Coal, Gas, and Water	177
Goods Returned to Suppliers . . .	74
Investment in Utopia, Ltd. . . .	600

The stock at April 30, 1934, was valued at £1,275.
(University of Birmingham.)

11. The following is the Trial Balance extracted at December 31, 1934, from the books of S. Printer, who carries on business as a manufacturer of sports equipment :—

	Dr. £	Cr. £
Petty Cash Book	28	
Nominal Ledger :		
Carriage Outwards	504	
,, Inwards	266	
Travelling Expenses	2,169	
Discount Allowed	933	
,, Received		218
Repairs and Incidentals	820	
Rent, Rates and Taxes	872	
Factory Wages	10,655	
Heating and Lighting	137	
Sales, less Returns		30,750
Factory National Insurance . . .	318	
Packing and Dispatch Expenses . .	1,252	
Purchases, less Returns	10,546	
Salaries and National Insurance . .	2,735	
Private Cash Book		853
Private Ledger :		
Stock, January 1, 1934	3,915	
S. Printer : Capital at January 1, 1934 .		10,000
,, Drawings	1,200	
Office Fixtures and General Equipment January 1, 1934	1,567	
Equipment Sold		136
,, Purchased	608	
Bank Interest Account	46	
Sales Ledgers :		
Accounts Receivable	6,002	
Purchase Ledger :		
Accounts Payable		2,616
	£44,573	£44,573

The stock at December 31, 1934, was valued at £5,200.
You are required to :—

(*a*) Prepare a Trading and Profit and Loss Account for the year ended December 31, 1934, and a Balance Sheet at that date.
(*b*) State the percentages of Gross Profit and of Net Profit to Turnover.
(*c*) Show the Office Fixtures and General Equipment Account as it would appear in the Private Ledger.

(University of Birmingham.)

12. The following is the Trial Balance extracted from the books of J. B. as at December 31, 1932.

	Dr.	Cr.
	£	£
Private Ledger :		
Capital, January 1, 1932		4,137
Drawings	1,000	
Stock, January 1, 1932	2,035	
Fixtures and Fittings, January 1, 1932	2,119	
Bills Payable		268
Bills Receivable	238	
Nominal Ledger :		
Purchases	5,911	
Sales		10,782
Discounts Allowed	223	
Discounts Received		104
Packing Expenses	192	
Office Expenses	74	
Salaries	826	
Repairs	58	
Lighting and Heating	87	
Rates	146	
Rent	200	
Wages (workpeople)	1,644	
Sundry Expenses	61	
Cash Book		781
Petty Cash Book	27	
Creditors (Personal Ledger)		1,433
Debtors (Personal Ledger)	2,664	
	£17,505	£17,505

The stock on hand at December 31, 1932, was valued by J. B. in the sum of £3,157.

Prepare Trading and Profit and Loss Account, and Balance Sheet.

(University of Birmingham.)

13. The following "Statements of Affairs" have been drawn up to give the financial position, as on March 31, 1931, and March 31, 1932, respectively, of A. Brown, who keeps his books on a single entry basis :—

STATEMENT OF AFFAIRS, MARCH 31, 1931.

	£		£
Capital . . .	6,192	Fixtures . . .	250
Creditors . . .	742	Stock . . .	2,305
		Debtors . . .	4,176
		Cash . . .	203
	£6,934		£6,934

STATEMENT OF AFFAIRS, MARCH 31, 1932.

	£		£
Capital . . .	5,933	Fixtures . . .	230
Creditors . . .	817	Stock . . .	2,562
		Debtors . . .	3,777
		Cash . . .	181
	£6,750		£6,750

Brown has transferred £100 a month regularly from his business banking account to his private banking account by way of drawings, and he has taken £25 worth of stock for his private use. The alteration in the value of the fixtures represents an amount written off by way of depreciation.

Calculate Brown's trading profit for the year.

(Royal Society of Arts.)

14. The only books kept by Brown are Personal Ledgers. At January 1 his position is as follows :—

	£		£
Cash . . .	17	Creditors . . .	635
Debtors . . .	3,109	Capital . . .	3,023
Stock . . .	102		
Equipment, at cost .	430		
	£3,658		£3,658

At December 31 following, he informs you that the following are the figures concerning his Assets and Liabilities :—

	£
Cash	15
Bank (overdraft)	230
Stock	98
Debtors	3,036
Creditors	502

He has had his equipment valued, and thinks that it is now only worth £350. He has taken notes as to his drawings, and informs you that he has spent £332 for household purposes, etc., £40 for a life assurance premium, and £10 for fire insurance for business assets. In addition, he has taken home goods, of which the cost price was £9 and the sale price £12.

Prepare a Statement showing Brown's profit for the year, and his general position at December 31. (University of Edinburgh.)

15. BALANCE SHEET.

	£		£
Creditors . . .	721	Freehold Premises .	1,560
Capital . . .	3,150	Machinery and Plant .	420
		Stock . . .	876
		Debtors . . .	982
		Cash . . .	33
	£3,871		£3,871

The above is a copy of Samuel Wood's Balance Sheet as on December 31, 1929. The only books kept are a Cash Book and a Ledger. The following is a summary of his receipts and payments for the year ended December 31, 1930:—

Receipts.	£	*Payments.*	£
Cash on account of Credit Sales .	4,276	Creditors for Goods Purchased .	3,954
Cash Sales . . .	1,863	Wages . . .	743
Capital paid in . .	200	General Expenses .	627
		Additions to Machinery . . .	160
		Drawings . . .	536
	£6,339		£6,020

On December 31, 1930, the amount due to Creditors was £816, and the Debtors and Stock amounted to £918 and £854 respectively. You are required to prepare Trading and Profit and Loss Accounts for the year ended December 31, 1930, and a Balance Sheet as on that date, after making adjustments in respect of the following:—

(*a*) Depreciation of 10% is to be written off the Machinery and Plant, including additions during the year.

(*b*) £150 is to be provided as a Reserve for Doubtful Debts.

(*c*) The sum of £38 for goods supplied to the proprietor was included in the Debtors' balances at December 31, 1930.

(Royal Society of Arts.)

F

CHAPTER XIV

ADJUSTMENTS IN THE FINAL ACCOUNTS

Question. You said (on page 135) that certain adjustments may be necessary in preparing the Final Accounts, and that the Trial Balance does not show what they are. Can we consider them now?

Answer. As we have dealt with the simple form of Revenue Account and Balance Sheet, in which no adjustments were called for, we may now look a little more closely at the problem of ascertaining **true Profit and Loss** as it arises in practice.

In the first place, our task is not merely to prepare the Final Accounts from the information given in the books of the business as they may stand. We must examine the Ledger Accounts, particularly the accounts in the Impersonal or Nominal Ledger, with a view to seeing that they are **complete so far as concerns the period under review.**

Question. Is there any likelihood of their being incomplete?

Answer. When we speak of the function of the Revenue Account, for example, as the statement of the Profit or Loss over a definite period, it is essential that we include in it **all the expenses incurred as well as the whole of the gross income** of the business.

If any expenses **attributable to the period** were inadvertently omitted, the final figure of Profit would be untrue, and would be **overstated.** Similarly, Profit is **understated** if we neglect to bring in every kind of income, however incidental to the main purpose of the business, which has been **earned** during the period and for which it may properly take credit.

Question. Can you give me examples of such items, and explain why they are termed " adjustments "?

Answer. One of the biggest single items of expense in a manufacturing business is **wages** paid to workpeople. In an ordinary case wages may be paid on Fridays in respect of the week ended on the preceding Wednesday. The wage sheets or cards for the week have to be checked and certified, the pay roll prepared, deductions made for National Insurance, and so on. Consequently, if the financial year ended on a Thursday, wages for a whole week and one day would be outstanding, no payment would have been made, and there would be no Credit entry in the Cash Book, and no Debit entry in the Wages Account for the amounts involved when the books were closed.

In effect, the **expense** figure for wages would be less than the true amount, and the fact that the workpeople were **creditors** of the business would be ignored. The former clearly has a bearing on the **Revenue Account** and the latter on the **Balance Sheet.** Therefore we must make an adjustment raising the wage figure to its true level (an additional Debit), and at the same time record the liability for wages in the Balance Sheet (an additional Credit).

Another instance arises in connection with the Book Debts, or "**Sundry Debtors,**" as we have more recently described them.

At the end of the financial year, a certain amount will be due from customers under this head for goods sold to them. The value of these goods appears as "**Sales**" in the **Trading Account,** as we have seen, and is the main source of Profit. Unless we are quite convinced that our customers are willing and able to pay what they owe, a part of the Book Debts may become **Bad Debts,** and any loss that is likely to arise in this way must be charged by way of **estimate** against the Profit earned in the period. Otherwise, such estimated loss, if and when it becomes an actual or ascertained loss, is a burden on the Profits of the **subsequent** trading year. Neglect to reserve an estimated sum for Bad or Doubtful Debts has then the effect of **overstating Profits,** and **overstating Assets also,** in that they appear in the Balance Sheets of the business at more than they will ultimately realise.

The adjustment required in this case is to **debit** a sum to **Revenue** by way of "Provision for doubtful debts," along with the debts actually written off as Bad during the period.

The corresponding Credit balance so created can be shown on the Liabilities side of the Balance Sheet, or better, as a **deduction** from the total Sundry Debtors on the Assets side, thereby reducing them to their estimated collectible value.

Question. With all these adjustments, then, both the Revenue Account and the Balance Sheet are affected?

Answer. Yes, either as a Debit to Revenue and a Credit on the Balance Sheet, with what is called a **Liability Provision,** or as a Credit to Revenue and a Debit on the Balance Sheet, in the form of an **Asset Provision.** The following are illustrations :—

Example. Merryweather & Co. pay a rent of £250 p.a. for their business premises, which are rated at £225 p.a. The local rates are 16*s*. in the £ payable half yearly in advance on March 31 and September 30.

The rent is payable on the usual quarter days, but on September 30, 1936, the firm sublet a part of the premises to Tenant & Co. at £50 p.a., the first half-yearly payment being due on March 31, 1937.

The Rent and Rates Account in Merryweather's books was as follows on January 1, 1936 :—

		£	*s.*	*d.*			£	*s.*	*d.*
1936 Jan. 1	To Balance b/d, Rates prepaid . .	45	0	0	1936 Jan. 1	By Balance b/d, Rent due December 25.	62	10	0

You are required :—

(*a*) To write up the account for the year, bringing down any necessary balances at December 31, 1936.

(*b*) To state in which section of the Final Accounts for the year 1936 these balances would appear, giving reasons in brief.

(Royal Society of Arts.)

Before we begin, let us take the information given, and consider it. The following points must be borne in mind :—

(*a*) The financial year end of the business is December 31, 1936.

(*b*) In the year ended on that date we shall expect to find in the **Profit and Loss Account** :—

1. An expense for rent payable of £250,
2. An expense for rates of £180 (16*s*. in £ on £225),

3. A profit for rent receivable from Tenant & Co. of £12 10*s*. (3 months at £50 p.a.),

(*c*) And in the **Balance Sheet :—**

4. An **Asset** or Debit Balance of £45 representing **rates paid in advance for the 3 months to March 31, 1937.**
5. A similar **Asset** of £12 10*s*., being rent accrued due at December 31, 1936.

The Rent and Rates Account in the Impersonal Ledger will then appear as on p. 166 assuming all payments are made on the due dates.

We notice in the above **account** that two columns may usefully be provided for rent and rates respectively, and that the **two provisions** carried down appear as the opening figures for the year 1937. Since they are Debit Balances they may rightly be described as **Asset Provisions.**

It is not usually the practice to journalise these provisions (as by entry in the Debit and Credit Journal) and to this extent we find one exception to the general rule that "nothing should be recorded in a Ledger Account which has not first appeared in a Book of Prime Entry."

One more illustration may be taken of a provision, which is in the reverse direction.

Example. During 1935, his first year of business, a merchant wrote off Bad Debts amounting to £100, and at December 31 made a provision for Bad and Doubtful Debts, amounting to £50.

During 1936, a final dividend, £30, was received in respect of one of the debts (£40) written off in 1935, further debts amounting to £60 were written off, and at December 31, 1936, the merchant considered it prudent to make a provision against existing debts of 60% for one of £40, and 30% for one of £30.

In addition it was estimated that a final dividend of 15*s*. in the £ would be received in 1937 in respect of a debt standing in the books at £28.

You are required to produce, for the two years, the Bad Debts Account, Provision for Bad and Doubtful Debts Account, and (as far as possible) Profit and Loss Account.

(Institute of Bankers.)

MERRYWEATHER & CO.

RENT AND RATES.

DR.

Date.		Rent.	Rates.
1936		£ s. d.	£ s. d.
Jan. 1	To Balance b/d, Rates prepaid.		45 0 0
„ 2	„ Cash, Rent . . .	62 10 0	
Mar. 25	„ Cash, Rent . . .	62 10 0	
„ 31	„ Cash, Rates 6 months to September 30, 1936 .		90 0 0
June 24	„ Cash, Rent . . .	62 10 0	
Sept. 29	„ Cash, Rent . . .	62 10 0	
„ 30	„ Cash, Rates 6 months to March 31, 1937 . .		90 0 0
Dec. 25	„ Cash, Rent . . .	62 10 0	
„ 31	„ Transfer to Profit and Loss A/c, Rent Receivable	12 10 0	
		£325 0 0	£225 0 0
1937			
Jan. 1	To Balance b/d:		
	Rent accrued due . .	12 10 0	
	Rates prepaid . .		45 0 0

CR.

Date.		Rent.	Rates.
1936		£ s. d.	£ s. d.
Jan. 1	By Balance b/d, Rent due December 25 . . .	62 10 0	
Dec. 31	„ Provision for 3 months' Rent accrued due from Tenant & Co. at this date at £50 per annum c/d .	12 10 0	
„ 31	„ Provision for 3 months' Rates paid in advance c/d .		45 0 0
„ 31	Transfer to Profit and Loss A/c:		
	Rent Payable . .	250 0 0	
	Rates . . .		180 0 0
		£325 0 0	£225 0 0

IMPERSONAL LEDGER.

BAD DEBTS.

DR. CR.

		£ s. d.			£ s. d.
1935 Dec. 31	To Sundry Customers' Debts written off .	100 0 0	1935 Dec. 31	By Transfer to Profit and Loss A/c .	100 0 0
1936 Dec. 31	To Sundry Customers' Debts written off .	60 0 0	1936 Jan. 1	By Cash, Final Dividend of 15s. in £ on debt of £40 written off in 1935 . .	30 0 0
			Dec. 31	„ Transfer to Provision for Bad and Doubtful Debts A/c .	30 0 0
		£60 0 0			£60 0 0

IMPERSONAL LEDGER.

PROVISION FOR BAD AND DOUBTFUL DEBTS.

DR. CR.

		£ s. d.			£ s. d.
1935 Dec. 31	To Provision c/d, being provision at this date .	50 0 0	1935 Dec. 31	By Transfer to Profit and Loss A/c.	50 0 0
1936 Dec. 31	To Transfer from Bad Debts A/c .	30 0 0	1936 Jan. 1	By Provision b/d .	50 0 0
„ 31	„ Provision c/d, being provisions at this date : X. 60% of £40 £24 Y. 30% of £30 9 Z. 25% of £28 7 —	40 0 0	Dec. 31	„ Transfer to Profit and Loss A/c.	20 0 0
		£70 0 0			£70 0 0
			1937 Jan. 1	By Provision b/d .	40 0 0

PROFIT AND LOSS ACCOUNTS (EXTRACT).

Year ended December 31, 1935.

DR. CR.

	£ s. d.		
To Bad Debts, including Provision . . .	150 0 0		

Year ended December 31, 1936.

	£ s. d.		
To Bad Debts, less Recoveries, and including Provision . . .	20 0 0		

In this illustration, we are instructed to open separately an account for the Provision for Bad and Doubtful Debts.

The recovery of £30 during 1936 serves to reduce the expense of £60 for debts written off during that year, and the balance is transferred at the year end to the Provision Account. The Provision required at December 31, 1936, is brought down as a **Credit Balance** on January 1, 1937, and may as such be termed a **Liability Provision.**

Tests and Questions

1. Explain briefly the object of a bad debts reserve. Upon what basis is it usually formed? How does it affect the Profit and Loss Account and the Balance Sheet? Illustrate your answer with a specimen account. (College of Preceptors.)

2. During the year ended December 31, 1929, C. P. Kilham made the following bad debts: A. B., £13 2*s.* 6*d.*; X. Y., £5 9*s.* 10*d.*; and R. Z., £12 18*s.* 4*d.*

Submit the entries Kilham should make when closing his books as on December 31, 1929. (Royal Society of Arts.)

3. X. sets up in practice as a doctor on January 1, 1932. During 1932 he received fees amounting to £545, and at the end of the year £237 was owing to him. During 1933 the fees received amounted to £831, and at the end of the year £364 was owing to him. His expenses amounted to £265 in 1932 and £320 in 1933, there being no liabilities outstanding at the end of either year.

Ascertain his profit for each of these years.

(Royal Society of Arts.)

4. On October 1, 1935, the Bad Debts Reserve Account of a business stood at £3,768. During the ensuing twelve months bad debts amounting to £3,389 were written off. On June 30, 1936, a payment of £80 was received on account of a debt which had been treated as irrecoverable two years previously. The debts outstanding at September 30, 1936, were examined, and the book-keeper was instructed to make a reserve of £3,400 to cover the anticipated loss.

You are required to show the Ledger Account or Accounts as they appear after the closing of the books had been completed.

(Royal Society of Arts.)

5. On January 1, 1936, H. Jacks owed J. Dixon £220. On March 31 Jacks purchased goods from Dixon valued at £246, of which he returned goods to the value of £16 on April 3. On April 6 Jacks paid Dixon £120 on account. On July 1 Dixon received notice of the bankruptcy of Jacks, and on October 5 he received first and final dividend of 6*s.* 8*d.* in the £ from the Trustee in Bankruptcy. Show the account of H. Jacks in the Ledger of J. Dixon as it should appear after Dixon had balanced his books at December 31, 1936. (Union of Educational Institutions.)

6. The Rates Account of G. Baker is shown in his Ledger as follows :—

RATES ACCOUNT.

1934	
Dec. 31.	To Balance, in advance, b/f £16.
1935	
May 31.	To Cash, half-year to September 30, 1935, £34 10*s.*
Nov. 18.	To Cash, half-year to March 31, 1936, £34 10*s.*

Balance the account by transfer to Profit and Loss Account at December 31, 1935, bringing forward the appropriate amount in advance. (Institute of Book-keepers.)

7. At December 31, 1931, the Ledger of T. Atkins contained the following balances for debts due to him :—

	£	*s.*	*d.*
Arthur	36	1	8
Charles	15	10	0
Henry	14	1	10
Percy	20	10	0

The estate of Arthur is being administered in Bankruptcy, and it is feared, pending realisation, that not more than 10*s.* in the £ will be recoverable. Henry has died and his estate has no assets whatever. For the sake of prudence 5% is to be reserved on the debts of Charles and Percy.

Show the four accounts, together with Bad Debts Account and Reserve for Doubtful Debts Account. Journal need not be given. (Institute of Bankers.)

8. In 1932 a trader, X., wrote off as a bad debt £19 15*s.* 4*d.*, the balance of an account due to him by Y.

In 1933 Y. paid the debt in full. Show by means of Journal entries how the recovery of this debt would be dealt with in closing X.'s books for 1933, on the assumption that :—

(*a*) The cash received was posted to the credit of Y.'s account.

(*b*) The cash was posted to a nominal account.

(Royal Society of Arts.)

9. The payments made by X., Ltd., to its travellers on account of commission and salaries during 1934 amounted to £1,547 3*s.* 9*d.* and during 1935 to £1,752 13*s.* 4*d.* The amounts accrued and unpaid under this heading were as follows :—

	£	*s.*	*d.*
December 31, 1933 . . .	36	19	1
December 31, 1934 . . .	41	3	7
December 31, 1935 . . .	22	17	10

Draw up a statement showing the amount to be charged against profits in 1934 and 1935 respectively, and show what would have been the effect of accidentally omitting to make the proper reserve at the end of 1934. (Royal Society of Arts.)

10. The Rent and Rates Account in the Ledger of Riley Bros. showed that on December 31, 1935, the rent for the quarter to Christmas was outstanding, and that the rates for the half-year

ending March 31, 1936, amounting to £76 7*s.* 6*d.* had been paid. During the ensuing year the following payments relating to rent and rates were made :—

		£	*s.*	*d.*
Jan. 4.	Rent for Christmas quarter	90	0	0
Mar. 29.	Rent for Ladyday quarter	90	0	0
June 26.	Rates for half-year ending September 30, 1936	74	14	8
July 7.	Rent for Midsummer quarter . . .	90	0	0
Sept. 30.	Rent for Michaelmas quarter . . .	90	0	0
Dec. 28.	Rent for Christmas quarter . . .	90	0	0

The rates for the half-year ending March 31, 1937, which amounted to £80 17*s.* 10*d.* were paid on January 6, 1937.

You are required to show the Rent and Rates Account as it would appear after the books for the year ended December 31, 1936, had been closed. Make any calculation in months.

(Royal Society of Arts.)

11. The financial year of Sanctions, Ltd., ended on December 31, 1935.

At that date, the following balances appeared, among others, in their Impersonal Ledger :—

Rates, £225 (15 months to March 31, 1936).
Wages, £7,098 (to December 27, 1935).
Stationery, Advertising, etc., £864.
Bad and Doubtful Debts, written off, £126.

The wages for the week ending January 3, 1936, were £63.

Stationery stocks for which an adjustment is required amounted to £117.

The Sundry Debtors totalled £5,660, and a reserve is to be made of 5% for doubtful debts, and 2% for discounts.

Show the Ledger Accounts involved after giving effect to the above.

(Royal Society of Arts.)

12. X. Y., who owed £200 to A. B. for goods supplied on June 1, 1934, became unable to pay his debts in full and offered a composition of 5*s.* in the £ to his creditors and this was accepted. A cheque for the dividend was received by A. B. on December 1, 1934.

When X. Y. called his creditors together, A. B. had on his premises a machine belonging to X. Y. and claimed a right of lien in respect thereof. This was admitted and the machine was valued at £80. A. B.'s claim was consequently reduced by this amount.

A. B. decided that instead of selling the machine he would retain it as part of his plant. When making up his annual accounts on December 31, 1934, the balance of X. Y.'s account was written off as a bad debt.

You are required to show, by means of Journal entries and Ledger Accounts, how the foregoing transactions would be recorded in A. B.'s books. (University of Manchester.)

13. In the books of Harry Holborn at December 31, 1936, the financial year end, the Ledger Account for "Heat, Light, Power

and Water" shows a Debit Balance of £253. Investigation discloses the following points :—

(a) A deposit of £10 (returnable on cessation of supply) was paid on April 1, 1936, in respect of electric power.
(b) The charge for electric power is made quarterly, and the last debit in the account is for the three months to November 30, 1936. The charge note for the three months to February 29, 1936, amounted to £36.
(c) A half-year's water rate, amounting to £14, was debited to the account in October, 1936, in respect of the period to March 31, 1937.

Make such adjustments in the Ledger Account as appear to you to be necessary and state how, if at all, they would be shown in Holborn's Balance Sheet at December 31, 1936.

(Birmingham Commercial College.)

14. On January 1, 1933, A. and B. go into business as advertising consultants, on the footing that each contributes £1,000 cash as capital, profits and losses to be shared equally.

The £1,000 provided by A. is borrowed by him privately from his bankers at 5% p.a. interest.

It is agreed that B., who devotes his whole time to the business, shall receive prior to the ascertainment of profit a management salary of £250 p.a.

Office accommodation is acquired on February 1, 1933, at a rent of £300 p.a., payable quarterly, the first payment to be made on March 31, 1933.

Furniture and fittings are purchased on the latter date from O. F., Ltd., for a sum of £72 cash, and B. introduces other similar equipment of a value of £36 to be credited to his Capital Account.

Apart from the above items, at December 31, 1933, there has been received in cash by A. and B. as consultants' fees the sum of £3,150, and at that date fees totalling £340 are outstanding and due to them.

Office salaries, heating, lighting, etc., amounted to £575 during the period, and A. and B. incurred travelling and entertaining expenses of £763 in connection with visits to clients, all of which has been duly paid.

Prepare a Revenue Account of the business of A. and B. for the year ended December 31, 1933, and a Balance Sheet at that date.

(University of Birmingham.)

CHAPTER XV

DEPRECIATION

We have seen in the preceding chapter how very important it is that all matters affecting the ascertainment of true profit shall be properly taken into account whenever an attempt is made to produce a Trading and Profit and Loss Account and Balance Sheet. Thus, any outstanding income, even though not actually received in cash, and any expense incurred but not yet paid must, if relating to the period under review, be provided for either as an **Asset or a Liability Provision.**

In so doing, we are taking steps to ensure **the genuineness of the profit figure** which the Revenue Account discloses, but we should not forget that the **Balance Sheet** drawn up at the end of the period likewise calls for attention. If the Balance Sheet is concerned with the proprietor's Capital, and the property or Assets by which it is represented, it is just as necessary to consider the correctness of the values put upon these Assets. Generally speaking, it is sufficient for the Assets as a whole to be shown at their **"going concern"** values, *i.e.* at a figure which reflects their worth to the business as an established concern, producing a normal and reasonable profit on the total Capital invested. By way of contrast we can speak of **break-up** values of the property, representing its realisable value if sold in the market for what it will fetch. Between the two, there is a very wide gap, particularly noticeable with **Fixed Assets,** as distinct from **Current Assets.**

Examples of Current Assets, as we know, are :—

(*a*) Stock in Trade, and
(*b*) Book Debts,

and we have seen that they are typical of the property **in which the business is dealing from day to day.** The Stock held by the business must be capable of sale at the prevailing market price ; Book Debts must also be capable of collection from customers at their full value, subject to any provision made for debts which are considered to be doubtful.

We can, therefore, appreciate that as regards Current Assets, the test of their **realisable value** is all-important, and their **book value** (as shown in the Books of Account) should be in line with it.

In the case of **Fixed Assets,** however, being property **purchased for retention** and **not** for resale, altogether different considerations apply. Of this class of property, examples are :—

(*a*) Plant and Machinery,
(*b*) Motor Vehicles for delivering goods to customers.

Without them, the business cannot begin to function, and they are clearly an essential part of its Capital equipment.

Because they represent property **used** for the purpose of the business, we have to recognise that there is in them **an element of impermanence,** and although they are retained within the business, a limit must be set to their **effective working life,** or the period of time during which they can be economically operated. Beyond that period, no matter how carefully they have been repaired and overhauled, it will probably be found that charges for renewals and replacements of parts to an increasingly large extent have to be met, so much so, that quite apart from the risk of their becoming obsolete, or out of date, **these Assets as a whole must be replaced.**

The effective working life will naturally vary as between one class of Fixed Asset and another; sometimes it may be from 20 to 30 years, while with motor vehicles, 3 years is often the maximum period during which useful service can be rendered to the business.

As a result, we can recognise a progressive shrinkage in value of these classes of property, which we term **depreciation,** and it is very important that we take a note of it as **a shrinkage of value caused by the use of the property for the purpose of profit-earning.**

We can even take the matter further, and argue that against the profits earned in each trading year should be put as an expense the depreciation estimated to have taken place.

In other words, we may say that the loss in value is just as truly a business expense as the wages paid to workpeople, or the charge for rent and rates.

The real working expenses will be understated if the factor of depreciation is ignored year by year, and ultimately, when the machinery is worn out, or obsolete, the proprietor of the business will have to introduce fresh Capital to replace it, or else shut down.

This point of view brings us to the second reason for charging depreciation. Net Profit as ascertained by the preparation of the Trading and Profit and Loss Account is the yield upon the Capital invested, and may be wholly withdrawn by the proprietor in the form of cash. If depreciation is charged as a business expense, this Profit figure will be accordingly reduced, and also the amount of **cash withdrawable from the business** on account of it. Put in yet another way, cash or its equivalent, representing the charge for depreciation, will be retained within the business, and may, over a period of time, accumulate to provide the moneys required for eventual replacement.

For these reasons, it is the general practice to depreciate or **write down** the Fixed Assets, usually on a percentage basis, at all times when the Final Accounts are to be prepared.

The result is that we have :—

(*a*) **A Debit to Profit and Loss Account,** and
(*b*) **A Credit to the particular Asset Account,** thereby reducing its book value, since Assets are Debit Balances in the Private Ledger.

The two methods most generally employed are :—

1. The Straight Line, or Fixed Instalment method.
2. The Diminishing Balance, or Reducing Instalment method.

They both have this in common, that a percentage of either the cost or book value of the Asset is written off against profits period by period, with or without allowance for any **residual** or **scrap** value.

The former, or straight line method relies on writing off yearly a part of the **original or purchase cost.** When the Asset is bought its effective working life is estimated as being a certain number of years, and the cost is recovered rateably over this period.

Example. Sanders and Son have a motor lorry which cost £285 on January 1, 1935. Depreciation is to be provided on the Straight Line method over a period of 3 years. Show the Ledger Account of the Asset in the firm's books.

PRIVATE LEDGER.

MOTOR LORRY.

Dr. Cr.

Date.	Details.	Fo.	Amount. £ s. d.	Date.	Details.	Fo.	Amount. £ s. d.
1935 Jan. 1	To Cash, Purchase cost		285 0 0	1935 Dec. 31	By Transfer to Profit and Loss A/c, Depreciation		95 0 0
				„ 31	„ Balance .	c/d	190 0 0
			£285 0 0				£285 0 0
1936 Jan. 1	To Balance .	b/d	190 0 0	1936 Dec. 31	By Transfer to Profit and Loss A/c, Depreciation		95 0 0
				„ 31	„ Balance .	c/d	95 0 0
			£190 0 0				£190 0 0
1937 Jan. 1	To Balance .	b/d	95 0 0	1937 Dec. 31	By Transfer to Profit and Loss A/c, Depreciation		95 0 0
			£95 0 0				£95 0 0

At December 31, 1935, the lorry would appear in the Balance Sheet as under :—

Assets

	£	£
Motor Lorry, at cost	285	
Less Depreciation written off . . .	95	
		190

i.e. its **book value** would then be £190 only.

Diminishing Balance Method

In this case, a **fixed percentage is written off the book value** of the Asset as it appears **at the commencement of each year.** This method is more popular than that just described, as there is no necessity to keep before us the original cost figure of each particular item, which with an Asset like Plant and Machinery, may be somewhat difficult, in the absence of a detailed Plant register.

Example. At January 1, 1936, the balance on the Plant and Tools Account was £4,730. During the year a lathe was purchased costing £75, and on March 31, 1937, three drilling machines were sold for £52. Ignore loss on Sale.

Show the Asset Account, reckoning depreciation at 5% p.a. (to nearest £) on the Diminishing Balance method.

PRIVATE LEDGER.

PLANT AND TOOLS.

DR. CR.

Date.	Details.	Fo.	Amount.			Date.	Details.	Fo.	Amount.		
			£	s.	d.				£	s.	d.
1936						1936					
Jan. 1	To Balance	b/d	4,730	0	0	Dec. 31	By Transfer to Profit and Loss A/c, Depreciation 5% on £4,730		236	0	0
June 30	„ Cash, Lathe .		75	0	0	„ 31	„ Balance .	c/d	4,569	0	0
			£4,805	0	0				£4,805	0	0
1937						1937					
Jan. 1	To Balance	b/d	4,569	0	0	Mar. 31	By Cash, 3 Drilling Machines.		52	0	0
						„ 31	„ Transfer to Profit and Loss A/c, Depreciation 5% on £4,569		228	0	0
						„ 31	„ Balance .	c/d	4,289	0	0
			£4,569	0	0				£4,569	0	0
1938											
Jan. 1	To Balance	b/d	4,289	0	0						

At December 31, 1936, the following would appear in the Balance Sheet :—

Assets

	£	£
Plant and Tools		
At Cost *less* Depreciation . . .	4,730	
Add Additions at Cost . . .	75	
	4,805	
Less Depreciation at 5% p.a. . .	236	
		4,569

The reducing instalment method is open to the criticism that Fixed Assets so depreciated tend to be dealt with in groups, and that with ordinary rates of depreciation its slowness in writing down the values is not sufficiently recognised. If the life of the asset is short the percentage required may be prohibitively high ; *e.g.*, to depreciate a tool having a life of 3 years only would require a 90% rate.

Sometimes the Debit and Credit Journal is used so as to avoid making a Prime Entry in the particular Ledger Account :—

Example.

		Dr. £	Cr. £
1935 Dec. 31	Depreciation A/c or Profit and Loss A/c . . . . Dr.	236	
	To Plant and Tools . . .		236
	Being depreciation at 5% p.a. now written off.		

As the illustration shows, an account for Depreciation as a business expense may be opened in the Impersonal Ledger, **but the Debit Balance on it must ultimately be transferred to Profit and Loss Account.**

Tests and Questions

1. How is the shrinkage in the value of fixed assets provided for in accounts kept on the double entry principle ?

Illustrate your answer by showing an account relating to an asset which has been written down in accordance with your suggestions.
(University of Manchester.)

2. Explain briefly, but as clearly as you can, why it is generally necessary, when preparing the accounts of a business, to make provision for depreciation of the fixed assets.

If you know of any exceptions to this general rule, mention them and give your reasons.

Note.—Goodwill is, for the purpose of this question, not to be regarded as a fixed asset. (Royal Society of Arts.)

3. On January 1, 1930, a business purchased a motor delivery van for £800.

Show how the account would appear in the books of the business for the four following years assuming that depreciation is written off (*a*) by the fixed instalment method, and (*b*) by the diminishing balance method, the rate of depreciation being 20% in each case.

State, giving your reasons shortly, which method of depreciation you consider is more appropriate for an asset of this sort.

(Royal Society of Arts.)

4. On January 1, 1932, Dix, Ltd., purchased machinery costing £240. For the years 1932, 1933 and 1934 depreciation was written off at the rate of 5% on the diminishing balance. During 1935, it became apparent that the machinery would not be of service after December 31, 1936, and for these latter two years the fixed instalment method was substituted. In December, 1936, the machinery realised £15 on sale. You are required to write up the Machinery Account from the commencement, reckoning depreciation to the nearest £. (Birmingham Commercial College.)

5. X., Ltd., purchased a seven-year lease of certain shop premises for £8,000. A further sum of £2,000 was expended in various alterations, and it was estimated that at the end of the lease the cost of restoring the premises to their original condition (for which the company were liable) would be about £500.

Show the Ledger Account for the first two years, providing for depreciation. (Royal Society of Arts.)

6. From the following particulars, write up the Machinery Account for the year ended November 30, 1936.

The balance from the previous year was £26,882.

On May 31, 1936, new machinery was purchased for £1,264, and wages amounting to £24 were paid for its erection. The old machinery replaced by the above was sold for £144, which was its written-down value on November 30, 1935.

Depreciation at the rate of 12½% per annum is to be written off.

(Royal Society of Arts.)

7. The Balance Sheet of P. Q. & Co., Ltd., drawn up as on March 31, 1930, showed plant and machinery valued, after writing off depreciation, at £25,500.

Depreciation had been written off regularly, from the dates of purchase of the various items, at the rate of 10% per annum on the diminishing value.

On June 1, 1930, a motor, which had been bought on November 1, 1925, for £750, was sold for £250 and replaced by a new one costing £1,100.

Show the Plant and Machinery Account as it would appear in the Company's books for the year ended March 31, 1931, after writing off the appropriate depreciation for the year.

(Royal Society of Arts.)

8. C. D. purchased factory premises (subject to a lease of 50 years from June 30, 1909) from the Liquidator of H., Ltd., on June 30, 1934, the purchase price being £2,500.

To enable him to complete the purchase, he borrowed £1,650 from Happy Bank, Ltd., the loan being repayable in three years by equal annual instalments of principal, reckoning interest at 5% per annum.

Provide depreciation on the fixed instalment basis, and show the Property Account and the Loan Account in C. D.'s books for the three years to June 30, 1937. (Birmingham Commercial College.)

9. On January 1, 1934, a manufacturer acquired a machine at a cost of £1,200.

During 1934 repairs to the machine cost £5 and a new attachment, which cost £25, was added to it.

The repairs during the year 1935 amounted to £18.

It was decided to depreciate the machine at the rate of 10% per annum on the reducing instalment method.

From the foregoing particulars you are required to write up the Machinery Account for the two years ended December 31, 1935.

(University of Manchester.)

10. The following was the Trial Balance of Mark Lane on June 30, 1935 :—

	Dr. £	Cr. £
Mark Lane : Capital		5,000
,, Drawings	600	
Debtors	6,000	
Purchases, less Returns	19,800	
Creditors		4,000
Furniture and Fittings	200	
Salaries	850	
Sales, less Returns		25,200
Rent, Rates and Insurance	430	
Stock, July 1, 1934	5,750	
General Expenses	350	
Carriage (Outward)	180	
Travelling Expenses	290	
Trade Marks	1,000	
Bad Debts	60	
Discount	140	
Cash	25	
Bank		1,475
	£35,675	£35,675

The stock on hand on June 30, 1935, was valued at £4,800.

Discount debtors and creditors at 2½%.

Provide for depreciation of furniture and fixtures at 20% and write £200 off trade marks.

Make an adjustment in respect of rates charged in advance, £60.

From the foregoing information you are required to prepare a Trading and Profit and Loss Account for the year ended June 30, 1935, and a Balance Sheet as on that date.

(University of Manchester.)

11. E. F. was in business as a merchant and on April 1, 1935, his position was as follows :—

Assets: Debtors £2,300; Stock £2,200; Furniture and fittings £500; Balance at bankers £1,650; Cash in hand £25.
Liabilities: Sundry creditors £1,375.

The following is a summary of his transactions for the year ended March 31, 1936:—

	£
Total of credit sales	11,350
Cash received on Sales Ledger Accounts	10,860
Salaries paid from bank	1,840
Discounts allowed on Sales Ledger Accounts	295
Cheques paid on Purchase Ledger Accounts	7,600
Cheques paid for expenses	1,275
Proprietor's drawings from bank	800
Discounts received on Purchase Ledger Accounts	420
Total of Purchase Book	8,030

Write off a debt of £50 which has proved to be bad.
Depreciate furniture and fixtures at the rate of 10% per annum.
Stock on hand at March 31, 1936, £2,100.

Complete the double entry and prepare a Trading and Profit and Loss Account for the year ended March 31, 1936, and Balance Sheet as on that date. (University of Manchester.)

12. The following is the Trial Balance extracted from the books of J. Falconer at December 31, 1936:—

	Dr. £	Cr. £
Salaries	2,414	
Discounts Received		132
Repairs and Renewals	318	
Sales		18,505
Carriage Outwards	163	
Creditors		674
Wages	6,116	
Sundry Expenses	86	
Sundry Debtors	3,445	
Commission	196	
Capital, January 1, 1936		7,200
Stock, January 1, 1936	1,572	
Discounts Allowed	578	
Returns Outwards		295
Plant and Machinery, January 1, 1936	1,460	
Cash in Hand	2 10	
Purchases	7,336	
Rates	175	
Warehouse Expenses	537	
Office Fixtures, etc., January 1, 1936	220	
Cash at Bank	1,200	
Rent of Premises	187 10	
Drawings	1,000	
Bad Debts Reserve, January 1, 1936		200
	£27,006	£27,006

You are required to prepare :—

(*a*) Trading and Profit and Loss Account for the year to December 31, 1936.

(*b*) Balance Sheet at December 31, 1936, showing per cent. net Profit to Capital at January 1, 1936.

(*c*) The following adjustments are necessary :—

(1) The stock on hand at December 31, 1936, was valued at £1,769.

(2) 3 months rates are prepaid in the sum of £35.

(3) The rent of premises is £250 per annum, payable quarterly, and has been paid to September 29, 1936.

(4) Depreciation is to be charged at 5% on plant and machinery, and 10% on office fixtures, etc.

(Birmingham Commercial College.)

13. Give the Journal entries necessary to record the following transactions :—

Dec. 2. Bought fixtures and fittings value £345 on credit from S. Maxton and Sons.

„ 15. A cheque value £76 5*s*. 4*d*. received from Perkins, Ltd., was wrongly posted to Brampton Bros.' Account.

„ 19. Exchanged one motor-car value £120 for three typewriters value £22 each and the balance in cash.

„ 31. Plant and machinery is to be depreciated by £73.

„ 31. O. Carfax, a debtor for £55, having become insolvent, pays 4*s*. in the £ in settlement of the amount owing.

(Union of Educational Institutions.)

14. A firm acquired a 25 years' lease of its business premises for £18,000. The firm's bankers advanced £12,000 towards the purchase price on the security of the lease.

Repayment of the Bank loan is made by quarterly instalments of £250 which the bank debit to the firm's current account together with interest at the rate of 6 per cent. per annum.

You are required to make the entries in the firm's books at the end of the first year to record the above arrangements, including depreciation of the lease according to the method you consider most suitable in the circumstances.

CHAPTER XVI

PARTNERSHIP

In the chapters that have gone before we have considered the business to be owned by a sole proprietor, or, as he is termed, a **sole trader.** This was the earliest form of proprietorship, and still exists in the typical small business, often of the merchanting and distributive type.

With the growth in the size of the business unit, the Capital required to provide the necessary equipment and to finance ordinary trading is usually found to be in excess of the resources of any one individual. A further handicap must be recognised in the fact that, in the event of the business failing, the proprietor is liable to his last penny for the payment of his business creditors. His liability is said to be **unlimited,** in contrast to that of the shareholders in a Limited Company, which is restricted to the amounts unpaid on the shares they have contracted to take.

Between these two extremes we have the partnership relation which, just as in the case of the Sole Trader, involves each partner in unlimited liability as regards the whole of the debts of the **partnership firm.**

It is a very suitable form of business proprietorship where—

(*a*) A large amount of Capital is not required.
(*b*) Liabilities to suppliers and others are unlikely to be considerable.
(*c*) The business is of a size in which each partner can take part in the general supervision.

For these reasons, partnerships are often found in the professions and in the smaller merchanting and manufacturing businesses.

Partnership Act 1890

A measure of statutory control was imposed by this Act, which defines partnership as **the relation which subsists between persons carrying on business in common with a view to profit.**

Not more than twenty persons may be partners in a trading firm, and the Act provides certain rules which, in the absence of written or verbal arrangement between the partners, can be applied in defining the duties of the partners to each other, and their responsibility to persons outside the firm with whom they have business dealings.

As it is in all respects desirable to make special arrangements in each individual case, and to have a permanent record of what is agreed upon, a **Deed, or Articles of Partnership,** is often drawn up by which each of the partners consents to be bound. These also provide for such modifications of the Act of 1890 as may be thought necessary.

The Deed may state :—

(*a*) The term for which the partnership is entered into.
(*b*) The nature of the business to be carried on.
(*c*) The amount of Capital to be introduced and in what circumstances it may be withdrawn.
(*d*) The ratio in which Profits and Losses shall be shared.
(*e*) How much each partner shall be entitled to draw on account of accruing profits.
(*f*) Whether Interest shall be allowed on Partners' Capitals.
(*g*) The salaries, if any, to be paid to individual partners.

As regards (*a*), if no term is stated, or the partnership is continued without any fresh agreement after the original term has expired, it is said to be a **Partnership at Will.**

Of the above, items (*c*), (*d*), (*e*), (*f*) and (*g*) have a special bearing on the **accounts,** and must therefore be considered separately.

Capital

The Capital brought in may take the form of cash, or property in kind, such as machinery, buildings, stock, etc.

In any event, the agreed value must be credited to the Partner's **Capital Account,** and the proper Asset Account debited. If the Capitals are **fixed** the profit shares and drawings on account thereof will be dealt with in separate **Current Accounts.** The form of the latter is exactly similar to what was described on page 150.

Profits and Losses

Partners may share Profits and Losses on any agreed basis. In the last resort the Partnership Act provides that they are entitled to share equally. Sometimes Profits and Losses may be divided in the ratio of the Fixed Capitals; in other cases where one partner takes a more active part than another, he may be rewarded with a bigger proportionate share.

Drawings

It is better to agree at the outset upon a limit for each partner's drawings. As the cash so withdrawn depletes the circulating Capital, interest may be charged thereon from the date withdrawn to the end of the firm's financial year. Drawings may be in the form of goods as well as cash, in which event **Purchases Account** will usually be credited and the partner's Current Account debited.

Interest on Capitals

Prior to the division of the Net Profit, the Deed may provide for charging Interest on the Capital of each partner. If this were not done in a case where, for example, Capital Accounts were unequal, but Profits and Losses were divided equally, the partner having the larger (or largest) Capital would lose.

Such Interest on Capital is in no sense a business expense, and would be debited in the Appropriation, or Net Profit and Loss Account.

Partnership Salaries

A management salary may be paid to one or more of the partners if they devote more time to the business than their co-partners, or if they are **active** as distinct from **sleeping** partners. The latter may be regarded as those who have contributed Capital, but take no part in the daily supervision of affairs.

Salaries paid or payable to the partners will, like interest on Capital, be debited in the Appropriation Account. They are, in effect, and as regards each partner, a part of the ascertained profit due to him as a proprietor.

Partners' Advances

If a partner, to assist the firm, advances cash by way of **loan,** it is probable that he will require it to be treated in the books in a manner different from the **Capital** invested by him. The amount should therefore be credited to a separate **Loan Account.**

The Act of 1890 provides that the partner making the **advance** shall be entitled to interest thereon at the rate of 5% per annum from the date of the advance.

Goodwill

Goodwill is a business Asset, which may be defined as the worth inherent in an established business producing a normal and reasonable profit on the Capital employed in it.

It is **worth** or **value** over and above that represented by the **Tangible** Assets, such as buildings, plant, stock and book debts, and can so be termed an **Intangible** Asset.

If the business were sold, it would clearly be to a purchaser's advantage to pay something for the right to enjoy a continuity of the profits arising, and this is well brought out in the case of a **partnership.**

An incoming partner can be expected to pay the existing partners for the goodwill represented by his profit share, and an outgoing partner is entitled to have goodwill taken into account in determining the sum due to him. The Deed of Partnership will often indicate how the value of the goodwill is to be ascertained, in these and similar circumstances, as by reference to past profits or an estimate of future maintainable profits.

Example. A. joins B. in partnership on January 1, 1935. The Capital is provided as to £5,000 by A., who is a dormant partner, and £500 by B., who devotes his whole time to the business and is wholly dependent on it.

Assuming the gross receipts for 1935 are £10,000, and the working expenses £9,000, prepare a Revenue Account incorporating these items, and also the distribution of profit, allowing 5% Interest on Capital, and dividing the balance equally.

(Royal Society of Arts.)

A. AND B.

PROFIT AND LOSS ACCOUNT.

Year ended December 31, 1935.

DR.	£ s. d.		CR. £ s. d.
To Working Expenses .	9,000 0 0	By Gross Receipts . .	10,000 0 0
„ Balance, Net Profit c/d	1,000 0 0		
	£10,000 0 0		£10,000 0 0
To Interest on Capital:		By Net Profit b/d . .	1,000 0 0
A. 5% on £5,000 .	250 0 0		
B. 5% on £500 .	25 0 0		
	275 0 0		
„ Balance:			
A. ½ share £362 10*s*.			
B. ½ share 362 10*s*.	725 0 0		
	£1,000 0 0		£1,000 0 0

In the above we see the benefit to A. of charging interest on Capital.

The interest due to each partner and the amount of his profit share can be carried direct to Capital Account, or alternatively credited to a Current Account.

Example. Rogers and Shaw enter into partnership on January 1, 1937, and agree to divide Profits and Losses equally, after charging Interest on Capital at 4% per annum.

On December 31, 1937, the following Balances are extracted from their books :—

	Dr. £	Cr. £
Rogers: Capital		3,000
,, Drawings	156	
Shaw: Capital		2,000
,, Drawings	156	
Sales		10.257
Discounts Received		81
Purchases	5,413	
Discounts Allowed	187	
Salaries	1,497	
Wages	2,500	
Sundry Debtors	2,200	
Rates	75	
Printing and Stationery	312	
Travelling Expenses	596	
Bad Debts	24	
Repairs and Renewals	133	
Cash in Hand	11	
Bank Overdraft		54
Subscriptions	8	
Bank Charges	10	
Legal Charges	15	
Audit Fee	21	
Sundry Creditors		662
Factory and Warehouse Premises	1,234	
Plant and Machinery	1,506	
	£16,054	£16,054

The stock at December 31, 1937, was valued by the partners at £1,125.

You are required :—

(*a*) To prepare Trading and Profit and Loss Account for the year to December 31, 1937, and a Balance Sheet at that date.
(*b*) To state the percentage of Gross Profit to turnover.
(*c*) To show the Partners' Current Accounts.

The following adjustments are necessary :—

1. Provide £50 for wages accrued due.
2. Provide 1% on the amount of the Sundry Debtors for Bad and Doubtful Debts.
3. Provide £100 depreciation in respect of Plant and Machinery.

Rogers and Shaw.

TRADING AND PROFIT AND LOSS ACCOUNT.

Year ended December 31, 1937.

		£	s.	d.		£	s.	d.
To Purchases		5,413	0	0	By Sales	10,257	0	0
„ Wages	£2,500				„ Stock, December 31, 1937	1,125	0	0
Add Provision	50							
		2,550	0	0				
„ Gross Profit c/d, $33\frac{1}{3}$% to turnover		3,419	0	0				
		11,382	0	0		11,382	0	0
To Salaries		1,497	0	0	By Gross Profit b/d	3,419	0	0
„ Travelling Expenses		596	0	0	„ Discount Received	81	0	0
„ Printing and Stationery		312	0	0				
„ Discounts Allowed		187	0	0				
„ Repairs and Renewals		133	0	0				
„ Rates		75	0	0				
„ Bad Debts	£24							
Add Provision	22							
		46	0	0				
„ Audit Fee		21	0	0				
„ Legal Charges		15	0	0				
„ Bank Charges		10	0	0				
„ Subscriptions		8	0	0				
„ Depreciation of Plant and Machinery		100	0	0				
		3,000	0	0				
„ Net Profit c/d		500	0	0				
		3,500	0	0		3,500	0	0
To Interest on Capitals:					By Net Profit b/d	500	0	0
Rogers, 4% on £3,000		120	0	0				
Shaw, 4% on £2,000		80	0	0				
		200	0	0				
„ Rogers, $\frac{1}{2}$ share	£150							
„ Shaw, $\frac{1}{2}$ share	150							
		300	0	0				
		£500	0	0		£500	0	0

Note.—In practice, the Provisions are seldom shown separately in the Revenue Account, *e.g.*, Wages would be shown in the one sum of £2,550 only.

ROGERS AND SHAW.

BALANCE SHEET AS AT DECEMBER 31, 1937.

Liabilities.		£	s.	d.	*Assets.*		£	s.	d.
Sundry Creditors .	£662				Cash in Hand . . .		11	0	0
Wages due . .	50				Sundry Debtors . .	£2,200			
		712	0	0	*Less* Provision	22			
Bank Overdraft . .		54	0	0			2,178	0	0
Current Accounts:					Stock in Trade . .		1,125	0	0
Rogers:					Plant and Machinery	£1,506			
Interest on Capital . .	£120				*Less* Depreciation	100			
One half profit .	150						1,406	0	0
	270				Factory and Warehouse Premises . .		1,234	0	0
Less Drawings	156								
		114	0	0					
Shaw:									
Interest on Capital . .	£80								
One half profit .	150								
	230								
Less Drawings	156								
		74	0	0					
Capital Accounts:									
Rogers . .	£3,000								
Shaw . .	2,000								
		5,000	0	0					
		£5,954	0	0			£5,954	0	0

ROGERS.

PRIVATE LEDGER.

DR. ROGERS—CURRENT ACCOUNT. CR.

		£	s.	d.			£	s.	d.
1937					1937				
Dec. 31	To Drawings . .	156	0	0	Dec. 31	By Interest on Capital, 4% on £3,000 . .	120	0	0
„ 31	„ Balance c/d	114	0	0	„ 31	„ One half Profit, year to date .	150	0	0
		£270	0	0			£270	0	0
					1938				
					Jan. 1	By Balance b/d	114	0	0

DR. SHAW—CURRENT ACCOUNT. CR.

		£	s.	d.			£	s.	d.
1937					1937				
Dec. 31	To Drawings . .	156	0	0	Dec. 31	By Interest on Capital, 4% on £2,000 . .	80	0	0
„ 31	„ Balance c/d	74	0	0	„ 31	„ One half Profit, year to date .	150	0	0
		£230	0	0			£230	0	0
					1938				
					Jan. 1	By Balance b/d	74	0	0

In this example we should be careful to note how the provisions for **wages, doubtful debts** and **depreciation** are dealt with in the Balance Sheet.

Tests and Questions

1. Give some reasons why interest is generally charged against the drawings of individual members of a firm, and also credited to their Capital Accounts.

(Union of Lancashire and Cheshire Institutes.)

2. Give two reasons why interest on Capital Accounts should be taken into account in dividing the profits of a partnership.

Mention a case, if you know of one, where one of these reasons does not apply. (Royal Society of Arts.)

3. Earle and Yeoman contemplate the establishment of a dairy to be carried on by them in partnership. Earle is to provide nine-tenths of the capital required, but, having no practical knowledge of the work, is not expected to take much active part in it. Yeoman is experienced in this direction and upon him will devolve the management of the undertaking.

If consulted by them with regard to the financial provisions to be embodied in the Partnership Deed, enumerate your suggestions.

(University of Manchester.)

4. In the absence of agreement, to what extent are partners entitled to interest on capital in and loans to the firm?

Illustrate your answer by reference to the following:—

	£
A. Capital	10,000
B. ,, ...	5,000
A. Loan	3,000

Profits of the firm (before charging any interest), £2,500.

(Royal Society of Arts.)

5. On January 1, 1936, A. and B. entered into partnership but without any formal deed of partnership. A. provided £10,000 as capital, and B. provided £500. On July 1, 1936, A. advanced £2,000 on loan to the firm.

Accounts were prepared and disclosed a profit of £3,000 for the year to December 31, 1936, but the partners could not agree as to how this sum should be divided between them. A. contended that the partners should receive 5% interest on capital and that he should receive 6% interest on his loan to the firm, and the balance then available should be divided equally. B. contended that, as he did most of the work, he should be paid a salary before any division of profit was made.

You are required to show how the profits of the firm should be divided and to state what different division, if any, would be made if A. had written a letter to B. agreeing that a partnership salary of £500 should be paid to him. (Royal Society of Arts.)

6. A., a sole trader, prepared accounts as on March 31, 1934, when his Capital Account showed a balance of £9,000. On April 1

he took in B. as a partner on the terms that before B.'s entry a Goodwill Account for £4,000 should be raised, that B. should bring in £3,000 in cash as his capital, interest at 5% per annum should be allowed on Capital Accounts and the balance of profit be divided between A. and B. in the proportion of 3 to 1.

The profit for the year to March 31, 1935, before charging interest, was £4,050. Show the division of this between A. and B. Show also what the division would have been had no provision been made as to goodwill, the other arrangements being as stated above.

(Royal Society of Arts.)

7. X. and Y. are partners, and they admit Z. as a partner, profits to be shared as follows: X. four-ninths, Y. three-ninths, Z. two-ninths.

Y. is credited with a partnership salary of £300 per annum, and X. and Y. guarantee that Z.'s share of profits shall not be less than £2,000 in any year.

The profits for the year ended December 31, 1929, prior to providing for Y.'s salary, amounted to £8,208.

Prepare the Appropriation section of the firm's Profit and Loss Account. (Royal Society of Arts.)

8. A., a sole trader owning an established business, took B. into partnership on January 1, 1933, at which date the goodwill of the business was agreed to be worth £6,000. A.'s capital (exclusive of goodwill) was £10,000, and B. brought in £3,000 as his capital. Interest on Capital Accounts was to be allowed at 5%, and A. and B. were to divide the remaining profit in the ratio of 2 to 1.

The profit for 1933, before charging interest, was £2,600.

Calculate the division of this sum between A. and B. on the alternative assumptions that:—

(1) Goodwill was ignored on B.'s entering the business.
(2) Goodwill was taken into account at its correct value.

(Royal Society of Arts.)

9. Bright and Smart carry on business in partnership, sharing profits in the proportion of three-fifths and two-fifths respectively.

On January 1, 1936, the Capital Accounts showed the following credit balances: Bright, £8,000; Smart, £6,000.

The Partnership Agreement provides that the partners shall be allowed interest on capital at 5% per annum and that Bright shall be entitled to a salary of £600 per annum and Smart to one of £400 per annum. During the year ended December 31, 1936, the partners' drawings were: Bright, £550; Smart, £425.

The profit for the year, prior to making any of the foregoing adjustments, was £3,500.

You are required to write up the Profit and Loss Appropriation Account and to show how the Capital Accounts of the partners would appear on the Balance Sheet at December 31, 1936.

(University of Manchester.)

10. A. and B. entered into partnership on January 1, 1936, sharing profits and losses equally.

A. contributed £5,000 as capital, comprising £2,000 in cash, and fixtures and plant valued at £3,000.

B. could only introduce £1,000 in cash, but it was agreed he should be given credit in the sum of £1,500 for his sales connection, and also receive a salary at the rate of £170 p.a.

On June 30, 1936, B. paid in an additional £500, and at the same date C. entered the firm, paying £1,600 for a quarter share of the profits and goodwill and bringing in £1,000 cash as his capital, all of which it was agreed should be left in the business.

A. and B. continued to share profits in the same relative proportions as before, and it was arranged that as from the date of C.'s entry, B.'s salary should cease, but 5% p.a. interest on capitals should be allowed.

The profits for the year to December 31, 1936, prior to charging such interest and B.'s salary, were £1,170. Draw up a Statement showing the division of this amount between the partners, making any necessary apportionments on a time basis, and open Ledger Accounts to record the whole of the foregoing.

(Birmingham Commercial College.)

11. Alfred White and George Gardiner, in partnership as merchants, extract from their books the undermentioned Trial Balance at December 31, 1935:—

	Dr. £	Cr. £
Capital Accounts:		
White		5,000
Gardiner		3,000
Stock, January 1, 1935	4,000	
Discounts Received		100
Salesmen's Salaries	1,000	
Rent	400	
Rates	200	
Carriage Inwards	1,000	
Sales		20,000
Balance at Bank	800	
Drawings:—		
White	500	
Gardiner	300	
Trade Creditors		2,400
Purchases	15,000	
General Expenses	500	
Trade Utensils	1,800	
Trade Debtors	5,000	
	£30,500	£30,500

Notes.—(1) One year's interest at 5% is due on the Capital Account of each partner but otherwise the Partnership Act, 1890, applies.

(2) Stock December 31, 1935, £5,000.

(3) Of the rates paid, one payment, £50, was for the half-year ended March 31, 1936.

(4) Depreciate Trade Utensils by 10%.

You are required to produce Trading and Profit and Loss Account for the year 1935 with Balance Sheet as at the end thereof.

(Institute of Bankers.)

12. James and John entered into partnership as merchants on January 1, 1936. James brought in cash £500 and stock-in-trade £1,000; John brought in cash £300 and a motor lorry £700. The agreement provided that John was to have a salary from the firm of £250 per annum and that each partner might draw (on account of salary and profit) £100 per month; otherwise the terms of the Partnership Act, 1890, were to apply.

At the end of 1936 the following Trial Balance was extracted from the books :—

TRIAL BALANCE, DECEMBER 31, 1936.

	Dr. £	*Cr.* £
Capital Accounts		2,500
Debtors	950	
Cash	25	
Carriage Inwards	500	
Bank		135
Stock	1,000	
Rent Paid	550	
Sales		16,000
Motor Lorry	700	
Carriage Outwards	130	
Discounts Received		575
Petty Cash Expenditure	52	
Purchases	11,500	
Drawings	2,400	
Creditors		697
Discounts Allowed	50	
Rates Paid	200	
Salaries (not Partners')	850	
Trade Utensils (cost)	1,000	
	£19,907	£19,907

Notes.—(1) Stock December 31, 1936, valued at £1,800.
(2) Rent accrued but not paid, £50.
(3) Rates paid in advance, £40.
(4) Depreciate the motor lorry at 10% per half-year on the diminishing balance system, and the trade utensils at 5% per half-year on original cost.
(5) Bank charges not yet entered in books, £50.

Prepare Trading and Profit and Loss Accounts for 1936 and a Balance Sheet at the end of the year. (Institute of Bankers.)

13. The following Trial Balance has been extracted as at March 31, 1937, from the books of C. Spargo and W. Penna—partners sharing profits and losses in the proportion of 2 to 1 respectively.

	Dr. £	s.	d.	Cr. £	s.	d.
Stock, April 1, 1936	3,690	0	0			
Purchases and Sales	36,892	15	9	49,469	19	4
Bad Debts written off	291	13	5			
Plant and Machinery (cost £7,000)	6,650	0	0			
Furniture and Fittings (cost £1,200)	1,164	0	0			
Returns	371	11	4	297	10	7
Discounts	351	14	2	403	13	8
Drawings: C. Spargo	560	0	0			
,, W. Penna	380	0	0			
Debtors and Creditors	5,620	0	0	4,872	13	7
Light and Heat	397	14	10			
Rent, Rates and Taxes	650	12	9			
Insurances	131	10	0			
Salaries	1,215	13	4			
Wages	6,394	18	7			
General Expenses	445	12	5			
Bad Debts Reserve				200	0	0
Commissions				363	19	5
Capital: C. Spargo				5,800	0	0
,, W. Penna				3,800	0	0
	£65,207	16	7	£65,207	16	7

Value of stock on March 31, 1937, £1,793.

You are asked to draw up Trading and Profit and Loss Accounts for the year, using the following data for making necessary adjustments :—

(*a*) Depreciate plant and machinery 5% on cost.
(*b*) Depreciate furniture and fittings 2½% on cost.
(*c*) Amount of insurance pre-paid, £31 15*s*.
(*d*) Amount of wages due but unpaid, £111 13*s*. 1*d*.
(*e*) The Bad Debts Reserve is to be increased to an amount equal to 5% of debtors' balances.
(*f*) Amount of commissions due but not received—£34 18*s*. 8*d*.
(*g*) Capital Accounts to be credited with interest at 5% per annum.

(No interest to be charged on drawings.)
No Balance Sheet is to be drawn up.
Instead, you are to show the following accounts in full for the year ended March 31, 1937 :—

(i) Plant and Machinery Account.
(ii) Insurance Account.
(iii) Bad Debts Reserve Account.
(iv) Commission Account.

(Union of Lancashire and Cheshire Institutes.)

14. The firm of John Smith & Sons, makers of engineering equipment, consists of John and Magnus Smith. They share profits equally, after each has been credited with interest at 5% on his capital at the beginning of the year.

At January 31, 1937, the end of the firm's financial year, the following are the balances in the Ledger :—

	£	£
Purchases : Raw Materials	18,562	
" Finished Goods	860	
General Office Expenses	934	
Returns Inwards	413	
Creditors, including an unsecured loan of £500, maturing in 1960		2,617
Bad Debts Provision		205
Stock : Raw Materials	3,906	
" Finished Goods	101	
Wages (Factory)	18,687	
Salaries (Factory)	1,252	
Rent, Insurance, etc. (Factory) . . .	1,246	
" " " " Prepaid .	25	
Net Rents from Workmen's Cottages . .		97
Fire Expense	750	
Carriage Outwards	909	
Factory Equipment and Machinery . .	14,315	
Factory Equipment and Machinery, Depreciation Provision		2,000
Cash	14	
Sales		45,200
Interest Paid on Overdraft, etc. . . .	61	
Debtors	4,135	
Capital : John Smith		12,420
" Magnus Smith		3,740
Drawings : John Smith	837	
" Magnus Smith . . .	371	
Bank		1,099
	£67,378	£67,378

The stock of raw materials at January 31, 1937, was valued at £4,310. There were then no finished goods on hand.

The "Fire Expense" Account shows the balance of a heavy loss from fire in 1932. £150 of this amount is now to be written off.

£22 of bank overdraft interest is accrued and has not been allowed for.

The Equipment Depreciation Provision is to be increased by £315.

A claim for £150 has been made against the firm under the Workmen's Compensation Act.

Prepare suitable Final Accounts and Balance Sheet.

(University of Edinburgh.)

CHAPTER XVII

THE CRITICISM AND INTERPRETATION OF ACCOUNTS

MUCH of what has been already written concerns the recording of business transactions from the earliest stage in the Books of Prime Entry to the preparation of the Final Accounts.

We must never lose sight of the fact that accounts are kept in order that they may assist the proprietor or manager of the business, and it will be time well spent to consider the work we have done from the point of view of those who are to make use of it.

If the accounts, or any part of them, have no meaning to us, they can have no meaning to others, and we must try to regard the records made as telling a story of what has happened, and telling it in a clear and intelligible manner.

A very simple instance of this is seen in the ordinary **Ledger Account.** Having regard to the subject-matter of the account as indicated by its heading, we should be able to describe not only the nature of the entries appearing in it, but also the final result of the transactions, both from the personal and the impersonal aspect.

Example.

H. BROWN.

DR. CR.

Date.	Details.	Fo.	Amount.	Date.	Details.	Fo.	Amount.
1937			£ s. d.	1937			£ s. d.
Jan. 1	To Balance .	b/d	50 0 0	Feb. 1	By Returns		10 0 0
Feb. 28	„ Goods .		25 0 0	Mar. 10	„ Cash on A/c.		20 0 0
May 3	„ Goods .		15 0 0	June 4	„ Bank .		19 10 0
June 7	„ Bank, cheque returned .		19 10 0		„ Discount .		10 0
„ 7	„ Discount .		10 0	Aug. 8	„ Bank, First and Final Dividend of 5s. in £		15 0 0
				„ 31	„ Bad Debts .		45 0 0
			£110 0 0				£110 0 0

The above is a customer's account as shown in the Sales Ledger. At the beginning of the year £50 was owing by him, and a month later he returned goods to the value of £10, further goods being supplied to him on February 28.

On March 10, he remits a sum of £20, which is stated to be "on account"—in itself often a sign of weakness. Despite this, goods are again invoiced to him on May 3, and on June 4 a cheque is received for the balance of what was due as far back as January 1.

The bank subsequently reports that the cheque has not been met, and Brown is accordingly debited with the amount of the cheque and discount.

Between then and August 8, he either compounds with his creditors as a whole, or is made bankrupt. A first and final dividend of 5*s.* in the £ is received, and 15*s.* in the £ has to be written off as a Bad Debt.

Criticism of the Final Accounts

It is, however, in regard to the Trading and Profit and Loss Account and Balance Sheet, as representing the logical conclusion of the book-keeping work, that the principal points for criticism arise.

To deal firstly with the **Trading Account,** the following may have to be considered :—

(*a*) How does the **sales** figure compare with that of the previous year, or other period, and how far have alterations in selling prices contributed to any difference noted ?

(*b*) Similarly as regards **purchases** and the cost of materials bought.

(*c*) Are the **closing stocks** much in excess of those held at the beginning of the year, and if so, in a manufacturing business, to what extent do they consist of raw material or the finished product ? In the former case, have purchases been made in anticipation of a rise in the price of materials ? In the latter case, is the turnover partly seasonal so that a large part of the stock is sold early in the following trading period ? What is the average stock carried, and what is its relation to the turnover ?

(*d*) Does the business earn a fairly consistent rate of

Gross Profit, expressed as a percentage to turnover? **If less than the usual Gross Profit is earned,** is it because selling prices have declined or because the closing stock is valued at the then market price which is below the original cost?

Should the Gross Profit percentage rise, is the cause to be found in more favourable selling prices, or in an improper inflation of closing stock values?

The following illustration may be helpful:—

Example. At January 1, 1937, T. Peters had a stock of 1,000 articles then valued at £1 per unit. During the year he purchased 10,000 articles at the same average cost. To arrive at his selling price he adds 50% to cost, his Gross Profit thus being 33⅓%. The sales amount to 9,000 articles. Show his Trading Account for the year assuming:—

1. Selling prices were advanced 10%, stock values remaining constant, and
2. Stock values at December 31, 1937, had fallen by 10%, which is to be provided for.

In the first case the Trading Account shows a Gross Profit of 39·4%, as follows:—

DR.	Units.	£		Units.	£ CR.
To Stock, Jan. 1, 1937	1,000	1,000	By Sales (at £1 13*s.* per unit) . .	9,000	14,850
,, Purchases . .	10,000	10,000	,, Stock (at cost, £1 per unit) . .	2,000	2,000
,, Gross Profit (39·4% to Sales) . .		5,850			
	11,000	£16,850		11,000	£16,850

In the second case, the stock provision will appear as a separate expense contra in the Profit and Loss Account:—

DR.	Units.	£		Units.	£ CR.
To Stock, Jan. 1, 1937	1,000	1,000	By Sales (at £1 10*s.* per unit) . .	9,000	13,500
,, Purchases . .	10,000	10,000	,, Stock (at current market price) .	2,000	1,800
,, Gross Profit (33⅓% to Sales) . .	—	4,500	,, P/L A/c contra, Stock Provision.	—	200
	11,000	£15,500		11,000	£15,500

The Profit and Loss Account

This section of the Revenue Account includes, as we have seen, the **indirect** or **"overhead"** expenses of the business.

To a large extent these do not vary in sympathy with the sales or turnover figure, and therefore it is always necessary to watch carefully the individual items, and the total to which they amount.

Broadly speaking, the Profit and Loss Account is concerned with the reconciliation of **Gross** and **Net Profit.** Stated in another way, Gross Profit may be said to consist of (*a*) the indirect expenses and (*b*) Net Profit.

Indirect Expenses

To assist scrutiny, some suitable arrangement of these expenses is most desirable. **Subheadings** may be inserted, such as :—

1. **Production Expenses.**
   Factory Rent, Rates, etc.
   Repairs to Plant.
   Depreciation of Plant, etc.
2. **Selling and Distribution Expenses.**
   Travellers' Salaries and Commission.
   Travelling Expenses.
   Rent of Show Rooms, etc.
3. **General or Administrative Expenses.**
   Office Salaries.
   Bank Interest.
   Depreciation of Office Furniture, etc.

A classification of the Profit and Loss Debits in this way is much more helpful than a mere haphazard listing of the balances on the various Ledger Accounts.

Net Profit

This is of importance because it represents :—

1. The amount which the proprietor may withdraw in the form of cash, **and still leave his Capital intact.**

2. The net yield on the Capital invested, which may conveniently be stated as **a percentage return on that Capital.**

The net earnings of the business can only be ascertained after including all expenses, and all forms of income, as we saw in Chapter 14, and clearly the proprietor will expect to receive something in excess of the rate of interest obtainable from the investment of an equivalent amount of capital in, say, gilt-edged securities. How much more will largely depend on the degree of risk to which his business Capital is exposed in each particular case.

The Balance Sheet

A point constantly to be borne in mind is that the Revenue Account and the Balance Sheet must be read together. Each serves to explain and interpret the other. As an example, if a profit is disclosed at the end of the period, it must be reflected in an increase of the Total Assets. If a loss has been sustained, these Assets will be less at the end of the period than they were at the beginning. Further, when depreciation is charged in the Profit and Loss Account, not only will the profit figure be reduced, but the book value of the Fixed Asset in question will similarly be reduced in the Balance Sheet.

The Balance Sheet is concerned with showing the position of the business **at a particular date.** That position may substantially alter on the day after its preparation, or it may be materially different on the day before it was prepared. The most informative Balance Sheet is that which gives the typical or average state of affairs.

In criticising a Balance Sheet we may well begin with the **Liabilities.**

Who is interested in the business as a provider of Capital? Apart from the liability to the proprietor on Capital Account, there may be amounts due to trade creditors, and to bankers. The latter liabilities rank ahead of the former, and the proprietor must wait until all these claims are met before he can recover any part of his original investment.

The proportion of the Proprietor's Capital to other liabilities should also be noted. If relatively large sums are due to suppliers and others, the position must be further investigated by reference to the total Assets available, and their division between **Fixed,** and **Current or Floating Assets.**

Just as liabilities may be divided as between Fixed or Deferred Liabilities—those in favour of the proprietors, and Current Liabilities—or the claims of creditors, so it is from the Current or Floating Assets that the creditors primarily look for payment.

We have already considered the distinction between Fixed and Current Assets, but as a final illustration, the following introduces other points :—

The Balance Sheet of T., a haulage contractor, at February 29, 1936, is as set out below.

		£	s.	d.			£	s.	d.
T. Capital:					Leasehold Warehouse, Offices, Sheds, etc., at cost, March 1, 1930 .		3,511	0	0
Balance forward	£7,350				Motor Vehicles, Wagons, etc., at cost, *less* Depreciation, March 1, 1935 .	£3,700			
Add Profit for year . .	750				*Less* Depreciation	37			
	8,100						3,663	0	0
Less Drawings .	600	7,500	0	0	Stocks of Fuel, Oil, Waste, etc., as estimated by T.		495	0	0
Trade Creditors .		2,118	0	0	Book Debts, Gross . .		2,606	0	0
Accrued Expenses . .		432	0	0	Insurance prepaid . .		15	0	0
Municipal Bank, Ltd. .		269	0	0	Cash in Hand . .		29	0	0
		£10,319	0	0			£10,319	0	0

You are required :—

(*a*) To comment carefully upon the position disclosed.

(*b*) To draw up a statement showing the amount of the—

(i) Fixed Capital.

(ii) Floating Capital.

(Royal Society of Arts.)

(*a*) **Criticism of Position Disclosed.**

The **Profit** for the year is rather more than 10% on the Capital. Before accepting it, we should look at the **Assets** of the business and the basis of their valuation.

The first item, **Leasehold Warehouse, Office, etc.,** is stated at cost six years ago. No provision for depreciation has been made by reference to the term of the lease.

By contrast, **Motor Vehicles and Wagons** have been depreciated, but in the past year at the rate of 1% only. A proper figure for depreciation would probably be from 15 to 20% of the original cost, *i.e.*, on the straight line method (see page 174).

The **Stocks** are shown " as estimated." Estimates may be of two kinds, good and bad, and information should be sought as to whether the quantities or values, or both, have been estimated, and whether the values are in line with cost or market price, whichever was the lower at the date of the Balance Sheet.

As the Book Debts are described " gross," their full face value has clearly been taken, and there is no provision for Doubtful Debts. The amount is large for a business of this kind, particularly in view of the Bank Overdraft.

It would thus seem that the profit for the year is overstated because of possible over-valuations of the Assets mentioned.

Lastly, there is a pressing need for the collection of the Book Debts to provide moneys out of which to pay the trade creditors and accrued expenses. The extent of this urgency will in part depend on the limit set to the Overdraft facilities.

(*b*) **Statement of Fixed and Floating Capital.**

This may be drawn up as follows :—

Fixed Capital.

	£
1. Leasehold Warehouse, Offices, Shed, etc., at cost March 1, 1930 . . .	3,511
2. Motor Vehicles, Wagons, etc., at cost, less depreciation	3,663
Total Fixed Capital	£7,174

Floating Capital.

3. Stocks of Fuel, Oil, etc., as estimated. .	495
4. Book Debts (gross)	2,606
5. Cash in Hand	29
	£3,130

Deduct—

		£	
6. Trade Creditors	. . .	2,118	
7. Accrued Expenses	. . .	432	
8. Municipal Bank, Ltd.	. .	269	2,819
Total Floating Capital	. . .		311
Fixed Capital, as above	. . .		£7,174
Floating Capital, as above	. . .		311
			£7,485

Represented by—

		£	
9. Capital Account	. . .	7,500	
Deduct—			
10. Insurance prepaid	. . .	15	
			£7,485

The Insurance prepaid cannot strictly be regarded as an Asset. It is merely the allocation of an expense from one Trading period to another.

Tests and Questions

1. A trader's Capital appears on the "liabilities" side of his Balance Sheet. In what sense is it true that the Capital is a liability of the business ?

What would you infer if the trader's Balance Sheet (assumed correctly drawn up) showed his Capital on the "Assets" side ?

(Royal Society of Arts.)

2. Give an example of one of each of the following :—

(*a*) Fixed Asset.
(*b*) Floating Asset.

Explain the difference (if any) in the purposes for which such Assets are held by a trader or manufacturer.

(Royal Society of Arts.)

3. Suppose that you have been newly appointed to an administrative position in a wholesale merchanting business. What data would you call for, and what tests would you apply to this, in order to find out if the general financial position of the business is sound and healthy ? (University of Edinburgh.)

4. The following is an account taken from the Sales Ledger of Herbert Charleston. Explain clearly what information this account gives you.

LEONARD BRYAN.

DR.				CR.		
1934		£		1934		£
Jan. 1.	To Balance	102		Feb. 3.	By Returns	21
Mar. 3.	„ Goods	336		April 4.	„ Cheque	401
					„ Balance carried forward	16
		£438				£438
April 4.	To Balance forward	16		Sept. 22.	By Cheque	164
June 23.	„ Goods	141				
Aug. 3.	„ Interest Charged	7				
		£164				£164
Sept. 26	To Cheque Dishonoured	164		Nov. 18.	By Bad Debts A/c	164
		£164				£164

(Union of Educational Institutions.)

5. Briefly explain the meaning of the items shown in the following Ledger Account.

E. SIMPSON—CAPITAL ACCOUNT.

DR.				CR.		
1932		£		1932		£
June 30.	To Cash Drawings	200		Jan. 1.	By Balance	3,636
Sept. 30.	„ Purchases, Motor car for self	60		June 30.	„ Cash	500
Nov. 30.	„ Balance	5,116		Sept. 30.	„ Freehold Property	1,225
				Nov. 30.	„ A. Graham	15
		£5,376				£5,376

Note.—On November 20, A. Graham, a creditor, for goods supplied had agreed to accept a cash payment of 10*s*. in the £ in full discharge of his account of £30. (University of Birmingham.)

6. Each year a firm calculates the following percentages :—

(*a*) Gross profit per cent. on sales.
(*b*) Net profit per cent. on gross profit.
(*c*) Net profit per cent. on capital.

What information do you think is obtained from these calculations ? (East Midland Educational Union.)

7. From the under-mentioned figures which were extracted from the books of a manufacturer you are asked to prepare an account or statement in a form which will give the proprietor the maximum information as to his trading results, including the percentages of the various items to turnover, and to state what conclusions can be drawn from the figures :—

	Year ended September 30, 1934. £	1935. £
Purchases of Material	5,823	6,494
Wages : Productive	5,064	6,768
„ Non-productive	620	984
Returns Inwards	472	1,903
Discount Received	180	36
Salaries	1,560	1,584
Selling Expenses	1,720	2,784
Discount Allowed	420	492
Works Expenses	3,176	3,456
Office Expenses	370	420
Stock at commencement of year	2,189	2,876
Sales	20,472	25,903

The stock of material at September 30, 1935, was valued at £1,882. (Royal Society of Arts.)

8. The following accounts showing the result of a year's trading, with comparative figures for the preceding year, have been submitted to the proprietor of a manufacturing business, who has forwarded them to you for criticism. Re-arrange the accounts in the form you consider will give the maximum information (showing also the percentages of the various debits on turnover), and state any conclusions which can be drawn from the figures.

Trading and Profit and Loss Accounts.

	Year ended Dec. 31, 1930. £	1931. £		Year ended Dec. 31, 1930. £	1931. £
To Stock	2,105	2,001	By Sales	20,000	18,000
„ Purchases	5,576	5,524	„ Stock	2,001	1,495
„ Wages (Productive)	5,500	5,400			
„ Works Expenses	960	909			
„ Gross Profit c/d	7,860	5,661			
	£22,001	£19,495		£22,001	£19,495
To Rent and Rates	700	720	By Balance b/d	7,860	5,661
„ Wages (Non-productive)	800	990			
„ Salaries	1,808	1,818			
„ Travellers' Commission and Expenses	20	900			
„ Office Expenses	272	270			
„ Bad Debts	200	414			
„ Net Profit	3,160	549			
	£7,860	£5,661		£7,860	£5,661

(Royal Society of Arts.)

9. Criticise, under the appropriate headings, any five of the items of the Balance Sheet of B. M. Downfield. In your opinion, is his financial position satisfactory? Give reasons for your answers.

BALANCE SHEET OF B. M. DOWNFIELD FOR 1935–1936.

Liabilities.	£	*Assets.*		£
Sundry Creditors	12,500	Cash		1,300
Bank	3,200	Bills Receivable		2,680
Capital	1,040	Sundry Debtors		3,200
		Stock		6,860
		Plant	£2,000	
		Add Cost of Repairs	200	
				2,200
		Fittings, Cost Price in 1930		500
	£16,740			£16,740

(Union of Lancashire and Cheshire Institutes.)

10. In the course of your audit of the accounts of a Trading Company the following comparisons are noted :—

	1939. £	1940. £
Sales	40,000	30,000
Stocks, closing	10,000	14,000
Gross Profit	8,000	7,800
General Expenses	2,500	1,800
Selling Expenses	1,000	1,100
Discounts to Customers	400	450
Bad and doubtful debts	200	100
Debtors	10,000	11,000
Trade and Sundry Creditors	5,000	3,000

Comment on the figures set forth above and indicate what, if any, special inquiries you consider the facts necessitate.

CHAPTER XVIII

LIMITED COMPANIES, AND THE COMPANIES ACT, 1948

THE limited company, as an artificial body corporate, owes its existence to registration under the provisions of the Companies Act, 1948, and must be considered apart from changing generations of shareholders. The latter, when subscribing for shares, are able to limit their liability to the nominal or "face" value of the shares taken by them. An applicant for 100 shares of £1 each has, when his offer is accepted by the company, a liability to pay £100 *and no more*, even if the company should in future be unable to meet the claims of its creditors. The creditors have contracted with the company, to which alone they can look for payment.

Thus limited liability has furnished an immense stimulus to the development of business because :—

(*a*) *The company*, unlike the Sole Trader, or Partnership firm, can obtain capital funds from a very large number of persons.

(*b*) *The individual shareholder* can take as many, or as few shares as he desires, and when once he has paid for them is protected from any further liability.

Public and Private Companies

All Companies incorporated under the Companies Act, 1948, are bound by its provisions and comprise two main classes:—

Public Companies and Private Companies.

A Private Company is one which, by its Articles, or Regulations :—

(*a*) Restricts the number of its shareholders (exclusive of employees or ex-employees) to fifty.

(*b*) Restricts the right freely to transfer shares issued by it.

(*c*) Forbids any appeal to the public to subscribe for its shares or debentures.

A broad distinction is that a Public Company is one in which the public are substantially interested as providers of capital, whereas in a Private Company management and proprietorship are often identical, the company having been formed chiefly to obtain the benefit of limited liability rather than the provision of new money.

Restrictions on the transfer of shares in a Private Company may mean that a would-be seller must first offer his shares to an existing shareholder, or accept a price determined in accordance with the Articles, etc.

The Memorandum and Articles of Association

Any seven or more persons, or where the company to be formed will be a Private Company, any two or more persons may form an Incorporated Company by subscribing their names to a Memorandum of Association and otherwise complying with the requirements of the Companies Act.

The Memorandum of Association is, in effect, the Charter of the Company, and must state :—

(*a*) The name of the company, with " Limited " as the last word of the name.

(*b*) The situation of the Registered Office of the company.

(*c*) The objects of the company.

(*d*) That the liability of the members is limited.

(*e*) The amount of the Share Capital with which the company proposes to be registered, and the division thereof into shares of a fixed amount.

No subscriber of the Memorandum may take less than one share.

As regards the Memorandum, note :—

(*a*) The name chosen for the new company must not so closely resemble that of an existing company as to deceive or cause confusion in the mind of the public.

The proposed name may in the first instance be submitted to the Registrar of Companies.

(*b*) The applicants for registration must state the objects which it is proposed to carry out. The company may only act in fulfilment of the objects stated. If the substratum of the business disappears, particularly where the company is a Public Company, it is only right that the directors should not be able to turn unhindered to some quite unrelated form of business with the residue of the funds originally subscribed.

Usually the opportunity is taken to provide for eventualities by adding to the main object a number of others which may be regarded as reasonably incidental to it.

(c) The Capital stated in the Memorandum of Association is variously styled the Registered, Authorised or Nominal Capital, but may be altered from time to time by the company in general meeting.

Articles of Association, or a series of regulations prescribed for the company, may be registered with the Memorandum, but failing this, a model set of articles, known as Table A (and given as an appendix to the Companies Act, 1948), is applicable.

The Articles may be likened to the rules of a club or society, and provide for the general conduct of the company's affairs.

All members of the company are bound by the Articles in force, even if they subsequently acquire their shares by purchase in the market, and were not original subscribers.

The Articles may be altered or added to by passing a special resolution of members in general meeting, a three-fourths majority being required and not less than 21 days' notice of the intention to propose the resolution as a special resolution having been given.

The Articles will concern the following, *inter alia* :—

Shares. Issue, transfer and voting rights.

Directors. Appointment, powers and remuneration.

Meetings. Procedure, and business thereat.

Finance. Preparation and circulation of Accounts, payment of dividends, etc.

Share Capital

Shares, as units of proprietorship, may be generally classified as Ordinary and Preference Shares. The latter carry a fixed rate of dividend and are known as a *e.g.* 6% Preference Share. Preference Shareholders have a priority for this dividend to the extent there are profits available. Ordinary Shares, subject to the placing to reserve of any part of the profits, take what remains, and may earn very large dividends in prosperous years. The Ordinary Shareholders have thus the opportunity of capital appreciation through an increase in market price.

With Cumulative Preference Shares any arrears of dividend are carried forward to the ensuing period.

Redeemable Preference Shares are those which are to be redeemed either out of *profits*, or from the proceeds of a fresh issue of *capital*; otherwise, the shareholder of any class may only realise his investment by sale in the market.

The two latter classes represent variations of the simple Preference Share, and are usually of importance in the case of a Public Company, whose appeal to the investor it is desired to frame in the broadest possible way.

Voting Rights are commonly restricted to the Ordinary Shareholders. Preference Shareholders may enjoy voting rights during any period when their dividend is unpaid.

It must be carefully observed that with both Public and Private Companies the boon of limited liability is only conferred on the understanding that the capital fund of the company is maintained intact.

The capital must not be returned to shareholders in dividend.

Dividends should only be paid out of profits periodically ascertained by preparing accounts, and as recommended by the directors and approved by the members in general meeting.

The Articles may give the directors power to pay *interim* dividends.

Dividends are usually paid according to the amounts from time to time *paid-up* on the Shares.

Debentures

In addition to issuing shares, a company may issue debentures, which are acknowledgments of *loans* made to the company. The debenture-holder, unlike the shareholder, is a *creditor*, with all a creditor's remedies.

Debentures issued by companies incorporated under the Companies Act are usually redeemable at a future date. Meantime the debenture-holder receives interest at a fixed rate per cent. whether or not profits exist out of which to pay it.

A further feature of debentures is that the holders are almost always *secured* creditors. This means that the company pledges or charges some part of its property (*e.g.*, its factory premises) in favour of such creditors specifically, who may, on default by the company, appoint a Receiver (Receiver for debenture-holders), realise the security to the best advantage and repay themselves out of the proceeds.

It will thus be appreciated that an issue of debentures, because of the minimum risk of loss to the holder, enables money to be *borrowed* at a rate of interest relatively low in comparison with the rate of dividend paid on Preference and Ordinary *Shares*.

Books of Account

Statutory Books.

The Companies Act, 1948, requires every company to keep proper books of account to record its :—

(*a*) Cash receipts and payments.
(*b*) Trading purchases and sales.
(*c*) Assets and liabilities.

Proper books of account are such as are necessary to give a true and fair view of the state of the company's affairs and to explain its transactions.

The *Statutory Books* of the company similarly required, chiefly comprise :—

(*a*) The Register of Members.
(*b*) The Register of Charges (*e.g.*, Debentures).
(*c*) The Register of Directors and Managers.
(*d*) Separate Minute Book for meetings of directors, and of shareholders.

The Register of Members is the principal statutory book, in which particulars are to be kept of members, their shareholdings, transfers, etc.

Access to the Register of Charges is clearly a help to an unsecured creditor or other person giving credit to the company, enabling him to see what part of the company's property is already charged.

Accounts and Audit

The directors of both Public and Private Companies must once in each year lay before the company in general meeting a Profit and Loss Account made up to a date not earlier than the date of the meeting by more than nine months.

A Balance Sheet made up to the same date must also

be presented, together with a report of the directors as to their dividend recommendations and the general state of the company's affairs.

The Balance Sheet must contain a Summary of the Authorised and Issued Share Capital of the company, and particulars of the general nature of its Assets and Liabilities. The Companies Act, 1948, in its Eighth Schedule, lays down detailed requirements as to the contents of Balance Sheets and Profit and Loss Accounts.

Every company must at each annual general meeting appoint an Auditor, or Auditors, who must in general belong to a body of accountants recognised by the Board of Trade. The Auditors are to report to the members on the accounts examined by them, and have a right of access at all times to the books, accounts and vouchers of the company.

From the following particulars, prepare a Balance Sheet of Wick, Ltd., at November 30, 1940, grouping the Assets and Liabilities in the form you think most desirable :—

	£
4% Debentures	20,000
Interest due thereon	400
Cash at bank	4,911
Reserve Fund	10,000
Calls in arrear on Ordinary Shares	100
Stock-in-Trade	24,009
Goodwill, at cost	30,000
40,000 5% Preference Shares	40,000
80,000 Ordinary Shares	80,000
Doubtful Debts Provision	500
Contingent Liability on Bills discounted	250
Preliminary Expenses, not written off	600
Sundry Debtors	12,350
Freeholds, at cost	32,750
Creditors	6,562
Profit and Loss Account, December 1, 1939 (Cr.)	5,000
Plant and Machinery, at cost, less depreciation, December 1, 1939	54,600
Reserve Fund Investment	9,800
Debenture Discount, not written off	200
Additions to Plant and Machinery at cost	742
Profit for the year, *less* Dividends on Preference Shares	7,600

Solution to Example No. 1 :—

WICK, LTD.

Balance Sheet as at November 30, 1940.

LIABILITIES.		£	£
(*a*) *Liability to Proprietors :—*			
Share Capital Authorised—			
50,000 5% Preference Shares of £1 .		50,000	
100,000 Ordinary Shares of £1 .		100,000	
			150,000
Share Capital Issued—			
40,000 5% Preference Shares of £1 fully paid		40,000	
80,000 Ordinary Shares of £1 fully paid		80,000	
		120,000	
Less Calls in Arrear . . .		100	
		119,900	
Reserve Fund		10,000	
Profit and Loss Account—	£		
Balance, December 1, 1939	5,000		
Profit for the year to date	9,600		
	14,600		
Less Dividend on Preference Shares .	2,000		
		12,600	
			142,500
(*b*) *Liability to Creditors, etc. :—*			
4% Debentures		20,000	
Interest due thereon		400	
		20,400	
Creditors		6,562	
			26,962
			£169,462

ASSETS.		£	£
(*c*) *Fixed Assets :—*			
Goodwill, at cost		30,000	
Freehold, at cost		32,750	
Plant and Machinery, at cost, less depreciation .	£ 54,600		
Add Additions, at cost.	742		
		55,342	
			118,092
(*d*) *Current Asset :—*			
Stock-in-Trade		24,009	
Sundry Debtors . . .	12,350		
Less Doubtful Debts Provision. . .	500		
		11,850	
Investment on account of Reserve Fund		9,800	
Cash at Bank		4,911	
			50,570
(*e*) *Fictitious Assets :—*			
Preliminary Expenses . . .		600	
Discount on Debentures . . .		200	
			800
			£169,462

Note.—There is a Contingent Liability of £250 in respect of Bills discounted.

The Authorised Capital of the company is 50,000 5% Preference Shares of £1, and 100,000 Ordinary Shares of £1.

Note :—

(*a*) Preliminary Expenses represent those incurred in connection with the formation of the company, stamp duty on the authorised capital, solicitors' and accountants' charges, etc.

(*b*) Discount on Debentures is a concession made by the company to the debenture-holders at the time of issue. The amount of cash received from them was to this extent less than their claim for ultimate repayment, viz. £20,000.

Example No. 2.

The following is the Balance Sheet at June 30, 1940, of Bleak, House & Co. :—

	£	£		£
To Sundry Creditors .		8,440	By Cash . . .	120
,, Bankers . .		18,600	,, Sundry Debtors .	20,780
			,, Stock-in-Trade . .	42,140
To Capital Accounts :				
B. Bleak . .	74,000		By Sundry Fixed Assets .	63,000
H. House . .	29,000		,, Goodwill . . .	4,000
		103,000		
		£130,040		£130,040

The partners shared profits and losses as to three-fifths to B. Bleak and as to two-fifths to H. House.

A Limited Company, Bleak House, Ltd., was formed to acquire the business as from July 1, 1940, the purchase consideration being £106,000. All the Assets and Liabilities were taken over at book values, except as regards the Goodwill and the Sundry Fixed Assets, which last were valued for the purpose of the Sale and Purchase Agreement at £58,000.

In respect of the amount due to him, B. Bleak received 20,000 5% Preference Shares of £1 each in the new company, and the balance in cash.

H. House received the whole of his share in £1 Ordinary Shares, allotted at par, except for £3,200 paid to him in cash.

In addition to the foregoing, 30,000 Preference Shares

Solution to Example No. 2.

BOOKS OF BLEAK HOUSE, LTD.

B. BLEAK AND H. HOUSE—VENDORS.

Dr. | Cr.

Date	Particulars	£	£	Date	Particulars	£	£
1940 July 1	To Sundry Creditors		8,440	1940 July 1	By Sundry Assets :—		
	,, Bankers		18,600		Cash	120	
	,, Balance, c/o		94,000		Sundry Debtors	20,780	
					Stock-in-Trade	42,140	
					Fixed Assets	58,000	
							121,040
			£121,040				£121,040
July 1	To *B. Bleak* :—			July 1	By Balance, c/o		94,000
	5% Preference Shares	20,000			,, Goodwill		12,000
	Cash	55,800					
			75,800				
	To *H. House* :—						
	Ordinary Shares	27,000					
	Cash	3,200					
			30,200				
			£106,000				£106,000

GOODWILL.

Dr. | Cr.

Date	Particulars	£	Date	Particulars	£
1940 July 1	To B. Bleak and H. House	£12,000			

Dr. 5% PREFERENCE SHARES. Cr.

			1940		£
			July 1	By B. Bleak	20,000
			,, 1	,, Applications and Allotments	30,000
					£50,000

Dr. ORDINARY SHARES. Cr.

			1940		£
			July 1	By H. House	27,000
			,, 1	,, Applications and Allotments	60,000
					£87,000

Dr. APPLICATIONS AND ALLOTMENTS. Cr.

1940		Ordinary. £	Preference. £	1940		Ordinary. £	Preference. £
July 1	To Share Capital A/cs	60,000	30,000	July 1	By Cash	66,000	30,000
,, 1	,, Share Premium A/c	6,000	—				
		£66,000	£30,000			£66,000	£30,000

Dr. SHARE PREMIUM ACCOUNT. Cr.

			1940		£
			July 1	By Applications and Allotments	£6,000

CASH BOOK.

Dr.		£	£		Cr.	£
1940 July 1	To B. Bleak and H. House		120	1940 July 1	By B. Bleak and H. House	18,600
" 1	" *Applications and Allotments* :—			" 1	" B. Bleak	55,800
	Ordinary Shares	66,000		" 1	" H. House	3,200
	Preference Shares	30,000		" 1	" Formation Expenses	1,300
			96,000	" 1	" Balance c/o	17,220
			£96,120			£96,120

BLEAK HOUSE, LTD.

COMMENCING BALANCE SHEET.

	£	£		£	£
Share Capital Authorised :—			*Fixed Assets*, at cost :—		
5% Preference Shares of £1	—		Goodwill	12,000	
Ordinary Shares of £1	—	—	Sundry Fixed Assets	58,000	70,000
Share Capital Issued :—			*Current Assets* :—		
50,000 5% Preference Shares of £1, fully paid	50,000		Stock-in-Trade	42,140	
87,000 Ordinary Shares of £1, fully paid	87,000	137,000	Sundry Debtors	20,780	
			Cash at Bank	17,220	80,140
Share Premiums		6,000	*Fictitious Asset* :—		
Creditors		8,440	Formation Expenses		1,300
		£151,440			£151,440

were issued to the public at par for cash, and 60,000 Ordinary Shares at a premium of 2*s.* per share; these issues were subscribed and paid up in full, formation expenses amounting to £1,300.

You are required to record the above in the books of Bleak House, Ltd., and to give the commencing Balance Sheet of the new company.

Note to Student.

	B. Bleak.	*H. House.*
	£	£
Prior to sale the partners' Capitals are	74,000	29,000
They share profits and losses as 3 is to 2.		
They *lose* £9,000 on revaluation of Goodwill, etc. . .	5,400	3,600
	68,600	25,400
The net worth of their business is thus reduced to £94,000.		
But the Purchase Price is £106,000, a *profit* of . .	7,200	4,800
	£75,800	£30,200

Further Exercises

1. A. B. & Co., Ltd., has an authorised Capital of £8,000, divided into 8,000 Ordinary Shares of £1 each. On December 31, 1940, 6,000 shares had been issued and fully paid, and there were also balances on the books of the Company in respect of the following :—

	£
Sales	10,350
Purchases	4,128
Wages	3,084
Stock (January 1, 1940)	746
Salaries	525
Rent	135
Rates	48
Insurance	29
Repairs	37
Debenture Interest, net.	75
Bank Charges	14
Travelling Expenses	197
Sundries	188
Goodwill, at cost	3,000
Patents, at cost	2,506
Plant and Machinery, at cost	1,240
Experimental Account (Asset)	1,777

	£
Trade Debtors	2,316
Trade Creditors	846
Bank Overdraft	187
5% Debenture	2,000
Preliminary Expenses	142
Profit and Loss Account (Liability) at January 1, 1940	804

Stock, as taken on December 31, 1940, amounted to £911, but includes an item of £65 for catalogues, the invoice for which has not yet been passed through the books.

The charges for Carriage Inwards, amounting to £102, have been debited to Sundries Account.

You are requested to prepare a Trading and Profit and Loss Account for the year ended December 31, 1940, providing 5% depreciation on Plant and Machinery, and £84 for Bad Debts. It is also required to provide $2\frac{1}{2}$% for discounts to be allowed to Debtors, ignoring any provision of a similar kind for Creditors.

2. Tompkins, the accountant of Gloria Tubes, Ltd., submits to you the following Revenue Account of the Company for the year ended February 29, 1940 :—

Dr.		£		Cr. £
To Wages		8,200	By Balance of Profit, March 1, 1939	1,250
" Purchases		12,500	" Stock, February 29, 1940	2,350
" Salaries		3,468	" Rates, Prepaid	21
" Commission		2,803	" Sales	27,550
" Rates		105	" Discounts Received	125
" Carriage Inwards		180		
" Repairs and Maintenance		217		
" Stock, March 1, 1939		2,120		
" *Depreciation*—	£			
Plant, 10%	110			
Fixtures, 5%	45			
Lorries, 20%	80			
		235		
" Directors' Fees		105		
" Packing and Carriage		486		
" Insurance		37		
" Debenture Interest		60		
" Bank Interest		22		
" Sundry Expenses		308		
" Profit		450		
		£31,296		£31,296

The authorised capital of the Company is £5,000, in shares of £1 each. Of these, 4,951 have been issued as fully paid to the vendor, who is the managing director, and his wife.

A 6% Debenture for £1,000 is outstanding in favour of the managing director's wife.

£1,452 is owing to suppliers, and £2,500 by customers, in respect of which latter 2% is to be provided. At February 29, 1940, the Company had £817 in the Bank, while at March 1, 1939, the book values of the Fixed Assets were :—

	£
Plant	1,100
Fixtures	900
Lorries	400

Prepare in proper form Trading and Profit and Loss Account for the year ended February 29, 1940, and a Balance Sheet at that date.

3. The authorised capital of the Waterloo Engineering Co., Ltd., is £80,000 in £1 shares. The following Trial Balance was extracted from the Company's books as on March 31, 1940 :—

	Dr. £	Cr. £
Issued Capital (60,000 shares) . .		60,000
Sales		138,980
Land and Buildings	30,000	
Machinery and Plant . . .	29,530	
Sundry Debtors and Creditors . . .	30,059	8,131
Purchases	46,150	
Interim Dividend	3,000	
Delivery Expenses	3,910	
Stock, March 31, 1939 . . .	5,782	
Discounts	1,537	729
Returns Inwards	1,110	
Salaries	2,697	
Travellers' Commission and Expenses	3,740	
Profit and Loss Account, March 31, 1939		2,530
Motor Lorries	3,987	
5% Debentures		20,000
Rent and Rates (Factory £1,650, Office £224)	1,874	
Wages	61,846	
General Expenses	892	
Factory Power and Light . . .	2,839	

	Dr.	Cr.
	£	£
Debenture Interest	500	
General Reserve		6,000
Repairs to Machinery . . .	1,421	
Directors' Fees	300	
Bank Deposit	3,500	
Bank Current Account . . .	1,696	
	£236,370	£236,370

You are required to prepare the Manufacturing Account, Profit and Loss Account and Balance Sheet of the Company after taking into consideration the following matters :—

(*a*) The item "Delivery Expenses" includes £175 in respect of the subsequent trading period.
(*b*) Wages £515 and Directors' Fees £100 are outstanding.
(*c*) No provision has been made for the half-year's Debenture Interest due on March 31, 1940.
(*d*) The Machinery and Plant is to be depreciated at the rate of 10% and the Motor Lorries are to be written down to £3,000.
(*e*) The Bank Pass Book shows on March 31, 1940, a credit of £15 for Interest on Deposit, but this item has not been entered in the Company's books.
(*f*) The General Reserve is to be increased by £2,000.
(*g*) The Stock held on March 31, 1940, was valued at £8,765.

ANSWERS

P. 56. (3) Debit.
do.
Credit.
Debit, if allowed : Credit if received.
Credit.
(5) (*b*) £101 8*s*. 11*d*.
(*c*) Brown is indebted.
P. 57. (6) Balance £1,002 10*s*. 7*d*.
(7) (*b*) Credit Bank. Debit Bank charges.
(*c*) Credit Motor Vans £25.
Debit Loss on Sale A/c £25.
(8) (*a*) Plant A/c. Debit.
(*b*) Robinson's personal A/c. Credit.
Cash £170 and Discount allowed £2 12*s*. 6*d*.
(*c*) Fire Loss A/c. Credit.
(*d*) Motor Van A/c. Credit.
(*e*) Fitter's personal A/c. Debit.
Cash £250 and Discount received £10 15*s*. 0*d*.
P. 75. (4) (*a*) Credit landlord.
Debit rent.
Credit cash.
Debit landlord.
(*b*) Credit cash.
Debit rent.
P. 76. (5) Dr. Bals. Cash £15 15*s*. 6*d*.
Bank £193 12*s*. 7*d*.
Discount. Dr. 18*s*. 7*d*. Cr. £2 6*s*. 6*d*.
(6) Dr. Bals. Cash £46. Bank £582.
Discount. Dr. £6 17*s*. 6*d*. Cr. £2 10*s*. 0*d*.
(7) Cheque payment £354 18*s*. 0*d*.
P. 77. (8) Dr. Bals. Cash £5 11*s*. 2*d*. Bank £24 7*s*. 2*d*.
(9) (*a*) Dr. side. Personal.
Impersonal.
Private.
Cr. side. Impersonal.
Personal.
Personal.
Impersonal.
P. 78. (10) Dr. Bal. Cash £43 15*s*. 11*d*.
Cr. Bal. Bank £222 6*s*. 10*d*.
Discount. Dr. £1 11*s*. 1*d*. Cr. £2 6*s*. 8*d*.
P. 86. (2) Favourable Bal. £65 16*s*. 5*d*.
(*b*) Unfavourable Bal. £233 19*s*. 4*d*.
(3) Favourable Bal. £80 8*s*. 0*d*.
P. 88. (9) Pass book. £914 17*s*. 6*d*.

P. 115. (1) Capital £1,100. Dr. Cash £25.
Cr. Bank £237.
T.B. Totals £2,115.
(2) Capital £5,000. Dr. Cash £10 13*s.* 4*d.*
Dr. Bank £3,142 5*s.* 7*d.*
Cr. Discount £20 4*s.* 0*d.*
T.B. Totals £5,160 19*s.* 6*d.*

P. 116. (3) Capital £1,650. Dr. Cash £40.
Dr. Bank £778 10*s.*
Cr. Discount 10*s.*
T.B. Totals £2,178 10*s.* 8*d.*
(4) Capital £854 2*s.* Dr. Cash £9 16*s.* 6*d.*
Dr. Bank £16 9*s.* 6*d.*
Cr. Discount £3 15*s.* 8*d.*
T.B. Totals £1,088 14*s.* 1*d.*

P. 117. (5) Capital £602. Dr. Cash £12 14*s.* 4*d.*
Cr. Bank £123 11*s.* 0*d.*
Dr. Discounts £5 14*s.* 7*d.*
T.B. Totals £1,116 7*s.* 2*d.*

P. 118. (6) Capital £1,000. Dr. Cash £13.
Dr. Bank £1,310 1*s.* 8*d.*
Cr. Discounts 19*s.* 2*d.*
T.B. Totals £1,664 17*s.* 5*d.*

P. 119. (7) Capital £1,184 7*s.* 4*d.* Dr. Cash £2 6*s.* 8*d.*
Dr. Bank £66 19*s.* 2*d.*
Cr. Discounts £5 10*s.* 3*d.*
T.B. Totals £1,320 16*s.* 3*d.*
(8) Capital £550. Dr. Cash £6 9*s.* 3*d.*
Dr. Bank £406 16*s.* 8*d.*
Cr. Discounts £3 18*s.* 0*d.*
T.B. Totals £669 7*s.* 2*d.*

P. 120. (9) Capital £2,250. Dr. Cash £10 10*s.* 1*d.*
Dr. Bank £214 5*s.* 3*d.*
Cr. Discounts 7*s.* 3*d.*
T.B. Totals £2,373 13*s.* 3*d.*

P. 127. T.B. Totals £165.

P. 130. (5) Short Credit £103 2*s.* 0*d.*
(6) Profit £3,500. Liabilities £2,000.
(7) (*b*) T.B. Totals £4,247.

P. 131. (8) (*a*) Short Dr. £12 5*s.* 0*d.*
(*b*) Short Dr. £5 7*s.* 6*d.*
(*c*) None.
(*d*) Short Dr. 10*s.*
(*e*) Short Cr. £4.
(9) (*c*) T.B. Totals £46,146 12*s.* 1*d.*

P. 132. (10) T.B. Totals £39,546.
(11) T.B. Totals £5,952.

P. 133. (12) (1) Originally short Dr. £122 7*s.* 6*d.*

P. 145. (6) (*b*) Closing stock £320.
(7) Claim £3,703.

P. 146. (8) (*b*) £9 3*s.* 4*d.*
(9) Net Profit. Dept. A £72.
B £710.
C £226.
Dr. P/L A/c £8 Bal.

P. 154. (1) (*a*) Short Dr. £100 : None : Short Debit £30.
(*b*) Debtors understated £100: Fixtures understated £12. Profit understated £12 : Bank balance understated £30.
(3) Pass Book Bal. £36 overdrawn.
(4) Bal. Sheet Totals £3,350.

P. 155. (6) T.B. Totals £853 12*s*. 5*d*.
Gross Profit £31. Net Loss £57 13*s*. 4*d*.
Bal. Sheet Totals £689 15*s*. 8*d*.
(7) Capital £2,041 4*s*. 10*d*.
Gross Profit £210 5*s*. 7*d*. Net Profit £197 18*s*. 7*d*.
Bal. Sheet Totals £2,424 5*s*. 6*d*.

P. 156. (8) Gross Profit £870. Net Profit £525.
Bal. Sheet Totals £1,275.

P. 157. (9) Gross Profit £1,155. Net Profit £110.
Bal. Sheet Totals £5,820.
(10) Gross Profit £108. Net Loss £1,769.
Bal. Sheet Totals £2,557.

P. 158. (11) Gross Profit £10,250 ($33\frac{1}{3}$%).
Net Profit £1,000 ($3\frac{1}{4}$%).
Bal. Sheet Totals £13,269.

P. 159. (12) Gross Profit £4,349. Net Profit £2,586.
Bal. Sheet Totals £8,205.
(13) £986 less £20 depreciation : £966.

P. 160. (14) Profit £125. Bal. Sheet Totals £3,499.

P. 161. (15) Gross Profit £1,261. Net Profit £426.
Bal. Sheet Totals £4,018.

P. 168. (3) Profits 1932 £517. 1933 £638.
(4) P/L Debit £2,941.
(5) P/L Debit £220.

P. 169. (6) P/L Debit £67 15*s*.
(7) Bad Debts £14 1*s*. 10*d*. Reserve £19 16*s*. 10*d*.
(9) P/L Dr. 1934 £1,551 8*s*. 3*d*.
1935 £1,734 7*s*. 7*d*.
Omission overstates 1934 Profits and understates Liabilities £41 3*s*. 7*d*.
(10) P/L Dr. Rent £360. Rates £153 7*s*. 4*d*.

P. 170. (11) P/L Dr. Rates £180. Wages £7,134.
Stationery, etc. £747.
Bad Debts and Reserve £409.
Discounts £107 10*s*. 10*d*.
(12) P/L Dr. £90.
(13) P/L Dr. £248. Prepayments, etc. £17
Accrued expenses £12.

P. 171. (14) Profit £1,627.
Bal. Sheet Totals £3,663.

P. 178. (4) P/L Dr. 1932 £12.
1933 £11.
1934 £11.
1935 £103.
1936 £88.
(5) P/L Dr. £1,500 p.a.
(6) Depreciation (nearest £) £3,432.
Profit on sale £9.

(7) Depreciation (nearest £) £2,602.
Loss on sale £214.

(8) Depreciation £100 p.a.
Interest 1935 £82 10*s*. 0*d*.
1936 £55.
1937 £27 10*s*. 0*d*.

P. 179. (9) Depreciation (opening Bals.): 1934 £120.
1935 £110 10*s*. 0*d*.

(10) Gross Profit £4,450. Net Profit £1,920.
Bal. Sheet Totals £11,695.

(11) Gross Profit £3,220. Net Profit £130.
Bal. Sheet Totals £6,015.

P. 180. (12) Gross Profit £5,545. Net Profit £900.
12½% on Capital.
Bal. Sheet Totals £7,836 10*s*. 0*d*.

P. 190. (4) Interest on Capital £150.
Profit Shares £1,175.

(5) (*a*) Interest on Capital £50.
Profit Shares £1,475.
(*b*) Salary £500.
Interest on Capital £50.
Profit Shares £1,225.

(6) (*a*) A. £2,437 10*s*. 0*d*. B. £812 10*s*. 0*d*.
(*b*) A. £2,587 10*s*. 0*d*. B. £862 10*s*. 0*d*.

P. 191. (7) X. £3,376. Y. £2,532. Z. £2,000.

(8) (*a*) A. £1,800. B. £800.
(*b*) A. £1,900. B. £700.

(9) Profit Shares:
Bright £1,080. Smart £720.

(10) A. Profit £370. Interest £145.
B. Salary £85. Profit £370.
Interest £95.
C. Profit £80. Interest £25.

P. 192. (11) Gross Profit £5,000. Net Profit £2,845.
Bal. Sheet Totals £12,445.

P. 193. (12) Gross Profit £4,800. Net Profit £3,250.
Bal. Sheet Totals £4,282.

(13) Gross Profit £4,099 11*s*. 2*d*.
Net Profit (before Interest) £988 7*s*. 0*d*.
Plant A/c £6,300. Insurance A/c £99 15*s*. 0*d*.
Bad Debts Reserve £281.
Commission A/c £398 18*s*. 1*d*.

P. 194. (14) Manufacturing A/c £39,561.
Gross Profit £4,265.
Net Profit (before Interest) £2,189.
Bal. Sheet Totals £21,029.

P. 218. (1) Gross Profit £3,136. Net Profit £1,763 4*s*. 0*d*.
Bal. Sheet Totals £11,690 4*s*. 0*d*.

P. 219. (2) Gross Profit £6,900. Net Loss £850.
Bal. Sheet Totals £7,803.

P. 220. (3) Gross Profit.
(Manufacturing A/c) £23,479
Net Profit £9,011.
Bal. Sheet Totals £103,787.

EXAMINATION PAPERS

ROYAL SOCIETY OF ARTS

STAGE I—ELEMENTARY

July 1953

[TWO AND A HALF HOURS ALLOWED.]

All questions are to be attempted.

1. John Doe is about to open a retail tobacconist's shop. All his sales will be for cash, but he expects to purchase supplies on monthly credit terms from wholesalers and manufacturers.

You are asked to write John Doe a brief note telling him what financial books he should keep, explaining the purpose of each and the kind of transaction it should be used to record.

2. Copy the form below on the two-column paper provided in your answer book, and complete it by inserting the figures from the information which follows and calculating the percentages asked for.

Sylvia & Co., Booksellers.	*Year ended March* 31, 1952. £	*Year ended March* 31, 1953. £
Sales for year		
Stock at commencement of year .		
Add Purchases (*less* returns) .		
Less Stock at end of year . .		
Cost of Sales		
Gross Profit for year . . .		
Gross Profit : percentage of Sales .	%	%
Gross Profit : percentage of Cost of Sales	%	%

Year ended March 31, 1952

	£
Stock April 1, 1951 . .	3,000
Purchases . . .	8,000
Returns outwards . .	500
Sales	9,750
Stock March 31, 1952 .	4,000

Year ended March 31, 1953	£
Purchases . . .	12,100
Returns outwards . .	800
Sales	11,600
Stock March 31, 1953 .	6,600

3. Nathan Grimes is a wholesale outfitter and divides his business into four departments : Suits, Shirts, Overcoats, and Sundries.

(*a*) Draft a suitable columnar sales day book for use in Grimes' business and record in it the following sales on credit :

Jan. 1. To N. Taylor, 6 Overcoats at £8 5*s*. 0*d*. each, *less* 10% Trade Discount.

„ 2. To T. Baker, one dozen Shirts at 12*s*. 11*d*. each.

„ 3. To B. Black, 8 Sports Suits, at £13 10*s*. 0*d*. each.

„ 4. To N. Taylor, 4 dozen assorted Ties at 25*s*. per dozen, 6 dozen Studs at 50*s*. per gross and 6 Shirts at 15*s*. each, the whole *less* 10% Trade Discount.

(*b*) Explain how the book-keeping process of double entry is completed in respect of the above transactions.

(Do not post the items to ledger accounts.)

4. Tom, Dick, and Bob go for a week's cycling and camping holiday. Bob is a student of book-keeping, and it is agreed that he should act as " book-keeper and treasurer " for the holiday and that all expenses should be shared equally (except the cost of bicycle repairs, which are to be charged to the owner of the bicycle concerned). At the commencement of the trip, Tom and Dick each advance £3 to Bob towards their share of the cost of the holiday.

From the information which follows, copied from Bob's diary, prepare a summarized statement showing the total cost of the holiday, how much it cost each person, and how much, at the end, Tom and Dick each owed Bob or were entitled to receive from him. What was the average cost of food per day ?

		£	*s.*	*d.*
1st Day.	Train Fares		15	0
	Food		17	9
	Beds at Hostel—4*s*. each			
2nd Day.	Food	1	0	6
3rd Day.	Food	1	3	6
	Visit to Pictures		4	6
4th Day.	Food		19	8
	Bicycle Repairs (Tom)		7	4
5th Day.	Food	1	4	4
	Bicycle Repairs (Tom)		5	0
	„ „ (Bob)		3	6
6th Day.	Food	1	4	6
	Beds at Hostel—4*s*. 6*d*. each			
7th Day.	Food		15	0
	Train Fares		18	6

During the holiday the boys earned 12*s.* 6*d.* for harvesting, and 15*s.* for fruit picking; this money was paid to Bob as Treasurer.

5. The following is the Balance Sheet of A. Smith :—

Balance Sheet, December 31, 1951.

	£		£
A. Smith : Capital .	2,000	Fixtures and Fittings (at cost) .	1,000
		Stock (at cost)	800
		Cash at Bank	200
	£2,000		£2,000

During the year 1952 :—

(*a*) A. Smith borrowed £500 for the business from L. Brown, which he had not repaid on December 31, 1952.

(*b*) Stock at December 31, 1952, at cost, was £1,200.

(*c*) On December 31, 1952, A. Smith owed to Trade Creditors £200 for goods supplied to the business.

(*d*) On December 31, 1952, he purchased a machine for the business for £300, paying for it from the business bank account.

(*e*) A. Smith's Net Profit for 1952 was £500 and his drawings £250.

All his receipts were banked and all his payments were made by cheque.

You are asked to prepare A. Smith's Balance Sheet on December 31, 1952.

6. A and B are in business sharing profits and losses equally. After their final accounts for the year ended April 30, 1953, had been prepared in draft form (without the books being closed) the following errors were discovered :—

(*a*) Stock at April 30, 1953, included 32 shades at 15*s.* each, which had been wrongly entered on the stock sheets as 320 shades at 15*s.* each.

(*b*) A motor van used in the business, which was purchased during the financial year for £200 had been charged to Motor Expenses, when in fact it should have been entered in an asset account and depreciated by £40 at the end of the year.

(*c*) At January 1, 1953, premises had been acquired at a rental of £75 per quarter payable in advance, the rent for the first quarter being paid on January 1, 1953. The rent for the quarter to June 30 was paid on April 1, but no adjustment had been made in preparing the draft final accounts at April 30, 1953, for the unexpired rent.

(i) What effect will the correction of the above errors have on the Net Profit of £450 shown by the draft Profit and Loss Account, and what will be the corrected net profit ?

(ii) Show the Motor Van Account and the Rent Account as they will appear when the corrections shown above have been made.

May 1953

[TWO AND A HALF HOURS ALLOWED.]

Questions 1 *and* 2 *must be answered first. The remaining questions may then be answered in any order*

1. The following is the Balance Sheet of E. Kent as at December 31, 1952.

Balance Sheet

	£	£		£	£
Creditors		2,640	Cash		80
Salaries owing		60	Bank		620
Capital (December 31, 1951)	5,000		Debtors	1,400	
Add Net Profit	500		*Less* Provision for Bad and Doubtful Debts	100	
	5,500				1,300
Less Drawings	700		Stock		2,000
		4,800	Land and Buildings		3,000
			Goodwill		500
		£7,500			£7,500

(*a*) What is the total of Kent's current assets?

(*b*) What is the total of his fixed assets?

(*c*) If he had valued his stock at £2,200 what would his net profit have been?

(*d*) Was Kent solvent or insolvent at December 31, 1952? Give your reasons.

(*e*) What would have been the effect on the Balance Sheet of writing £50 off Goodwill?

(*f*) Was Kent overtrading in the year 1952? Give reasons for your answer.

2. W. Barker and L. Harrison are in business as wholesalers, sharing profits and losses in the ratio of their capitals. On December 31, 1952, the following Trial Balance was extracted from their books:

	Dr. £	Cr. £
Stock (January 1, 1952)	3,056	
Purchases and Sales	28,000	33,600
Returns Inwards and Outwards	242	424
Wages	1,112	
Carriage Inwards	624	
Carriage Outwards	780	
Discount Received		265
Rates and Taxes	241	

	Dr.	Cr.
	£	£
Bad Debts	100	
Salaries	1,946	
Advertising	482	
Insurance	89	
Sundry Trade Expenses	278	
Cash in hand	15	
Bank Overdraft		1,240
Loan—S. Gibbons		3,000
Debtors and Creditors	2,500	2,306
Plant and Machinery, at cost	2,000	
Land and Buildings	5,000	
Goodwill	500	
Current Accounts: W. Barker	—	—
L. Harrison	20	
Drawings: W. Barker	500	
L. Harrison	350	
Capital Accounts: W. Barker		4,000
L. Harrison		3,000
	£47,835	£47,835

From the above information prepare the partners' Trading and Profit and Loss Accounts for the year ended December 31, 1952, and the Balance Sheet on the closing date, taking into account the following :—

(*a*) Stock at December 31, 1952, was valued at £3,710.

(*b*) Make a Provision for Bad and Doubtful Debts of 5% of the Debtors.

(*c*) Provide for £56 Interest owing on the loan.

3. (*a*) From the following details prepare the Petty Cash Book of M. Stocks to show in columnar form the expenses of Office Expenses and Salaries.

May	1.	Balance in hands of the petty cashier, £1 17*s*. 6*d*.
„	1.	The balance is made up to £15.
„	4.	Paid Office Expenses, £2 19*s*. 6*d*.
„	6.	Paid Office Expenses, £1 4*s*. 7*d*.
„	8.	Paid Salaries, £3 10*s*. 0*d*.
„	12.	Paid Office Expenses, 12*s*. 6*d*.
„	16.	Paid Salaries, £3 15*s*. 0*d*.

(*b*) Give the postings that should be made before a trial balance, dated May 16, is prepared.

(*c*) How would you deal with the balance of unexpended petty cash at May 16 ?

4. (*a*) Show by means of journal entries how the following would be recorded or, if necessary, corrected, in the books of S. Shepherd, a wholesaler.

1952

Oct. 1. Omission of 12½% trade discount on sales of £120 to G. Thomas.

Nov. 1. Sale on credit for £140 to E. Wilson of furniture which had cost Shepherd £120.

Dec. 31. Transfer of Discount Received, £80, to the Profit and Loss Account.

„ 31. Shepherd wrote off a debt of £25 owing by B. Lewis.

(*b*) By how much would the net profit of Shepherd for the year ending December 31, 1952, be increased or decreased as a result of posting the above entries?

5. Distinguish between capital and revenue income and expenditure in relation to a firm which builds and lets out on hire holiday cruisers and yachts.

6. (*a*) On January 1, 1950, a trader purchased a machine for £1,000 and decided to depreciate it at the end of each year by 10% of its original value. Show the Machinery Account for the two years ending December 31, 1952.

(*b*) Show the entry made in the trader's balance sheet dated December 31, 1952, in respect of this asset.

March 1953

[TWO AND A HALF HOURS ALLOWED.]

Questions 1 *and* 2 *must be answered first. The remaining questions may then be answered in any order you like.*

1. (*a*) What is an Income and Expenditure Account, and how does it differ from a Trading and Profit and Loss Account?

(*b*) From the following information, prepare the Income and Expenditure Account of the Opal Social Club for the year ended March 31, 1953:—

Membership: 224 full members each paid £1 10*s*. 0*d*. subscription and 48 junior members each paid 15*s*.
Income from dances, £146—dance expenses, £122.
Income from whist drives, £83—whist drive expenses, £23.
Rent of Hall, £50.
Lighting and Heating, £42.
Secretarial and other expenses, £39.
The Club owned fixtures and furniture valued at £300, and in respect of these the Income and Expenditure Account is to be charged with 15% as depreciation.

2. L. Brown is in business as a wholesaler and on February 1, 1953, his financial position was :—

	£	s.	d.
Assets			
Fixtures and Fittings	395	0	0
Trade Debtor : R. Reed	156	0	0
Stock	672	1	8
Petty Cash	7	10	0
Liabilities			
Trade Creditors : W. Whiting	87	0	0
B. Black	197	3	6
Bank Overdraft	146	8	2

Open by journal entry the accounts necessary to record the above in L. Brown's books and post through proper subsidiary books the following transactions :—

Note : A Petty Cash Book with two analysis columns, (1) Wages, (2) Sundry Expenses, is to be employed to record cash payments. Cash and cheques received are banked on day of receipt.

1953

Feb. 1. R. Reed paid the amount due from him, less 5% Cash Discount, and was supplied with goods invoiced at £108, less 10% Trade Discount.

„ 2. Drew and cashed cheque for petty cash, £15.
Paid from Petty Cash—Wages, £9 10*s*. 0*d*., and Expenses, £2 6*s*. 3*d*.

„ 3. Paid Rent, £62 10*s*. 0*d*. (by cheque).
Received cheque, £350, as loan from L. Light.
Bought from H. Wills, on credit, counter for shop for £85, paying (by cheque) £15 on account.

„ 4. Received for Cash Sales, £96.
Sold goods on credit to A. Bridge, £63.

„ 5. Purchased on credit from B. Black for £43 goods for re-sale.

„ 6. Paid to W. Whiting by cheque the amount due to him on February 1, less 2½% Cash Discount.
Paid to B. Black, £97 3*s*. 6*d*. on account (by cheque).

„ 9. Paid from Petty Cash—Wages, £7 18*s*. 6*d*., and Expenses, £1 2*s*. 1*d*.

„ 11. R. Reed paid for goods sold to him on February 1, less £5 4*s*. 0*d*., agreed allowance for faulty goods, and 5% Cash Discount.

Balance the Cash Book, Petty Cash Book and Personal Ledger Accounts, bringing down the balances, and extract a Trial Balance as on February 11, 1953.

Note : No Trading Account, Profit and Loss Account or Balance Sheet is to be prepared.

3. The following account appears in the books of a wholesale merchant :—

Bad Debts

		£			£
1953.			1952.		
Mar. 31.	To Transfer from Sales Ledger, being Bad Debts written off .	168	April 1.	By Balance brought forward, Provision for Bad and Doubtful Debts . . .	325
„ 31.	„ Balance carried forward, Provision for Bad and Doubtful Debts . . .	450	June 30.	„ Cash . . .	16
			1953. Mar. 31.	„ Profit and Loss Account . . .	277
		£618			£618

(*a*) Explain the nature of this account and the transactions recorded by the entries in it.

(*b*) If the Provision for Bad Debts on March 31, 1953, was equal to 5% of the total debts outstanding, what was the latter figure ?

4. A is the owner of a business and the following is his Trading Account for the year 1951 :—

Trading Account for the Year ended December 31, 1951

	£		£
To Stock at Cost—Jan. 1, 1951 .	500	By Sales for the year . . .	4,000
„ Purchases for the year . .	2,900	„ Stock at Cost—Dec. 31, 1951 .	600
„ Gross Profit . . .	1,200		
	£4,600		£4,600

From January 1, 1952, A. employs a new manager, and at the end of the year it is found—

(*a*) that the sales for 1952 were one and a half times those for the previous year ;

(*b*) that the rate of Gross Profit on sales was 10% better (on sales) in 1952 than in 1951 ;

(*c*) that the Stock on December 31, 1952, valued at cost, was one-third more than it was on December 31, 1951.

You are asked to prepare the Trading Account of the business for 1952.

5. (*a*) What do you understand by the expression " Working Capital " ?

(*b*) From the following state A.B.'s working capital on January 1, 1952.

A.B.

Balance Sheet, January 1, 1952

	£		£
A.B. Capital Account . . .	2,350	Fixed Assets	1,500
Sundry Trade Creditors . .	550	Stock in Trade	800
		Trade Debtors	250
		Cash at Bank	350
	£2,900		£2,900

(*c*) If during 1952 A.B. purchased and paid for, from the business bank account, additional fixed assets for the business for £250, and raised £500 for the business by a mortgage, what would be the effect of these transactions on his working capital?

6. From the information below prepare the account of B. Wagstaff as it would appear in the books of the Quilter Co. for the month of March 1953.

1953			£
March	1.	Balance due from Wagstaff	80
,,	5.	Wagstaff purchased 20 dozen saws at £30 a gross (*less* 20% trade discount) and was charged £2 10*s*. 0*d*. for case and packing.	
,,	9.	Wagstaff returned the case and was credited with £1 10*s*. 0*d*.	
,,	15.	Wagstaff paid cheque to settle balance due on March 1, deducting 5% cash discount according to terms.	
,,	25.	The Quilter Co. purchased on credit from Wagstaff a second-hand machine for £50.	

Balance the account on March 31, 1953, and state whether the Quilter Co. is due to pay or receive the balance.

November 1952

[TWO AND A HALF HOURS ALLOWED.]

1. (*a*) Distinguish between Fixed Assets and Current Assets.

(*b*) Give *one* example of a current asset and *two* examples of fixed assets that you would expect to find in each of the balance sheets of a wholesale grocery concern and a garage.

2. Show by means of journal entries how the following would be recorded or, if necessary, corrected, in the books of F. Waller, a retailer.

1952.

Aug. 1. A loan of £200 made by cheque to his brother, George Waller.

Sept. 1. 15% Trade Discount on credit purchases of £180 from Wholesalers, Ltd., was not deducted in the Purchase Day Book.

Oct. 1. Goods valued at £120 sold on credit to T. Allen had been debited to T. Allman.

Nov. 1. The transfer to the Trading Account for the year ending June 30, 1952, of stock in hand at July 1, 1951, valued at £2,500.

3. From the following details prepare :—

(*a*) the current accounts of Albert and William Howard, who share profits in the ratio of three-fifths to two-fifths.

(*b*) the appropriation section of their Profit and Loss Account.

	Albert.	*William.*
	£	£
Capital Account balances, December 31, 1950	6,000	4,000
Current Account balances, December 31, 1950	240 (*Cr.*)	100 (*Dr.*)
Drawings during 1951 . . .	700	500
Additional fixed capital brought in during 1951	—	1,000
Salaries for the year 1951 . .	200	150

Interest on capital should be credited to the partners at 5% per annum, calculated on the opening balances.

The divisible profit for the year ending December 31, 1951, *after* allowing for salaries and interest on capital accounts, was £600.

Exercise I

M. and L. Lucas are in business as wholesalers, sharing profits and losses five-ninths to four-ninths respectively. On June 30, 1951, the following Trial Balance was extracted from their books.

	Dr.	Cr.
	£	£
Stock in hand (July 1, 1950)	8,928	
Purchases and Credit Sales.	19,000	28,000
Cash Sales		1,200
Returns Inwards and Outwards	343	303
Wages	2,495	
Carriage Inwards	111	
Carriage Outwards	191	
Rates and Taxes	528	
Discounts Received		107
Rent Received		520
Commissions Received		72

	Dr.	Cr.
	£	£
Salaries	1,825	
Sundry trade expenses	247	
Depreciation—Motor Vehicles	150	
Insurance	86	
Bad Debts	124	
Cash in hand	182	
Bank	700	
Debtors and Creditors	2,242	1,827
Current Accounts: M. Lucas		126
L. Lucas		26
Drawings: M. Lucas	805	
L. Lucas	874	
Capital Accounts: M. Lucas		10,000
L. Lucas		8,000
Land and Buildings	7,500	
Machinery	6,500	
Motor Vehicles *less* depreciation	1,350	
Loan		1,000
Mortgage		3,000
	£54,181	£54,181

On June 30, 1951, the stock was valued at £6,526.

Note: Two-thirds of the Rates and Taxes should be charged to the Trading Account.

You are required from the above information to prepare Trading and Profit and Loss Accounts for the year ending June 30, 1951, and a Balance Sheet on the closing date.

Exercise II

On October 1, 1952, the assets of C. Curry, a trader, were: Sundry Debtors: S. Stead £47 7*s*. 6*d*.; T. R. Brooker £31 10*s*. 0*d*.; Stock £500; Bank £86 12*s*. 6*d*.; Premises £1,000 and Furniture and Fittings £175 0*s*. 0*d*. His liabilities were: Sundry Creditors: L. Richards £42 0*s*. 0*d*. and D. Hart £98 10*s*. 0*d*.

Open by journal entry the accounts necessary to record the above position in C. Curry's books, and post thereto, using the proper subsidiary books, the following transactions:—

Note: A Petty Cash Book with analysis columns for (1) Salaries, and (2) Office Expenses, is to be used for recording payments in cash. All cheques received are paid to bank on the day of receipt and no "cash" column is, therefore, required in the main cash book.

1952

Oct. 1. Drew and cashed a cheque for £15 for petty cash expenses.
Received a cheque from T. R. Brooker for the amount due from him, less 5% cash discount.

1952

Oct. 2. Accepted Fittings, valued at £45, from S. Stead in full settlement of his debt.

„ 3. Paid by cash: Salaries £5 10*s.* 0*d.* and office expenses £1 18*s.* 9*d.* Received from R. Tennant a cheque for £35 for rent in respect of part of the premises sub-let to him.

„ 7. Paid Hart by cheque the amount due to him less 5% cash discount. Cash sales £76 12*s.* 9*d.* banked.

„ 9. Purchased from T. R. Brooker on credit goods invoiced at £104 less 12½% trade discount.

„ 10. Paid by cash: Salaries £5 10*s.* 0*d.* Sold to F. Walters certain fittings in exchange for cheque, £20.

„ 14. Purchased from W. Woodhouse on credit goods invoiced at £160 less 15% trade discount and from R. Richards goods valued at £8 net.

„ 16. Paid by cash: Office expenses £1 13*s.* 3*d.* Drew and cashed a cheque to restore the petty cash balance to £15.

„ 21. Returned to W. Woodhouse goods invoiced at £16 and sent him on account a cheque for £75. Banked cash sales £45 7*s.* 3*d.*

„ 24. Drew a cheque for £200 in favour of Builders, Ltd., for extensions to premises, and arranged for the bank to meet it.

Balance the Cash Book and the Petty Cash Book, and personal ledger accounts, bringing down the balances, and extract a Trial Balance as on October 24, 1952.

Note: No Trading Account, Profit and Loss Account or Balance Sheet is to be prepared.

July 1952

[TWO AND A HALF HOURS ALLOWED.]

1. The following is a list of balances extracted from the books of T. Bisk on March 31, 1952. You are asked to arrange them in a Trial Balance:

	£
Capital (T. Bisk)	650
Discount Received	28
Freehold Shop Premises	2,500
Loan from K. Rusk	150
Purchases	1,200
Rates and Insurance	247
Salaries	836
Sales	2,950
Stock	621
Bank Overdraft	1,626

2. Explain the difference between "Cash Discount" and "Trade Discount," and state how each should be recorded in the books of a trader. Can both discounts be secured in respect of the same transaction?

3. Give journal entries to correct the errors noted below, which have been made in the books of P. Tapp, a wholesaler :—

(*a*) Mar. 16, 1952. A cheque for £16 10*s.* 0*d.* paid to L. Green had been posted to purchases instead of to his personal account.

(*b*) Apr. 10, 1952. J. Rudd had sent a cheque for £10, which had been credited to his personal account, in respect of a debt due from him which P. Tapp had previously written off as a bad debt.

(*c*) June 16, 1952. £500 paid for an extension to the warehouse had been charged to Repairs Account.

4. L. Proudie, a trader, had in stock on March 1, 1952, 4,000 articles valued at 2*s.* 6*d.* each. During March he purchased a further 8,000 costing 3*s.* 0*d.* each, but was given an allowance of 2*s.* 0*d.* each on 500 of these, as they arrived in a damaged condition. His sales during the month were 7,000 articles at 5*s.* 0*d.* each, and 340 of the damaged articles at 2*s.* 0*d.* each. Undamaged articles in stock at March 31, 1952, were valued at 3*s.* 0*d.* each, and the damaged articles at 9*d.* each.

Show L. Proudie's Trading Account for the month of March 1952.

Exercise I

The following Trial Balance for March 31, 1952, was extracted from the books of D. and N. Sowerby, who are in business as wholesalers, sharing profits $\frac{3}{5}$ths and $\frac{2}{5}$ths. From the information given, you are asked to submit the final section of the Profit and Loss Account for the year ended March 31, 1952, showing the distribution of the net profit, the partners' Current Accounts for the year and the firm's Balance Sheet on the closing date.

	Dr. £	Cr. £
Capital Accounts : D. Sowerby . . .		2,000
N. Sowerby . . .		2,500
Current Accounts as on April 1, 1951 :		
D. Sowerby . . .		800
N. Sowerby . . .	150	
Drawings Accounts : D. Sowerby	750	
N. Sowerby	550	
Profit and Loss Account for the year ended March 31, 1952		2,800
Loan Account—D. Sowerby		500

	Dr.	Cr.
	£	£
Motor Cars (at cost less depreciation) . .	825	
Debtors and Creditors	2,760	1,026
Stock, March 31, 1952	3,100	
Fixtures and Furniture (at cost less depreciation)	1,225	
Cash at Bank	250	
Cash in Hand	16	
	£9,626	£9,626

Note : In preparing these accounts interest is to be provided as follows :—

		£
On Capital :	D. Sowerby	100
	N. Sowerby	125
On Loan Account :	D. Sowerby . . .	20

Exercise II

On February 1, 1952, J. Overend went into business as a retailer. You are asked to record the following transactions in the proper subsidiary books, posting them to the necessary ledger accounts.

Note : A petty cash book having two analysis columns—(1) Wages, (2) Sundry Expenses—is to be used for recording payments in cash. Cheques and cash received are banked on the day of receipt, and no " cash " column is therefore required in the main cash book.

1952

Feb. 1. J. Overend paid to the business bank account a personal cheque for £500 as his capital; he also brought in a motor van, value £300, for the use of the business.

Received by cheque a loan of £250 from L. Tubbs.

Paid, by cheque, rent £20.

Drew and cashed cheque for £25 for petty cash imprest.

Purchased on credit from N. Fish goods valued at £120, less 10% trade discount.

" 2. Bought furniture for use in the business from L. Brown, invoice price £65, paying £20 on account, balance due on March 31.

Paid from Petty Cash, Wages £5, Sundry Expenses £1 18*s*. 0*d*.

" 4. Purchased on credit from T. Crabbe goods for £60.

Received for shop sales £30.

" 5. Sold goods on credit to K. Smith for £19 and to Y. Netherby £26.

Purchased a job lot of goods for £120, paying for them by cheque.

1952

Feb. 6. Returned to N. Fish one fourth of the goods purchased from him and sent cheque for balance due, less 5% cash discount.

„ 7. K. Smith sent cheque in payment of his account, deducting $2\frac{1}{2}$% cash discount.

„ 8. It was agreed this day that L. Tubbs should become a partner in the business; the amount received from him on February 1 to be transferred to his capital account. L. Tubbs also contributed, as part of his capital, goods (stock) costing £150 for future sale by the firm.

„ 9. Paid from Petty Cash, Wages £5 10*s.* 0*d.*, Sundry Expenses £4 6*s.* 0*d.*
Received for shop sales £35.
Paid by cheque to O. Ormerod £75 for shop furniture.

„ 11. Purchased on credit from L. Bodkin goods invoiced at £25.

„ 12. N. Fish wrote that he was unable to allow the cash discount from the payment of 6th as it was contrary to terms, and that the amount deducted was being carried forward as outstanding.
Received for shop sales £42.

„ 13. Drew and cashed cheque for petty cash purposes to restore imprest.

Balance the Cash Book, Petty Cash Book and Personal Ledger Accounts, bring down balances, and extract a Trial Balance as on February 13, 1952.

Note : No Trading Account, Profit and Loss Account or Balance Sheet is to be prepared.

May 1952

[TWO AND A HALF HOURS ALLOWED.]

1. For what purposes is stocktaking carried out periodically and on what bases may the stock be valued?

2. Show by means of journal entries how the following would be recorded or, if necessary, corrected in the books of L. J. Silver :—

(*a*) Jan. 1. £75 paid to S. Sinding, a creditor, but debited to B. Britling.

(*b*) Feb. 1. 10% trade discount on credit sales of £85 to D. Debtor was not deducted in the Sales Day Book.

(*c*) Mar. 1. The sale on credit to Preston, Ltd. of some of Silver's fixed equipment valued at £300.

3. (*a*) State how *each* of the following errors, made during the year ending December 31, 1951, would affect the Net Profit of M. Martyn for that period :—

(i) Stock at January 1, 1951, under-valued by £176.

(ii) Interest on Martyn's bank deposit, £28, debited to his Profit and Loss Account.

(iii) The omission of credit purchases of £180 from the Purchase Day Book.

(iv) Discounts Received, £370, debited to Profit and Loss Account.

(v) A loan of £1,000 made to Martyn during 1951 was credited to his Profit and Loss Account.

(*b*) If the incorrect Net Profit obtained after committing these errors was £2,000, calculate what the correct amount should be.

Exercise I

A. Henson carries on business as a wholesaler. On December 31, 1951, the following Trial Balance was extracted from his books :—

Trial Balance, December 31, 1951

	£	£
Capital (January 1, 1951)		12,500
Mortgage on Property		1,200
Drawings	3,400	
Debtors and Creditors	2,961	2,650
Stock (January 1, 1951)	3,535	
Purchases and Sales	13,500	21,000
Returns Inwards and Outwards	439	362
Wages : Warehousemen	2,000	
Carriage Inward	777	
Discounts Allowed and Received	414	260
Rent Received		130
Office Salaries	898	
Mortgage Interest	60	
Advertising	306	
Bad Debts	117	
General Expenses	595	
Depreciation of Buildings	100	
Cash in hand	85	
Bank balance	315	
Motor Vans	700	
Land and Buildings *less* depreciation	6,900	
Goodwill	1,000	
	£38,102	£38,102

On December 31, 1951, the value of Stock in hand was estimated at £3,939.

You are required to prepare Trading and Profit and Loss Accounts for the year ending December 31, 1951, and a Balance Sheet as on that date.

Exercise II

On January 1, 1952, the assets of R. Read were: Cash in hand, £12 14*s.* 6*d.*; Cash at Bank, £297 5*s.* 6*d.*; Stock at cost, £1,250; Fittings, £202 10*s.* 0*d.*; and L. Howard owed him £37 10*s.* 0*d.* His sole liability was a debt to E. Edwards of £100.

Open by journal entry, the necessary accounts to record the above in Read's books and post thereto, using the proper subsidiary books the following transactions:

1952

Jan. 1. The premises occupied by Read were flooded and stock costing £250 was rendered valueless. He claimed on his insurance company. Read withdrew £20 from the bank for office use.

„ 3. Purchased on credit goods from E. Edwards £180 and from R. Ray £190, both subject to 10% trade discount.

„ 5. Paid Salaries by cash, £8. Paid by cheque, Rent £20.

„ 8. Paid Edwards by cheque the amount owing at January 1, *less* 5% discount and returned him goods invoiced at £10. Withdrew £10 cash for private expenses.

„ 12. Cash Sales of £42 15*s.* 6*d.*, of which £35 was banked. Paid Ray by cheque, £51. Edwards stated that only £4 of the discount deducted on the 8th could be allowed.

„ 19. Agreed to accept Fittings from L. Howard in full settlement of his debt at January 1 and sold him goods on credit £48, subject to 12½% trade discount.

„ 22. Agreed to lend his brother, W. H. Read, £100. Cheque despatched.

„ 31. Received a cheque £225 from the insurance company in settlement of the claim made on January 1.

Balance the Personal Accounts and Three-column Cash Book, bring down the balances, and extract a Trial Balance as on January 31, 1952.

Note: No Trading Account, Profit and Loss Account or Balance Sheet is to be prepared.

March 1952

[TWO AND A HALF HOURS ALLOWED.]

1. The Profit and Loss Account of A.B. shows a net profit of £507 for the year ended December 31, 1951, but after its preparation the following errors are discovered:—

(*a*) £65 paid in June 1951, for repairs had been charged to Plant and Machinery Account instead of Repairs Account.

(*b*) Stock at December 31, 1951, was under-valued by £80.

(*c*) Rent was paid quarterly in advance on January 1, April 1, July 1, and October 1, 1952, at the rate of £200 per annum. The rent for the quarter commencing January 1, 1952, was paid on December 31, 1951, and included in error in the charge for 1951.

(*d*) An allowance of £20 to a customer for goods returned by him was entered in the Returns Inwards Book, but credited to Purchases Account instead of to the customer.

You are asked to state the effect of each of the above errors on the computed net profit for 1951 and give the corrected net profit for that year.

2. State briefly what is meant by the following terms in connection with book-keeping :—

(*a*) Credit Balance.

(*b*) Subsidiary Book.

(*c*) Nominal Account.

(*d*) Drawings Account.

3. Jones is in business as a printer and stationer, and the following information relates to the year 1951 :—

(*a*) He pays rent at £80 per annum at the end of each quarter on March 31, June 30, September 30, and December 31.

(*b*) Rates were paid on January 1, 1951, £135 6*s*. 0*d*., and July 1, 1951, £142 3*s*. 0*d*.

(*c*) Jones sub-lets one room to a tenant for a rent of £45 per annum, which was received on December 31, 1951, in respect of the year ended on that date.

From the above information prepare Jones' Rent and Rates Account for the year ended December 31, 1951, and close it off on that date, one-third of the balance being charged to Profit and Loss Account and the remainder to Trading Account.

In which of Jones' ledgers would you expect to find the account ?

Exercise I

P. and B. Hill are in business as wholesalers sharing profits and losses equally and on March 31, 1951, the following Trial Balance was extracted from their books :—

Trial Balance, March 31, 1951

		Dr.	Cr.
		£	£
Capital Accounts (April 1, 1950) :	P. Hill .		3,200
	B. Hill .		3,000
Current Accounts (April 1, 1950) :	P. Hill .		350
	B. Hill .	130	

Trial Balance, March 31, 1951 (contd.).

	Dr. £	Cr. £
Stock (April 1, 1950)	1,862	
Purchases and Sales	8,537	13,326
Carriage and Distribution Expenses .	647	
Returns Inwards	563	
Depreciation—Furniture and Equipment .	215	
Salaries	750	
Lighting and Heating	318	
Furniture and Equipment	2,165	
Bad Debts	18	
Discounts Allowed and Received . .	483	95
Rent, Rates, and Insurance . . .	976	
Debtors and Creditors	2,389	1,067
Motor Vehicles	1,320	
Cash in Hand	51	
Bank Overdraft		186
Drawings : P. Hill	320	
B. Hill	480	
	£21,224	£21,224

On March 31, 1951, the stock was valued at £2,364.

You are required from the above information to prepare Trading and Profit and Loss Accounts for the year ended March 31, 1951, and a Balance Sheet on the closing date.

Exercise II

On February 1, 1952, the position of T. Brown, a trader, was as follows: Sundry Debtors: M. Malloy, £26 10*s.* 0*d.*; B. Sape, £41 7*s.* 10*d.* Sundry Creditors: D. Dawe, £31 6*s.* 5*d.*; L. Horner, £101. Stock, £473 15*s.* 0*d.*; Furniture and Fittings, £575; Bank Overdraft, £347 10*s.* 6*d.*

Open by Journal entry the accounts necessary to record the above position in T. Brown's books, and post thereto, using the proper subsidiary books, the following transactions :—

Note : A Petty Cash Book with analysis columns for (1) Wages, and (2) Office Expenses, is to be used for recording payments in cash. All cheques received are paid to bank on the day of receipt, and no "cash" column is therefore required in the main cash book.

1952

Feb. 1. Drew and cashed cheque for £25 petty cash.

„ 2. Received cheque from M. Malloy for the amount due from him, less 5% cash discount.

„ 3. Purchased from D. Dawe on credit goods invoiced at £80, less 15% trade discount.

1952

Feb. 4. Paid L. Horner a cheque for £101 in settlement of his account.

„ 5. Sold to M. Malloy on credit goods invoiced at £35. Paid from petty cash wages, £7 10*s.* 0*d.*—office expenses, £1 19*s.* 0*d.*

„ 6. L. Horner wrote stating that the payment made on February 4, should have been less 5% for cash discount and that he was crediting T. Brown's account with this amount.

„ 7. Sold to J. Ruffle on credit goods invoiced at £121 6*s.* 10*d.* Received from M. Maude, who became a partner from this day, £500 as Capital.

„ 8. Agreed to allow B. Sape £2 10*s.* 0*d.* in respect of faulty goods delivered to him last month and received his cheque for the remainder of the balance due from him.

„ 9. Paid from petty cash, offices expenses, £1 2*s.* 5*d.* Sold to B. Bax various second-hand fittings and furniture from the office in exchange for cheque, £15.

„ 12. Paid from petty cash, wages £7 18*s.* 9*d.*; office expenses, £2 1*s.* 0*d.*

„ 13. Purchased from T. Tucker goods invoiced at £83 2*s.* 7*d.*

„ 14. Sent to T. Tucker a cheque for £50 on account.

„ 15. Paid cheque for £8 2*s.* 9*d.* in respect of electricity, and drew and cashed cheque to restore petty cash balance to £25.

Balance the Cash Book and Petty Cash Book, and Personal Ledger Accounts, bringing down the balances, and extract a Trial Balance as on February 15, 1952.

Note: No Trading Account, Profit and Loss Account or Balance Sheet is to be prepared.

November 1951

[TWO AND A HALF HOURS ALLOWED.]

1. Give Journal entries in the books of R. Redgrove for the following items:—

(*a*) Redgrove received and banked a cheque for £50 from S. Miles in full settlement of the latter's debt of £60.

(*b*) Redgrove wrote 7½% depreciation off his Machinery which stood in his books at £4,000.

(*c*) An invoice of goods sold on credit to E. Wilson was found to have been overcast by £20.

2. State briefly the purpose of a Bank Reconciliation Statement.

3. Copy out the following, and, in the columns provided, state: (1) the name of the account, and (2) the side of the account to which each of the items would be posted :—

	Name of the Account.	*Dr. or Cr. side.*
(*a*) The total of the Returns Inwards Book		
(*b*) A payment in the Cash Book for a Motor Lorry purchased on credit		
(*c*) A receipt in the Cash Book for goods sold on credit . .		
(*d*) The total of the Discount column on the credit side of the Cash Book . .		

4. From the following details prepare the Trading Account of R. Allen for the year ending June 30, 1951 :

	July 1, 1950.	*June* 30, 1951.
	£	£
Stock	3,643	2,080
Debtors	1,600	1,705
Creditors	2,906	3,104

[Transactions during the year]	£
Cash paid by and discount allowed to debtors	8,815
Cash paid to and discount allowed by creditors	5,002
Bad Debts written off	80
Cash Sales	1,000
Wages	1,237

5. A. Archer and D. Dale are in partnership as warehousemen. Profits and losses are shared: A. Archer three-fourths; D. Dale one-fourth. On December 31, 1950, the following Trial Balance was extracted from their books :—

Trial Balance, December 31, 1950.

	£	£
Capital Accounts (January 1, 1950) :		
A. Archer		8,000
D. Dale		2,000
Current Accounts (January 1, 1950) :		
A. Archer		900
D. Dale	100	
Drawings : A. Archer	500	
D. Dale	400	
Cash in Hand	100	
Cash at Bank	900	

Trial Balance, December 31, 1950 (contd.).

	£	£
Debtors and Creditors	2,904	4,304
Stock (January 1, 1950)	1,895	
Purchases and Sales	16,562	22,045
Returns Inwards and Outwards	290	333
Carriage Inwards	656	
Carriage Outwards	416	
Rates	800	
Insurance	196	
Heating and Lighting	1,204	
Warehouse Wages	2,900	
Office Salaries	433	
Postage, Telephone, etc.	155	
Travelling Expenses	327	
Loan Interest	80	
Discount Received		326
Commission Received		180
Motor Vehicles, *less* Depreciation	700	
Depreciation	70	
Fixtures	600	
Land and Buildings	7,500	
Loan		1,600
	£39,688	£39,688

The stock at December 31, 1950, was valued at £2,700. Three-fourths of the Rates is to be charged to the Trading Account.

You are required to prepare Trading and Profit and Loss Accounts for the year ended December 31, 1950, and a Balance Sheet as at that date.

6. From the following information, write up the three column Cash Book of N. North, indicating against each item the account to which it would be posted in the ledger. Balance the Cash Book at September 25, and bring down the balances. You are NOT required to post the items to the ledger.

1951			£	*s.*	*d.*
Sept.	1.	Cash in Hand	5	10	4
,,	1.	Overdrawn balance at the Bank	97	16	8
,,	3.	Arranged and received a loan of £300 from N. North. Cheque banked	—	—	—
,,	3.	Withdrew cash from bank for office use	20	0	0
,,	4.	Paid to the Petty Cashier	3	2	6
,,	12.	Paid electric light account	10	7	8
,,	13.	Cash sales of 3 dozen articles at 3*s.* 6*d.* each	—	—	—
,,	14.	Paid by cheque, deducting 2½% discount, E. South's account of £45	—	—	—

1951		£	s.	d.
Sept. 15.	Received from W. West, who had deducted 2½% discount, a cheque in settlement of his account of £18. Cheque banked	—	—	—
„ 15.	Paid by cash salaries	8	12	6
„ 17.	Purchased for cash 6 dozen articles at 4*s.* 4*d.* each	—	—	—
„ 22.	Received and banked a cheque from E. East in part payment of his account	42	6	5
„ 24.	Bank notified its charges	3	6	2
„ 25.	N. North became a partner bringing in £500. Cheque banked	—	—	—
„ 25.	Sold Office Furniture, cheque banked	10	10	0

July 1951

[TWO AND A HALF HOURS ALLOWED.]

1. On January 1, 1950, the book value of a firm's stock was £5,000, but on December 31, 1950, after stocktaking it was valued at £4,500. Show the firm's Stock Account recording these facts.

2. Give the journal entries necessary to record or correct the following in the books of J. Dixon, a decorator :—

(*a*) E. Francis, a creditor, stated that £4 which had been deducted as cash discount could not be allowed.

(*b*) Dixon accepted a typewriter, valued £25, from E. Underwood in part payment of a debt.

(*c*) A purchase of equipment, £75, for use in the business had been debited to Purchases Account.

3. Record the following in E. Harding's account in L. Astell's Ledger :—

1950	
Jan. 1.	Balance owing by Harding £53 10*s.* 0*d.*
„ 5.	Harding paid by cheque the amount owing less 2½% cash discount.
„ 6.	Harding was sold goods, catalogue price £75 less 12½% trade discount.
„ 6.	Carriage of £1 5*s.* 0*d.* was charged by Astell.
„ 8.	Harding returned goods, catalogue price £8 16*s.* 0*d.*
„ 11.	Harding paid the amount owing less 2½% cash discount.
„ 16.	The bank returned Harding's cheque dishonoured.

4. For what do the following abbreviations stand: Dr.; %; E. & O.E.; I.O.U.; Div.?

Exercise I

L. Dale carries on business as a retailer. On December 31, 1950, the following Trial Balance was extracted from his books:—

Trial Balance, December 31, 1950

	£	£
Capital (January 1, 1950)		7,500
Drawings	675	
Cash	26	
Bank	210	
Stock (January 1, 1950)	2,400	
Fixtures	343	
Premises	7,000	
Debtors and Creditors	1,001	2,155
Wages	1,296	
Rent		70
Carriage Outwards	172	
Salaries	325	
Loan Interest	80	
Loan		2,000
Advertising	97	
General Expenses	308	
Bad Debts	206	
Discount	174	
Commission	276	
Purchases and Sales	17,139	20,200
Returns Inwards and Outwards	335	276
Carriage Inwards	138	
	£32,201	£32,201

On December 31, 1950, the value of Stock in hand was estimated at £2,300. Two-thirds of the Wages is to be charged to the Trading Account and one-third to the Profit and Loss Account.

You are required to prepare Trading and Profit and Loss Accounts for the year ending December 31, 1950, and a Balance Sheet as on that date.

Exercise II

On January 1, 1951, the assets of D. Baker were: Cash in hand £19 14*s*. 6*d*., Stock £1,426 12*s*. 6*d*. and Furniture and Fittings £150. His liabilities were a Bank Overdraft of £382 17*s*. 0*d*. and £13 10*s*. 0*d*. owing to R. Saunders.

Open by journal entry, the necessary accounts to record the above in Baker's books and post thereto, using the proper subsidiary books, the following transactions :—

1951

Jan. 1. Entered into a partnership agreement with his brother Charles who invested £600 in the business. This sum was banked.

„ 2. Paid Saunders, by cheque, the amount owing to him on January 1 less 5% discount and purchased further goods on credit, valued at £25 10*s.* 0*d.*

„ 2. D. Baker withdrew £5 cash for private expenses.

„ 3. Sold to M. Stanley on credit goods to the value of £164 subject to trade discount of 25%.

„ 4. Bought for cheque, £50 goods from H. Miller.

„ 5. Paid wages in cash £4 12*s.* 6*d.* Paid by cheque, Rent £10. Cash Sales £24 16*s.* 9*d.*

„ 8. M. Stanley paid the amount owing by him less 2½% cash discount. The cheque was banked, together with £30 cash. Bought Stationery £2 18*s.* 9*d.* cash.

„ 8. Sold for £20 cash some of the Furniture.

Balance the Personal Accounts and Three Column Cash Book, bring down the balances and extract a Trial Balance as on January 8, 1951.

Note : No Trading Account, Profit and Loss Account or Balance Sheet is to be prepared.

May 1951

[TWO AND A HALF HOURS ALLOWED.]

1. State, giving briefly the reasons for your answer, whether you consider the following statements to be true or false :—

(*a*) " If the totals of a Trial Balance agree it proves that no errors have been made in the book-keeping."

(*b*) " A debit balance on an account shows that the person whose account it is, owes a debt to the owner of the business."

2. E. Raeburn is in business as a wholesaler. From the following information prepare L. Hexham's account as it would appear in Raeburn's ledger :—

1951

Jan. 1. Balance due from Hexham, £135.

„ 15. Hexham paid £27 and was allowed £3 discount.

„ 20. Hexham sold Raeburn a second-hand motor van for £300 and spare parts for £21.

„ 21. Raeburn sold on credit to Hexham goods invoiced at £45.

1951

Jan. 26. Hexham returned goods and received a credit note for £4.

(*a*) Balance the account, bringing down the balance.

(*b*) State whether Raeburn has to pay or receive the amount of the balance.

3. N. Boffin is a furniture and musical instrument dealer, and divides his business into three departments—(1) furniture, (2) radio, and (3) musical instruments, etc. He purchased for re-sale the following goods on March 1, 1950 :—

From R. Riderhood :	12 Chairs at £1 3*s*. 0*d*. each.
„ T. Harmon :	3 Radio sets at £15 5*s*. 0*d*. each, *less* 10% trade discount.
„ S. Wegg :	One gross of Violin strings at 1*s*. 5*d*. each.

Rule a suitable Purchase Day Book and record therein the foregoing transactions.

Exercise I

A. and B. Wilfer are in partnership as printers and stationers, sharing profits and losses: A. Wilfer $\frac{2}{5}$ths and B. Wilfer $\frac{3}{5}$ths. Having extracted and agreed the Trial Balance at March 31, 1951, the book-keeper prepared the statement shown below. It contains a number of errors, and you are asked : (1) to correct and re-draft the account in a proper form, to show the gross profit and net profit for the year, and the allocation of the net profit to the partners; (2) to show the partners' current accounts for the year ended March 31, 1951.

A. & B. Wilfer

Trading Statement as at March 31, 1951

	£	£		£	£
To Stock March 31, 1951 .		3,600	By Sales for year . .	15,000	
„ Carriage outwards . .	148		*Less* Purchases . .	10,600	
„ „ inwards . .	312				4,400
		460	„ Stock March 31, 1950 .		1,800
„ Returns outwards . .	295		„ Interest on Partners' capital for year :		
Less Returns inwards .	100				
		195	A. Wilfer . .	300	
„ Discount Received . .		325	B. Wilfer . .	250	
„ Printers' Wages . .	750				550
„ Office Salaries . .	225		„ Balance, net profit :		
		975	A. Wilfer . .	516	
„ Rent and Rates . .		350	B. Wilfer . .	774	
„ Office Expenses . .		820			1,290
„ Depreciation—Printing Machinery . . .		215			
„ Drawings : A. Wilfer .	500				
B. Wilfer .	600				
		1,100			
		£8,040			£8,040

Note : The balances on partners' current accounts at March 31, 1950, were : A. Wilfer £350 (credit); B. Wilfer £50 (debit).

EXERCISE II

On January 1, 1951, the position of N. Smith, a trader, was as follows: Cash at Bank £189 12*s.* 6*d.*; Debtors: G. Brown £28 10*s.* 0*d.*, M. Black £127 15*s.* 0*d.*; Creditor: R. Green £118 15*s.* 0*d.*; Stock £376 12*s.* 11*d.*; Furniture and Fittings £750.

Open by journal entry the accounts necessary to record the above position in N. Smith's books and post thereto, using the proper subsidiary books, the following transactions:—

Note: A Petty Cash Book having two analysis columns for (1) Purchases, and (2) Office Expenses, is to be used for recording payments in cash. All cheques received are paid to bank on day of receipt and no " cash " column is therefore required in the main cash book.

1951
Jan. 1. Drew and cashed a cheque for £25 for petty cash.

,, 2. Received cheque from G. Brown for the amount due from him less 5% cash discount.

,, 3. Sold to D. Russell on credit goods invoiced at £120 less 15% trade discount.

,, 4. Paid from Petty Cash: Wages, £8; Purchases, £5 10*s.* 0*d.*

,, 5. D. Russell returned one half of goods invoiced on January 3 as being in excess of order.

,, 6. Purchased on credit from L. Lunn goods for £125.

,, 7. Sold goods on credit to T. Jones for £130.

,, 8. M. Black sent a cheque for amount due from him.

,, 9. D. Russell sent his cheque for amount due from him, less 5% cash discount.

,, 10. Paid Furniture, Ltd., a cheque for £50 for office furniture.

,, 10. Paid rent for quarter to March 25, 1951, £120.

,, 11. Paid from Petty Cash: Wages, £7 15*s.* 0*d.*; Office Expenses, 10*s.* 6*d.*

,, 12. Paid L. Lunn the amount due to him, less 2½% cash discount.

Balance the Cash Book and Petty Cash Book and Personal Ledger accounts, bringing down the balances, and extract a Trial Balance as on January 12, 1951.

Note: No Trading Account, Profit and Loss Account or Balance Sheet is to be prepared.

March 1951

[TWO AND A HALF HOURS ALLOWED.]

1. The following account is in the books of T. Jones :—

K. Brown

DR. 1951.		£	1951.		CR. £
Jan. 15.	To Returns . . .	20	Jan. 1.	By Balance . . .	120
„ 20.	„ Contra Account .	95	„ 10.	„ Goods . . .	340
„ 20.	„ Discount . . .	5			
Feb. 10.	„ Cash . . .	323			
„ 10.	„ Discount . . .	17			
		£460			£460

Explain what is recorded by each entry in this account, from what subsidiary books the postings are made and where the corresponding double entry would be found.

2. A trial balance was extracted from the books of Z. Moloney and failed to balance. The following errors were later found in the books and after their correction the trial balance agreed :—

(1) The Sales Day Book was overcast by £100.

(2) £25 received from P. Peters was entered correctly in the cash book but posted as £52 to the credit of Peters' account.

(3) £10 allowed to a debtor, K. Bennet (for faulty goods sold to him) was included in the Returns Inwards and Allowances Book but debited to Bennet's account.

State the effect of each error on the balancing of the books and the amount of the difference on the trial balance extracted before they were corrected.

3. Show by means of journal entries how the following would be recorded in the books of J. and B. Gold, a partnership :—

(*a*) J. Gold had goods for his personal use from the business costing £38.

(*b*) £80 was paid by T. Smithson, a customer, but credited to T. Smith.

(*c*) The dishonour of a cheque for £22 10*s*. 0*d*. received from a customer; discount amounting to £2 10*s*. 0*d*. had been allowed on the receipt of the cheque.

Exercise I

L. Lionel is in business as a wholesaler. From the following trial balance prepare his trading and profit and loss account for the year ended December 31, 1950, with a balance sheet on the closing date.

Trial Balance, December 31, 1950

	£	£
Capital Account (January 1, 1950) . .		5,000
Drawings during year	950	
Freehold Land and Buildings—Cost . .	2,650	
Stock, January 1, 1950	2,789	
Returns Inwards	576	
Purchases and Sales	18,647	29,276
Fixtures and Fittings (cost *less* depreciation December 31, 1949)	1,300	
Discount allowed and received . . .	307	181
Interest on Bank Deposit		19
Wages—Warehousemen	1,800	
Insurance	176	
Rates and Water	580	
Office Salaries	2,165	
Office Cleaning and Expenses . . .	1,278	
Sundry Debtors and Creditors . . .	2,675	3,712
Cash at Bank : Current Account . .	795	
Deposit Account . .	1,500	
	£38,188	£38,188

Depreciation of 10% is to be written off the fixtures and fittings. Stock at December 31, 1950, was valued at £1,522.

Exercise II

G. Gibbons carries on business as a retail music dealer. On January 1, 1951, his assets were: Shop Fixtures and Fittings £1,000 12*s.* 3*d.*; Trade Debtors—T. Wright £180, P. Wing £75; Stock £955 11*s.* 6*d.*; Petty Cash in hand £1 8*s.* 6*d.* His liabilities were: Trade Creditors—Music Supply Co. £91, Trumpet Stores £150; Bank Overdraft (on current account) £28 6*s.* 9*d.*

Open the accounts necessary to record the above position and post through the proper subsidiary books the following transactions :—

Note : A Petty Cash Book is to be used for recording payments in cash, with analysis columns for (1) Wages, (2) Purchases, and (3) Office Expenses. All amounts received are paid to bank and no "cash" column is therefore required in the main cash book.

1951

Jan. 1. Received cheque from T. Wright for the amount owing, less 2½% cash discount.

„ 2. Drew and cashed cheque for £25 for petty cash purposes. Shop sales, £28 3*s.* 9*d.*

„ 3. Sold to P. Wing on credit: three tenor trombones at £50 each, less 10% trade discount, and a parcel of sheet music for £5.

1951

Jan. 4. Received from P. Wing, £100 on account.

„ 5. Paid from petty cash: wages £5 10*s.* 0*d.*, purchases £8 16*s.* 0*d.*, shop cleaning £1 8*s.* 0*d.*, and office teas £1 7*s.* 6*d.* Shop sales, £107 14*s.* 7*d.*

„ 8. Sold to B. Roberts, on credit: two saxophones for £65.

„ 12. Paid from petty cash: £5 15*s.* 0*d.* wages, and £1 7*s.* 0*d.* travelling expenses.

„ 19. Received from A. Arne a loan of £500.

„ 20. Bought on credit from Music Supply Co., goods invoiced at £120.

„ 21. Returned to Music Supply Co., goods invoiced at £8 10*s.* 0*d.*, and sent cheque for the balance less 5% cash discount. Shop sales, £97 4*s.* 6*d.*

„ 21. Purchased from Fittings, Ltd., a new display table for the shop, £140 7*s.* 7*d.* (paid by cheque).

Balance the Cash Book, Petty Cash Book and Personal Ledger Accounts, bringing down the balances, and extract a Trial Balance as on January 21, 1951.

Note: No Trading Account, Profit and Loss Account or Balance Sheet is to be prepared.

November 1950

[TWO AND A HALF HOURS ALLOWED.]

1. Give Journal entries for the following items :—

(*a*) The correction of a credit of £60, made to the personal account of E. Kemp instead of to E. Kempster.

(*b*) A lorry stood in the books of C. Phillips at £190. It was taken by Garage Ltd. at an agreed value of £150, in part exchange for a new lorry valued at £650.

(*c*) The sale of goods to L. Bates valued at £88 8*s.* 0*d.*, but subject to a trade discount of $12\frac{1}{2}$%.

2. Record the following facts in the personal accounts of A. and B. Moore, two partners, who share profits and losses in the ratio of 5 to 3; and allow interest on capital at the rate of 4% per annum. No interest is to be allowed on current accounts or charged on drawings. B. Moore is to be credited with a salary of £300 for the year.

		A. Moore.	*B. Moore.*
		£	£
Jan. 1.	Capital accounts . .	4,000	3,000
June 30.	Additional capital brought in and banked . .	1,000	—
Jan. 1.	Current accounts . .	72 (*Dr.*)	100 (*Cr.*)
,, 1.—Dec. 31.	Drawings . .	650	650

The partnership's total divisible profit for the year, after charging the salary, was £1,188.

3. State precisely what you would do if the trial balance extracted from a set of books did not agree.

4. W. Milton and M. Wordsworth are in partnership as manufacturers. Profits and losses are shared: W. Milton, $\frac{3}{5}$ths; M. Wordsworth, $\frac{2}{5}$ths. On December 31, 1949, the following Trial Balance was extracted from their books:—

Trial Balance, December 31, 1949.

	£	£
Capital Accounts (January 1, 1949):		
W. Milton		10,000
M. Wordsworth		7,500
Current Accounts (January 1, 1949):		
W. Milton		230
M. Wordsworth	100	
Stock (January 1, 1949)	1,246	
Wages	3,000	
Power	744	
Carriage Inwards	232	
Purchases and Sales	11,046	20,000
Carriage Outwards	170	
Returns Inwards	232	
Depreciation	200	
Debtors and Creditors	3,520	1,876
Salaries	1,700	
Lighting and Heating	241	
Patents	180	
Insurance	216	
Bad Debts	73	
Discounts Allowed and Received	195	295
Drawings: W. Milton	1,700	
M. Wordsworth	950	
Cash in Hand	95	
Cash at Bank	1,261	
Machinery	6,000	
Land and Buildings	6,800	
	£39,901	£39,901

The stock at December 31, 1949, was valued at £1,500. You are required to prepare Trading and Profit and Loss Accounts for the year ended December 31, 1949, and a Balance Sheet as at that date.

5. How would each of the following affect—

(*a*) The net profit of a business for the year 1949.

(*b*) The assets as given in the firm's Balance Sheet dated December 31, 1949.

1. Over valuation of stock at December 31, 1949.
2. An amount debited to a nominal account instead of a real account.
3. An amount credited to a debtor instead of to the account of a creditor.

6. At January 1, 1950, a firm's stock of a product was 3,600 units, which were valued at 10*s*. each. During the first six months of the year 7,000 additional units were purchased at 12*s*. each, but 150 of these were returned to the makers and retained by them. Carriage inwards and other expenses amounted to 2*s*. 6*d*. per unit bought. By June 30, 8,200 units had been sold at 16*s*. each, but 200 were returned, and a further 150 were rendered valueless. It was decided to value the stock on hand at June 30, 1950, at 12*s*. 6*d*. each. Prepare a Trading Account for the above period and insert columns to show the number of units handled.

ROYAL SOCIETY OF ARTS

BOOK-KEEPING—ELEMENTARY

July 1953

THE COMPLETELY WORKED PAPER

1. John Doe, Esq.

Dear Sir,

In reply to your inquiry I have pleasure in suggesting that the following financial books may be kept in connection with your new business :—

(1) As all your sales will be for cash, it will be convenient to have a separate Cash Sales Book into which the total of each day's takings can be entered. This total may be analysed in separate columns to any extent you wish, *e.g.* sales of tobacco, cigars, smoker's requisites, etc.

If you bank the proceeds weekly, or two or three times a week, the total so paid to bank should be ruled off at that point in the Cash Sales Book, and debited in the " Bank " column in your main Cash Book.

In the " Bank " column on the credit side of the latter you will enter cheques drawn in payment of suppliers' monthly accounts, as well as payments of rent and rates, insurance, heat, light, etc.

(2) Smaller and more frequent outgoings in cash should be recorded in a Petty Cash Book kept on the imprest system, and I understand that these payments will be made by you or under your supervision. The imprest system involves the maintenance of a fixed cash float, reimbursed from time to time to the extent of the actual expenditure, and it has the advantage of being always represented by cash or a record of expenses paid, for some of which it should be possible to obtain receipts, *e.g.*, carters' receipted bills.

(3) If you can possibly accept the suggestion, it is better to bank cash sales intact without any deduction for the purpose of paying suppliers or meeting your own private drawings.

(4) A Purchase Day Book, with total and analysis columns, must be kept to record the details of suppliers' invoices once these have been checked for price, quantity, etc.

It will probably be sufficient to rule this off at monthly

intervals, posting the monthly totals to the debit of the "Tobacco Purchases" or "Requisites Bought" accounts in your ledger.

But in order to ascertain how you stand in relation to each supplier, you must post the individual invoice totals to the credit of a personal account with him either in that ledger or—if the number of suppliers is large—in a separate Bought Ledger.

(5) I understand that you have opened a business bank account by paying in from your private resources the sum of £1,000, and have duly debited this in your main cash book, in the "Bank" column.

This amount represents your commencing capital, and you must record the fact in a Capital Account in the ledger by posting the £1,000 to the credit thereof.

(6) To complete the double-entry, the various expense payments I have referred to at the end of (1) above should be debited in correspondingly headed ledger accounts.

Thus, in the ledger you will have the material to enable a complete statement of your business's position to be prepared assuming the records are written up to date, and subject to information being available as regards your stock from time to time on hand.

As the business grows it will certainly be advisable to subdivide the ledger, keeping one section for personal accounts with suppliers, another for sales and expenses and a third for private and capital items, including shop fittings, etc.

Please let me know if I can give you any further help.

Yours very truly,

2.

Sylvia & Co., Booksellers.	*Year ended March* 31, 1952.	*Year ended March* 31, 1953.
	£	£
Sales for year	9,750	11,600
Stock at commencement of year	3,000	4,000
Add Purchases (less returns)	7,500	11,300
	10,500	15,300
Less Stock at end of year	4,000	6,600
Cost of Sales	6,500	8,700
Gross Profit for year	3,250	2,900
Gross Profit: percentage of Sales	$33\frac{1}{3}$	25
Gross Profit: percentage of Cost of Sales	50	$33\frac{1}{3}$

3. (*a*)

Sales Day Book

Date.	Name.	Details.		S.L. Fo.	Total.	Suits.	Shirts.	Overcoats.	Sundries.
			£ s. d.		£ s. d.	£ s. d.	£ s. d.	£ s. d.	£ s. d.
Jan. 1	N. Taylor	6 Overcoats at £8 5*s*.	49 10 0						
		Less 10%	4 19 0						
					44 11 0			44 11 0	
" 2	T. Baker	12 Shirts at 12*s*. 11*d*.			7 15 0		7 15 0		
" 3	B. Black	8 Suits at £13 10*s*.			108 0 0	108 0 0			
" 4	N. Taylor	48 Ties at 25*s*. dozen	5 0 0						
		72 Studs at 50*s*. gross	1 5 0						
		6 Shirts at 15*s*.	4 10 0				4 1 0		5 12 6
			10 15 0						
		Less 10%	1 1 6						
					9 13 6				
					£169 19 6	£108 0 0	£11 16 0	£44 11 0	£5 12 6

(*b*) Weekly the sales made to the various customers named above will be debited to their accounts in the Sales ledger, *e.g.* £9 13*s* 6*d*. to N. Taylor.

(*c*) Monthly the totals of the sales analysis columns will be posted to the credit of the relative accounts in the Nominal (or Impersonal) ledger.

4.

	s. d.	£ s. d.
Train fares		1 13 6
Food		7 5 3
Beds at hostel		1 5 6
Sundries :		
Bicycle repairs	15 10	
Cinema	4 6	
		1 0 4
		£11 4 7
Less receipts :		
Harvesting	12 6	
Fruit-picking	15 0	
		1 7 6
Total cost of holiday		£9 17 1

	Tom. £ s. d.	*Dick.* £ s. d.	*Bob.* £ s. d.
Bicycle repairs	12 4		3 6
One-third share of £9 1*s.* 3*d.*, *i.e.* £9 17*s.* 1*d.* less 15*s.* 10*d.*	3 0 5	3 0 5	3 0 5
	3 12 9	3 0 5	3 3 11
Less Advanced . .	3 0 0	3 0 0	
Owing to Bob . .	12 9	5	

Average cost of food per day, £1 0*s.* 9*d.*

5. A. Smith

Balance Sheet, December 31, 1952

	£	£		£	£
Capital	2,000		Fixtures and Fittings at Jan. 1, 1952 . .	1,000	
Add Profit . . .	500		*Add* Addition . .	300	
	2,500				1,300
Less Drawn . . .	250		Stock at Cost . . .		1,200
		2,250	Balance at Bank . .		450
Loan from L. Brown .		500			
Trade Creditors . .		200			
		£2,950			£2,950

6. (i) (*a*) Profit overstated by £216.

(*b*) Profit understated by £160.

(*c*) Profit understated by £50.

On balance, therefore, profit is overstated by £6, and the corrected figure is £444.

(ii) *Motor Van*

	£		£
Transfer from Motor Expenses A/c .	200	Profit and Loss A/c—Depreciation .	40
		Balance c/d	160
	£200		£200

Rent

1953.		£	1953.		£
Jan. 1.	Cash	75	April 30.	Profit and Loss A/c .	100
April 1.	Cash	75		Balance c/d . . .	50
		£150			£150

INDEX

Account, Appropriation, 144
,, Current, 135
,, Drawings, 135
,, Final, 137
,, Impersonal, 36
,, Ledger, 32, 196
,, Personal, 32
,, Profit and Loss, 141, 199
,, Revenue, 137
,, Trading, 137, 197
Accounts, Company, 211, 212
Adjustments, 162
Agreement, Bank, 80
Articles of Association, 208, 209
,, of Partnership, 183
Asset, 15
,, Fixed, 15, 173
,, Floating, 15
,, Intangible, 185
,, Liquid, 59
,, Tangible, 185
Auditor, 212
Authorised Capital, 209

Bad Debts, 163
,, ,, Reserve, 163
Balance Sheet, 147, 148, 200
Balance, Trial, 114, 122
Bank Commission, 82
,, Interest, 82
,, Pass Book, 79
,, Reconciliation, 80
Book-keeping, 9
"Break-up" Values, 172

Capital, 14, 15, 16
,, Interest on, 184
,, Partners', 184
,, Purchases, 39
,, Sales, 43
,, Working, 59
Cash, 59
,, Book, 19, 68
,, Discount, 60
,, Journal, 19
,, Paid Journal, 65
,, Petty, 89
Cash Received Journal, 61
Commission, Bank, 82
Compensating Error, 123
Credit, 33
,, Note, 22, 28, 34
Cumulative Preference Shares, 210
Current Account, 135

Debentures, 210, 211
Debit, 33
Debit and Credit Journal, 95, 144
Debit Note, 28
Debtors, 13
Deed of Partnership, 183
Depreciation, 172
Diminishing Balance Method, 176
Discount, Allowed, 72
,, Cash, 60
,, Received, 72
,, Trade, 20, 60
Dividends, 210
Double Entry, 10–12
Drawings Account, 135
,, Partnership, 184

Error, Compensating, 123
,, of Omission, 122
,, of Principle, 123

Final Accounts, 137
First Entry, 12
Fixed Asset, 15, 59, 173
,, Instalment Method, 174
Floating Asset, 15, 59
Four-Column Trial Balance, 128

"Going Concern" Values, 172
Goodwill, 185
Gross Profit, 137, 138, 198

Impersonal Accounts, 36
,, Ledger, 40, 45
Imprest System, 92
Intangible Asset, 185
Interest, Bank, 82
,, on Capital, 184

Journal, 17
,, Cash, 19
,, Cash Paid, 65
,, Cash Received, 61
,, Debit and Credit, 95, 144
,, Purchase, 19
,, Purchase Returns, 23
,, Sales, 19
,, Sales Returns, 23

Ledger, 9, 32
,, Accounts, 32
,, Impersonal, 40, 45
,, Nominal (*see* Impersonal).
,, Private, 40, 45
,, Purchase, 40
,, Sales, 40, 56
Liability, 16
Limited Companies, 207
,, Liability, 207
Liquid Asset, 59
Lodgment, Bank, 79
Loss, 134

Manufactured Goods, 13
Memorandum of Association, 208, 209
Merchanted Goods, 13

Narration, 95, 96
Net Profit, 199
Nominal Capital, 209
,, Ledger (*see* Impersonal).

Omission, Error of, 122
Ordinary Shares, 209, 210

Partnership, 182
,, Act, 183
,, at Will, 183
,, Capital, 184
,, Deed, 183
,, Drawings, 184
Pass Book, Bank, 79
Personal Accounts, 32
Petty Cash, 89
Postage Book, 93
Preference Shares, 209, 210
Prime Entry, 12
Principle, Error of, 123
Private Companies, 207, 208
,, Ledger, 40, 45
Profit, 134
,, Gross, 137, 138, 198
Profit and Loss Account, 141, 199
Public Companies, 207, 208
Purchase, Capital, 39
,, Invoice, 31
,, Journal, 19
,, Ledger, 40
,, Returns Journal, 23, 24

Receiver for Debenture-holders, 211
Reconciliation, Bank, 80
Redeemable Preference Shares, 210
Reducing Instalment Method, 176
Register of Charges, 211
,, of Members, 211
Registered Capital, 209
Reserve for Bad Debts, 163
Revenue Account, 137

Sales, Capital, 43
,, Journal, 19
,, Ledger, 40, 56
,, Returns Journal, 23, 35
Shares, 209
Sole Trader, 182
Special Resolution, 209
Stamp Book, 93
Statutory Books, 211
Stock-in-Trade, 13, 135, 138, 139
Straight Line Method, 174
Subsidiary Books, 11

Table A, 209
Tangible Asset, 185
Trade Discount, 20, 60
Trading Account, 137, 197
Trial Balance, 114, 122
,, ,, Four Column, 128

Values, "Break Up," 172
,, "Going Concern," 172
Voting Rights, 210

Will, Partnership at, 183
Working Capital, 59

ADVERTISING & PUBLICITY ALGEBRA AMATEUR ACTING ANA
BOOK-KEEPING BRICKWORK BRINGING UP CHILDREN BUSINE
CHESS CHINESE COMMERCIAL ARITHMETIC COMMERCIAL AR
COMPOSE MUSIC CONSTRUCTIONAL DETAILS CONTRACT BRIDGE
SPEEDWORDS ECONOMIC GEOGRAPHY ECONOMICS ELECT
ENGLISH GRAMMAR LITERARY APPRECIATION ENGLISH RENASC
REVIVAL VICTORIAN AGE CONTEMPORARY LITERATURE ETCHI
FREELANCE WRITING FRENCH FRENCH DICTIONARY FRENCH
LIVING THINGS GEOLOGY GEOMETRY GERMAN GERMAN
GOOD CONTROL OF INSECT PESTS GOOD CONTROL OF PLANT DISE
GOOD FARMING BY MACHINE GOOD FARM WORKMANSHIP GOO
GOOD MARKET GARDENING GOOD MILK FARMING GOOD PIG KE
GOOD ENGLISH GREEK GREGG SHORTHAND GUIDEBOOK TO T
GREAT BOLIVAR BOTHA CATHERINE THE GREAT CHATHAM CLEM
LIBERALISM HENRY V JOAN OF ARC JOHN WYCLIFFE LENIN LOUIS
ROBES HASTINGS
HOUS REPAIRS
WRIT ND TOO
MECH LCRAFT
MOTO FICIENCY
PHYSI DESIGN
ADMI NG RE
PHRA OOK SAILING SALESMANSHIP SECRETA ACTICE
DEBAT SPELLING STAMP COLLECTING STUDE DE ST
TYPEWRITING USE OF GEOGRAPHY WAY TO POETR WRIT
COOKERY FOR GIRLS DOGS AS PETS FOR BOYS AND GIRLS KNIT
PHOTOGRAPHY FOR BOYS AND GIRLS RADIO FOR BOYS RIDING F
SOCCER FOR BOYS STAMP COLLECTING FOR BOYS AND GIRLS WO
ACTING ANATOMY ARABIC ASTRONOMY BANKING BEE
CHILDREN BUSINESS ORGANISATION CALCULUS CANASTA C
COMMERCIAL ART COMMERCIAL CORRESPONDENCE COMMERC
CONTRACT BRIDGE COOKING CRICKET DRAWING DRESSM
ECONOMICS ELECTRICITY ELECTRICITY IN THE HOUSE ELOCUT
ENGLISH RENASCENCE ENGLISH RENASCENCE TO THE ROMANTIC
LITERATURE ETCHING EVERYDAY FRENCH TO EXPRESS YOURSE
DICTIONARY FRENCH PHRASE BOOK GARDENING GAS IN TH
GERMAN GERMAN DICTIONARY GERMAN GRAMMAR GERMAN
CONTROL OF PLANT DISEASES GOOD FARM ACCOUNTING GO
GOOD FARM WORKMANSHIP GOOD FRUIT FARMING GOOD GRAS
GOOD MILK FARMING GOOD PIG KEEPING GOOD POULTRY KEEP
GREGG SHORTHAND GUIDEBOOK TO THE BIBLE HINDUSTANI
CATHERINE THE GREAT CHATHAM CLEMENCEAU CONSTANTINE COO
ARC JOHN WYCLIFFE LENIN LOUIS XIV MILTON PERICLES PETER THE
USE OF HISTORY WARREN HASTINGS WOODROW WILSON HOCKEY
HOUSEHOLD ELECTRICITY HOUSE REPAIRS ITALIAN JOINERY
MANAGEMENT MATHEMATICS HAND TOOLS ENGINEERING
DRAUGHTSMANSHIP METEOROLOGY MODELCRAFT MODERN DAN
MUSIC NORWEGIAN PERSONAL EFFICIENCY PHILOSOPHY PHOT
SHORTHAND PLANNING AND DESIGN PLUMBING POLISH POP

GIVE INSTRUCTION TO A WISE MAN . . .

NOW THE SYNTHESIS

Capitalism, Socialism and the New Social Contract

NOW THE SYNTHESIS

Capitalism, Socialism and the New Social Contract

Richard Noyes, editor

CENTRE FOR INCENTIVE TAXATION

SHEPHEARD-WALWYN · LONDON
HOLMES & MEIER · NEW YORK

177 Vauxhall Bridge Road
London SW1V 1EU

This edition first published 1991
in the United Kingdom by
Shepheard-Walwyn (Publishers) Ltd
26 Charing Cross Road (Suite 34)
London WC2H 0DH
and in the United States by
Holmes & Meier Publishers, Inc.
30 Irving Place
New York NY 10003

British Library Cataloguing in Publication Data
Now the synthesis: a new economic model.
1. Economics. Theories
I. Noyes, Richard
330.1

ISBN 0-85683-124-7 (UK edition)
ISBN 0-8419-1300-5 (US edition)

Typeset by Alacrity Phototypesetters,
Banwell Castle, Weston-super-Mare.
Printed and bound in Great Britain by
BPCC Wheatons Ltd, Exeter.

Contents

Introduction
RICHARD NOYES 1

I A HOLISTIC PHILOSOPHY

1 Dialectics and the Millennium:
emergence of the Synthesis
RICHARD NOYES 13

II THE TRANSFORMATION OF PROPERTY RIGHTS

2 Property Rights and the Social Contract:
the constitutional challenge in the USA
NICOLAUS TIDEMAN 47

3 'Planning Gain': the making of a tax or
land values in Britain
FRANCIS M. SMITH 60

III THE EVOLUTION OF SOCIAL SYSTEMS

4 Post-socialism and the Single Tax:
a holistic philosophy
FRED HARRISON 77

5 Conflict, Ideology and Hope in Latin America
JAMES BUSEY 112

6 Land Policy and the Economics of Colonial
Exploitation
JEROME F. HEAVEY 136

IV ECOLOGY AND ECO-POLITICS

7 The Greens and the Tax on Rent
DAVID RICHARDS 155

8 Incentive Taxation and the Environment: complex — yet feasible
JURGEN BACKHAUS AND JACOB JAN KRABBE 174

V INTERNATIONAL TRADE

9 Protectionism, Rent and the Dynamics of Agricultural Degradation
RICHARD BODY 207

10 Trade and Investment: preserving the fruits of liberty
C. LOWELL HARRISS 215

Appendix: Open Letter to Mikhail Gorbachev 225

About the Authors 231

Index 235

Introduction

THE world is at the crossroads of a new epoch. Old orders are crumbling fast, and necessity will surely spawn new social and economic systems as we arrive at the dawn of a new millennium. Whether the changes will be for good or bad depends on the nature of the philosophies that triumph on the streets. This book articulates an applied philosophy which, the authors suggest, offers the best prospect for peaceful, evolutionary development.

The crises that challenge the peoples of the world today may be summarised in these terms. The old orders exaggerated the potential for conflict by over-simplifying, through their institutions and social processes, the rights and obligations of the individual and of the State. In the West, at the beginning of the modern period of history, we defended the rights of the individual to the point where the supportive role of the community was all but buried. The social side of life was only grudgingly re-introduced, in the form of the bureaucratically administered Welfare State. East of Warsaw, an alternative solution was adopted in which the individual was buried in favor of the power of the State. Again, the bureaucracy came out on top.

How, then, do we re-work the relationship between the individual and society in terms of a creative partnership that is capable of meeting the needs of people in the 21st century? The time for recondite philosophising has gone: we are in a period in which people need guidance from an applied philosophy, one that offers practical solutions to conflicts over such vexed issues as property rights and the distribution of income, and which does so by addressing the heartfelt need for justice.

But the challenge goes deeper than that. In recent years, a powerful awareness of our obligations to nature has emerged to add a serious complication to the problems that now confront mankind. A relevant philosophy has to offer solutions to the systemic abuses that threaten our ecological environment. With the enormous pressure for change building up, it is not possible to deal with social issues as separate from the environmental ones. In other words, what we need is a holistic philosophy; one that will 'work' in the modern era.

It is not with a sense of misplaced nostalgia that I say we have to go back in time, to rediscover the secrets of our forefathers. They developed cultural formulae that successfully guided them through evolutionary timescales, permitting them to experiment with increasingly complex social structures without undermining the integrity of Mother Earth. We now need to unearth those rules and translate them into a modern form. The overall objective: to liberate each person so that he can relate peacefully to other men and women ('the community') and harmoniously to his ecological habitat.

The solutions will have to be expressed in terms that are relevant to contemporary problems, display flexibility in the processes of decision-making and resilience in the social structures to ensure stability. This means that the favored solutions will be simple to apply but comprehensive in their relevance. In institutional terms, that means democratic politics and market economics. But if that was *all* that we needed, there would be fewer problems in the world today. Something fundamental has evidently been missing, these past two centuries of industrial life and strife.

The authors of these essays believe that an applied philosophy appropriate to the times is ready and waiting in the wings. Indeed, they go further than that. They claim that history is actually unfolding in the direction of the kind of social system that would be prescribed by that philosophy. This is another way of saying that, in historical terms, the philosophy articulated in this book has a certain preferential validity. Its principles must be tested and retested; but to ignore the lessons of that philosophy would be to risk the future wilfully.

Although the essential elements of that philosophy can be traced back several thousand years — the formula did not come out of a magician's hat, or off the mathematician's blackboard — they found their modern expression in the writings of Henry George. In this book, no attempt has been made to select contemporary issues merely to parade the genius of one social reformer. The authors chose those topics that are of central relevance to the public dialogue. Then they applied the harsh test: to what extent were these events foreshadowed by Henry George? Alternatively, could these developments benefit from the insights which the American offered a century ago?

Many current issues are not addressed here, because of the constraints of space. For example, Henry George sought to stimulate political activity that would lead to greater efficiency in the actions of government, a full century before that subject became a popular policy issue when Margaret Thatcher became Prime Minister of Britain in 1979.[1]

The authors are drawn from a wide variety of disciplines, and each was free to bring his individualistic style and point of view to bear on his subject. The overall objective was to discern the prospects of qualitative change — of progress, social evolution — in the world today; or, where these signals were weak or absent, to apply the Georgist critique in such a way as to illuminate the debates in the parliaments and coffee shops around the world. In other words, this volume is not merely a record of current events; it is also a manual offering principled guidance for the policymakers who are now confronted with harsh choices.

The epic debate focuses on the challenge confronting the leaders of the Soviet Union and Eastern Europe. The reformist zeal of Mikhail Gorbachev and his advisers was tempered, from the outset, by the inability of conventional economics to guide the transformation of the command economy into a free market system. The debates in Peking, in the 1970s, and in Moscow, in the 1980s, were not directly influenced by Henry George. This is ironic, because both Russia (through Leo Tolstoy) and China (through Sun Yat-sen) have Georgist traditions.

Fred Harrison (chapter 4) does not share the view that economic theory is unable to formulate a model for a relatively smooth transformation of the socialist system into a post-Marxist society. In his view, the classical concepts and theories of Adam Smith and David Ricardo, if applied in a consistent manner, could smooth the transition from the antithetical economy. But to what should the peoples of the eastern countries aspire? A carbon copy of the western model? Or should they synthesise the best elements of the past into a new social system, one that would find its central expression in the fiscal policy for which Henry George is best known: the Single Tax on the rental value of land? This latter option enjoys a high prospect of realisation because, in the Soviet Union at least, land is already in the public domain, and is the one to which Mikhail Gorbachev has been intuitively guided. His one sticking point over the Shatalin 500-Day Plan — an emergency program to transform the command economy into a free market — was the issue of land ownership.

Land, in Gorbachev's view, ought to remain in social ownership, but with the individual user having secure possession of the sites he needed upon which to live and work, paying the community a rent in return for this privilege — a solution straight out of Henry George's *Progress and Poverty*. Boris Yeltsin, the President of the Russian Federation, impatient though he was with the reform process — an impatience that brought him into serious political conflict with Gorbachev — nevertheless agreed that the ownership of land was not negotiable. Yeltsin was quoted as stating: 'People here do not understand the concept of buying and selling land. The land is like a mother. You don't sell your mother.'[2] That philosophy is a primitive one, which has found its expression in numerous declarations by the leaders of aboriginal societies; Henry George acknowledged it, and had the imagination to clothe it in a fiscal policy that was suitably adapted to the needs of industrial society.

Gorbachev, in promoting the virtues of the market economy and the individual ownership of capital, was so adamant about the land question that he declared a willingness to stage a nationwide referendum in defence of the principle that land should remain in social ownership. The prospect of building western-style poverty and unemployment into the structure of the new Soviet Union will turn on the outcome of this debate.

Doubts about the nature of 'the system' are not confined to the East. The London *Financial Times* editorialised the following warning to the leaders of the capitalist West on May 26, 1990:

> To hold a nationwide referendum on the case for a market economy in a country where people have been subjected to decades of anti-market propaganda is, to put it mildly, a high-risk strategy. The irony is that if market economics were put to a test in the west similar to that proposed by the Soviet Government last week, the outcome might be less clear cut

> than the recent rhetoric of western politicians would tend to imply . . . are the instincts of those Russians really so different from those of their American counterparts who are now having to confront the unhappier consequences of Reaganomics? The model of capitalism that delivered a boom under Reagan and an impending slowdown under President Bush is not one which the average American would necessarily wish to sell to the Soviets.

All bets are off; at the level of the street, there is a deep-seated anxiety about the quality of life in the West. Materialism has eclipsed much of the spiritual side of life, but without the compensation of spreading its benefits to every able-bodied man and woman willing to work for wages.

In the view of our authors the best prospects for defining a new approach have long been nurtured in the West, which retained the Lockean spirit of liberty, a spirit that was progressively suppressed after 1917 in the East. In the free expressions of individual men and women we discover the seeds that, as they germinate, appear to propel society towards the realisation of the synthesis. Central to the prospect of social evolution is the vexed question of property rights, the maldistribution of which is at the heart of most of today's social and individual traumas. Representative of the dissatisfaction with the simple-minded perception of individual property rights is the Chief Judge of the Court of Appeals of New York. Judge Breitel's seminal words were voiced in his judgment in a suit brought by Penn Central Transportation Company, which challenged the right of New York City to impose a landmark order on Grand Central Station. That order meant that the company could not construct a building above the terminal. In his judgment, the judge — whether or not he realised it — articulated the view most eloquently stated by Henry George that the community was a partner in the creation of wealth, and was therefore entitled to share in the stream of income generated by a particular enterprise. Judge Breitel said:

> Although government regulation is invalid if it denies a property owner all reasonable return, there is no constitutional imperative that the return embrace all attributes, incidental influences, or contributing external factors derived from the social complex in which the property rests. So many of these attributes are not the result of private effort or investment but of opportunities for the utilization or exploitation which an organized society offers to any private enterprise, especially to a public utility,

> favored by government and the public. These, too, constitute a background of massive social and governmental investment in the organized community without which the private enterprise could neither exist nor prosper. It is enough, for the limited purposes of a landmarking statute, albeit it is also essential, that the privately created ingredient of property receive a reasonable return. It is that privately created and privately managed ingredient which is the property on which the reasonable return is to be based. All else is society's contribution by the sweat of its brow and the expenditure of its funds. To that extent society is also entitled to its due.[3]

The judge did not use the technical terms of the economist, but his message was clear: 'It is exceedingly difficult but imperative, nevertheless, to sort out the merged ingredients and to assess the rights and responsibilities of owner and society. A fair return is to be accorded to the owner, but society is to receive its due for its share in the making of a once great railroad.' In fact, for the clear-thinking economist, the process of disentangling the 'merged ingredients' is not a difficult one at all; it can be done in terms of the flow of income — a fact to which Judge Breitel drew attention when he declared: 'To recapitulate, a property owner is not absolutely entitled to receive a return on so much of the property's value as was created by social investment.' The clearest statement of the dues of the individual and of society appears in *Progress and Poverty:* people are entitled to a fair return on their labor and their capital investments, but the rental value of land is a measure of the wealth created not by the individual property owner but by the community; and that rental value properly belongs to the community.

Judge Breitel's analysis remains controversial, but it is one of the many chinks in the door that is opening up a debate for change. In Nicolaus Tideman's view (chapter 2), however, the redefinition of property rights ought not to take place within the courtroom, through legal precedent, but through amendment to the constitution. This strategy commends itself for the prospect of a principled debate on the rights of the individual and the nature of the good society.

But the identification of communally-created land values as a fund over which society has exceptional rights does not rely on future action for its expression: the process has already begun in Britain, explains Francis Smith, through deals that are called 'planning gains' (chapter 3). While defective in many respects, this policy at least has the virtue of pointing us in the right direction, in that it employs an *ad hoc* system of taxation on the economic rent of land to fund the provision of social amenities such as roads, recreational facilities and housing. Prof. Elson, in a new assessment of planning gain, predicts that in the 1990s this levy on land values will be used increasingly to underwrite the public's desire for conservation of the natural environment.[4] This mechanism for capturing some of the increases in land values that occur from the growth of the community is still a controversial one, however,[5] and is likely to be a focus for fresh political debate over the rights of the individual against the rights of the community.

Foreshadowing the current concern with the well-being of the natural environment by a full century, Henry George voiced this warning about the fate of trees and the fertility of the soil in *Social Problems*:[6]

> We do not return to the earth what we take from it; each crop that is harvested leaves the soil the poorer. We are cutting down forests which we do not replant; we are shipping abroad, in wheat and cotton and tobacco and meat, or flushing into the sea through the sewers of our great cities, the elements of fertility that have been embedded in the soil by the slow processes of nature, acting for long ages.

Sir Richard Body, a British parliamentarian and working farmer, offers a powerful critique of agri-business (chapter 9). He demonstrates that the beneficiary of government policies has been the landowner, rather than the farmer, laborer or consumer. Surprisingly, however, as David Richards reports (chapter 7), ecologists — with the notable exception of the British Green Party — have yet to appreciate that land value taxation, aligned with the free market, is the most powerful tool for conserving our natural environment. The penetrating analysis by Prof. Backhaus and Dr. Krabbe (chapter 8) illuminates the scope for using the tax on the economic rent of land as an instrument for financing socially-necessary expenditure while simultaneously protecting and conserving the natural environment.

In advancing the proposition that society is evolving inexorably in the direction of a Georgist synthesis, we are not denying that there is still much to be done by the philosopher and the reformer. The cries of despair from the Third World are particularly harrowing. Yet there is hope, for the analytical tools for laying bare the structural problems are at our disposal. Professors Busey (concentrating on Central America) and Heavey (analysing the origins of the problems in the former European colonies) offer critiques in terms of misaligned land tenure systems. If malnutrition and death by hunger are to be banished, action will have to focus on land tenure and fiscal policy. In the view of our authors (in chapters 5 and 6), the principles articulated by Henry George will serve as the benchmarks for reform.

But just how free is the market? Seen from an international perspective, the answer is not an unmitigatedly bright one. The industrialised countries continue to flirt with the idea of imposing limits on trade with each other on the basis of spurious notions of self-interest and 'fairness.' In the 1980s, arguments between the United States and Japan (over semi-conductors) and with the European Economic Community (over protection accorded to its farmers) threatened the outlook for free trade. Lowell Harriss reminds us (chapter 10) that Henry George's unremitting advocacy of that policy in *Protection or Free Trade* was sound then and is of salutary significance now: the living standards of many people improved as the opportunities to exchange wealth across national boundaries were enlarged over the past century. To retrace our steps now would be a tragic mistake. The hard choices over the shape of society in the 21st century presented themselves sooner than the authors of these essays anticipated when the negotiations over free trade (under the umbrella of the General Agreement on Tariffs and Trade; GATT) broke down in December 1990. As the disputing nations sought a solution to the impasse, they were constantly reminded of the cost of failure; at stake was an estimated $4,000 billion, the value of trade that would be lost to the world during the 1990s if the multilateral trading system was dismantled. The hidden interest behind the brinkmanship is worth noting, here, for the way that this case underlines the importance of the Georgist critique.

The conflict within GATT stemmed from objections to the protection accorded to the European Economic Community's farmers, and in particular the EEC's practice of dumping food on the world markets at prices well below their production costs. The economic benefits of this protectionism were not reaped by the working farmer (through higher profits on his capital equipment), or by his laborers (through higher wages). As Sir Richard Body (chapter 9) reminds us, the economic value of subsidies and the other devices that raise the price of food is capitalised into higher land prices. The landowner is the primary beneficiary — in return for what services to the consumer or the community?

It is not only the EEC that is at fault: agricultural protectionism in the industrialised world costs taxpayers and consumers an estimated $250m a year. Little wonder that the price of farmland is so high! The benefits of free trade in food would be reflected in lower land prices: thus, the pressure to over-exploit the soil would be taken off farmers, freeing them to use ecologically benign methods for nurturing food out of the land. Free trade would also lead to an increase in the output of food, to the value of an estimated $100 billion a year. Third World farmers would be able to compete on the world markets, and therefore earn the incomes that they are at present banned from receiving by the policies of protectionism. The prospect for abolishing malnutrition (which is measured in the tens of millions) and mass death by starvation, are self-evident.

Agricultural protectionism, then, is yet another reminder of the timely relevance of the philosophy of Henry George. His vision of a new society built on social justice and economic efficiency rests on two inalienable rights: the freedom of the individual, and the right of equal access to the fruits of nature. Expressed in such abstract terms, it would be difficult to find many people who would disagree. But it was the genius of George, through prose that was at once poetic in its beauty and scientific in its rigor, that he was able to offer a practical definition of a social and economic system that would provide men and women with the means for realising that vision.

President George Bush promoted the notion of a 'new world order' in the wake of the concerted military opposition to Iraq's annexation of the land of Kuwait. The mobilisation of armies in the shifting sands of the desert, however, could not provide a firm foundation for a sustainable social order that achieved the twin goals of eliminating poverty and protecting our natural habitat. And yet, there is reason to be optimistic: the undercurrents of change are shifting their direction towards a set of institutions and relationships that augur well for mankind and the evolution of society in the 21st century.

RICHARD NOYES
Salem, New Hampshire
January 1991

NOTES

1. *Social Problems* (1883), centenary edition, New York: Robert Schalkenback Foundation, 1989, Ch. 17.
2. Yeltsin's attitude did not stop the Congress of Russian People's Deputies from passing a resolution giving peasants a share of their collective farm's land for life, with the right to pass it on to their heirs. See Jonathan Steele, 'Russia allows private land,' *The Guardian,* London, Dec. 4, 1990.

   But as Henry George was at pains to point out, what mattered was not who owned the title deeds, but who benefitted from the rental income. Yeltsin and his colleagues evidently failed to spot the difference. Their legislative action provoked a remonstration from Ivan Polozkov, the Communist Party leader, who wrote a letter protesting against the Russian parliament's decision to allow peasants to 'own' land. See Mark Frankland, 'Lipstick-deep revolution holds kiss of death,' *The Observer,* London, Dec. 9, 1990.

   Polozkov cited a letter written by Tolstoy to Pyotr Stolypin, the Czar's reformist Prime Minister who believed that his plan to alienate village common land would lead to the enhancement of the status of peasants. Tolstoy, taking a radically different view of the historic consequences of this action — a view that was inspired by his close study of the writings of Henry George — told Stolypin in his letter dated July 26, 1907, that Russia had the option of 'taking the lead among all the countries of Europe' by striving 'to abolish the oldest and greatest injustice of all, which is common to all peoples; the individual ownership of land.' Tolstoy, whose advice was rejected, understood that there was a difference between the secure individual possession and use of land, and the exercise of rights over land that gave owners the power to exploit others.
3. Penn Central Transp. Co. v City of New York, 366 N.E. 2d 1271, 42 N.Y. 2d 324 (1977).
4. Martin Elson, *Negotiating the Future: Planning Gain in the 1990s,* Gloucester: ARC Ltd, 1990.
5. Samantha Jenkins, 'Moves to stamp out planning gain abuse,' *Estates Times,* July 20, 1990.
6. *Social Problems,* p.27.

I
A HOLISTIC PHILOSOPHY

1
Dialectics and the Millennium: emergence of the Synthesis

RICHARD NOYES

I

THE WORLD has been, for most of this century, divided into two camps with sharply differing creeds (or differing 'certainties', an alternative choice of word to be justified in what follows): the communists as the 'evil empire', and the capitalists as 'exploiters'. But now, suddenly, in a matter of only a few months, events have taken place around a world-growing-smaller which few could have imagined, and which even those few would not have guessed could happen so soon. The warring certainties are dissolving, their ability to satisfy even their advocates is collapsing and only the diehards in both camps are left clinging to the old certainties. Everything still intact seems so unfamiliar. 'What in the world,' one is entitled to ask, 'is happening?'

There is an elemental answer: history is giving birth.

History, which some first thought might be 'ending', is instead bearing us a future. Something new is surely coming for human society. It would be rash to insist on foretelling exactly, in minute detail, what to expect, or even to know if the birth will be easy or will be difficult. But there is good reason to sense, and this book insists, that what is emerging from the present chaos is an idea long in coming: a well-seasoned concept of how the human race can live at peace and with justice on an earth made even smaller by our growing population and our burgeoning technology. There are long foreshadows of a synthesis soon to emerge out of the two ageing certainties — out of the tension between the reasoned idea of individual freedom and the revolution spawned by indignation over capitalism's failure to nourish both rich and poor alike.

All this is happening in the closing decade of another thousand years on our calendar — another millennium. That word is so freighted with meaning that to use it is to risk dismissal in the minds of some. There is, however, an essential core to the word in its generic (as opposed to its narrower eschatologic) sense which makes it almost obligatory in considering something so fundamental as historical evolution. I am not suggesting, nor are the other authors of this book, a vision of the future rooted in any particular religious system of beliefs, although that seems to be the starting point for the concept of the millennium. We do insist, however, upon a level of historical consequence which the word implies, and I will argue that it is appropriate, after first laying an adequate foundation.

History does give birth to new concepts, although not often enough to make the process seem familiar to people in their everyday lives who may be living through such an epoch. Such sea changes are separated by long stretches of flattened time. Evolution, slow though it be, is the only ground for hope for a species as troubled as ours. One of the more recent realisations is the process by which history does give birth. The gestation period in cultural evolution, when measured against the life span of any single individual among the concurrent five and a half billion of us, is so long, skipping some entire lifetimes and being lost against the busy background for others, that revelation when it emerges comes as a surprise. It was as recent as the early years of the last century that the philosopher George Hegel first saw the process of evolutionary birth clearly enough to give it a name: dialectics. Thesis, antithesis and synthesis — the continuity I am suggesting here. Initially, for Hegel, this was just his own method for reasoning. Hegel was struck by the inevitability of contrast, the clash between opposites, and arising out of them a synthesis which contains within it the essence of both. Only out of that personal view of individual thought, quite logically, did the concept grow in his mind into the architectonics of historical evolution.

The idea that history is once again giving birth was a working hypothesis for the present authors well before the social avalanche of the last few months of 1989. The confluence of a wide variety of trends and events suggested the possibility of a millenarian change of direction that could take the form of a new social contract to guide mankind through the 21st Century. That new philosophy is encapsulated in the works of an American social reformer, Henry George, whose radical proposals are based on nothing less than the transformation of both social relationships and the way mankind relates to his natural habitat.

John Locke, Adam Smith and others gave us the thesis during what Paine called the Age of Reason. Karl Marx and Friedrich Engels, feigning cold rationality to mask seething anger at the plight of poor people whom 'capitalism' had apparently excluded from the new riches, called for revolution: the antithesis which has scarred so much of the 20th Century. Henry George's realisation about how mankind must live on a God-given planet, although it has roots that go back a millennium or more, is only now at long last timely as the wedding of reason and revolution. George painstakingly probed history's first full manifestation of individual liberty as the founding fathers had laid it down, and as we have come to know it. Perplexed at the riddle of how some were excluded from the fruits of a new social contract that for others was working so well, he was able to identify the one great imperfection, the snag on which freedom catches: the idea that any individual can monopolise even a part of the earth we share.

The burden of this opening effort is as follows. In section II, I review discoveries made since Hegel's initial revelation about the process by which history gives birth. In sections III and IV, I examine the proposition that Henry George's prospectus is the synthesis to which the world is tending, tracking the continuity through two unmet provisions — or 'provisos' — which were spelled out in the original thesis but never resolved. Finally, in section V, we face up to the challenge of the word millennium and place the studies that follow in the context of the overall proposition that history is moving on to a qualitatively new social framework.

II

George Hegel's dialectics — the first formal analysis of the manner in which history gives birth — grew out of his belief that all ideas worth talking about are relationships, and that the most universal of all such relationships is contrast or opposition. History is being made only at those times when contrasting ideas are at war. It is in that sense that we might be able to justify the suggestion that, with the collapse of socialism, history has come to an end. The suggestion that the collapse of socialism has left the world without a struggle is a superficial one; it misses a major point. It is not the struggle of opposing philosophies that leads to transition from thesis to antithesis to synthesis, but the collapse of belief in the certainty that happens to be predominant at the time which creates the vacuum of uncertainty. Succession — what comes next — has more to do with continuity of thought than with struggle.

Hegel's writings have been called 'masterpieces of obscurity', and his dialectics have been both debated and adapted for other purposes. The concept has persisted, however, and a more recent American student of philosophy with a unique ability to simplify and qualify, Will Durant, has some things to say about Hegel and his dialectics that will help us here.[1]

> The movement of evolution is a continuous development of oppositions, and their merging and reconciliation. Schilling was right — there is an underlying 'identity of opposites'; and Fichte was right — thesis, antithesis and synthesis constitute the formula and secret of all development and all reality.
>
> History is a dialectical movement, almost a series of revolutions in which people after people, genius after genius, become the instrument of the Absolute. Great men are not so much begetters, as midwives, of the future.

Just as dialectics was the work of Hegel and Schilling and Fichte, working together, talking together, so some of the essential elements of Henry George's realisation, to which he was originally drawn out of his life's experience, were already familiar to a long list of other reasoners: the French physiocrats, Tiberius Gracchus, and a Spartan king named Agis, to suggest a few. He was surprised to learn he had predecessors some years after having drawn *Progress* and Poverty[2] out of his own heart and head, and in *The Science of Political Economy*[3] he credits the physiocrats and others.

Such is the way with cultural evolution — it is a shared process, a social development in which individuals may play a role, but are never enough in themselves — and it is the way with our understanding of the manner in which history gives birth, a process Hegel first suggested but which others have helped us to understand more clearly since. There are two important aspects of it that we will do little more at this point than to name, planting them in the reader's awareness until such time as their significance emerges: continuity and fallibilism.

Continuity in particular is a key element because it is a necessary ground for the concept of order, whether in space or in time. If it were not for continuity there would be chance, history in random sequence. There is clearly a continuity of time from past through the present to the future; but is there continuity in social events? If not, the idea of dialectical history falls apart.

Fallibilism is linked to Durant's observation above, that great men are the midwives, not the seers, of the future. Men, even the great men, are not themselves the Absolute, but simply the instruments. Their ideas are not perfect revelation, but concepts built up gradually, those of current thinkers standing on the shoulders of thinkers who came before them.

One philosopher who dealt scrupulously with both concepts was Charles Sanders Peirce, who was born, as was Henry George, in the year 1839. There have been intriguing hints of chronological mystery down through the course of human events, concurrent phenomena which seem to suggest something about determination (maybe even continuity) which we have yet to understand. The discovery almost simultaneously by Charles Darwin and Alfred Russel Wallace of natural selection in evolution is one example. Another is the haunting deaths of John Adams and Thomas Jefferson within hours of each other (although miles apart) on the Fourth of July just exactly half a century after the Fourth of July they had earlier shared. They do, at least, suggest order and pattern in the course of human events; as does the fact that two of America's most fertile minds — two thinkers whose realisations are still coming to public awareness — were born within only eight days of each other, one (George) at Philadelphia on September 2, 1839, the other (Peirce) at another 'cradle' of American liberty in Massachusetts on September 10 of that same year. Peirce was born not at Boston, but just across the Charles River in Cambridge, where General Washington had earlier made his headquarters in his fight with the British redcoats. A seldom remembered logician, philosopher and physicist, Peirce must nevertheless be credited with the most familiar philosophical structure in this century: pragmatism. George Gilder is one who has called him 'America's greatest philosopher.'

In his writings, Peirce clarified the process of how history gives birth. The only readily available collection of his work is *Chance, Love and Logic*[4], which amounts to a midwife's manual on the mechanics of evolutionary birth.

It is doubt and uncertainty, and nothing else, says Peirce, that trigger thought; and it is thought that leads ultimately to new belief. Or more exactly, in words from a seminal essay of 1878[5] called 'How to Make Our Ideas Clear': 'The action of thought is excited by the irritation of doubt, and ceases when belief is attained; so that the production of belief is the sole function of thought.' Belief, in turn, creates habit, and thus determines the regularity that continues unbroken until doubt once again arises.

Pragmatism began, it can be clearly established, with a definition of belief that Peirce and others received from the Scottish educator, Alexander Bain. A belief, he said flatly, 'is that upon which a man is prepared to act.'[6] So the emergence of a widely shared, or popularly held, belief is as near as we can come to the birth of a social idea. And it arises only out of the kind of doubt or uncertainty in which our world suddenly finds itself in the dying years of the 20th Century. We maintain and continue to carry out habitual behavior so long as creeds or 'certainties' remain intact, shedding them and searching with all our rational powers for new beliefs only with the onset of doubt.

Where, though, does doubt come from? Any man able single-handedly to bring about in society full and authentic doubt (for there are such things as false or simulated doubt) would, of course, wield a powerful political tool; but the great mass of people is not easily herded into uncertainty. We all cling to belief with tenacity, as the two camps have done through most of this century. 'You can fool some of the people all of the time, and you can fool all of the people some of the time,' but in historical fact it is social experience that leads to the kind of wholesale uncertainty in which the world is now caught up. 'Genuine doubt arises only in response to an experiential challenge or obstacle,' according to Thomas S. Knight in a clarification of his thinking to be found in a biography of Peirce.[7]

There is another important element in pragmatism — or, more specifically, in pragmaticism — that should be noted in this recitation of the generalities. While it was Peirce who originated this now-popular way of thinking, it was the product of many minds, some of them better known than Peirce: William James, for instance, and John Dewey. It was some of the others who put the word deeply enough into the popular vocabulary so that now it does not seem unusual to hear one say, 'we are all pragmatists now,' or 'let us be pragmatic about this.' While the originators all agreed that a true statement is one that produces satisfactory results, they differed on the question of 'satisfactory results for whom?' Peirce insisted the satisfaction could not be restricted to one individual, and as biographer Knight has put it, 'For a proposition to be true, its results must be considered satisfactory by the whole community of competent observers.'[8] Knight explains:

> When Peirce concluded in his (essay) 'Fixation of Belief' that truth is a stable set of beliefs or a state of satisfaction, he did not mean the satisfaction of one person but 'the satisfaction which would ultimately be found if the inquiry were pushed to its ultimate and indefeasible issue.' This qualification distinguished his theory of truth from that of James, F. S. C. Schiller and others who, under the name 'Pragmatism', held a true proposition to be one that results in satisfying conduct for desirable results for the individual.

Peirce was patient about this misuse of his term for a while, but when it began to appear in literary journals with the individualistic slant he came up with a new term: Pragmaticism. It is just this social transition, this broader understanding of the process — belief, habit, regularity, emerging dissatisfaction, uncertainty, irritation, thought and back once again to full, social belief and freshly taken habit — that we are here likening to historical birth.

Is the astonishing avalanche of current events which assumed an almost daily manifestation in the second half of 1989, an example of uncertainty? In mid-August of that year, *The Economist* carried on its cover an illustration suggesting a vast, smouldering wasteland and the headline: 'The century that purged itself.'

'The triumph of the twentieth century,' explained the magazine in its lead editorial, 'is that it has purged itself of certainty.' If that conclusion were legitimate then, how much more so is it now that socialism has collapsed in eastern Europe and the capitalist West is staggering under budgetary deficits, increasing homelessness, banking failures, the bankruptcy of prestigious investment firms already weakened by malpractice, and growing unemployment? The uncertainty that will lead beyond thesis and antithesis to a synthesis is not a breakdown of belief in just one or the other creed, but in both.

This has indeed been, as *The Economist* editorial claimed, a century of uncertainty. It has been marked not by one certainty, but by two. Nations have been torn internally, as well as externally, by the 'conflict of visions' that Thomas Sowell has described.[9] The vast majority of people have been so captivated by one certainty or the other for so many years that there has been all too little critical thought. Belief is resilient. It lasts longer than it ought to because we hold onto it tightly as a bandage against the irritation of doubt. It closes its eyes to uncertainty as long as there is the vestige of an excuse, even longer, even to the extent of misrepresenting to itself. Cerebration on behalf of existing certainty is not to be mistaken for authentic thought.

III

The focus of our enquiry is summed up by this proposition: *Henry George is our contemporary synthesis in the course of human events.* The words are chosen carefully. The closing phrase is taken from Philadelphia history, having been used there so many years earlier, when the thesis of this structure was being put in place in the United States. It was prefaced in that case by a critical conjunction: 'When in the course of human events'. The phrase is important for several reasons, not the least of them being to establish continuity. Henry George is most apt to be remembered as the advocate of the 'single tax', which one recent writer (apparently trying to be friendly) has described as the 'confiscatory and unworkable single-tax panacea.' Others speak of it as his 'remedy.' George's full fiscal remedy is, in fact, relatively simple and concise, but slightly longer: 'We must abolish all taxation save that upon land values.' But it is not George's alleged 'remedy', the single-tax, that is here presented as the synthesis and historical progeny. It is his full realisation about the course of human events. That is the sense in which continuity can be seen.

Steven Cord highlighted the issue with this account: 'When William Lloyd Garrison (the younger), an avid supporter, told George that he did not believe the single tax to be a panacea, George replied, "Neither do I: but I believe freedom is, and the single tax is but the tap-root of freedom".[10] Thus, it is as a new phase, on a higher altitude of achievement in the continuing march toward individual freedom, that George's realisation must be seen.

A key word in our exploratory proposition is 'contemporary'. It is only as a logical and relevant realisation in the here and now that Henry George's ideas can be seen as a synthesis that may properly arise out of the current disenchantment with both Reason and Revolution. George can be seen as 'contemporary' only over a long stretch of time. The important ideas in history always overlap. Hegel's dialectics are not entirely neat.

It could accurately be said that George's realisation, here being claimed as the contemporary synthesis growing out of Reason and Revolution, is 'the beginning of now.' This raises another critical question: 'How long is "now"?' It may seem an esoteric question, but it is critical in this matter of pragmaticism, continuity and historical birth because 'now' in the broad social sense under consideration is something in the nature of a consensus. *Now*, strictly speaking, is a point in time — a point often called the present — from which index the long stretches of time past and future are measured. But for thinking people it has its own fourth dimension. Philosophers have insisted upon it. If the present were without dimension, if it were literally 'now' and nothing else, then it would be reduced to what Jonathan Edwards said of that empty abstract, 'nothing': that which 'the sleeping rocks do dream of.' But we are conscious and we observe, holding a present sensation in temporary memory while a new one comes along with which it can be compared; and on the basis of that comparison we predict yet another sensation still to come.

Charles Peirce, who realised thought 'cannot be immediately present to us, but must cover some portion of the past or future'[11] illustrated this insight in his essay, 'How to Make Our Ideas Clear.'

> In a piece of music there are separate notes, and there is the air. A single tone may be prolonged for an hour or a day, and it exists as perfectly in each second of that time as in the whole taken together; so that, as long as it is sounding, it might be present to a sense from which everything in the

> past was as completely absent as the future itself. But it is different with the air, the performance of which occupies a certain time, during the portions of which only portions of it are played. It consists in an orderliness in the succession of sounds which strike the ear at different times; and to perceive it there must be some continuity of consciousness which makes the events of a lapse of time present to us. We certainly only perceive the air by hearing the separate notes; yet we cannot be said to directly hear it, for we hear only what is present at the instant. These two sorts of objects, what we are *immediately* conscious of and what we are *mediately* conscious of, are found in all consciousness.[12]

'Now,' as the word is being used here, be it agreed, is that range of experience of which society as a whole (for we are talking pragmaticism, as opposed to pragmatism) is aware at any given point in time. Now is all the time of which history is conscious at any moment.

In the individualistic sense of the word — in ordinary pragmatism — Henry George's realisation about how our world works may or may not be new. That depends upon the point in time at which the individual becomes aware of it. It is in the broader sense of pragmaticism that his full realisation marks the beginning of now, linked to the closing decade of the 20th Century along a continuity which has been built up gradually by a team of thinking 'midwives of the future' (using Will Durant's term). The concept precedes George. It was a refinement of ideas alive and kicking with the French physiocrats, who are said to have founded the science of economics more than a century before George wrote *Progress and Poverty.* They, too, were trying to find the way out of poverty and misery, but at a time when Louis XV had nothing more profound to say on behalf of his people than '*Après moi le déluge.*' They elaborated something similar to the remedy that George later discovered on his own, and their successor, Jacques Turgot, as finance minister to Louis XVI, saw the need for a tax on land values and urged that such a tax be put into effect. He did so as early as the year 1776 — at another of those times in the course of human events when history was giving birth. But it was not original even then. History was not ready for Turgot, any more than it was ready for George in his day, or than it had been for Tiberius Gracchus ever so much earlier.

The previous glimpses of George's full realisation are more fleeting, less exact, couched in simpler terms than the jargon of economic science, and therefore not ready for historical birth. It has to do with fallibilism: the fact that no man, even any great man, can see ahead absolutely. Henry George was standing on the shoulders of these earlier thinkers, whether or not he was fully aware of their contribution. There is a common element in their several 'realisations', however; and it is for this reason that we must be concerned with the relationships not just between individual people, but between all individuals in society and our shared planet. Locke and Smith saw economics from the standpoint of the free individual. Marx saw it from that of society. George, like François Quesnay before him, saw what Tiberius Gracchus had been concerned about so much earlier when he described the plight of the poor in this way.[13]

> The wild beasts of Italy have their caves to retire to, but the brave men who spill their blood in her cause have nothing left but air and light. Without houses, without any settled habitations, they wander from place to place with their wives and children ... The private soldiers fight and die, to advance the wealth and luxury of the great; and they are called the masters of the world, while they have not a foot of ground in their possession.

What, though, is it that might justify our claim that history may at long last be ready for what Henry George had seen ahead? What leads us to conclude that George's awareness is the beginning of now? A phrase employed by Nicolaus Tideman in a paper he delivered at a seminar at Dartmouth College in 1987 first suggested it to this writer. Tideman was one of several scholars addressing the problem of land takings, about which there had been some surprising legal rulings which appeared to favor the collective rights of the community against the proprietorial claims of the individual. Those rulings, he argued, could not be understood except in terms of a 'not yet acknowledged idea' that seemed to be catching hold.

By the time Tideman had reshaped the paper to fit the *Columbia Law Review*,[14] he had worked it out this way: 'We are on the verge of understanding that land and natural resources are the common heritage of humanity and must be managed in a way that provides equal benefits for all persons in all generations.' Tideman saw it as the only logical explanation for the turn of events in the judicial system of the United States — a new appreciation of rights (as between individuals) and duties (towards the planet) that spills into a wide variety of new concerns, which also encompassed a number of additional developments. How else can we explain the proliferation within the past two decades of local planning boards? How else are we to understand the emergence of new political groupings known as the Greens? And what about the new sympathy for aborigines around the world, whose primordial relationship with nature is now the subject of a new appreciation, which finds its healthy expression in the collective desire to preserve the time-honoured traditions that served the evolution of the human species so well?

It is not surprising that both thesis and antithesis, originating as they did out of the Enlightenment, should have been concerned primarily with mankind, and to have overlooked the planet. From Condorcet's deep concern with *The Progress of the Human Spirit*[15] all the way to the more recent popular self-assuring slogan, 'Every day in every way I grow better and better,' there were straws in the prevailing wind of those earlier days. Thinkers up until the beginning of now were not faced with a crowded and polluted planet, except perhaps in their imagination. They had no ready reminders that the fixed size of our shared earth was a factor. Man, we were in those earlier days just discovering, could do hitherto undreamed of things, and did. But those accomplishments in turn have brought us back to a less euphoric awareness. Still — there has been no change — it is through our senses that we drink in data, and in particular through the gift of sight. Images impel. A picture is worth a thousand words. Having reached all the way up to where we can look at our small earth, and watch its diaphanous atmosphere swirling — the only place, anywhere, we can exist — man is astonished . . . and chastened. The word Hubris comes back into fashion.

IV

Reason, mankind's power to think, is fallible. The Age of Reason gave us a thesis with flaws. The Marxist Revolution, as the antithesis, grew out of those faults. It drew emotional strength from man's powerful sense of indignation at injustice. The outrage was generated by faults in the original thesis which led to the failure of the capitalist system to provide for all people the wealth and prosperity it was able to provide for some. Its authors, Marx and others, devised a program of opposition which did not, alas, rest on a firmer foundation of reason — as the systemic collapse of socialism has so conclusively demonstrated. Consumed by anger, they urged not incremental reforms but outright rejection. Dialectically, it would seem, it could not have been otherwise!

Reason's limitation, its fallibility and its power to mislead, has been known all through the dialectical process with which we are here concerned. It was explicitly recognised by the 'founding fathers' when they wrote America's constitution, the delegates having been reminded by John Dickinson of Delaware on Monday, August 23, 1787, that 'Experience must be our only guide. Reason may mislead us.'[16] His was practical advice. The constitutional authors had to devise something that was not necessarily perfect, but which provided the best frame of government on which they could agree. Experience was the practical guide. Virtually all the delegates had labored on their own state constitutions before assembling in Philadelphia; and they were led by that earlier experience. But in the long haul mankind has no choice but to return to reason; for it is the only creative process capable of delivering new solutions when, say, the advance of technology changes the economic facts of life. Reason, while fallible, can be shared and enhanced. Today's thinkers can stand on the shoulders of their predecessors. Faults in theory, given time, have a way of revealing themselves in practice, raising doubts and uncertainties, which provoke thought and new beliefs.

The central question now before us, as the collapse of certainty drives us to think, is this: where did Reason go wrong? It is an exploration of that problem that will provide us with the signposts that will make continuity possible.

* * *

The fatal faults in two seminal documents link Locke and Smith to Marx and Engels and thence to George. One is to be found in John Locke's *Second Treatise on Civil Government*, which was as nearly as any single document the blueprint on which the thesis was built. The other is to be found in Adam Smith's *An Inquiry into the Nature and Causes of the Wealth of Nations,* which continues to be an owner's manual for the western world. While neither of these is a 'fault' in the narrow sense, each of them articulated a provision which, because it was left unresolved, served to undermine the emergent mode of production and distort the appropriate system of property rights.

Locke's *Second Treatise* was almost as familiar to the founding fathers as the Bible. Each had his copy and knew it well. The *Second Treatise* grew out of the public dialogue of Locke's day, an exchange of views which hypothesised the free individual and which identified the role of property as a crucial element of that freedom.

Locke's thinking started with a 'state of nature,' which was made to seem real by the discovery of an apparently unsettled continent ready to be explored across the ocean to the west. His thesis boils down to the idea that a social contract is necessary to harmonise relations among individuals rising out of that state of nature. 'The great and chief end, therefore, of men's uniting into commonwealths, and putting themselves under government, is the preservation of their property;'[17] with life and one's whole self being a part of one's property. Only through the guarantee of property rights could the individual really be free.

So the dialectic which followed can be reduced to this. Individual liberty entails property rights. These rights made possible a level of prosperity which had never existed before. But this liberty (as written into the contract) was not available to everyone. Some were condemned to lifelong poverty. Marx's antithesis turned on the argument that the whole concept was wrong. There could be no such thing as property, because some people abuse it (or use it to abuse) and anyway the individual was subordinate to society.

Henry George resolved these contradictions with a sophisticated solution which, because of its uniqueness in the history of ideas, justifies our claim to represent it as a synthesis. George realised that there were two kinds of property (beyond one's self), and thus two kinds of property rights. In his view the distinction was essential if we are to secure either one. It was through this deeper appreciation of property rights that the appropriate reforms could be formulated and implemented.

The flaw in Locke's reasoning, the root of so much trouble, is to be found in the section headed 'Of Property.' There, he readily concedes that God 'hath given the world to men in common.' God did not give us the world merely to admire. He gave it to us to use, including all the 'fruit or venison' and other such goods as were to be found there. In the course of taking them, a person mixed his labor with them and made those goods his property. George agreed with Locke: the foundation of an individual's property rights was the fact that 'every man has a "property" in his own "person"', so that anything a man has 'removed from the common state,' anything with which he has 'mixed his own labour', rightfully belongs to him. The duty of government is to secure that right.

Locke's first examples were acorns and apples, deer and the hare, all of which once captured and held over time may spoil. That was the first fact of life that gave rise to a qualification, or provision: the first of what have been called Locke's two provisos. He held that a man could mix his labor with these things and make them his own, provided he did not claim so many that they would spoil.

Locke understood, and George reminds us in the synthesis, that such improvements as one can make by mixing labor with the natural thing are only one kind of property: 'The chief matter of property being now not the fruits of the earth and the beasts that subsist on it, but the earth itself.'

The earth does not spoil, but it has another little problem. It is limited: fixed in quantity. As Will Rogers has put it: they aren't making land any more. Locke had no quick answer for that one. He was just as sure the earth was there to be used as was the hare and the apple, so it was not acceptable even in a state of nature for vacant land to be left idle while people had unmet needs. At this point he developed the second proviso: it was all right for the individual in a state of nature to mix his labor with land and so call it his own, '*since there was still enough and as good left, and more than the yet unprovided could use.*'

There is the rub. Locke's reason began to mislead him because he failed to think through the problem. The fact that there is not 'enough and as good' of the earth and its fulness for the unprovided is what creates the proletariat. It was the dilemma which troubled Tiberius Gracchus, the one which angered Marx. In the 1930s it is what led to so many unemployed people that a welfare state had to be created in the United States, 'the land of the free.' These days, it has led to the homeless, the street people, food stamps.

Locke (writing in secret, because there was civil strife and he could not be sure of the outcome) moved on within a few pages in the

Second Treatise, inching his way down the course of human events, to the invention of money. Money took care of the first proviso: spoilage. The individual who was better able than others to pick up acorns and catch the hares could do so and sell them to someone else for money before they spoiled. Locke did not explain how money could be used to resolve the problem with the second proviso. Even in his day there was no longer 'enough and as good' left for the unprovided. With an expanding population the crisis would inevitably intensify. That is the heart of our problem today. Unused land, being scarce, is available only at a premium which few can afford.

Locke failed to think through the inexorable course of history to the situation in which an expanding population and the favored system of land tenure would leave an army of people unprovided with 'enough and as good'. The ancient word, proletariat, came once again into common usage. The failure of Locke's followers, down through the years, to heed the plight of the unfree (who did not own property), served to deepen the economic trauma in which progress and poverty were handmaidens. Grinding poverty, which the industrial revolution intensified. Enter Marx and those who shared his indignation. It was the visible injustice which drove them and fuelled the antithesis which captured half the world until the last months of 1989. Hungry, compassionate people struggled to make socialism work, because there had to be an answer, and, until experience became 'our only guide', the possibility remained as the dream of so many that socialism might be the viable answer.

The truth with which we are faced now is that socialism has not worked: attention has shifted back to the thesis. But doubt and uncertainty also surround the founders' prototype model of free enterprise, giving rise once again to genuine thought. It is the contention in this book that doubt will drive us, in our restless search for the relief and comfort of new belief, to take yet another look at Locke's unresolved second proviso.

It is not an intellectually unexplored region. Locke's failure to think his concept through has been the subject of persistent study and endless debate. It has been dismissed and explained away in a tortuous manner which confirms Mr Dickinson's warning that reason can mislead. But the 'unprovided' do not go away. Poverty persists and deepens. The gap between the haves and have nots widens, and the vast sums of money being spent by fiat to keep the two halves together threatens to break the back of free enterprise. The United States wrestles with a budget deficit in which the most unresolvable ingredient is 'entitlements', which are nothing more than the value of the denial of opportunity inflicted on the many citizens who are 'unprovided' with the proprietorial rights of access to the resources of life.

Karen I. Vaughn is the author of a bibliographical essay on Locke's *Second Treatise*,[18] in which she exhaustively reviews the topic with which we are dealing here: property, and Locke's theory of it. She discusses the book-length ideas of at least three other scholars who have dealt with Locke and property. And she nails down the significance of property, calling it 'the linchpin of Locke's political thought.'

'The very reason, then, that men form societies and governments,' she concludes from all these sources, 'is to protect their property which Locke takes to include life, liberty and estate.' Vaughn notes that it was the invention of money that provided Locke with a resolution to his first proviso, but she points out the ironic fact that money, far from resolving the first proviso, in fact made it worse.

> However, the cost to mankind of the use of money is the increasing dissension brought about by increasing resource scarcity and great inequality of income. Although by using money, men tacitly consent to the unequal distribution of wealth and hence should have no cause for complaint, in fact 'men are no great respectors of equity and justice' and the enjoyment of property becomes less and less secure.

Vaughn unfortunately pays almost as little attention to the second proviso as did the historical midwife whom she had set out to study. 'Locke does not stress this limitation, but puts most of the force of the limitation on' that other class of property which is the province of the first proviso: improvements. She pays scant attention, moreover, to the fact which Locke noted: that there are two great classes of property, oftentimes designated indiscriminately by the same unqualified word. She sees the difference in the ways the word property may be used, but then faults C. B. MacPherson for taking 'a very narrow view of the meaning of property,' a narrowness which, if historic errors are to be corrected, economists will eventually have to adopt. MacPherson, she points out, 'consistently interprets (Locke) to mean solely estate, and landed estate at that.' Since it is land, not personal property or any improvements to land, which is at the heart of the second proviso, there is reason to wish Vaughn had been more tolerant of MacPherson for his discrimination.

James Madison, often called the Father of the American Constitution, is another historical midwife who clearly saw the significance of the dilemma foreshadowed in the unresolved second Lockean proviso: the fact that, with the passage of time, more and more people would be marooned on the face of Earth without 'enough and as good'. He said little about it during the Constitutional Convention at Philadelphia, there being so many other fine points to be debated. He did take the floor to talk about it on Tuesday, August 7, 1787, when the issue was suffrage. Recording his comments in his *Notes,* referring to himself in the third person, Madison set out his concerns.[19]

> Whether the Constitutional qualification (for voting) ought to be a freehold, would with him depend on the probable reception such a change would meet with in the States where the right is now exercised by every description of people. In several of the States a freehold was now the qualification. Viewing the subject in its merits alone, the freeholders of the Country would be the safest depositories of Republican liberty. In future times a great majority of the people will not only be without landed, but any other sort of property. These will either combine under the influence of their common situation, in which case the rights of property and the public liberty will not be secure in their hands: or, which is more probable, they will become the tools of opulence and ambition, in which case there will be equal danger on another side.

All too few of the delegates at Philadelphia had the inclination to be concerned with the Lockean proviso. Many of them were land speculators and proud of it. There was surely 'enough' land left on the continent, certainly land that was 'as good' as anything which had yet been claimed, probably some that was even better. But Madison, adopting a longer time horizon, correctly calculated the outcome. The 'free' land would eventually be appropriated by new owners. Some people would be left without land — the proletariat — which threatened the 'more perfect Union' which the delegates were trying to establish.

This struggle between those who owned land and those who did not is one of the great threads that bind the continuity of American history. Jefferson wanted land ownership to be the basis of society, but he saw that government would then have a responsibility to see that every family owned land. Where vacant land and property existed together, he knew, the natural right of all men to own land was out of adjustment. The Louisiana Purchase helped, as did the gradual opening up of the continent, but even in their presidencies Madison and Jefferson both knew that the amount of free land was finite. Horace Greeley's advice to 'go west, young man,' George Evans's claims in the *Workingman's Advocate* that land monopoly was the root cause of poverty and inequality, George Washington Julian's fight for the Homestead Act, the railroad grants, the post-Civil War calls for 'forty acres and a mule,' and Frederick Jackson Turner's frontier thesis, the early statements of which were based in no small part on the writings of Henry George: all these elements are facets of the ongoing struggle Madison foresaw.[20]

Finally, in 1829, when Madison was back home at Montpelier, and his home state of Virginia was examining once again its own Constitution, the ageing statesman wrote some notes which take up nine pages of the *Letters of Madison* published in 1865.[21]

'The United States have not reached the stage of society in which conflicting feelings of the class with, and the class without property, have the operation natural to them in countries fully peopled,' he realised, as the young country continued to expand westward. The continent had not yet been filled up. But it must inevitably happen.

> And whenever the majority shall be without landed or other equivalent property, and without the means or hopes of acquiring it, what is to secure the rights of property against the danger of an equality and universality of suffrage, vesting complete power over property in hands without a share in it; not to speak of danger in the meantime from a dependence of an increasing number on the wealth of a few?

Madison was deeply concerned about that ultimate cleavage between the propertied and propertyless — the 'haves' and the 'have nots'. He wondered, first of all, when it might be expected to happen. His arithmetic led him to believe that by the year 1929 there would be some 192,000,000 people in the United States, by which time the continent would have been filled up. He missed his target by a few years, as it turned out; it was not until the sixties that the population topped 190,000,000 although it was in the year 1929 that another, closely related, event took place. It was well before that year that others in America began to be worried about the danger Madison had foreseen. Frederick Jackson Turner was a little-known professor of history from Wisconsin in 1893 when he made a speech at the Columbian Exposition at Chicago that eventually made him famous. Turner's frontier thesis, explaining the American character in terms of the availability of free land (so long as there continued to be 'enough and as good' left to be had) became a dominant idea among American historians for some years.

Turner said that the continent had already been filled up. He had been studying the federal census for 1890 and had noted that, for the first time, the Census Bureau had seen fit to omit the 'frontier' as a category. It did not exist any more, as far as the census takers were concerned; and that troubled Turner, because he felt sure the American character would change. (Hasn't it?) Franklin D. Roosevelt thought it might present a problem too, and in 1932, when speaking to the Commonwealth Club (before his long tenure in office began) he said, 'Our last frontier has long since been reached. There is no safety valve in the form of a Western Prairie . . .' George Gilder was still saying it only a few years ago when he published a best-seller, *Wealth and Poverty.* He writes, two pages from the end of the book, 'It is said we must abandon ecnomic freedom because the frontier is closed.'

But it was not just property rights that were coming into the picture as more and more thinkers came to be concerned, but the right to liberty itself. Turner, having deliberated about it for years, was specific about the threat to liberty after World War I, when he was asked to deliver a series of six lectures on liberty at Harvard University. He said flatly that, once the continent had been filled up and all the free land was gone, there would no longer be any hope of the unrestrained economic liberty with which Madison had been familiar. In its place, he predicted, must come an 'adjusted liberty' as government controls were extended in the interests of society as a whole.

In 1936 the public domain was officially closed. I do not believe it to be a coincidence that, about then, the 'welfare state' was being brought into existence.

This brings us back to the present, and to the closing years of a century which is said to have 'purged itself of certainty.' An avalanche of astonishing events may once again be triggering thought. What will contemporary thinkers find if they go back to Locke and his second proviso: Enough (land) and as good?

The word 'enough' is a challenge, of course, but the words 'as good' would have seemed in Locke's day even harder to resolve. Who knows exactly how good one tract of land is, to say nothing of whether or not another tract of land may be 'as good?' Surprisingly, perhaps, an open-minded thinker will find, if he goes at the questions in these days when history is ready for a new beginning, that the market knows the answer. It fixes them in terms of money:land values. So money, ironically, can do for poverty — destitution, and the second proviso — what it has already done for spoilage and the first. It is not through confiscation and redistribution, which are features of the welfare state, that money will resolve the second proviso, however, but by means of the remedy articulated by Henry George in 1879: what was then called the 'single tax', but is now called land value taxation. This is the fiscal representation of the synthesis for which the public dialogue is ready.

'It is not necessary to confiscate land,' said George. 'It is necessary only to confiscate rent,' which can be collected in units of money, assessed with precision by the invisible hand of the market. The earth is ours to use, as Locke insisted, but not just by the few. Everyone must have access to its fullness which, as it turns out, is metered in what economists call economic rent. Let society share economic rent, instead of leaving it in the hands of the few, and there need no longer be any who are poor.

The market decides exactly how good any particular tract of land is, and the extent to which it is worse, better than or as good as another. David Ricardo helped us to understand the process. This measure of value enables us to resolve the second proviso. Economic rent, left uncollected by society — which has the only clear title to it, since the earth belongs morally to us all — shows up as the price at which land is traded. It is this price that leads to trouble. Economic rent is land's value in productive terms, but left uncollected as price, it creates new temptation. The uncollected price of land fattens as it accumulates an outer husk of speculative value — the possibility of resale, at a premium, to someone who may need it and be willing to pay not just for its productive value but for the privilege as well.

George's synthesis integrates with Locke's thesis at this point. It nurtures reason by eliminating a central defect. It matches up with Marx's antithesis by eliminating poverty, and thus the destructive roots of indignation and envy. The continuity is indisputable, and must eventually be appreciated. No one can be sure how long comprehension will take; nor is there any way to be sure whether the birth will be easy or difficult. But as with any birth, it is unavoidable.

* * *

The unmet provision in Adam Smith's reasoning, which is the integral part of the framework of this continuity, is to be found in his discussion of 'Systems of Political Economy.'[22] It is not as famous as the Lockean proviso, but its implications are far reaching, and have left their mark. After making the point that no political system needs to be perfect in order to function, Smith offers these observations.

> In the political body ... the wisdom of nature has fortunately made ample provision for remedying many of the bad effects of the folly and injustice of man; in the same manner as it has done in the natural body, for remedying those of his sloth and intemperance.
>
> It is thus that every system which endeavors, either, by extraordinary encouragements, to draw towards a particular species of industry a greater share of the capital of society than what would naturally go to it; or, by extraordinary restraints, to force from a particular species of industry some share of the capital which would otherwise be employed in it; it is in reality subversive of the great purpose which it means to promote. It retards, instead of accelerating, the progress of the society towards real wealth and greatness; and diminishes, instead of increasing, the real value of the annual produce of its land and labor.
>
> All systems of preference or of restraint, therefore, being thus completely taken away, the obvious and simple system of natural liberty establishes itself of its own accord. Every man, *as long as he does not violate the laws of justice,* is left perfectly free to pursue his own interest in his own way, and to bring both his industry and capital into competition with those of any other man, or order of men.

Smith calls for a balance between self interest and the laws of justice which is not easy to strike. One facet of human nature that has evidenced itself through history, which can be traced back long before the Enlightenment or even Christianity — one particular 'folly and injustice of man' for which the wisdom of nature has not provided protection — is greed. It is widely accepted that man is a predatory animal, uniquely capable of turning against and even killing the weaker of his own kind. And there is inescapable evidence in all history to show that men — or some men, at least — are unable to prevent their drive to satisfy self interest from spilling over into greed. The Calvinists who first settled the bleak northeastern coast of what has become the United States were convinced that 'unregenerate man is half beast and half devil,' and their earliest social contracts included guarantees protecting one against another. America's first written constitution, in fact, the temporary social contract written in New Hampshire to guide that colony through the War of Revolution, included in its statement of purpose a phrase that grew directly out of that Calvinist creed: the need to protect prople in a state of nature 'from the Machinations and evil Designs of wicked men.'[23] The 'liberty' we so highly treasure is really a freedom from each other — freedom from coercive behavior, one manifestation of which is greed.

As society has evolved, and as mankind has become better acquainted with itself, there have been discovered all manner of ways in which 'self interest' impels the discovery of tools and advantages by which to exploit others. One of the worst has been the State, which Franz Oppenheimer has defined as an institution 'forced on a defeated group by a conquering group, with a view only to systematising the domination of the conquered by the conquerors, and safeguarding itself against insurrection from within and attack from without. This domination had no other final purpose than the economic exploitation of the conquered group by the victorious group.'[24] Albert Jay Nock, like Oppenheimer, differentiates between the '*economic* means' of satisfying our self interests (which he defines as the production and exchange of wealth) and the '*political*' means (which he describes as the 'uncompensated appropriation of wealth produced by others.')[25] The several ways in which powers held aside for the State (or for any form of government whether autocratic, aristocratic or democratic) can be used as a club for the strong against the weak were widely discussed by the

American delegates at the constitutional convention and in the *Federalist Papers* written to convince the people of a nation then being born of the wisdom of that convention's product. The concepts adopted to protect against any such abuse include the separation and the balance of powers, and the Bill of Rights.

The primary instrument of coercion, and thus of injustice between people, is through the control of natural resources, land, the earth, access to which is the indispensable condition for existence. 'Everybody has to be somewhere.' Man without access to land is a slave. And so it is that virtually every written code of laws — the predecessors to constitutions and the more formal social contracts — has included some provision for guarding justice in land. The codes of Moses (1500 B.C.?), Lycurgus (900 B.C.?), Solon (600 B.C.?) and Licinius (300 B.C.?) all recognise the common rights of the world to a fair share in the earth.

We can now see that there is no way in which Smith's proviso requiring justice as a restraint on self interest, to enable the 'invisible hand' to operate efficiently, can be satisfied until the contradiction in the Lockean proviso has been resolved.

With the collapse of the socialist antithesis, some people advocate that society should return to the thesis as it was originally set down. That cannot be. 'You can't go home again.' Anyone who believes it possible must at least examine the record of how the appetite for speculative gains from land has, through all the years of free enterprise, torn the social fabric. The gradual appropriation of England's commons over many painful years is a chapter in that story, and Oliver Goldsmith's poem, *The Deserted Village,* is eloquent testimony to it. Land hunger and the appropriation of land value was a deep concern for colonial America's Calvinist leaders long before there were states to send delegates to a constitutional convention where other human foibles could be discussed. The Rev. Jonathan Edwards, for instance, who has been called America's outstanding theologian, and who served the New England colonies as its conscience in those early years, lashed out against the greed of the 'river gods' who so ruthlessly ruled the Connecticut River valley. It was Edwards who delivered at Enfield, Connecticut, the challenging sermon, 'Sinners in the Hands of an Angry God.' He preached against fornication, 'night walking', and irresponsibility towards honest debts; but in his mind sharp practice in land speculation was as great an evil as any other. When his patron and uncle, Colonel John Stoddard, died in 1748, and left the still young minister at the mercy of strong men whom he had chastised, it fell to the Rev. Mr. Edwards to deliver a funeral sermon over the Colonel. Perry Miller, a leading scholar in the roots of American religion, dramatises it in *Errand into the Wilderness.* Here is what Edwards thought of land speculators 240 years ago.[26]

> It is particularly unbecoming of them to be of a mean spirit, a disposition that will admit of their doing those things that are sordid and vile; as when they are persons of a narrow, private spirit, that may be found in little tricks and intrigues to promote their private interest. Such as will shamefully defile their hands to gain a few pounds, are not ashamed to grind the faces of the poor, and screw their neighbors; and will take advantage of their authority or commission to line their own pockets with what is fraudulently taken or withheld from others.

Were those early 'river gods' an exception in the evolution of the Locke/Smith thesis? Speculation in land, with all its sharp practices, has been a major factor throughout American history. Charles Haskins, a professor of history at the University of Wisconsin in 1891, analysed a shocking episode called the Yazoo Land Companies which carries this overview.[27]

> The spirit of speculation in land was a prominent characteristic of the United States at the close of the last century. Although the Crown had received frequent petitions for land grants in the West, there was little westward migration until the time of the Revolution. Then the number of emigrants, the cheapness of the lands, and the lack of an established system of sale in small quantities offered many inducements for the formation of great land companies whose opportunities for speculation were increased by the depreciated currency and the general ignorance concerning the west. So strong did the spirit of speculation become that in 1796 an English traveller would say: 'Were I to characterise the United States, it would be by the appellation of the land of speculation.' In spite of its exaggeration this assertion contained much truth. 'All I am now worth was gained by speculation in land,' wrote Timothy Pickering (then about to become Secretary of State under President John Adams) in the same year, and many eminent men could have said the same, often with a later experience quite similar. Land speculation involved Washington, Franklin, Gallatin, Patrick Henry, Robert Morris and James Wilson, as well as many less widely known.

The point here is not to moralise but to trace the continuity through history of greedy behavior, which time and again showed up in the grasp for speculative land values, even on the part of good, even great and otherwise decent men. It is as much a part of human nature as the hunger for power — the political means of satisfying needs from which protection has been sought in such devices as separation, balance and the Bill of Rights. Speculative greed can be satisfied by the accumulation of economic rent, but the price of this right is the denial of freedom of those who are excluded from a share in the fruits of Mother Earth. It is the chief human 'folly and injustice' against which the social contract has not yet struck a balance. The solution is Henry George's fiscal remedy which, elegant in its simplicity, is comprehensive in its power to unleash the talents of individuals while protecting the rights of everyone as members of a community.

Charles Peirce — not an economist, although he was the author of pragmaticism and an acknowledged authority in at least six scientific disciplines — was among those indignant about greed at a time when the American continent was finally filling up. He wrote about greed in his essay, 'Evolutionary Love.'[28] 'The twentieth century, in its latter half, shall surely see the deluge-tempest burst upon the social order — to clear upon a world so deep in ruins as that greed-philosophy,' he says after a long passage tracing the effects of unbridled 'self interest' then predominating as the robber barons fed off the system of capitalism and free enterprise which were pushing toward supremacy.

Peirce could not have known that Vladimir Ilyich Lenin, in his early twenties, was, at exactly the time Peirce was lamenting greed, himself feeling the same indignation welling up. It was in the year Peirce published 'Evolutionary Love' that Lenin became a member of an underground revolutionary group engaged in the distribution of literature among factory workers. And so, as it has turned out, it was earlier than the 'latter half' of the twentieth century that the 'deluge-tempest burst upon the social order' in the form of the antithetical Revolution; but here we are again with the same indignation over greed still welling up in compassionate people all over a small world growing smaller. This time, however, something else seems ready to happen to it.

Socialism may have collapsed, but the indignation is still there, and will remain there so long as Smith's proviso regarding the balance between self interest and justice remains unmet. That is a claim that can be supported in any country of the western world on any single day in the public prints. Laurence Harris, for example, explaining in the pages of London's *The Guardian* 'Why I remain a small 'c' communist,'[29] says it is 'because the vast mass of lives are materially, physically and spiritually impoverished. They are profoundly unfree. I don't think capitalism is able to overcome that blight, and in many ways it perpetuates and worsens it.' In fact, capitalism could overcome the blight if it were to do about greed what democracy has done about the hunger for power. It is towards the resolution of this problem that history now appears to be moving, and to the clarification of which this book is dedicated.

V

A certain spiritual yearning implied by the concept of the millennium — a fervor — is essential to the generic sense of the word as it relates to a consideration of social evolution. One of its accepted meanings is the imminence of 'a period of general righteousness and happiness,' the widespread hope for which seems not uncommon in historical dialectics. The millennial hope has been a factor in the dialectical stages under consideration here — the reasoned thesis and the revolutionary antithesis.

John Winthrop surely felt something of it when he preached a lay sermon aboard the flagship *Arabella* in 1630, when the first Puritans were sailing towards the new continent, partly because 'wise men thought that England was overpopulated and the poor would have a better chance in the new land.'[30] The sentence is not Winthrop's, but that of historian Perry Miller. A careful reading of his book supports the claim that for Miller's words 'the poor' one could correctly substitute 'the as yet unprovided.' It was the group of people Marx and others would later call the proletariat.

Winthrop, who was trying to articulate for his adventurous colleagues just what it was they were seeking to accomplish, assured them '... wee must Consider that wee shall be as a Citty upon a Hill, the eies of all people are uppon us.'[31] His words foreshadowed the thesis, Winthrop's sermon having been delivered two years before John Locke was born.

A better case, much more specific, for the millennial concept as an element in the dialectical thesis can be made for that much later period of authorship, during which free enterprise and the market system was being spelled out into the world's first written social contracts: the American constitutions. These were being written, debated and voted into existence by free people over a period of 15 years beginning in 1775 and continuing through the belated adoption by Congress of the American Bill of Rights. The most persistent constitutional author in the state of New Hampshire (where the first temporary Plan of Government was adopted just after New Year's Day in 1776, and where the second oldest constitution still in effect was finally accepted by voters in 1784) was a man named Benjamin Giles.[32] He was a new light Calvinist, clearly motivated by what is still called the Great Awakening. A study of the primary sources makes it clear that the reason why Giles travelled on horseback over the mountains and through the woods, winter and summer, between his farm at Newport and the constitutional conventions in Exeter and Concord, was the millennial hope of bringing into existence a better way of life for all people. Giles was certainly influenced by Jonathan Edwards's book on *Freedom of Will*, which historian Alan Heimert has called 'the Calvinist handbook of the Revolution.'

The *Federalist Papers* and the famous exchange of letters between John Adams and Thomas Jefferson,[33] most of them written after their years as president, provide ample evidence that the driving force behind the implementation of the dialectical thesis in the United States was a will to create a better organisation of society, fairer and more fruitful for everyone, than the ones from which they had fled in the Old World.

James Turner, having studied what he calls 'modern belief' in America between the years 1500 and 1865,[34] was willing to report that, 'Near the end of the (18th) century, hope for progress began to feed heavily on religious beliefs, especially in America, where Protestantism harbored a pronounced streak of millennial expectation. This hope gradually took a form among some believers that dovetailed with the idea of steady human improvement culminating in a perfected society.' He nailed it down more exactly in the closing decade of that century, a period just 200 years ago. There was a belief that 'The millennium itself would emerge not all of a sudden, but as a gradual perfecting of earthly life through human effort, inspired by divine grace.'[35]

It is not the theological basis of the millennial concept that is being explored here, but the fervor — spiritual energy as a driving force. And for the socialist antithesis that element is nowhere better developed than in a book called *The God that Failed*,[36] edited by an Englishman and including chapters by literary figures in several western countries. The book was pulled together in the years immediately after World War II, and was published in 1950. When it was republished in 1983 it carried a new foreword by Norman Podhoretz in which he acknowledges 'the susceptibility of intellectuals to communism.' But there is more than theory or even ideology behind the vigor with which the socialist antithesis went into effect in the first half of this century. It was a 'god' that had failed. Podhoretz, reconsidering the book a quarter of a century after it was written, sees the major element in whatever it was that drew six literary men from different countries into communism as '... the struggle for social justice.' Marx's and Lenin's versions of socialism were even then beginning to lose support, and Podhoretz was obviously clinging to the possibility that the synthesis eventually to emerge would be a mixture he called 'democratic socialism.'

The editor, Richard H. Crossman, who first saw the need for such a book, suggests the millennial concept as a motivation by singling out a common ground between the six contributors. They 'saw it first from a long way off — just as their predecessors, 130 years ago, saw the French Revolution — as a vision of the Kingdom of God on earth.' It was his concern with 'the lives of the oppressed and the isolated' that drew the American Richard Wright into it. French novelist and playwright André Gide said he initially supported the antithesis because he saw it as 'an impulse capable of sweeping along the whole of humanity.' Each of the seven writers was ready to admit that his god had failed; each was concerned with all humanity, for equality and justice, rather than prosperity for the few while the majority were excluded.

The mainspring of the thesis is liberty. The maispring of the antithesis is equal justice for all. They are the essentials. The synthesis, when and if it emerges, must accommodate them both. The claim made here is that Henry George's realisation about the practical terms on which people must relate to each other, and to the planet, stands the test on both counts. The Georgist philosophy also provides the vision that nurtures the fervor and the spiritual yearning that are the driving force of millennial hopes, which are the emotional responses of human beings to the concepts of liberty and justice.

If Charles Peirce is correct, and if doubt and uncertainty do give rise to thought, then truth will be found. Like an undiscovered continent, it must eventually be stumbled across. A new belief in a better world will be attained and acted upon. In that sense the word millennium seems allowable and is employed here.

NOTES

1. Will Durant, *The Story of Philosophy*, revised edition (Garden City, N.Y. Garden City Publishing Co. 1938) pp.322, 323.
2. Henry George, *Progress and Poverty*, 1879 (centenary edition New York: Robert Schalkenbach Foundation, 1987).
3. Henry George, *The Science of Political Economy*, 1898 (reprint edition New York: Robert Schalkenbach Foundation 1981).
4. Charles S. Peirce, *Chance, Love and Logic*, Harcourt, Brace and World Inc 1923 (reprint edition New York: Barnes & Noble Inc)
5. Ibid, p.38.
6. Thomas S. Knight, *Charles Peirce* (New York: Twayne Publishers Inc., 1965) p.45.
7. Knight, supra.
8. Ibid, p.61.
9. Thomas Sowell, *A Conflict of Visions* (New York: William Morrow and Company Inc., 1987).
10. Steven B. Cord, *Henry George: Dreamer or Realist?* (Philadelphia: University of Pennsylvania Press, 1965), p.202.
11. Peirce, op cit., p.40.
12. Ibid., pp.39-40.
13. Plutarch, *The Lives of the Noble Grecians and Romans*, The Modern Library edition New York: Random House Inc.) p.999. The translation quoted is that of John and William Langhorne (London: George Routledge & Sons, Limited, 1904).
14. T. Nicolaus Tideman, 'Takings, Moral Evolution and Justice,' *Columbia Law Review*, Vol.88 No. 8 (December 1988) pp.1714-30).

15. Marie Jean Caritat, Marquis de Condorcet, *Sketch for a Historical Picture of the Progress of the Human Mind.* 1795.
16. James Madison, *Notes of Debates in the Federal Convention of 1787.* The Norton Library edition, New York: W. W. Norton & Company 1966) p.447.
17. John Locke, *Of Civil Government: Second Treatise,* (Gateway edition, Chicago: Henry Regnery Company, 1955) p.102.
18. Karen I. Vaughn, 'John Locke's Theory of Property: Problems of Interpretation,' *Literature of Liberty,* (Menlo Park, California: Institute for Humane Studies) Vol. III, No. 1, Spring 1980, pp.5-37).
19. Madison, op cit., pp.403-4.
20. The greed-driven struggle for 'free land' as the American continent was taken up has been amply documented, for examples: Alfred N. Chandler, *Land Title Origins: A Tale of Force and Fraud,* (New York: Robert Schalkenbach Foundation, 1945); Leslie E. Decker, *Railroads Lands and Politics: The Taxation of Railroad Land Grants 1864-1897,* (Providence, Rhode Island: Brown University Press, 1964); Benjamin Horace Hibbard, *History of the Public Lands Policies,* (New York: The Macmillan Co., 1934); Homer Hoyt, *One Hundred Years of Land Gambling in Chicago,* (Chicago: University of Chicago Press, 1934); Shaw Livermore, *Early American Land Companies,* New York: The Commonwealth Fund, 1939); Roy M. Robbins, *Our Landed Heritage,* Princeton: University of Princeton Press, 1942); and Frederick Jackson Turner, *The United States, 1830-1850,* (New York: Henry Holt & Co., 1935). For a more extensive bibliography, see Chandler, supra.
21. James Madison, *Letters and Other Writings,* (Philadelphia: J. P. Lippincott & Co., 1865) Vol. 4, pp.21-30.
22. Adam Smith, *Wealth of Nations,* 1776, The Harvard Classics edition (New York: P. F. Collier & Son Corporation, 1909) p.445.
23. Richard Noyes, 'A Note on a Founding Father's Library: The Books of Benjamin Giles,' *Historical New Hampshire,* Vol. XXXIV, Nos. 3 & 4, Fall/Winter 1979, pp.244-252.
24. Albert J. Nock, *Our Enemy the State,* 1935, Free Life edition (New York: Free Life Editions, Inc., 1973) p.20.
25. Ibid., p.26.
26. Jonathan Edwards, 'God's awful Judgment in the breaking and withering of the Strong Rods of a Community,' in *The Works of Jonathan Edwards,* Edward Hickman edition (Carlisle, Pennsylvania: The Banner of Truth Trust, 1974) Vol.II, p.37. Perry Miller discusses it in *Errand into the Wilderness* (Cambridge, Massachusetts: The Belknap Press of Harvard University Press, 1956) p.165.
27. Charles Haskins, 'The Yazoo Land Companies,' *American Historical Association Papers* (New York: 1891) Vol.5, pt 4, pp.393-437.

28. Peirce, op cit., p.274.
29. Laurence Harris, Professor of Economics at the Open University, in *The Guardian,* London, January 4, 1990.
30. Perry Miller, op cit., p.4.
31. Ibid., p.11.
32. Noyes, op cit.
33. Lester Cappon, Jr., ed., *The Adams-Jefferson Letters,* (Williamsburg Virginia: The University of North Carolina Press, 1959).
34. James Turner, *Without God, Without Creed: The Origins of Unbelief in America,* (Baltimore: The Johns Hopkins University Press, 1985) p.42.
35. Ibid., p.87.
36. Richard H. Crossman, ed., *The God that Failed,* (New York: Harper and Row, 1949) republished in 1983 (Chicago, Regnery Gateway, Inc.) with a new foreword by Norman Podhoretz.
37. Social Problems (1883), centenary edition, New York: Robert Schalkenbach Foundation, 1989, Ch.17.
38. Penn Central Transp. Co. v City of New York, 366 N.E. 2d 1271, 42 N.Y. 2d 324 (1977).
39. Martin Elson, *Negotiating the Future: Planning Gain in the 1990s,* Gloucester: ARC Ltd, 1990.
40. Samantha Jenkins, 'Moves to stamp out planning gain abuse,' *Estates Times,* July 20, 1990.
41. *Social Problems,* p.27.

II
THE TRANSFORMATION OF PROPERTY RIGHTS

2

Property Rights and the Social Contract: the constitutional challenge in the U.S.A.

NICOLAUS TIDEMAN

IN A MANNER reminiscent of Socrates, the proponents of land value taxation strive to convince people of the validity of ideas that lie on the edge of their consciousness, not yet acknowledged. Because no one made the land, a person can have a respectable claim to the use of more than a proportionate share of land only if he or she compensates those who thereby have less than proportionate shares. Thus the rent of land must be collected socially. But when people begin to entertain this idea, and realize that it implies that the sale price of unimproved land would fall to practically nothing, they often are brought to a halt by the thought that this would constitute a 'confiscation of the property of landowners,' and therefore could never be acceptable.

My purpose is to analyze in detail the concern that land value taxation would be confiscation. I will begin by discussing the theory of confiscation, and then consider how this theory applies to land value taxation. I will argue that by using a constitutional amendment it is possible to implement 100% land value taxation, without compensation for the virtual disappearance of the sale value of land titles, while still being faithful to the values that lie behind the concern for confiscation.

There is a good side to the concern about confiscation. This concern reveals an understanding that there is potential for governments to intrude upon what properly belongs to individuals, and that such intrusions ought not to be allowed. Such an understanding is one of the requirements for successful democracy.

But why does the prospect of land value taxation trigger the concern for confiscation? Why is it *not* generally seen to be confiscation when a government appropriates to itself a substantial fraction of what individuals earn from their labor and capital? To persuade the people who talk of 'confiscation' that land value taxation ought not be regarded as confiscation, we must understand what they mean by this term.

The fifth amendment to the U.S. Constitution ends with the words, 'nor shall private property be taken for public use, without just compensation.' This clause reflects the understanding that governments are capable of taking what belongs to individuals, and the desire to prevent this abuse of power. But a constitution can only express principles in the broadest terms. The detailed meaning of a constitution emerges over time, as its principles are interpreted in legislation and legal cases. And the 'takings clause' has been at the center of a great deal of debate and numerous legal challenges to government action.

One of the most widely respected analyses of the body of law that has emerged from cases involving the takings clause is a 1967 paper by Frank Michelman in the *Harvard Law Review*.[1] One of Michelman's principal conclusions was that if one wished to state rules that would distinguish the cases where courts had decided that a government action constituted a taking of property, for which compensation was required, from cases that courts had decided did not constitute takings, and therefore did not require compensation, then the following rule was central:

If a government action reduces the value of something that a person owns to nothing or nearly nothing, then that action is a taking of the person's property, and the government must provide compensation. On the other hand, if a government action reduces the value of something a person owns only partially, leaving a significant fraction of the original value in the hands of the owner, then that action is not a taking of property, and no compensation is required.

In a more recent review of the law of takings, Michelman summarized the apparent current position of the Supreme Court as follows: For activities that are nuisances there is no issue of takings. For other activities, a government action is a taking if it involves permanent physical occupation of property or if it eliminates all economic value of the affected property.[2] There is one further test to which the court may have given the same authority.[3] A government action may be a taking if it represents a reversal of an earlier government position on which an aggrieved person relied in making an investment.

This summary of the existing rules is consistent with regarding a tax that collects all the rent of land as confiscation, while not regarding as confiscation a tax that collects half the return to capital. When all the rent of land is collected by a tax, the sale value of unimproved land can be expected to fall virtually to nothing, so by the stated rules the tax is a taking that requires compensation. On the other hand, a 50% tax on the return to capital is not a taking by this rule, because capital still retains a significant fraction of its original sale value.

But why, it might be asked, do we tolerate government actions that eliminate substantial fractions of the value of property when we do not tolerate government actions that take all the value of property? To answer this question I shall first address the question of why it is that government actions that eliminate all the value of things are unacceptable.

The reason, I believe, is that we understand that one of the ways in which democratic decision-making can go awry is that a 'tyranny of the majority' may develop. That is, a faction that constitutes more than half of the legislature may take over and make all decisions in whatever way suits themselves, without taking any account of consequences for those outside the faction. Our expectation that legislative bodies will operate through political parties reflects an acceptance of factions, although the rarity of straight party votes is an indication that the legislative process generally involves more than a simple imposition of the will of a majority faction on the whole group.

If a majority faction were to take over a legislative process completely, then one of the things that they might do, in the absence of a constitutional constraint, would be to pass laws by which the property of people who were not supporters of the faction was appropriated for their purposes. We know that this would involve unnecessarily unfair discrimination against those whose property was appropriated, because if the property in question actually were needed for public purposes, then it would be possible to call on everyone to contribute to a fund from which those whose property was to be taken could be compensated. And so to prevent unnecessarily unfair appropriations by a majority faction we forbid the taking of property for public purposes without compensation.

Why, though, is the same analysis not applicable to actions that take part of the value of things? Indeed, there are some legal scholars, notably Richard Epstein of the University of Chicago Law School, who assert that the requirement of compensation for takings *should* be understood to apply to all diminutions of value from public actions.[4]

I believe that there are two reasons why Epstein's view has not generally prevailed. First there are the 'transactions costs' of implementing universal compensation. If anyone who had property that was adversely affected in any noticeable way by government actions was eligible for compensation, there would be substantial additional administrative costs of processing all the claims. The possibility of receiving compensation could be expected to give rise to artificial claims and to exaggerated statements of the magnitude of valid claims. If the administrative costs of dealing with claims of compensation for partial losses of value are large relative to the magnitude of the claims, and if partial losses of value of property are a commonly recurring phenomenon, then the uncompensated losses will be sufficiently equally distributed for nearly everyone to benefit more from not having to contribute to the compensation of others than he would lose from not being compensated himself, and none of those with net losses would lose all that much.

A second reason for not compensating for partial losses is that these losses may reflect coherent decisions about who should bear which costs. For example, we are now in the process of limiting the use of chlorofluorocarbons (known as CFCs), to avoid further damage that CFCs do to the ozone layer of the atmosphere. This development is likely to reduce the value of equipment that has been created for the sole purpose of manufacturing CFCs. If we do not compensate the owners of such equipment for the losses they incur as a result of the phasing out of CFCs, then the producers of other substances will be motivated to be more concerned about the potential harmful consequences of their own products. It is as if we were saying that the past existence of a particular state of affairs does not create an entitlement to the perpetuation of that state. What people are entitled to is an evolving best guess as to what is in the general interest. If people develop expectations that go unfulfilled because of an evolution in our understanding, we can classify those expectations as ones that should not have been developed in the first place.

Thus it is that a distinction is made between a government action that eliminates all the value of something, which is regarded as a 'taking,' and would be regarded as confiscation if compensation were not provided, and an action that reduces the value of something, which is not considered a taking, and for which no compensation is required.

This distinction between actions that take all the value of things and actions that take only part of the value of things has been challenged recently by the introduction of the concept of 'conceptual severance.' This idea is best explained with an example. Suppose that a local government passes a regulation stating that no buildings taller than 100 feet may be built. From what has been said so far, it would appear that this is not a taking of property. The new regulation may diminish the sale value of some land, but there will still be many ways in which it can be used. Suppose however that some people, concerned about shadows, have been purchasing from others easements specifying that no building taller than 100 feet will be built on specific sites. Occasionally someone who has a site for which such an easement has been sold buys it back again so that he will be able to construct a building taller than 100 feet. At the time when the new regulation is passed, there is someone who has just repurchased such an easement and is about to begin construction. The regulation can properly be said to take 100% of the value of the easement that he has just purchased. This would appear to mean that the regulation constitutes a taking, at least as far as he is concerned, and that he is therefore entitled to compensation. More generally, for any regulation that restricts the use of property, there is a possibility of a contract in which the right to precisely that action is exchanged. Therefore, we can 'conceptually sever' the right at issue from the remainder of the property, and the regulation will properly be described as taking all the value of what has been conceptually severed. And if such contracts *could* exist, what difference should it make whether they *actually* exist for the issue of whether compensation must be paid?

An example of conceptual severance becoming actual severance, and threatening to intrude upon the issue of compensation, arose in the recent case of Keystone Bituminous Coal Association versus DeBenedictus.[5] This case arose from a Pennsylvania law that requires coal companies to leave in the ground enough pillars of coal to insure that the ground will not collapse. This seems like an eminently reasonable regulation, which would diminish the value of coal holdings by little enough not to qualify as a taking. But there is more to the story. Many years earlier, the coal companies had purchased, along with mineral rights, what in Pennsylvania is known as the 'support estate,' by which is meant the right to be assured that the surface will not cave in. Somewhat remarkably, people built extensively even though they knew that coal companies held the support estates. Such building is not necessarily financially irrational. If it was reasonable to expect that any mining that did occur would be far enough in the future that the investments in improvements could be recouped before the mining started, then it was not irrational to improve the land without owning the support estates. But as the years passed, the holders of the surface rights came to rely on an indefinite postponement of the mining that had earlier been contemplated.

While permitting limited mining, the Pennsylvania law had the same effect as a law prescribing that every coal company that held support estates without the corresponding surface estates was required to turn the support estates over to the holders of the surface estates. If the law had been written in that fashion, the court would almost certainly have declared that it served private rather than public purposes and was therefore a deprivation of property without due process of law. With the law written as it was, however, the Supreme Court said that the law could be justified by a State's power to regulate nuisances, and even if the caving in of the surface had not been a nuisance, it would not have been a taking in any case since the coal involved consituted only about 2% of the companies' total holdings. The Court thus rejected the notion that the severability of the support estate might transform a permissible regulation into a taking. The distinction between government actions that take some of the value of things people own and those that take all their value was maintained by the courts, though at some cost of apparent obtuseness. The court was saying, in effect, 'We all know what a "thing" is, so we all know what it means to take all the value of a thing.'

Michelman has an explanation of why the courts would refuse to deal with conceptual severance. According to Michelman, the protection of property against confiscation is the manifestation of a desire by our constitutional founders to provide 'a private sphere of individual self-determination securely bounded off from politics by law.'[6] The concept of property, existing apart from law, seemed entirely natural and unproblematic to our constitutional founders. For modern legal thinkers, on the other hand, property is made murky not only by conceptual severance, but also by the possibility of treating as property any advantage that accrues to individuals by virtue of legislation (tobacco acreage allotments, import quotas, broadcasting licenses, etc.).

An intractable problem is created, Michelman says, by the fact that we want both popular sovereignty — rule by the people— and limited government, and these two ideals must inevitably conflict. We use the idea of property to manage the conflict between popular sovereignty and limited government to specify the boundary between a region of activity that can be controlled by legislation and a region where individuals are free from legislative intrusions. Because of the great importance of this rôle of the idea of property, courts resist such notions as conceptual severance that would tend to undermine the coherence of the concept. To preserve the boundary-identifying rôle of property, courts search for formal tests like 'permanent physical occupation' and 'elimination of all economic value' that connect with common understandings of what property is all about.

To show how 100% land value taxation can be acceptable despite its virtual elimination of the sale value of titles to unimproved land, I must explain how the function of preserving the boundary between where individual rights prevail and where democratic process prevails can be sustained, even though the ban on actions that eliminate all the values of things is apparently violated. For this purpose it is useful to examine in more detail the limitations of democratic decisions.

A well-functioning government is understood to be a device through which people pursue the common good. In an ideal world, everyone would have the same perception of the common good, and all government actions would be approved unanimously. In our less-than-ideal world, on the other hand, we are rarely able to achieve unanimity, for two distinctly different reasons. First, people may have the best of intentions but still have differing perceptions of the common good. Second, people may pursue their selfish individual ends rather than the common good in their democratic participation. Whichever reason is the cause of departures from unanimity, there are things to be said in favor of democratic process. If the departures from unanimity are caused by differing perceptions of the common good, by people who have no selfish intentions, then democratic process is a useful way of settling on the view that is most likely to be right. On the other hand, if departures from unanimity are caused by the pursuit of divergent selfish purposes, it can still be said that, if the average advantage to those who favor a measure is the same as the average disadvantage to those who oppose it, then a democratic decision among the affected persons will reveal whether the measure is in the overall net advantage of the group.

These arguments in favor of democratic process do not prove that if a proposal is adopted by a democratic process, then it is necessarily the best thing to do. Sometimes the option favored by the minority will be better, either because the majority, though unselfish, happen not to be such good judges, or because the majority are selfishly intruding on the minority in ways that harm the minority much more than the majority would benefit if they were to prevail. The selected course of action expresses what the group has decided it *shall* do, and the possibility that the group actually *should* do something else cannot be precluded. There is no infallibility in democratic process. Rules like the prohibition of takings without compensation are intended to identify classes of cases where the likelihood of the action being an inappropriate pursuit of selfish advantage is so high that better results can be expected on the whole if these actions are precluded.

What makes the institution of 100% land value taxation an appropriate democratic action despite its apparent violation of the proscription of uncompensated takings is that it is pursued for reasons that have nothing to do with selfish advantage. Land value taxation is concerned with insuring that all receive their shares of our common heritage, and that all are able to decide for themselves how the wages of their labor and the interest from their capital shall be used.

Nevertheless, for those who do not yet see the merit of land value taxation, the claim that its advocates are not pursuing selfish advantage is easily doubted. The political landscape is full of proposals that cloak selfish advantage with claims of high purpose. How are the advocates of land value taxation to demonstrate their *bona fides* and distinguish their proposal from all these others?

The answer to this question, I believe, lies in the writing of another modern legal scholar, Bruce Ackerman. In a series of lectures titled 'Discovering the Constitution,' Ackerman elucidated the argument that James Madison used to defend the Constitution against charges that it could not be valid because the body that drew it up was not authorized to do so.[7] What Madison said was that the validity of the foundation of a nation came not from its adherence to a pre-established protocol, but rather from ability of a proposal to gain the respect of people despite its lack of proper antecedents.

As Ackerman explains, Madison was expounding a theory of political participation that dovetails with the distinction between legislation and constitutional provisions. The consideration of legislation is an activity that is so unending that it would be unreasonable to expect citizens to devote enough time to it to be able to participate in all issues on a truly informed basis. Politics is an occupation for some, a hobby for others, and for most of us an activity with which we have only a passing acquaintance. As a result, the legislative process becomes dominated by political specialists and special interests. Because it would be unreasonable to expect voters to devote enough time to political questions to prevent this, it is not something that can be corrected; it must simply be accepted.

On rare occasions, however, a political question comes to be so prominent in public discussion that nearly everyone comes to have a reasonably well informed opinion on the subject. It is only on these occasions that The People of a nation can be said to have spoken. The constitution of a nation, on this view, is a device for limiting the range of action of those who tend to politics between the times when The People speak.

What this means for land value taxation is that its introduction would not be barred by the constitutional prohibition of uncompensated takings if it were introduced as a constitutional matter rather than a legislative matter. There are several perspectives from which this makes sense.

First, as a matter of logic, constitutional amendments are on the same footing. One constitutional amendment cannot preclude another. Second, there is precedent. It is embarrassing to admit that the original American constitution provided for the perpetuation of slavery. When slavery was renounced at the end of the Civil War, the Fourteenth amendment provided that, '. . . neither the United States nor any State shall assume or pay ... any claim for the loss or emancipation of any slave.' Not only did it happen that no compensation was paid, but the possibility was explicitly ruled out. In adopting this provision we were as much as saying that those who held slaves should have known that it is not possible for one human being to own another. Any 'losses' arising from the social recognition that all humans are free cannot be the basis of valid claims for compensation. As Henry George pointed out, the introduction of land value taxation has much in common with the freeing of slaves.[8] Both involve the restoration to individuals of their birthrights — to the disposition of their time and talents, and to their shares of the heritage that Nature provides to sustain us. For the same reason that slave holders did not have a respectable claim to compensation, neither do landholders. It should be obvious that no one can have a claim to own land, because no one made the land. The fact that land titles happen to have permitted individuals to use excessive shares of our common heritage, without compensating those who thereby have less than their shares, cannot oblige us to perpetuate this unjust arrangement indefinitely.

Another way of putting this point is to say that a framework specifying the requirements of justice must provide for the possibility of moral evolution. To insist that a particular arrangement must be perpetuated because of its past existence, irrespective of the moral understanding of the current generation, would be nothing but ancestor worship. If, upon examination of the way that rights are allocated, the current generation discovers an impropriety, they must rectify it. If the granting of their just deserts to those who were previously deprived requires that someone else receive less than he or she had previously expected, then there is no one more suited to bear this disappointment than those who claimed more than their shares in blind disregard for justice.

This does not mean that the poor widow whose life savings were used to buy land titles (if there really is such a person) must starve. We have an obligation to provide for all who cannot provide for themselves, for whatever reason, and in any case the poor widow would be entitled at least to her share of the rent of land.

This defense of 100% land value taxation, without compensation, has implications for the way that this idea ought to be pursued. It means, first, that it is inappropriate to suggest that any individual ought to favor 100% land value taxation because he or she will pay less in total taxes. Attention to such selfish considerations is inconsistent with the justification for not paying compensation. Furthermore, while there are good arguments for land value taxation from the perspective of promoting the overall efficiency of an economy, it is out of order to dwell on these. If 100% land value taxation is required by justice, then 100% land value taxation would be required even if it imposed an economic burden on an economy. Also, it would be inappropriate to pursue political stratagems that might make it possible to achieve 100% land value taxation as the program of a narrow coalition of political activists. It is only the change in society's consensus regarding the requirements of justice that makes it just to institute the change without compensation. The primary task of the advocates of 100% land value taxation must be to spread the understanding that the earth is the heritage of all humanity. We must seek the grand coalition of all rather than a narrow majority.

These remarks on the ethics of advocating 100% land value taxation, it is to be noted, do not apply to the proposal to reform the property tax in urban areas by shifting taxes from improvements to land. The reason for this is that if the property tax were replaced entirely by a tax on land that yielded the same revenue, there would be little if any fall in land prices. In fact, the shifting of taxes from improvements to land probably causes land prices to rise on average. This is because the average piece of land pays the same tax as before, but now land is more valuable because it can be improved without creating additional tax liability. Any losses in property values would be inconsequential. It is this absence of anything like a taking that makes the proposal for property tax reform fair game for ordinary politics, where it is permissible to suggest that people vote in terms of their self interests and to seek victory through a coalition of activists.

Returning to the issue of 100% land value taxation, the idea that the earth is our common heritage leads to a different understanding of the boundary between what is politically permissible and what is an impermissible intrusion upon individuals. The idea of not taking property without compensation is fundamentally linked to preserving the property arrangements of the status quo. The alternative perspective, consistent with 100% land value taxation, is that no individual can have a just claim to any special advantage. The only claims that individuals can make are upon the products of their labor and capital, and upon equal shares of what nature provides. What must be shared equally is not only the advantage from using land, but also the advantages from using such things as radio and TV broadcasting opportunities, zoning exceptions, taxicab licenses if they are limited, fishing permits, and so on. Justice is then maintained not by preserving the distribution of advantages described by the status quo, but by preserving equality in the distribution of returns from government grants of rights.

NOTES

1. F. Michelman, 'Property, Utility and Fairness: Comments on the Ethical Foundations of 'Just Compensation' Law,' *Harvard Law Review* 80 (1967) 1165-1258.
2. F. Michelman, 'Takings 1987,' *Columbia Law Review* 88 (Dec. 1988) 1602-04, 1622.
3. *Ibid.*, 1604, footnote 21.
4. R. Epstein, *Takings, Private Property and the Power of Eminent Domain* (Chicago, University of Chicago Press), 1985, p. 349.
5. *Supreme Court 107* (1987), 1232.

6. F. Michelman, 'Takings 1987,' *Columbia Law Review* **88** (Dec. 1988) 1626.
7. B. Ackerman, 'Discovering the Constitution,' *Yale Law Journal* **92** (1984), 1013, 1039-43.
8. H. George, *Progress and Poverty* (New York, Robert Schalkenbach Foundation), 1979, p. 362-63.

3

'Planning Gain': the making of a tax on land values

FRANCIS M. SMITH

PLANNING GAIN is the benefit accruing to a local community in exchange for planning permission for a development. The increasing use of this procedure in Britain draws attention to a principle that has not been fully articulated in the democratic process, but which has a measurable impact on the rights of landowners: namely, that developments permitted by the local authority release profits which the public, through its elected representatives, intuitively believes should — in some measure — accrue to the community as a whole. We have here, then, the operation of a hidden tax, which finds its expression in a variety of ways. The developer provides or pays for specific benefits such as roads or other infrastructure, a leisure centre, low cost housing or in some cases training programmes and jobs. The costs of these amenities are deducted from the price that a developer is willing to pay to the landowner.

This is a partial demonstration of the principle that Henry George established, i.e., that the value of land is created by the community and should justly be returned to the community. This value must be identified and drawn out from the emotional and business turmoil in which it is often concealed, and recognised as another of those 'not yet acknowledged ideas' which mark the emergence of George's realisation as the current synthesis.

The use of land and property development in the UK is controlled by local government authorities who, under the Town and Country Planning Acts, are expected to grant planning permission 'having regard to all material circumstances, unless there are sound and clear-cut reasons for refusal.' Through the operation of this system, the general public have become aware of the enormous increases in land values which are released by the grant of planning permission where this involves a significant change of use. This is most obvious when farm land is converted to housing or commercial use, where the increase in land values can be a thousandfold. At first sight, it might appear that this increase in value is the Planning Gain, but it is not so. The Planning Gain is in fact the opposite, namely the benefit which the *local authority* can obtain from the developer at the time planning permission is granted. In the USA this is called financial exaction.

The simplest instances arise in quite a small way when a house builder wishes to develop a new estate and the local authority, unable to afford the necessary service roads and sewerage, is forced to refuse planning permission. These situations have become more frequent since central government has cut back grants to local authorities. The builder, mindful of his future potential returns and the state of the market, has been able to include the costs of roads and sewerage in his own costs and thereby obtain planning permission. As this method of operating has grown, developers have been quoted as saying: 'We have to be seen to be giving something back to the community.'

If a developer is refused planning permission by the local authority there is an appeal system which can be invoked. The Secretary of State for the Environment, if he thinks fit, can appoint an Inspector from his Department to hold an enquiry. The Minister may or may not accept the recommendation of his Inspector, but in any case the developer or the local authority can proceed to appeal to the High Court.

Throughout the 1980s the system has been frequently used by developers to appeal against refusals. Local authorities would, for example, refuse an application for an office block in the Green Belt surrounding a town, on the grounds that it was contrary to the locally agreed and government approved strategic plan for the area. On appeal, the Inspector might argue that the development would create employment and that this was an over-riding justification for allowing the appeal.

This sort of situation has discouraged local authorities from refusing planning applications, particularly since they can be penalised for cases which they lose. Furthermore, with declining financial resources owing to government cut-backs and refusal of government to allow them to spend even the resources gained from the sale of their own council houses, there has been even less capital available for essential local authority provision of new infrastructure and up-dating of aging facilities. It was therefore not surprising that local authorities came up with ideas for improving developers' prospects of obtaining planning permission. Developers could offer not only to pay for infrastructure but also to provide a village by-pass or re-furbish the Town Hall. In addition they had the option of including these extras in their plan or of making a separate legal agreement. If the extras were in the plan and became the subject of a disagreement over the plan, it might have to go through the appeal system, thereby causing delays which could be financially disadvantageous to the developer. A separate legal agreement that was not included in the planning application was not subject to appeal and thus to potential delay.

It is apparent that these arrangements were first of all considered illegal and secondly labelled as extortions applied by an over-zealous or unscrupulous local authority.

The legal position was supposedly answered by a series of Circulars from the Department of the Environment which attempted to clarify the Town and Country Planning Acts. In addition, a body of case law was established by Departmental Inspectors at appeals. It finally became a question of accepting that some form of contribution by a developer *was* valid, but deciding what form it should take became a further problem.

After an enquiry by the Property Advisory Group appointed by the Department of the Environment in 1981, the Department attempted clarification by producing Circular 22/83. Planning Gain was described as

> Obligations and benefits which extend beyond the development for which Planning Permission has been sought

and gave the definition:

> 'Planning gain' is a term which has come to be applied whenever, in connection with a grant of planning permission, a local planning authority seeks to impose on a developer an obligation to carry out works not included in the development for which permission has been sought or to

> make some payment or confer some extraneous right or benefit in return for permitting development to take place.

The circular gives some rather unclear guidelines and declares 'The essential principle to apply is that the facility to be provided or financed should be directly related to the development in question or the use of the land after development.' 'But this does not mean that an authority is entitled to treat an applicant's need for permission as an opportunity to exact a payment for the benefit of ratepayers at large.'

But this is exactly what has happened in practice. Thus the planning system does not attempt to handle the economic consequence of its land use control. The original 1947 Act had introduced the ideas of betterment and compensation but these have long since been abandoned. Betterment was defined as 'any increase in the value of land resulting from the granting of planning permission'. The Development Land Tax introduced in 1976 was an attempt to restore to the community the increase in the value of land arising from planning permission but it was ineffective and was abolished in 1985. Since then Planning Gain has been an informal means of securing benefits for the community in association with a proposed development. In order to save time on planning discussions and to avoid the appeal system, developers will now readily enter into negotiations with local authorities (LAs). Some agreements are well in excess of the guidelines contained within Circular 22/83 mentioned above.

The Environment Secretary himself subsequently appeared to recognise Planning Gain by giving the go-ahead for a mixed business park and residential development on a 30-acre green belt site in Langley, Berkshire (*Estate Times,* March 3, 1989). The Planning Gain includes a five-acre park provided by the developer for public use with additional funds for future maintenance, infrastructure, and two acres to be sold to a housing association.

The London Docklands Development Corporation

The authority for the development of the huge, derelict London Docklands site in the East End has been vested in the London Docklands Development Corporation (LDDC) and not with the

LAs covering the area. Nevertheless, in 1987 one of these LAs, Tower Hamlets Borough Council, was able to make an agreement with the developers of the 71 acre Canary Wharf site in which they would provide 2,000 jobs for local people (and a penalty of £7,000 for each job below this figure) and £2.5m over an eight-year period for the training of local people in high tech. and other skills. Although this may have seemed a great victory for Tower Hamlets at the time, the developers will hardly notice the cost.

In a similar agreement the London Borough of Newham and the LDDC have a 'social and community compact' for the provision of 1,500 new homes at fair rent, 25% of jobs for local residents and £10m for community facilities and an equity stake in certain developments. In this way the case for providing some benefit to the community is being publicly recognised.

Social and Economic Aspects

Whilst there is much anguish amongst many property developers about the inclusion of social and economic aspects and 'politicisation' of planning which they regard as exclusively a quasi-technical subject, some developers are taking the initiative. For example, the Chairman of a development company offered Camden Borough Council the sum of £2m and a proportion of the site for public open space in return for planning permission to develop the former St. Columbia Hospice on Hampstead Heath.

At the same time the Property Advisory Group established by the Department of the Environment who had said that 'We are unable to accept that, as a matter of general principle, planning gain has any place in our system of planning control' were completely ignoring the social and economic aspects of Town and Country Planning. In practice Local Authorities are more and more taking advantage of the opportunities presented by planning applications to supplement their funds and at the same time to gain some benefit for their community. As yet there is no sign that the benefits that they are seeking relate to the real, much greater long-term benefits that accrue to the developer. Any return is seen by the Local Authorities as a share of the short-term or immediate 'betterment' conferred.

Many councillors are largely ignorant of the benefits that are being lost.

It is, however, amazing to observe how financial considerations are being recognised by the Inspectors appointed by the Department of the Environment to consider appeals. A private school in Berkshire wished to allow a development of private houses on part of its playing fields in an area designated for conservation. The money derived, it was claimed, was to fund an expansion and improvement of the school which would not otherwise be possible. The planning permission refused by the Local Authority was granted in the appeal. Although in this example the gains to be made are recognised, they were given back to the developer!

The Royal Opera House

The most notorious case is that of the Royal Opera House in Covent Garden, London. The proposal to extend the Royal Opera House was described by the Covent Garden Area Plan of the Westminster City Council as 'probably the most significant single project in the area'. That it was essential to undertake a program of modernisation and reconstruction to ensure the Royal Opera's future national and international reputation was accepted. However, the local authority considered the proposed development scheme to be a radical departure from the Action Plan because of the element of office accommodation to be provided on part of the site, and damaging because it also involved the near-total demolition of the Floral Hall, a listed building. The Opera House had estimated that the improvement would cost £56m, of which £33m would be met by profits from the commercial element of the proposed development, with the balance of £23m being raised privately. The authority accepted that 'in the current climate the project will not be able to rely on public funds'. There were therefore uncertainties with regard to securing the substantial amount of additional funding required. The Covent Garden Community Association opposed the development on the grounds that the inclusion of the office accommodation for financial reasons was impermissible and was not a 'material consideration'. However, the appeal was granted by the High Court and typical of the nonsensical arguments used is the final summing up:

> Financial constraints on the economic viability of a desirable planning development are unavoidable facts of life in an imperfect world. It would be unreal and contrary to common sense to insist that they must be excluded from the range of considerations which may properly be regarded as material in determining planning applications. Where they are shown to exist they may call for compromises or even sacrifices in what would otherwise be regarded as the optimum from the point of view of the public interest. Virtually all planning decisions involve some kind of balancing exercise. A commonplace illustration is the problem of having to decide whether or not to accept compromises or sacrifices in granting permission for development which could, or would in practice, otherwise not be carried out for financial reasons. Another, no doubt rarer, illustration would be a similar balancing exercise concerning composite or related developments, ie, related in the sense that they can and should properly be considered in combination, where the realisation of the main objective may depend on the financial implications or consequences of others. However, provided that the ultimate determination is based on planning grounds and not on some ulterior motive, and that it is not irrational, there would be no basis for holding it to be invalid in law solely on the ground that it has taken account of, and adjusted itself to, the financial realities of the overall situation.

Thus we have the extraordinary situation where the financial needs of the developer are recognised as a justification for developments that are socially, environmentally and economically against the interests of the community. However, it is generally the more obvious cases of windfall gains by local farmers whose land is used by developers that strikes home to the general public and particularly to local councillors who are frustrated by seeing it happen and are helpless to alter the situation, in which domination by central government continues.

One year later the arguments over the developments of the Royal Opera House still continue.

Nevertheless, in this way, those who have never heard of Henry George and land value taxation are instinctively aware of the injustice of such a situation and are demanding some recompense to the community. The Georgist case is being made and its natural justice is becoming apparent.

In the Counties

A more parochial example is given typically by a local authority in the North West of England where permission has been granted for a supermarket in the center of one of its towns, Knutsford in Cheshire County. The site is the only remaining open space in the center of the town and the Planning Gain is to finance the building of tennis courts in the outskirts, which is a directly related benefit, and the renovation of the Civic Hall, which is not. The local Knutsford Town Council and the townspeople are violently opposed to the plan but are powerless to stop it. The Macclesfield Local District Authority, which gave the permission, will have acted under potential government pressure because they would have to pay all the legal costs if they lost an appeal against it. Presumably the benefits gained for the community represent the best deal that could be obtained in the circumstances.

Disparity in Land Values

The huge differences in land values between the South and the North of England provide another example of the relationship between land values and the local communities.

Since 1985, land values have roughly doubled in the South East of England, whereas in the derelict formerly industrialised areas of the North some sites, damaged by pollution, they have often fallen considerably. The difference between the two is strikingly visible.

Thus in Wokingham, Berkshire, near London in the South East, a new industrial estate is being built on farming land near the village. The government, having approved the plan, is standing aside as 'only a regulator'. The developer is happily contributing £10m for roads out of his land value gains.

On the other hand, in Stockton-on-Tees in the North East of England where there are 34,000 unemployed, the LA is clearing four feet of concrete from a site which was formerly iron and steel works and a shipyard. Plenty of government money is available to subsidise the new industries that will, it is hoped, follow. The Tees-side Development Corporation has been set up and is undertaking river-bank strengthening, road construction and infrastructure provision;

huge waste tips are being cleared. In this way negative land values are being eliminated. The local Member of Parliament sees nothing wrong with this government intervention — it is his party's government and he has a marginal seat.

The point is that the difference between the two sites in the South East and the North East is apparent for all to observe. The developer in the S.E. pays some of the value back, called Planning Gain, and in the N.E. the developer is a government sponsored body and the builders and businesses, far from contributing Planning Gain, will be compensated for the low land values despite the future potential gains.

It should be observed, however, that although the impact of land values and *increasing* land values is now widely recognised and seen to be unfair, it is only quantified when sales are made and windfall gains are publicised. The facts are established and the injustice exposed but the solution still has to be proclaimed.

Change of Land Use

The net result of the intervention by government in planning decisions and improvement programs is to bring about changes in land use, thereby considerably increasing land values for the benefit of developers. One of the most striking examples of such intervention was the pronouncement by Nicholas Ridley, Secretary of State for the Environment who said (*Financial Times*, 8/9 July 1989) he was 'minded' to approve plans by Consortium Developers, a group of 10 British housebuilders, which wants to build a new town of 4,800 homes called Foxley Wood in north Hampshire. The application had already been rejected by the Local Authority and by a public enquiry Inspector appointed by the Minister who had said that the harm the development would inflict on conservation interests, the countryside and highways outweighed the benefits of granting planning permission. The Junior Environment Minister said (*Financial Times*, 8 July 1989).

> The settlement could make an important contribution to meeting housing needs in north-east Hampshire and would be preferable to the further large-scale expansion into open countryside of existing towns and

villages, where there are already problems of congestion and overloading of local services.

The Planning Gain in Foxley Wood was to be a complete settlement with all its necessary infrastructure. Subsequently Mr Ridley's successor as Secretary of State 'has minded not to give planning permission'. More publicity.

Donation of Public Land

Another government move that recognises land values is the invitation to private developers to build community facilities for mentally ill people in return for being given prime housing land now occupied by the big Victorian asylums in which the mentally ill were housed. They call this maximising value for money but it is in reality short-term political gain in return for long-term community loss of increased land values.

A particularly interesting recognition of the actual value of land by people who have previously claimed that it cannot be properly valued has also come from the Department of Health Services. In a supposed attempt to make the hospital service more financially accountable and efficient, it has been instructed to work out the cost of all its individual services; these will ultimately be published for doctors who will thereby know where to send patients for the most cost-effective treatment. Hospitals have been told to include in their costings interest and depreciation of buildings and land. Buildings and land in use are to be valued at market rates for existing use; surplus land and buildings will be valued on the basis of alternative speculative use. 'Ministers hope this will act as an incentive to managers to use capital assets efficiently' (*Financial Times*, 20 June 1989). Thus although the value of land in relation to planning use permission is recognised, land is not distinguished from capital.

Good Design Constrained by Land Values

Architects and local authorities are in conflict over good design. Redevelopment of offices in Gloucester Road, London was rejected by Westminster Council on grounds of poor design, overdevelopment, excessive plot ratio and failure to provide sufficient planning advantages. However, on appeal, the Inspector said the Council 'was overzealous in its exercise of development control, and aimed at a standard of design that was unnecessarily high.' Undoubtedly high land purchase prices put pressure on funds that might otherwise be used to produce better design and construction.

Land Values Recognised as Company Assets

In the economic boom years of the late 1980s there was considerable activity in both company take-over struggles and in corporate strategies to avoid being taken over. The revaluation of a company's assets for either purpose was commonplace, and the sudden realisation that property and land shown in the company accounts at purchase price was worth a lot more money drew attention to the significance of land values.

A typical property developer, Chesterfield Properties, revalued its net assets at the end of 1988 by £5 to £14 per share. Shares leapt by £1 to £9.50. Independent revaluation of its investment properties on an open market value basis threw up a surplus of £77m. The total includes the value of One Buckingham Gate just opposite Buckingham Palace, which is their prestige office development.

Other companies were drawn into the land speculation game. *The Financial Times*, 12 July 1989 said:

> It would have been difficult five years ago to have imagined that British Aerospace would become controversial not because of its mainstream business but because of its desire to exploit property assets which had fallen into its lap through the purchase from the Government of Royal Ordnance.
>
> Its control of sites at Enfield and Waltham Forest, in north and north east London, and their long-term potential for mixed development following the closure of RO plants, has (sic) been the subject of parliamentary scrutiny and angry debate.
>
> In the same way, the privatisation first of AB Ports and then of BAA, once British Airports Authority, has led to a re-rating on the market because of their extensive property assets.
>
> Simply by virtue of the commercial activity at airports, BAA is an important landlord of retail property. AB Ports, on the other hand, has waterside holdings which can be, indeed are being, steadily developed. Both groups have acquired property development companies — Lynton

> by BAA and Grosvenor Square by AB Ports, the better to harness their opportunities.
>
> In similar vein, the privatised National Freight Corporation has found that extensive landholdings adjacent to railway stations have justified the establishment of a separate company which not only looks after NFC operational needs but develops in its own right.

and on the 20th July:

> BAe has 37 sites scattered round the UK, of which six are surplus to its manufacturing needs. Five of these have come into its hands through its takeover of Royal Ordnance for £190m in April 1987 and Rover for £150m in August 1988.
>
> It is the exploitation of these five sites — Waltham Abbey, Enfield and Patricroft from RO and Bathgate and Cowley South from Rover — which have excited political controversy. The arguments have circled around the issue of whether BAe paid a fair price for state assets or whether, given property development potential, it got them on the cheap. The Government has continually pointed to the fact that the sale of Royal Ordnance was by open competitive tender.

But the greatest public outcry was caused by the privatisation of the 10 Water Boards of England and Wales. The new owners inherited millions of acres of land, some of which will be potentially saleable at enormously increased prices. The general public appeared to be incensed, not only because they saw this land as their natural birthright but because they knew that it was bought by local authorities with their (ratepayers') money. It was also clear to any observer that this was unadulterated land and not buildings or 'property'.

There is a twist in the tail of this story: monies derived by the new water companies from the sale of land will be used to improve water purity to European standards. The alternative would be to increase charges or to subsidise with taxpayers' money.

Traditional Landowners

One might imagine that with all the business activity involving land speculation and property development, the traditional land owners were disappearing. Nothing could be further from the truth.

Of the 200 wealthiest people identified by the *Sunday Times* in 1989 there were:

57 landowners
53 retailers, distributors or service companies who own city sites
31 property developers or builders
14 publishers or owners of communication fortunes
5 bankers
6 brewers
19 financial dealers or traders.

More than half represent old or inherited money. The newspaper itself draws the conclusion that 'The ducal fortunes are all based on holding on to large amounts of land and property.'

For example Gerald Grosvenor, Sixth Duke of Westminster, is easily Britain's richest person next to the Queen. The 300 golden acres of Mayfair owned by the Grosvenor Estate form the linchpin of his fortune. These were the dowry of Mary Davies, the 12-year-old bride of Sir Thomas Grosvenor, in 1677. Today the family estate also embraces 13,000 acres outside Chester, including the family home Eaton Hall, 100,000 acres of Scottish forest, 12,000 acres of Vancouver, Hawaii office blocks and an Australian sheep station.

But what has happened to the large fortunes amassed by the cotton and woollen industrial barons? Where are the iron and steel manufacturers and the big shipyard owners? Many of these entrepreneurs returned to the community some of the wealth they had acquired. They presented or bequeathed parks, churches, libraries, art galleries and schools, and thereby recorded their names and their generosity for posterity. No doubt their benevolence was a form of paternalism rather than a recognition of the benefits they derived from the exclusive use of land and its products.

The great industrial fortunes of the 19th and early 20th centuries have gone or are seriously diminished. They obviously did not transfer their wealth to the land when they could. The only old industrial family left in the top 200 is that of the Pilkingtons who maintained their position by a technical innovation — the introduction of float glass.

Conclusion

The key rôle of land in the affairs of the Dukes, the newly privatised companies, the board room struggles and the windfall gains by farmers provided by the planning decisions of local government are regularly drawing attention to the significance of land values. The gains by the owners are regarded by many as a reward for shrewdness, the natural gains of a public lottery. The Planning Gain that retrieves some of these increases for the community is regarded by some as a form of extortion.

Nevertheless there is an increasing recognition of the need for a national strategy in the planned use of land in the national interest. It is but a short step to the realisation that the benefits should accrue directly to society as a whole, which has the moral right to them, rather than — as now — being drawn off by private individuals as the fruits of privilege.

APPENDIX

Government Support for Planning Gain

The implications of Planning Gain were high-lighted at a conference held in London on 2nd March 1990 (Henry Stewart Conference Studies). It was reported that many Local Authorities now provide guidelines on the Planning Gains that they will consider favorably; they may even be sub-divided into Planning Requirements (which relate to a site and its use), Planning Benefits (related to a development, and sought as site conditions and local needs dictate), and Planning Gain (for a shopping basket of community needs negotiated on an ad hoc basis), the latter often blatantly beyond what the Department of the Environment might be expected to agree to on appeal.

However, the chances of appeal are low because, as one speaker (Charles George, a barrister) said: 'The profits of development are usually such that they are scarcely dented by the financial sweeteners that local planning authorities require of developers, whereas the *costs* of delay which are inherent in legal challenge can be considerable in terms of profits deferred and market-opportunities missed.'

The political implications were not neglected. It was recognised that a developer might be expected to contribute directly to a local community that suffered local drawbacks (e.g. additional traffic) in a development that may have only wider benefits (e.g. regional employment). This is in line with a desire on the part of central government that major infrastructure projects should be 'contributed to' by major private developers. By cutting finance for local government at the same time, the government is practising the transfer of land value gains to local community benefit, albeit in a roundabout way and to a thoroughly inadequate extent. It does, however, seem unlikely that the Planning Gain procedure will be abolished.

The Conference drew attention to an excellent example of the way this concept is being extended to draw in private money to support an extension of the London Underground System:

> This is an example of the ultimate in Planning Gain. After a number of studies the government has accepted the need for a new tube line to connect central London with the inner south east and inner north east London but has also said that the tube line will have to be partly funded by the private sector. The government is reported as having suggested that the private sector will be considerable beneficiaries of the new line and therefore they should contribute to it.
>
> No detailed costings of the line are yet available but figures of £15bn have been reported. In addition a figure of £400m contribution to the cost from one of the largest developers has been reported and it appears that the developer may be prepared to make this contribution. Other developers may not be so willing to contribute but at the end of the day their land may be worth significantly more with the line than without.
>
> The question at issue is: Should the private sector be asked to contribute to something that would traditionaly have been provided by the state via a public transport undertaking?

The implication of this question is that the community should pay and that the businesses who benefit should make their contribution through their profits tax. How much fairer and more straightforward it would be if the land values were taxed on an annual basis. In this way, the landholders' payments would accurately reflect the benefits they derived from their holdings.

III
THE EVOLUTION OF SOCIAL SYSTEMS

4

Post-socialism and the Single Tax: a holistic philosophy

FRED HARRISON

MIKHAIL Gorbachev had a problem. He wanted nothing less than the transformation of Soviet society, but his aspirations were not synchronised with a relevant cosmology. He sought some semblance of continuity with the past, by wistfully invoking Lenin's vision of socialism. On economics, he acknowledged that the new system would have to evolve within a market framework, though he persisted in using the notion of a 'social market'. He recognised that internal transformation could not be approached in isolation from the rest of the world; that the benefits of change would be restricted if sovereign nations continued to adopt aggressive postures in defence of their land.

But there was more. Uniquely, he declared an intention to progress beyond social and economic reforms, for intuitively he was aware of the need to elevate natural resources to the centre of the strategy for transformation. He was aware that the damage to the natural environment would lead to a rapid depletion of Earth's ability to sustain life. His program was vague, but courageously he sought to link international political relations with ecological imperatives.

Could he knit this catalogue of concerns into a coherent, practical philosophical framework? He had no answer, yet this child of the planned society was willing to leap into the dark without the aid of the holistic philosophy that was a pre-condition of success.

By 1990, five years after the announcement that the USSR would break with the past, no-one had presented to the Soviets for their consideration an appropriate philosophy that could match the aspiration to create a post-socialist society.

The search for a hard-headed philosophy which, in its visionary grandeur and practical formulations matches the *perestroika* prospectus, need not have taken him further than the Kremlin archives. A statement of that philosophy was presented as a viable social and economic system in St Petersburg a decade before the 1917 revolution. A considerable part of the literary activity of Leo Tolstoy, during the years leading up to his death in 1910, consisted in expounding the ideas of the social reformer Henry George. So convinced was Tolstoy that the American had developed a program that would meet the then needs of the empire, that he used his influence to lay the plan before the Czar; to no avail.

Eighty Years later, the USSR has a new czar. In the fall of 1990, Mikhail Gorbachev was granted almost absolute power. With the Soviet empire crumbling, the republics reluctanctly handed over almost complete authority to one man, in the hope that he would get them through the hungry winter months. Pressed by the elementary need to eat and remain alive, Gorbachev had little time to reflect on philosophical issues. And yet he was aware that, without the appropriate philosophy, his search for a human society, one that bound nations together and corrected man's abuse of the natural environment, his society would disintegrate in civil violence.

Henry George's philosophy is not produced here as if a rabbit from the magician's hat. A hard-headed assessment of contemporary realities in the Soviet Union suggests that this philosophy addresses the immediate needs of hungry people while also addressing Gorbachev's larger vision. It is a holistic program, readily available to guide the emergence of post-socialist society.

In laying bare some of the essentials of that philosophy, testing the principles against the facts of Soviet life, we bear in mind the possibility that the market economies of the West are also in urgent need of reform. The attempt at a counter-revolution against the Welfare State in the 1980s by the New Right, led by Ronald Reagan and Margaret Thatcher, failed. It failed in its ultimate goal (diminishing the size of the public sector) because it had no answers to the problems of the causes of poverty and unemployment. Indeed, material and spiritual deprivation deepened, despite significant achievements in the labor and capital markets. The record of the capitalist mode of production remains a blemished one, despite 200 years of scientific and technological progress. One of the awesome questions, then, is whether Mikhail Gorbachev can avoid the pitfalls that entrap so many western citizens in poverty, now that he has accepted that the answer was not to be found in socialism.

An Appropriate Path to Freedom?

The absence of a clear vision of the *practical* steps they would have to traverse to the new society left Soviet reformers in a state of depression that found its expression in political fractiousness. With food stocks diminishing, the social situation would get 'out of control', warned Deputy Prime Minister Leonid Abalkin (reported in *Pravda*, Nov. 11, 1989). That was one reason why, when the 13th 5-Year Plan was unfolded by Prime Minister Nikolai Ryzkov on December 14, 1989, the Kremlin disclosed a continued dependence on central regulation. Western analysts interpreted this as a betrayal of *perestroika*. In fact, Mikhail Gorbachev was buying time.

Despite five years of *glasnost*, by the end of 1990 the coterie of advisers around Gorbachev had failed to formulate an effective strategy. The Politburo did not want to risk social chaos in a rush for directionless change, yet something had to be seen to be happening. That was why Gorbachev was handed full authority to create a new government and quickly define some political solutions to the immediate economic crises.

The price of a misaligned program of change was already being paid by the other Warsaw Pact countries. They were sinking into economic turmoil, the price they had to pay for help from the International Monetary Fund. To secure the massive loans that were needed to bail out their bankrupt economies, the popular leaders of Poland, Hungary and Czechoslovakia agreed to telescope changes into a short time frame. These changes took the form of higher prices and lower living standards.[1] At the heart of the process was the removal of state subsidies, so that resources could be allocated by the market on the basis of their costs — and used according to the preferences of consumers.

This rush to change led to the first error. The nature of the challenge before the liberated governments of Eastern Europe necessarily entailed the introduction of a system of taxation that corresponded to the needs of a market economy in which the individual, and not the all-wise planner, was the primary decision-maker. The fiscal question — as well as the liberty of the individual — was intimately bound up with the financial mess of the former communist countries, but the reformers were too anxious to escape the clutches of socialism to worry much about the nature of a post-socialist society.

Setting the pace was Poland's Solidarity government, which aimed to switch from a command to a market economy by the beginning of 1991. Without time to consider its new fiscal system, the leaders of the workers' union who filled the ministerial posts moved in favor of income taxes and the Value Added Tax. The first is a payroll tax, which implied that fewer workers would find jobs during the period of transition than might otherwise have been the case. VAT is a tax that raises the price of the consumer goods that the government ostensibly wanted to place within the reach of its citizens: this tax-push to prices meant extra downward pressure on the real value of wages that were already very low.

These fiscal choices were not consistent with economic aspirations, but was there an alternative on offer? The answer to that question begins to emerge as we re-examine the character of a Marxist society.

Under Marxism, the state appropriates people's incomes. Legitimacy for this action is provided by the fiction that individual contributions to the process of wealth creation cannot be differentiated: hence the justification for the collective ownership of the means of production. With all money accruing to the public sector, the distribution of income (and the standard of living) is in the gift of the state. The bureaucracy determines the allocation of resources, including the spending power of individuals. Amenities that are deemed to be the essential requisites of life — food, housing, medicine, the 'goods' that free men and women would prefer to provide directly for themselves — are 'subsidised', to put them within the reach of everybody. No-one is poor, because no-one grows rich by exploiting others.

The claim that the state 'subsidises' the essential needs of its citizens is also a fiction, employed to disguise the fact that the incomes generated by individuals are spent on their behalf by the state. East Germany, for example, devoted 65 billion marks each year to food and clothing. This was not an act of distribution in favor of the workers, for they were the ones who generated the income in the first place. Wages had remained fixed at the level of the 1950s; as incomes rose over time, they were captured by the state. The bureaucracy and its political masters decided how the money would be spent. The 'subsidies', then, were not a redistribution of income in favour of those in need, but a measure of the servile dependence of the worker on the state.

But it is not possible even for the command economy to do away completely with wages, so each worker is provided with pocket-money to exercise a limited discretion over his life. In these circumstances, the tax-take from 'pay' packets is necessarily a token sum — in the USSR, about 8% of what is characterised as 'nominal wages' (Aganbegyan and Timofeyev 1988: 33).

To move to a market-based system in which the individual is free to express his preferences, the state has to give up its power over people's incomes. For the state to continue to function, however, a new tax structure has to be created. Rationally, this ought to be consistent with the logic of the market and the financial obligations of the public sector, a primary one being the need for massive investment in infrastructure, to accommodate the market economy. The adjustments that were accepted by the East European countries in 1989 were undoubtedly necessary. The fatal mistake, however, was to accept the view of western financiers that the adjustments (characterised as 'stabilisation' programs) were preconditions to the move to the market economy. In fact, these austerity measures ought to have been postponed until the governments had formulated a coherent vision of the substantive institutions and policies that would constitute the new social foundations; to be implemented as part of the creation of an integrated system of pricing (in the private sector) and taxation (for funding the public sector). Prices and taxes are inextricably related, and they have a crucial effect on the levels of employment and investment.

Instead, the rush to obtain money from western bankers exposed the East Europeans to the crude model favored by capitalist ideology, a model built around the concept of privatisation of industrial enterprises and state property. This western influence planted in Eastern Europe the philosophical flaws that are built into the foundations of the capitalist nations (Harrison 1991; and below). The newly-liberated nations were not encouraged to differentiate between man-made capital and the resources that are provided by nature. This, as we shall see, now means they are denied the best chance of accelerated change in the desired direction. Instead, the East Europeans are creating carbon copies of an imperfect market. This system is a vast improvement on the command economy; but despite the modifications associated with the emergence of the Welfare State, the capitalist system has lamentably failed to free every able-and-willing person to work for money to pay for his basic needs without the need for charitable hand-outs from more to less fortunate citizens.

The fundamental structural defect in the western model is the way in which land and natural resources are used and abused. A particular combination of tax-and-tenure arrangements has conspired in the land market to assign monopoly power to a small class of people who exercise the right to prevent the economy from operating efficiently (Harrison 1983). The USSR, however, retains the opportunity to create the first system built on rational economic principles and ethics. The test of the integrity of that system, however, is its further capacity to guarantee both the integrity of the natural environment and the rights of future generations to inherit Earth in a state that is capable of sustaining life for as long as the sun shines benignly.

The 'Braking Mechanism'

Marx's labor theory of value provided the theoretical flaw that institutionalised the waste of the rich natural endowments of the USSR. Mikhail Gorbachev, as he scaled the heights of power in the Kremlin, did not articulate the problem in these terms, but he was uncomfortably aware that there was something seriously wrong:

> A kind of 'braking mechanism', affecting social and economic development, formed. And all this happened at a time when scientific and technological revolution opened up new prospects for economic and social progress (Gorbachev 1988: 19).

Marxist theory had caused the planners who commanded the mighty Soviet economy to shadow those errors in the capitalist economies that permitted owners to underuse urban sites and over-exploit the fertility of farmland (see Chapter 9). In the Soviet Union, the absence of market prices — rental values — encouraged planners to use natural resources as a costless substitute for improvements in the productivity of labor and capital. The planners did not impute rental values to land and natural resources, for the simple reason that — according to the labor theory of value — land *had* no value! So the planned targets were achieved by the *extensive* — that is, wasteful — use of the resources of nature.[2]

This approach, now characterised as the 'spend-away' economy (Gorbachev 1988: 46), forced itself on the collective consciousness of the Moscow mandarins through the accumulation of the brutal facts. Gorbachev admitted:

> We spent, in fact we are still spending, far more on raw materials, energy and other resources per unit of output than other developed nations. Our country's wealth in terms of natural and manpower resources has spoilt, one may even say corrupted, us. That, in fact, is chiefly the reason why it was possible for our economy to develop extensively for decades. Accustomed to giving priority to quantitative growth in production, we tried to check the falling rates of growth, but did so mainly by continually increasing expenditures: we built up the fuel and energy industries and increased the use of natural resources in production. As time went on, material resources became harder to get and more expensive ... So the inertia of extensive economic development was leading to an economic deadlock and stagnation ... An absurd situation was developing. The Soviet Union, the world's biggest producer of steel, raw materials, fuel and energy, has shortfalls in them due to wasteful or inefficient use (Gorbachev 1988: 19-21).[3]

In 1985, Gorbachev, as General Secretary of the Communist Party, moved swiftly. Wielding the long knife, to overcome political resistance, he recruited a new team of advisers into the inner circles of the Kremlin. His chief economist was Abel Aganbegyan, the portly academic from Novosibirsk who was flown to Moscow to chair the Commission for the Study of Productive Forces and Resources. He was also appointed head of the economics section of the Academy of Sciences of the USSR.

Had they rediscovered the lessons that flowed from the theory of rent, which was developed by David Ricardo in his *Principles of Political Economy and Taxation* (1817)? The opportunity to test the depth to which new thinking may have penetrated was afforded by the 27th Party Congress in Moscow, which endorsed Gorbachev's *perestroika* plan. In an early example of *glasnost* in action, the Foreign Ministry agreed to present Abel Aganbegyan at a Press conference on March 5, 1986. This was the first opportunity for western correspondents to probe Aganbegyan's thinking on the use of land and natural resources, which had been used to undermine the aspirations of Lenin's legions. Aganbegyan's answers reflected the shallowness of the prevailing theoretical perspectives. He replied, in answer to a question from me:

> As of today and the existing system of accounting, the price of land is not included in the overall system of pricing. Maybe an experiment will be conducted in the nearest future — for example, in Estonia — where a new system of taking into account all the factors of production wil be adopted with payments for all the resources utilised in production (Harrison 1986: 44).

Despite Gorbachev's attempts to initiate qualitative changes, the key constraint on the Soviet economy was still at work. Three years later, a dismayed Aganbegyan reported that, between 1985 and 1988, the major brake on growth was the failure to improve on the efficiency with which natural resources were used (Aganbegyan 1989: 243-44). This failure distorted investment and production in the urban/industrial sector, it slowed the pace of change and retarded living standards. He noted of the attempts at reform during the early years of *perestroika*:

> The gross inbalance in favor of our raw materials production is a burden to the whole structure of our natural economy, retarding it and preventing its development (Aganbegyan 1989: 244).

This defect could be remedied only after people were required to pay the price — rents — for using natural resources. But this, in itself, would not be sufficient. *For even if a market in land and natural resources had been created, the historical evidence from the market economies demonstrates that the privatisation of rents generates frictions which obstruct the optimum use of natural resources and full employment levels of economic growth.*

The logic of history and of economics, therefore, dictates that fiscal policy must intersect the debate on *perestroika* because of its central importance in the redefinition of legal rights to, and efficient use of, the resources of nature.

The importance of the appropriate definition of property rights was appreciated in Moscow. According to Abalkin:

> The diversity of the forms of property, their equality and competition, is the fundamental condition for the economic freedom of citizens which ensures the best possible utilisation of their abilities (Peel 1989).

In the capitals of Moscow's erstwhile satellites, however, there was no similar appreciation of the importance of appropriate fiscal policies. Gorbachev, who had by now emerged as President of the Soviet Union, was more shrewd and patient.

> We must enter the next five-year period, having a smoothly operating mechanism of financial relations between enterprises and the state budget. In this connection there is a need to speed up the working out of scientifically substantiated rates of income tax and rental payments to go to the budget. It is of paramount importance to establish a procedure for replenishing the local Soviets' budgets (Gorbachev 1989: 32-33).

This realisation of the importance of fiscal policy explains why we believe it made strategic sense for the USSR not to jump feet first into the hands of western financiers.

As a contribution to *perestroika*, an attempt to prescribe the relevant policies and institutional arrangements is outlined below. Our analysis begins with the agricultural sector. Gorbachev (1989: 4-5) acknowledged the crucial role of agrarian policy, which would identify 'the main direction of our entire political course.' He also saw that the inadequate supply of food was 'our society's biggest wound.' But there is also a heuristic reason for considering this sector first: the relevant economic principles — and policy solutions — emerge here with the fullest clarity.

Food for Thought

The quality of food was in inverse ratio to the quantity of vodka consumed by Soviet citizens. Despite the grandest of plans, insufficient food was placed on the tables of the proletariat. The reasons were not difficult to determine, but anyone who might have developed a critique of Marxism soon found himself consigned to a mental hospital or a Siberian work camp.

The waste of lives and precious capital found its corresponding expression in the countryside, where the planners wasted millions of hectares of rich soil. Gorbachev confessed to this in the lengthy analysis that he presented to the Plenary Meeting of the CPSU's Central Committee in March, 1989:

> In the past 25 years, 22m hectares of farmland have been lost; nearly 12m hectares of that area were used for industrial construction and roads, and more than 6m hectares were neglected — left to be overgrown with shrubs. At the same time, huge sums of money were spent to develop millions of hectares of new land. The fertility of fields is declining in most regions. More than 3m hectares of irrigated land — the 'golden fund' of every state — have practically dropped out of cultivation due to mismanagement. It should be added that the country has lost more than 10m hectares of flood meadow and pastures during the past two decades due to ill-conceived hydropower generation projects (Gorbachev 1989: 6).

The farmland of the Soviet Union was abused on an official basis.[4] Abolishing the centralized administrative structure is the starting point of any plan to raise productivity and reduce the massive damage to the countryside.

Speed of implementation is vital. Success, in the form of immediate and visible benefits, would buy time (through the goodwill of consumers) for changes in other sectors where progress is necessarily slower. The output of food can be markedly increased in a single growing season, sufficiently to make a measurable impact on supply and prices in the shops. To do so, however, and to create a competitive economy within which enterprise can flourish and the material needs of consumers be satisfied, the USSR has to transfer the means of production to individual users. Gorbachev acknowledged this by declaring that farmers had to become 'masters of their land.' This is a hazy concept, but it does convey the impression that the tiller has to be more deeply associated with the fields than is possible under the collective structure. At the same time, however, Gorbachev — while demanding the display of 'independence, enterprise and initiative' from farmers — has continued to promote the virtues of collective farms, albeit in the form of 'co-operatives of leaseholders.' Nevertheless, he is not dogmatic; and following Lenin, he is willing to 'let life have the last word' (Gorbachev 1989: 24, 25). This implies a pragmatism that augurs well for *perestroika*.

The first problem for the policy-makers is this. After 70 years of dictatorship, the USSR is devoid of entrepreneurial skills based on the exercise of individual initiative. What mechanism would recreate the willingness of people to take risks, re-cultivate innovation, encourage hard work for just rewards and guarantee the use of finite resources on the basis of conservation of, and respect for, man's natural habitat?

The output of food increases markedly when land is cultivated by farmers on an individual basis, and the most productive and ecologically-sound unit is the family-sized farm. The first problem, then, is to transfer possessory rights to farmers. An appropriate mechanism for enabling the state to reallocate tracts now held by collective farms has to be devised. This is a critical issue, because there is a danger that, for the sake of either speed or the appeasement of entrenched conservative interests, the state may adopt a second-best formula for the redistribution of land.

The most efficient method for allocating land would be by locally-administered *auctions*. Farmers should be free to bid a rent for the right to *possess* and *use* (but not own) land. This process would define the first benchmarks of a unique system that was consistent with both economic efficiency and the spirit of communalism.[5]

Farmers — and not the bureaucrats — would determine the initial level of rents. These bids measure the commitment of individuals to use land in an optimal way to produce the highest financial surplus consistent with acceptable levels of wages and ecologically-sound methods of farming.

Farmers having set the benchmark rents, it would then be incumbent on the state to publish a cadastral survey. The information should include the classification of all sites (as to quality and use) and annual rental values. This data is essential, the lifeblood for new institutions that would be charged with the task of monitoring trends in rental values and reallocating land to new users. Prospective users need this information if they are to bid for the right of access to land; and it is the raw material that both current users and the taxing authorities need, to ensure that appropriate adjustment (upwards or downwards) are made to the tax liability (= rents).[6]

Auctions also serve a crucial sociological purpose. They would help to differentiate the workforce, by identifying those who wished to remain as employees from those who wished to become risk-takers. It is a mechanism for enabling potential business leaders to come forward of their own volition.

This approach removes the risk that the bureaucracy might corruptly favor one individual as against another. Favoritism does not necessarily result in resources being placed in the hands of the most efficient users. Thus, market-based auctions would guarantee that public assets were allocated fairly and according to the expressed preference of consumers.

The auction room becomes the focal point for establishing the legitimacy of competition and the pricing mechanism. In a society where there is no private market for the sale of land, *the auction room becomes the local marketplace for socially-owned sites.*[7]

This formula creates a competitive *milieu* which excludes the excesses associated with market economies. In the ideal market *there are no losers.* The auction system is a win-win arrangement. Farmers who fail to secure use rights would be compensated by the knowledge that the winning rents bid by their competitors were going into the government exchequer to finance socially-necessary programs, from which they would benefit directly and equally.

China: a Missed Opportunity

The history of attempts to reform Communist China highlight some of the conclusions that flow from our theoretical framework.

China launched her reforms in 1978. Within 10 years, agriculture doubled its output. This remarkable success was achieved by re-creating family farms. But there were serious shortcomings in the measures adopted by Peking, and these reflect the failure to adopt appropriate tax-and-tenure measures.

The state did retain legal ownership of land, which was leased to users. A series of defects were built into the Chinese model, however. First, rents were not charged at market level. This provided lease-holders with an unintended windfall — they retained part of the unearned income and became a new class of rich people. Discontent in the countryside was the result. The differences in income were not based on special skill or hard work, but originated with the appropriation of part of the rent — the surplus value that is not created by any one person's labor or the investment of his capital. This illustrates the critical rôle of rent, which can be taken into account by the appropriate fiscal policy only if former communist countries are to adopt market-based systems without also incorporating the deep-seated inequities that mar the record of the industrially developed societies.

But there was also an efficiency problem with the Chinese model. During the early phase of the reforms, leaseholders were not confident that they would be allowed to retain possession of their fields. They were reluctant to invest their savings in land which might be taken away from them. The peak in the grain harvest was in 1984, when 407m tons were produced. From then on, millions of acres were allowed to fall into disuse and exposed to climatic erosion. Farmers invested their capital, instead, in the construction of new houses. The supply of food to the towns was dislocated, which forced up prices and sparked social discontent.

The Chinese had failed to learn the Georgist lessons which, through the writings of Sun Yat-sen, were buried in the Peking archives: that security of tenure — not ownership — is both a necessary and sufficient condition for farmers to invest their labor and capital into, and on, the land. Tenant farmers in the market economies are as productive as owner-occupiers. So long as they pay the rents, they retain the use of land and are compensated for the undepreciated value of capital investments when they relinquish their leases. To *whom* they pay the rents is irrelevant, so far as their wilingness to grow food efficiently is concerned.

Gorbachev (1989: 26) recognised the psychological importance of security of tenure; this is not surprising, for his parents were peasants who worked their own holding before being moved on to a collective farm. China's simple mistake was that she failed to reassure farmers that they would retain legal possession for as long as they paid the full current rent to the community. Her remedy was to create 50-year leases; and then make these inheritable. For all practical purposes, land that was ostensibly owned by the community was transformed into private property.

Efficiency was further compromised by the continued interference with prices. A free market would have led to optimum output at lowest costs (to the producer) and maximum surplus income (rent) for the community. Holding prices below market levels does curtail rents, but this is a very inefficient way of influencing the distribution of income or allocation of resources. By contrast, the model based on a 100% tax rate on the market-determined rent of land (which excludes, we emphasise, the interest payments for man-made capital investments on the land) harmonises the conflicting needs of farmers and consumers, and ensures a balanced distribution of income based on work and investment.

In China, social discontent in the countryside soon found its expression in the towns, where it was most brutally repressed in Tiananmen Square. This encouraged the Chinese Communist Party to unwind its reforms. The brunt of that reactionary process, ironically, fell on industry. The main charge against the nation's 14.5m privately-owned businesses was that many of them avoided the payment of taxes (a problem that could not arise, were the tax liability based on the value of land). Renewed interference with free enterprise led to a contraction in the private sector. Over 2m individually owned businesses disappeared by the end of 1989, which cost an estimated 3.5m jobs. One result was quick to emerge: in October 1989, negative growth was reported for the first time in 10 years.

Chinese society seems destined to foster private enterprise in the rural areas, in which a class society based on the privatisation of unearned income will store up the potential for another violent eruption; and collectivised production in the urban sector, with an ever-diminishing capacity to satisfy consumers. This will produce a dangerously lopsided economy, which will necessarily rely on increased state violence to contain the social dissatisfaction.

Soviet reformers have discussed the possibility of adopting 'leaseholds in perpetuity' (Peel 1989). This sounds remarkably similar to the Chinese model; the Soviet politicians who frame the new property laws should examine the empirical evidence from China very carefully.

Privatisation of Industry

Critically important lessons in the culture of enterprise and initiative would be provided by participation in auctions. Diffused into the urban sector, they would accelerate both the privatisation of enterprises and the efficiency with which capital was deployed.

If the wage-earner and the consumer are to derive maximum benefits, this process must be based on an appreciation of market values — that is, the prices that people are willing to offer for the right to own or lease premises and equipment. This lesson was not learnt during the early stages of change in Poland, where publicly-owned assets were alienated for less than their real value. In one case, a member of the Communist Party acquired a machine tool factory that was formerly state-run. 'He fixed things so that he could lease the land — formerly state propety — for a nominal sum,' reported *The Guardian* (London, August 28, 1989). If the land is leased, of course, it is not 'formerly' state property. But if the rent payable under the terms of the lease is nominal, the state might just as well hand over the title deeds, for possession of the income generated by land is what ultimately matters.

Apart from equity considerations, what are the economic ramifications implicit in such cases? The most obvious one is that the rents that ought to be paid to the asset owner (the community) can be used to subsidise the wages and profits of a company which, because it is not satisfying its customers, must be deemed to be inefficient. The receipt of rents disguises this inefficiency. The community is materially poorer than it need be; and the tax burden on labor and capital is necessarily higher than it otherwise would be. This absurd chain of events stems directly from the failure properly to value land and charge the user the full annual rent for the right of possession.[8]

Even isolated examples of such corruption or economic inefficiency gain wide publicity. This jeopardises the goodwill of the public, whose sense of fairness is outraged. The practical consequences, in times of uncertainty, ought not to be under-estimated.[9]

So there are lessons to be learnt by both government and citizen. In the government's case, it is crucially important that the alienation of publicly-owned resources should be on the basis of their full opportunity costs — that is, the price that others would be willing to pay for the resources. Where this is not done the national exchequer is deprived of revenue which then has to be raised from labor and capital, which retards economic development.

In the case of the citizen, the process of bidding rent for land forces prospective entrepreneurs to calculate 'the bottom line' of the enterprise. They are obliged to come to terms with the pricing system, calculating how much is needed for wages and to finance working capital, and what the revenue would be (given the price that can be charged in relation to the market that is to be serviced). Armed with this information, entrepreneurs arrive at the figure which is the surplus to these costs of production — i.e., the rental income.

If the citizen, as a resource user, and the government, as guardian of the social interest, discharged their responsibilities towards the use of the community's resources, a creative dynamic would be set in motion based on organic adaptation to changing tastes and rising living standards. This would ensure a constant reallocation of resources to meet new challenges. This necessarily entails change, a process which in the West is explicitly held to be obligatory for the labor and capital markets but which is not properly monitored and enforced in the land market. In the same way that a firm can be liquidated if its workers are unwilling to be as productive as their competitors; or if capital can be withdrawn in favor of uses that more efficiently meet the needs of consumers; so the current use of land should be abandoned in favor of uses that will yield the full rent to the community. That the latter does not occur as efficiently as it should is a serious restraint on the operation of the market economy.

Starting at the End

Armed with these insights, the historic conditions confronting the Soviet Union could turn economics on its head. The classical theorists recognised that rent was the surplus income; the *end result* of production and pricing, after all the costs of labor and capital had been met in a competitive environment. For the Soviet Union, however, which is obliged to conflate change into a relatively brief period, it is conceptually most useful to treat the determination of rent as the *starting point* in the joint venture between the state (the exclusive owner of natural resources) and citizen (who wants to obtain and use those resources at a competitive rent). If this appears to be a topsy-turvey approach, it is one that works. It was adopted by the Japanese reformers in what is known as the Meiji revolution, the lessons from which would serve Gorbachev well.

In the 1870s, feudal Japan decided to modernise in double-quick time. She needed an industrial economy to resist the aggressive trading overtures of foreign powers. At the heart of her strategy was the fiscal policy that captured rent (Harrison 1983). Japan's land tax, because it fell on the *surplus* income after all the costs of production had been met, achieved some remarkable results. First, it provided farmers with the incentive to improve productivity. This raised incomes and lowered prices for urban consumers. This tax-and-tenure approach encouraged the retention of family farms and protected the right of the rural community to keep the income that it *earned*. There was a mirror-image effect in the urban sector, where a balanced distribution of wage-bargaining power between employees and employers was established in the labor market. For there was no captive pool of unemployed laborers in the towns to exploit (as happened with the Enclosures in Britain at the turn into the 19th century, which conveniently provided Marx with his stereotype of the exploited proletariat). So short of workers were some capitalists that they had to resort to kidnapping people! A rise in the real value of wages followed.

The fiscal lessons are also crucial for the USSR. The tax fell on a buoyant base. The government invested the revenue in infrastructure and the educational needs of the formerly agrarian workforce. This removed the need to adopt forms of taxation that deter the formation of fixed capital and the creation of jobs; the logic of the land-value tax was exactly correct for this critical transitional period from feudalism to capitalism.

The fiscal policy proved to be catalytic. It laid the foundations for the unique Japanese industrial system (this contention needs further elaboration elsewhere). It can be contrasted with the approach adopted by Stalin in 1924-32. His brutal solution was to kill the rural wealth-creators (the entrepreneurial *kulaks*) and plunder everything that could be removed from them. This was not a rational program of incentives designed to increase productivity and economic development.

After 20 years, however, the Japanese model was compromised. A new class of landlords emerged. They did so by taking control of the political process and reducing the share of government revenue derived from rent. This produced a disastrous shift in the distribution of power, and it was to bequeath to the Japanese people a land market that was every bit as inefficient and socially destructive as its western counterparts.

We can now relate this fiscal policy to the two topics on which Soviet citizens will place the greatest emphasis in the 1990s — prices, and the redeployment of employees to new jobs. In doing so, it is worth re-emphasising that, economically, the only frictionless fiscal policy is the tax on the rent of natural resources. This is acknowledged in the standard textbooks on economics. Milton Friedman, an arch exponent of minimal government, concedes that governments have to raise revenue — in which case, he grudgingly admits, there is a rational method for doing so:

> There's a sense in which all taxes are antagonistic to free enterprise — and yet we need taxes . . . So the question is, which are the least bad taxes? In my opinion the least bad tax is the property tax on the unimproved value of land, the Henry George argument of many, many years ago (quoted in *Human Events*, November 18, 1978).

The lessons that can be learnt from the western tax system are those of fiscal failure or inefficiency. Capitalist societies extract exchequer revenues from earned income, consumption and profits on the basis of taxes that obstruct growth and prosperity. By adopting Henry George's land-value tax, the USSR would be creating the first coherent tax structure in the world.

Prices Other forms of taxation are treated as costs of production. They are incorporated into product prices and passed on to consumers. This raises the general level of prices. Such an effect would be disastrous for the USSR, for it would compound the consequences of cutting subsidies. It would be irrational to aggravate this process by adopting taxes that raise prices higher than is necessary for the sake of the efficient use of scarce resources. In contrast, the tax that falls on rent — after the appropriate structural adjustments in the market — cannot be shifted on to either the wages of labor or on to the profits of capital. It is a tax that remains where it falls — on the rent of land. Since this fact is not clearly understood by the public, it would be as well to digress, briefly, into the theory of rent.

Landowners *per se* do not make a practical contribution to the wealth-creating process. The receipt of rent (we are here excluding the income that a landowner can with justice claim in return for his capital improvements upon the land) is a privilege derived from a particular legal system, which permits the owners of the resources of nature to privately levy a land tax without sharing the proceeds equally with others.

Rent is treated as a *cost*, by firms or households, but only for accounting purposes; it is *not* a cost of production. Natural resources are literally provided free by nature (which is not the same thing as saying that they have no value). The costs of recovering them — for example, subterranean minerals which have to be hauled to the surface — are the costs of labor and capital. In a fully competitive system these have first claims on the revenue of an enterprise, before the residue, or rent, can be calculated.

The rent of natural resources, therefore, does not enter into the price that is charged for individual products that are either made or sold on a particular site, thanks to competition. Thus, a tax on the pure surplus income (rent) is unique in that it cannot be shifted to customers through higher prices. So in the West, today, if a tenant was required to pay the land tax, he would reduce the rents he paid to his landlord. His total costs of occupation would remain the same; the higher the land-value tax payable to the state, the lower the rent that could be claimed by the landlord. This is a well-attested fact in economic literature. The essence of the reasoning was explained in a technical note by the British Treasury in these terms:

> The effect of taxes depends upon the demand and supply elasticities of the commodity being taxed. For example if the supply is very elastic the main effect of a tax is to increase the market price; if the supply is very inelastic the main effect of the tax is to decrease the net of tax price. The supply of land, for example, is relatively inelastic and the usual long term effect of property rates [taxes] is largely to reduce rents and land values (Treasury 1984: 9).

In a local market, under certain circumstances, the elasticity of supply of one of the other factors of production — labor or capital — can be artificially altered (through, for example, the exercise of trades union power; or international barriers to the free flow of capital). But this is not an unalterable situation: labor and capital are reproducible. Land is finite; so, in the economist's term, its supply is inelastic. All the more reason, therefore, that the land market should be efficient enough to recycle sites quickly in response to the organically changing needs of the community.

The effect of taxation on prices must be borne in mind as a major consideration in the reform of the Soviet economy. It is a reality that cannot be avoided by inaction. The failure of government to take the impact of fiscal policy into account does not thereby mean a neutral response in either the market for land and natural resources, or the consumer markets. There is a reciprocal impact on the way that the private sector uses land and distributes income (Banks 1989: 149-53), and on the pricing structure for consumer goods and services, if an alternative fiscal policy — such as the income tax — is adopted.

Redeployment of employees The large-scale reallocation of labor is socially traumatic, but the damage can be minimised and even turned into an exhilarating and rewarding experience. It all depends on whether the time spent out of work is brief (no more than is necessary to find alternative work) or protracted (which is evidence of institutional barriers to the efficient use of resources). *Perestroika* may force employees to abandon the security of the old system, but there is no excuse for aggravating their plight by the adoption of misaligned policy. Taxes that raise prices above costs of production cause unemployment, because higher prices restrict demand: less can be bought by consumers than would be the case if price = cost.

A tax on land values represents a positive incentive to growth and the rational deployment of resources at the lowest possible prices. The implications for increasing the Soviet Union's share of international trade — providing an export-led thrust to growth — are plain: a country that heavily exploits land value taxation acquires a major advantage in price competitiveness.

Fiscal Policy & the Transitional Stage

We can now take a closer theoretical look at the holistic dimensions of our developmental model based on land value taxation (LVT), bearing in mind that Gorbachev sought broadfront solutions that integrated social, economic and ecological objectives into a single thrust.

Psycho-dynamics of LVT Personal fears stemming from the uncertainties of the future generate a 'conservative' reaction. LVT would play a significant part in ensuring the continuity of social cohesion, by minimising those anxieties. Consensus support of the population would be retained if people were assured that they had an equal claim on the cash value of common property — the natural resources of their community — whether through social expenditure or the distribution of land-value revenue in the form of a guaranteed minimum income for everyone.

Infrastructural investment The value of that common inheritance, of course, would rise as the economy developed. This would not only serve the material interests of the individual, but would also meet the budgetary needs of the Soviet Union, whose infrastructure was built to accommodate heavy industry rather than the consumer. A great deal of money will have to be spent on infrastructure. The Soviet Union entered the 13th Five-Year Plan period with the intention of building 226,000 kilometres of hard-surface roads in the rural areas, to assist farmers to transport their increased output of food to towns in a marketable condition. In one area alone, in what is called the non-black-earth zone, over 35 billion roubles were allocated for improving the road network. The impact of this investment on land values is of supreme importance, but the risks are those of a double-edged sword: handled incorrectly, it can injure the person wielding it. This point must be stressed, for it identifies one of the key weaknesses in the structure of the western market economies.

If rising values are reflected in higher government revenues, taxes on labor and capital are rendered unnecessary. Furthermore, the rise in rents proves that sound projects are self-financing: they pay for themselves through the increased benefits they generate (as measured in the land market), which means the government can accelerate its program of investment in socially-necessary infrastructure without burdening the wealth-creators with the damaging taxes that are employed in the west.

Where, however, the tax structure permits individuals to speculate in future rental values, it pays to hoard land that ought to be brought into use in the current period; this is a feature of western societies, and is most visible in the dereliction of the inner cities of

Europe and North America. This behavior alters the distribution of income between the factors of production (for artificial restriction of the supply of land pushes rents up even further); it results in the waste of capital (through the extensive provision of amenities required by communities that have been forced to sprawl into the countryside); and leads to a degeneration in the living environment. This prospect is now opening up for Poland, Hungary and Czechoslovakia, for they have failed to think through the consequences of the rush into the arms of the IMF.

Ecological imperatives Land-value taxation is an environmentally-friendly fiscal policy; it actively encourages users to conserve resources (Harrison 1991). We need not labor this point, for the benign influence of LVT on the environment is explored below, in Chapter 8. The Green Party in Britain adopted LVT, which it calls Community Ground Rent, because of its impact on both the environment and the social structure of the countryside.

The devolution of power We live in a world of interdependent nations. This urgently requires a redefinition of *rights* and *responsibilities* that correspond with a strategy of global harmony built on sustainable relationships (both as between sovereign nations, and as between mankind and his habitat). A practical test of how LVT can be used to harmonise political relationships is offered by the tensions between the 15 republics of the USSR that first emerged in 1990.

The defining characteristic of the nation-state is its ability to defend a precisely-demarcated area of land. But the origins of territorial conflicts are complex, for cross-border disputes often stem from an unequal distribution of rights of access to natural resources within societies. Through a complicated sequence of internal repression, this deprivation eventually finds its release in armed conflict with neighbors.

In the Soviet Union's case, the most dangerous points of conflict arise over escalating demands for improved living standards and job opportunities from ethnic minorities; and pressure for greater autonomy from republics which believe that, economically, they can fare better if power is devolved to them.[10] Can these demands be satisfied, while at the same time the republics are encouraged to remain united under the umbrella of a benign union of republics?

The dynamics, here, are of the spin-drier; the tendency to want to break out (centrifugal force generated by unsatisfied demands) working against the pressure from the federal superstructure, which seeks to contain the elements within it (the centripetal force). These oppositional pressures can be harmonised by a bold initiative that satisfied material needs and fulfilled a symbolic function. Such a vision, we believe, could be built on the concept of LVT. The acknowledgement that natural resources are a common heritage can be placed at the heart of a new political contract between ethnically diverse peoples.

The USSR could establish a Development Fund, into which each republic would annually contribute a percentage of the market value imputable to its natural endowments. The Fund would serve both *symbolic* and *developmental* purposes. The resources of the Fund could be used to alleviate short-term distress (natural calamities, such as famine), pay for the clean-up of the polluted environment, and to finance the economic development of regions with the lowest *per capita* incomes. Because the citizens of each republic would see that they were contributing to this humanitarian Fund, on the basis of ability, and that the money was controlled and allocated democratically, on the basis of need, the sense of a personal and collective identification with the goals of *perestroika* would be shared by everyone. There would be a general awareness that resources were being mobilised for the general good, and that every person benefited equally.

Some republics are rich in high-value minerals; their contributions would be proportionately greater than those from others. The resource-rich regions would not be net 'losers', under this formula. For if their economies were relatively undeveloped, they would be entitled to a disproportionate claim on the resources of the Fund to assist in their economic development. This meets the objection, for example, that Russia is resource-rich, but is relatively poor in *per capita* terms, compared with some of the other republics. The formula outlined here, then, restores a balance between the inflow and outflow of cash, but in the process it reinforces the restructuring of the domestic economy to generate balanced growth. As economically disadvantaged regions grew in prosperity, the monetary value of their land would correspondingly increase. Their contribution to the Fund would consequently rise, thereby tending to equalise the contributions from all the republics into a synchronised growth path based on mutual advantage and respect. The Development Fund, then, would also enhance the prospects of political integration.

The symbolic value of sharing in the rent of natural resources is crucial. It is the first step in the development of the practical recognition of the rights — and obligations — of individual cultural entities *within the framework of the union of republics.* If the Fund was financed by taxes on the work of individuals or enterprises, resentment would be a legitimate result, which would color the prospects of social harmony. Absent would be the identification with the Fund based on the concept of a mutual sharing of commonly-owned resources.

The USSR, having adopted the auction system for reallocating land at the micro-economic level, would be able to build on that fiscal philosophy to harmonise living standards, political relationships and psychological expectations between republics within the Soviet Union.

Marx and the Single Tax

Orthodox market economists lack the credibility to instruct the Soviets on how to transform their economy.[11] But if our model of an ethical and efficient economy is so good, why was it not adopted before now?

First, it has to be conceded that there never was any mystery about the essential elements of an efficient market system. The classical economists described the ideal model; it was simply not translated into the 'real world'. Nor was there any mystery about why the market consistently failed to deliver full employment. Successive governments conspired with vested interests to create and preserve the structural defect in the foundations. The western model guaranteed that, no matter how diligent the worker or productive the capital, no matter how innovative the scientist and technologist, no matter how sophisticated the business manager, government (through the tax system) and an inefficient land market, continuously bore down on the economy.

From the outset of the Industrial Revolution, entrepreneurs were deterred from expanding productive capacity to optimum levels.

And capital that should have been invested to encourage the use of the best techniques to conserve natural resources and preserve the environment was not invested because the 'commons' (rivers, oceans, skies) could be depleted and polluted at little or no cost. The cyclical propensity to speculate in land, which dislocated incentives and the pattern of growth, was also actively encouraged. And because labor was denied access to some of the land that it needed, structural unemployment was ingrained into the system.

The second distortion was through the pricing mechanism. By placing the burden of taxation on labor and capital, governments wilfully established a permanent ratchet for raising prices, by the process we have already described. This created its own vicious dynamic. After a period of human suffering and the waste of capital and natural resources (recessions), governments intervene in the market process and artificially stimulate demand — to shorten the queues at the soup kitchens. This encouraged inflation and further reduced the efficiency of the market. Band-aid tinkering with symptoms necessitated a new round of increases in either taxes or the national debt, to fund the public make-work measures. And so the vicious downward spiral continued, for the new tax increases forced up labor costs and factory-gate prices, which in turn triggered restraints on consumption, investment and commerce — and a new round of unemployment. Keynesianism and the Welfare State were, in the Hegelian sense, historically inevitable; for the logical demand for them was built into the imperfect foundations of the industrial economy 200 years ago.

It need not have happened. The economic insights into how taxes were passed on by workers and capitalists, through the pricing mechanism, were available in the original treatise on economics by Adam Smith (1976, Vol. II: 400). That manual also spelt out the appropriate remedial policies. Smith pointed out, at the beginning of the Industrial Revolution, that the correct fiscal policy was one that built on the tax that could be directly levied on economic rent:

> Both ground-rents and the ordinary rent of land are a species of revenue which the owner, in many cases, enjoys without any care or attention of his own. Though a part of this revenue should be taken from him in order to defray the expenses of the state, no discouragement will thereby be given to any sort of industry. The annual product of the land and labour

> of the society, the real wealth and revenue of the great body of the people, might be the same after such a tax as before. Ground-rents, and the ordinary rent of land, are, therefore, perhaps the species of revenue which can best bear to have a peculiar tax imposed upon them.
>
> Ground-rents seem, in this respect, a more proper subject of peculiar taxation than even the ordinary rent of land ... Ground-rents, so far as they exceed the ordinary rent of land, are altogether owing to the good government of the sovereign ... Nothing can be more reasonable than that a fund which owes its existence to the good government of the state, should be taxed peculiarly, or should contribute something more than the greater part of other funds, towards the support of that government (Smith 1976: Vol. II, 370-71).

Adam Smith provided the clearest warnings to those who held the fate of the trading nations in their hands. The adoption of the superior method of raising revenue would have led to a qualitatively different growth path for the economies of Europe and North America; one that would provide, on a sustainable basis, for full employment, decent wages and stable prices. That is why, today, at this late stage, the adoption of LVT would entail a radical departure from the model that has operated for 200 years. For example, the imposition of a high tax on the annual rent of land would lead to the spontaneous elimination of dereliction in the city through the creation of a competitive *milieu* in the land market. This policy, in turn, would generate so much revenue, as has been noted (Banks 1989), that corresponding cuts in the taxes on wages and profits would transform the capitalist countries, leading to a reduction in the level of prices and so eliminating the principal motive force behind what is popularly characterised as 'inflation'.

Karl Marx, in 'The Communist Manifesto' (1848), had once advocated this policy himself. Would that he had continued to do so! Instead, he chose to ridicule Henry George (Harrison 1979). The two philosophers were the leading critics of the results produced by the first century of the industrial mode of production. Henry George realised that there was no need to throw the baby out with the bathwater. He perceived the advantages of the free market, and sought to build on them by reform. Marx would have none of that: he sought revolution. His scathing attack on Henry George will return to haunt his ghost.

The Single Tax was elaborated in Henry George's *Progress and*

Poverty (1879). For Marx, the book was 'the capitalist's last ditch'. The march of history, as he saw it, precluded the reform of the market economy, and would guarantee the triumph of socialism. Under Marx's influence, socialism became the dominant alternative philosophy in the West. The Georgist critique was given a good run by the Liberal Party in Britain, under the leadership of Lloyd George and Winston Churchill, but despite a constitutional victory in the 1909 election against their opponents, the aristocratic landowners, the Georgist program was allowed to lapse in the face of the rise of the socialist Labour Party.

What of the prospects, now, for the Soviet Union? Gorbachev tried to preserve a sense of socialism. After all, insisted an editorial in *Pravda* (Aganbegyan and Timofeyev 1988: 73), *perestroika* was the product of the dialectical method of Marx and Lenin. Socialism would triumph — but 'with a human face', and within the context of a market economy; or at least, by whatever emerged after the demise of what Gorbachev called 'the command-administrative model, which was contrary to the original idea of socialism'.[12]

For Henry George, socialism was not a viable social system. He understood the essential nature of the human relations that would emerge in a system in which the superstructure of the state was given precedence over the rights of the individual:

> The proposal which socialism makes is that the collectivity or state shall assume the management of all means of production, including land, capital and man himself; do away with all competition, and convert mankind into two classes, the directors, taking their orders from government and acting by governmental authority, and the workers, for whom everything shall be provided, including the directors themselves ... It is more destitute of any central and guiding principle than any philosophy I know of ... It has no system of individual rights whereby it can define the extent to which the individual is entitled to liberty or to which the state may go in restraining it. (George 1981: 198).

The course of history has demonstrated that Karl Marx had might on his side; Henry George had to settle for being right.

But the directors of the socialist state have capitulated. The leading rôle of the Communist Party was abandoned in the glow of flickering candles in the squares of Budapest and Prague, and the flash of gunfire in Romania. And herein lies an irony. In the headlong rush to abandon socialism, Poland, Hungary and Czechoslovakia may have willy-nilly accepted the cyclically-discredited formulas of western economics, but the Soviet Union, by cautiously retaining the instruments of the command economy for the 13th 5-year Plan (1991-95), bought time for mature reflection. Academicians who scoured the world for solutions were confronted with the need to re-evaluate the Single Tax. This necessarily challenged them with the uncomfortable task of deciding whether Marx was premature in his dismissal of *Progress and Poverty* as 'the last ditch' of capitalism.

They ought not to have been too embarrassed, however, for the Supreme Soviet independently arrived at a law on property rights with which Henry George would not have argued. The Property Law came into effect on July 1, 1990. Article 20, on the 'Ownership of land and other natural resources,' declared that 'The Land and its contents, water, flora and fauna are the inalienable property of the peoples residing in a given territory.' Apart from defining special rights for peasant farmers, the law affirmed that all land continued to be owned by the state.

The legal basis for the first Single Tax society now exists. All that remains is for the Soviet Union to be consistent in the implementation of its law.

Mikhail Gorbachev, if he were to explicitly identify himself with the full richness of the Single Tax philosophy, would place at the disposal of his peoples the most powerful tool possible for them to transform the social, political and economic system. The end result would not be recognisable to Marx, but neither would it be the authoritarian, inefficient creature now championed by the advocates of capitalism. It does not matter what such a society is called, so long as it liberated further the individual and made the best use of the resources of nature for the collective good of everyone, and not just a privileged class.

NOTES

1. Poland was the first to settle with the IMF. Arrangements reached over the Christmas holiday in 1989 brought them $725m in stand-by loans, which triggered additional western aid. The price was a heavy one. Unprofitable enterprises had to be closed. The IMF predicted job

losses of about 1m. Government subsidies on consumer goods had to be cut from 31% to 14%, and wages had to be frozen (producing a predicted drop in real incomes of about 20%).

In Hungary, Prime Minister Miklos Nemeth resigned from the presidium of the Socialist (formerly Communist) Party, because he failed to get his comrades to support the austerity measures, which included a 35% increase in the rents of state housing. Parliament, however, endorsed the austerity budget on Dec. 21, 1989, which cleared the way for $350m in stand-by credits and an injection of $1 billion in European Community funds.

2. The degree to which market economies waste natural resources is not one that can be measured with confidence because of the paucity of information. This ought not to astonish anyone. Reforms to the land market have been successfully opposed by the simple expedient of placing limits on the availability of data. This preserved the privileges of owners. Britain serves as an excellent example.

For a survey into the failures of the corporate sector, see Avis *et al.* (1989), who conclude that most companies cannot relate the cost of property to their overall performance because they do not have internal property management accounts. Most companies do not even know the opportunity cost (the current market rent) of the space they occupy. Without this information there can be no accurate measurement of corporate performance.

These shortcomings were also present in the public sector. For an authoritative analysis, see various reports published by the Comptroller and Auditor General during 1988-89. The Auditor (John Bourn) succeeded in penetrating the Whitehall defences to measure the economic loss arising from the undervaluation of land that was privatised by the Thatcher government. The bureaucratic response was predictable: a new category of file was created for the use of civil servants: 'Not for National Audit Office Eyes.' See David Hencke, 'State files kept from watchdog,' *The Guardian*, London, January 3, 1989.

The Auditor, in the annual report for 1989, bluntly declared: 'Land and property are presented often as free goods in the culture; not as something out of which you could earn money.' In its practical effects, this 'capitalist' attitude towards natural resources coincides with Marxist theory.

3. Readers who imagine that the United States, which hitherto has been the leading market economy, is exempt from economic sclerosis, should consult Paul Krugman (1990). His analysis and forecasts yield a picture that has remarkable similarities to the account that emerged in the late 1980s for the Soviet Union. When the full history of the USA is finally written, the rôle of expansion based on under-priced/

over-exploited natural resources will figure prominently. The decline in growth rates in the productivity of labor and capital will, we suspect, be closely related to the rate of increase in the depletion of natural resources. The decline in overall growth rates will be related to constraints imposed by the finite nature of those resources.

4. Western governments have also been guilty of failing to identify large-scale destruction of natural resources. The starting point for this waste may have been the multiplicity of decisions taken by individuals and firms at the micro-economic level, rather than state-owned collectives; nonetheless, western governments fail to employ a system of national income accounts capable of identifying the defects in their tax-and-tenure policies. If the rental value had been correctly imputed to all natural resources, auditors could have drawn the waste to the attention of policy-makers.

National income accounts measure changes in short-term economic activity. They are largely illusory documents, however, for they do not taken into account considerations of long term sustainable growth. This is even a serious defect in the UN System of National Accounts, in which we might reasonably have expected an attempt at presenting realistic global evaluations of resource depletion. The point is highlighted by Serafy and Lutz (1989: 3):

> Underlying this asymmetry is the implicit, as well as inappropriate, assumption that natural resources are so abundant that they are costless or have no marginal value. Historically they have been regarded as free gifts of nature — a bias that provides false signals for policymakers. This approach ignores the depletion of valuable resources and confuses the scale of commercially marketable natural assets with the generation of income. Thus it promotes and seems to validate the idea that rapid economic growth can be obtained by exploiting a resource base that may be rapidly diminishing. The growth can be illusory, and the prosperity it engenders transitory, if the apparent gain in income means permanent loss in wealth, that is, if at least part of the receipts is not redirected into new productive investments. As income is inflated, often consumption is also, and the country concerned gets complacent about its economic performance; as a result the adjustment in economic policy gets delayed by the seeming prosperity. In this regard, proper income accounting is an aid to better decisionmaking, but, of course, it does not guarantee that improved decisions will actually be made.

The World Resources Institute, and the International Institute for Environment and Development, collaborating with the UN Environment Programme, have published a report that demonstrates how ecological vandalism is inextricably associated with the failure to charge the full economic rent of natural resources (*World Resources 1988-89*, esp. Ch. 12). The users of natural resources who are allowed privately to appropriate economic rent find that it pays them to destroy forests, debase the growing powers of the soil, denude the hillsides, deplete the supply of potable water, pollute the rivers and turn the skies into acid baths. This propensity is evident in both the industrialised regions and the Third World. These acts of destruction are supported by the structure of fiscal policies. The process of environmental degradation would be reversed if governments were to restructure their tax systems in favor of one that valued and taxed the natural resources on the basis of current market values (see Harrison, 'Ecology, Politics and the Theory of Rent', in Banks, 1989).

5. It might be argued that the auction system has greater relevance for Soviet agriculture than for the East European countries such as Yugoslavia and Hungary, where much of the agricultural land continued in private ownership, despite the postwar influence of the Marxist régimes. In Poland, 2.7m small private farms cover 76% of arable land; private farmers are free to buy and sell land, so the institutional arrangements of a market system already exists. This would be a spurious argument, however; the fact that much of this land remained in private ownership does not alter the fiscal logic that underpins the taxation of rents, as we will show.

   Note, however, that the failure to charge a tax on the realisable value of land (rent) means that a socialist society cannot escape the consequences of the private appropriation of rent. Vietnam is an illuminating example. She charges farmers a 'fixed' rent, in the form of rice delivered to the state. By failing to recognise that the productive capacity of land varies between one site and another, the state permits some users to capture part of the rental value of land. (Another example, discussed on pages 88-90, is that of Communist China.)

   The lesson is further illustrated in the urban land market. In Belgrade, when publicly-owned property was transferred to new users, the occupant who relinquished possession charged the prospective occupier a 'premium' before transferring his possessory rights. This 'premium' was the capitalised value of that part of the economic rent of land that was not taxed by the state (Harrison 1983: 178-181).

6. This mechanism is sufficiently effective and simple to meet the immediate needs of the USSR in the earliest stages of the transitional phase. Trying to create a more sophisticated framework at the outset would be so daunting for the policy-makers, that there is a risk they might opt for alternative fiscal policies. The latter, which may make for a simpler

life for bureaucrats (the costs of administering the payroll or sales tax can be imposed on the private sector), would be far more damaging to the economy and the freedom of citizens.

Evidence that efforts are being made in the right direction has already emerged, in the decision by officials in Leningrad to dust off the land-value map which pre-dated the revolution. Dr John Parker, a London architect, reports that this exercise was designed to rediscover the relative rental values of property in the city.

Ted Gwartney, one of the most experienced of assessors in the US in the field of land-value taxation, has devised a simple, practical protocol for assigning rental value to land in the USSR, under proto-market conditions. But if the Soviet Union were to proceed down the Single Tax road, it would quickly acquire the capacity to develop a system for continuous revaluation of rental values even more sophisticated than the methods employed elsewhere for property tax purposes. Such a model has been described by Prof. Nic Tideman. (Papers by Parker, Gwartney and Tideman were presented to a conference on August 22-24, 1990, on 'Concepts and Procedures for the Social Collection of Rent in the Soviet Union.' This was held in New York under a grant from the Robert Schalkenbach Foundation. See also Tideman [forthcoming].

7. Provision would have to be made for dealing with mischievous bidders who might try to force rents above the economic levels, which farmers could not pay. Winning bidders would be legally required to pay the rent (= tax) that they bid, even if they did not take possession of the land.
8. Proof of similar failure in the market economies emerges when the tax authorities finally consent to discharge their legal duty to revalue real estate for the purpose of property taxation. When this happens, it is sometimes discovered that relative property values have adjusted quite markedly. This gives rise to extreme dissatisfaction among those whose properties have risen in value, but whose bills were formerly at an artificially low level.

   This occurred with the revaluation of commercial and industrial property in Britain in 1989. Some firms claimed that they would have to shut down, because of the large and sudden upward revision of their tax liability. In at least some cases, closure was evidence that the firm had been allowed to employ labor, capital and land in an inefficient combination; i.e., their flow of income was evidence of their failure to satisfy customers. They had survived because wages and profits were subsidised by the artificially low property tax, a subsidy which was at the expense of the taxpayer. (Asset strippers, of course, make their fortunes by spotting this under-valuation of assets relative to the cash-flow of the business.)

9. The political reaction emerged in November 1990. In Poland, Prime Minister Tadeusz Mazowiecki was crushed into third place in the country's first presidential elections. He announced the resignation of his government on Nov. 26, declaring that the result expressed the public's disaffection with the IMF-backed austerity measures. In the same month, local elections in Czechoslovakia disclosed a new surge in support for the Communist Party, which observers interpreted as public anxiety about the IMF's formula that was due to take effect in January 1991.
10. In Mikhail Gorbachev's draft treaty for the union, published on Nov. 23, 1990, republics were said to be 'owners of the land and natural resources on their own territories.' This was not an uncontroversial solution to republican claims on natural resources, however, for the treaty imposed limits on these rights. The use of gold and diamond reserves, for example (produced by Russia) would have to be agreed with the union and the other republics. The fiscal question remained vague: taxation was addressed in two short paragraphs.
11. This was secretly acknowledged in a paper on the transformation of the Polish economy that was prepared for the Warsaw government by the economists of the Paris-based Organisation for Economic Co-operation and Development, which represents the industrially-advanced countries. The document was leaked to the *Financial Times*. This admitted that the OECD 'does not have, and cannot have, the degree and breadth of knowledge that would truly be required to address all the problems associated with such change' (Norman 1990).
12. In the draft of the new treaty for the USSR, Gorbachev dropped the word socialist in favor of the Union of Sovereign Soviet Republics.

Lenin remains a poor guide to land and tax policy. His analysis is redolent with confusion. For example, he confused the equalised *use* of land with problems associated with ownership (1965: 9). Henry George showed that the use of money and tax policy resolved the problem of an unequal distribution of land with no disruption other than to the power base of the privileged class that appropriated unearned income. For George, rent was at once the problem and the solution. Lenin sought the easy way out: he advocated the abolition of rent (ibid: 116). Rent cannot be abolished; but economic efficiency and social justice can be destroyed by those who try to act on Lenin's advice.

Lenin's myopia further emerges in his analysis of what the proletariat needed to do on behalf of the exploited peasants. Peasants had to be granted the 'free use of the lands they formerly rented, since no other economic or technical basis exists' (ibid: 120). In that case, how does such a society resolve the problem of having to favor some users with lush fertile soil, while consigning others to the harsher tracts? The economic basis (the free market) and technical solution (tax policy) did exist, for resolving such problems; Lenin ignored them because they conflicted with his ideology — Marxism.

BIBLIOGRAPHY

Aganbegyan, Abel, and Timor Timofeyev (1988), *The New Stage of Perestroka*, New York: Institute for East-West Security Studies

(1988), *The Challenge: Economics of Perestroika*, London: Century Hutchinson.

(1989), *Moving the Mountain*, New York: Bantam.

Avis, Martin, Virginia Gibson and Jenny Watts (1989), *Managing Operational Property*, Reading University: Department of Land Management and Development.

Banks, Ron (1989), *Costing the Earth*, London: Shepheard Walwyn/CIT.

George, Henry (1979), *Progress and Poverty* (1879), New York: Robert Schalkenbach Foundation.

(1981), *The Science of Political Economy* (1898), New York: Robert Schalkenbach Foundation.

Gorbachev, Mikhail (1988), *Perestroika*, London: Fontana.

(1989), *On the Agrarian Policy of the CPSU in the Present Conditions*, Moscow: Novosti Press Agency Publishing House.

Harrison, Fred (1979), 'Gronlund and Other Marxists,' in R. V. Andelson, *Critics of Henry George*, Rutherford: Fairleigh Dickinson UP.

(1983), *The Power in the Land*, London: Shepheard Walwyn.

(1986), 'Change of heart by classless society', *Land and Liberty*. London, May-June.

(1991), 'Geonomics: The Making of a Post-Socialist Society', in Sara Parkin and David Fernback, *Green Light over Europe*, London: Heretic.

Krugman, Paul (1990), *The Age of Diminished Expectations*, MIT.

Lenin, V. I. (1965), *The Land Question and the Fight for Freedom*, Moscow: Progress Publishers.

Norman, Peter (1990), 'OECD team will advise Poland on switch to

market economy,' *Financial Times*, London, January 3.
Peel, Quentin (1989), 'The battle lines are drawn,' *Financial Times*, London, November 20, p. 24.
Serafy, Salah El, and Ernst Lutz (1989), 'Environmental and Resource Accounting: An Overview,' in Yusuf J. Ahmad, Salah El Serafy and Ernst Lutz, editors, *Environmental Accounting for Sustainable Development*, Washington, DC: World Bank.
Smith, Adam (1976), *The Wealth of Nations* (1776), Chicago: Univ. of Chicago Press.
Tideman, T. Nicolaus (forthcoming), 'Integrating Land Value Taxation with the Internalization of Spatial Externalities,' *Land Economics*.
Treasury (1984), *Investment Appraisal in the Public Sector: a Technical Guide for Government Departments*, London: HM Treasury.
World Resources Institute (1988), *World Resources 1988-89*, New York: Basic Books.

5

Conflict, Ideology and Hope in Central America*

JAMES L. BUSEY

IN THE face of the ongoing collapse of rigid Marxism-Leninism-Stalinism, it is intriguing to return to the concepts of the Hegelian dialectic. Hegel taught that history evolves via the emergence of apparent 'syntheses' of thought or action that arise out of contests between initiating concepts or 'theses' and contrary concepts or 'antitheses'.[1]

Marx turned this mental process, this contest between great philosophies, into a materialistic clash between economic classes, wherein the final 'synthesis' would arise out of the victorious struggle by the working class (antithesis) against the ruling capitalist class or bourgeoisie (thesis). The Marxist 'synthesis' would be rule by the working class, or 'dictatorship of the proletariat' as Lenin, Stalin, and their successors described it. This would conclude the materialist dialectic, and would terminate all such theses and antitheses.

Now we know that this glorious Marxist synthesis, the final conclusion of all class struggle ('freeman and slave, patrician and plebian, lord and serf, guildmaster and journeyman, in a word, oppressor and oppressed') was nothing of the sort.[2] Rather, it produced a fantastic concentration of power in the hands of a small, self-appointed ruling élite; and under the surface of dogmatic propaganda and brutality, there boiled a seething hatred against fanatic

* I am most grateful to our editor, Richard Noyes, for his insights and encouragement; to my valued colleague, Professor Alfred G. Cuzán, Department of Political Science, University of West Florida, for the many suggestions that he will recognize I have incorporated into this paper; and as always, to Marian Busey for her recommendations about syntax and correction of typographical errors. — jlb.

ideologues who uprooted whole social systems, families, beliefs and entire populations, in an incredible zeal to achieve goals they thought had been set by their revelation of absolute truth.

Is it conceivable that classical social theory, especially that of an almost forgotten eighteenth century French physiocracy as further refined at the hands of Henry George (which I shall call geocracy), might fill a doctrinal gap and be suitable both for the preservation of freedom and for the resolution of human travail?[3]

Geocracy is not related to the materialistic Marxist interpretation of the Hegelian dialectic. It is very much related to, and a part of, the contest of ideas which was at the heart of the Hegelian concept. With this dissolution of Marxism as a viable doctrine for much of the world, could geocracy become a major conceptual antithesis to a reign of unprincipled self-aggrandizement into which the world might otherwise descend?

To help us find at least a partial answer to this question, we can devise a case study out of the profound dilemmas of Central America.

During most of its history both before and after independence from the Spanish colonial system in 1821 and Mexico in 1823, Central America has been plagued by socio-political adversity. This has included internal conflict, lawless dictatorships, foreign intervention, and prevalence of social systems and doctrines inimical to the rational solution of its problems.

The appalling economic and social travails of most of Central America are well known, or at least have been reported thoroughly by scholars and other observers.[4] Therefore, this paper will not undertake detailed description of these features, significant though they may be to an understanding of the persistent Central American malaise.

However, it is important to note here that Costa Rica has been, since the very earliest days of its history, a partial exception to this pattern of unremitting misery. This has to do with a wider distribution of land and therefore of other property than is the norm in Central America — factors that arose out of lack of mineral resources, struggles with Indians who refused to be enslaved, and almost total lack of interest on the part of Spanish *conquistadores* and exploiters.[5]

Also, it is not a disconnected coincidence that by comparison with the other four Central American republics (Guatemala, El Salvador, Honduras, Nicaragua), Costa Rica has been the least subject to internal or external violence, or to ideological extremism.[6]

In the remaining four countries, large majorities of their populations have been afflicted by inadequate health care, poor or no housing, massive unemployment or underemployment, and low levels of educational opportunity including widespread illiteracy — all in sharp contrast to conspicuous opulence enjoyed by tiny but influential minorities;[7] and governments have been too often marked by callous political repression and brutality, persistent domination by uncouth military elements, corruption and violence.

Central America, like the rest of Latin America, was settled by Spain (or in the case of Brazil, by Portugal) in the fifteenth and sixteenth centuries. When the British landed on the New England coasts in 1607 (Jamestown) and 1620 (Plymouth), the Spanish had already been in the Americas over a century; and Spain herself did not fully emerge out of medievalism and authoritarianism until modern times.

Contemporary Spanish socio-economic structures have little if any similarity to those of the nation that conquered a large part of the Americas — and established its authoritarian system of land monopoly, serfdom in the guise of the *encomienda* and peonage, and hierarchical domination in her realms in this hemisphere.[8]

Thus, the whole period of modern democracy, market economy, and liberty of persons and beliefs, simply passed by the old Spanish colonies. To this day, and no matter how called, a pervasive monopoly of land and power by tiny minorities of exploitive elements still is a characteristic feature of a large part of Latin America.[9] In several major cities, however, capitalism has evolved as a significant economic element; and concepts of market economy, in a crude sort of piratical form, is taking shape in the heads of politicians in Argentina, Brazil, Chile, Peru and elsewhere, including Central America.

The United States and Central America

Also, the causes of unfortunate Central American conditions go very far back to the period of the Spanish conquest, long before the United States existed. It is of course true that individual U.S. commercial enterprises have taken advantage of prevailing patterns of wages and working conditions as they found them, though in many instances improving on them; but awful economic conditions have long prevailed in Central America, with or without involvement by U.S. corporate elements. Nor is it accurate to contend that U.S. relations with all Central American republics have always been marked by insensitivity bordering on arrogance, heavy-handed 'diplomatic' intrusions and even direct armed interventions.

In greater or lesser degree, however, all the countries have experienced episodes of heavy pressure imposed by U.S. diplomatic representatives, or intrusions by secret agents, which in some instances have resulted in changes of governments. In 1954, for example, the CIA played a significant rôle in the overthrow of the Marxist-leaning régime of Jacobo Arbenz by Guatemalan dissidents under command of Colonel Carlos Castillo Armas.[10] Costa Rica and El Salvador were relatively free of excessive U.S. influence until the last decades, but are now being especially sensitized to the presence of the North American giant — Costa Rica, because of massive U.S. economic aid, and El Salvador as a consequence of large doses of both economic aid and military assistance and advice.[11] Honduras must now undergo ubiquitous U.S. presence in the form of airstrips, radar installations, training camps and personnel to man them — to say nothing of thousands of uprooted *contras,* most of whom were until recently fighting against the *sandinistas* of Nicaragua.[12]

Of the Central American republics, Nicaragua has had the most direct experience of various forms of United States intervention.

During 1856-57, a band of filibusterers under command of William Walker invaded the country upon invitation by Nicaraguan dissidents, and for a short time Walker even had himself set up as the English-speaking *presidente de la república.* It took the combined armed forces of Central America, led by Costa Rica and with financial help from William Vanderbilt, to throw out the intruders. The Walker episode, inspired by pro-slavery sentiment and a wild plan to set up some kind of slave territory in Central America, occurred without official connivance of the U.S. government; but, it is understandable that Central Americans think of it as having been an American invasion. Anti-U.S. elements do nothing to dissuade them from this notion.

Because of political instability that threatened economic interests, the U.S. marines were landed in Nicaragua in 1912; and with one brief interruption remained until 1933, when the commander of the National Guard, Anastasio Somoza, was on his way to power. In February of 1934, an early order of business for the emerging Somoza dictatorship was to assassinate the nationalist revolutionary, Augusto César Sandino.

Until the Carter administration decided at the last minute that the time had come to sever connections with the unsavory family dictatorship, most U.S. diplomacy in Nicaragua carried on an unusually cozy relationship with the successive Somoza régimes. In this respect, the most notorious U.S. ambassador was Thomas Whelan, who during 1951-63 made the United States synonymous in most Nicaraguan minds with the Somozas themselves. Whelan's period was exceptional in terms of the degree to which U.S. diplomacy and a hated dictatorship became indistinguishable from each other; but other U.S. ambassadors, before and after Whelan, differed from him only in the degree to which they carried on their friendly dealings with a dynasty whose stability was thought to be good for U.S. investments and national interest.

Of course news about the U.S.-Somoza affair was not confined to Nicaragua, but spread throughout Central America, into Mexico, and southward to the far reaches of Latin America.

Thus, in this as in so many other instances, the United States must carry a heavy load of historical baggage.[13]

The Marxist Theoretical Message

Under the conditions prevailing in Central America, and in the light of such limited experience with contemporary alternative theories, the Central American environment would be hard to beat for spreading strong support for Marxism. First, there is the terrible poverty, often coupled with brazen human exploitation by powerful monopolists of both land and capital (both fused in the uninformed mind as 'capital'), which can be utilized by Marxist ideologues to promote their doctrine. Secondly, political power, whether civilian or military, is often rightly seen outside Costa Rica as a creature of the same exploitive elements. Thirdly, and most significantly in Central America, the great 'capitalist Yankee' power is perceived by influential opinion-makers to have both worked in close collusion with oppressive, anti-popular régimes, and to have offended Central American sensibilities by intruding into their internal affairs, even to the extent of establishing unwanted régimes and occupying their republics with *yanqui* armed forces.

The scene was made for emergence of Marxist revolutionary leadership, and that is exactly what happened. There was no other visible social message, so the advocates of radical change took the only route they knew.

In Guatemala, this has been true of the Guatemalan Labor Party, the Armed Revolutionary Forces, the Guerrilla Army of the People, and the Organization of the Armed People. Until recently it was true in Honduras, where the persistent presence of U.S. armed forces and *contras* put new life into the Morazán Front for National Liberation; as also in El Salvador, where the Farabundo Martí National Liberation Front (FMLN) derives its name from a Communist insurrectionist executed in 1932, combines five different Marxist armies and parties (including the Communist party of El Salvador), and the hammer and sickle emblazon its banners. Until recently, it was conceivable that the FMLN could take over the country, and turn it into a slaughterhouse reminiscent of Pol Pot's regime in Cambodia.

It would be odd if the *sandinistas* of Nicaragua, the republic most abused by U.S. interventionist activities, should be an exception to this rule, and they were not. Begun by young students of the 1950s who knew no other doctrine of social change except Marxism, the FSLN (Frente Sandinista de Liberación Nacional; Sandinist Front for National Liberation) was overwhelmingly Marxist-Leninist from the start. At least five of its major leaders had already studied or consulted in Cuba, the U.S.S.R., or Eastern European satellite states before the 1979 overthrow of the Somoza regime.[14]

Two years prior to overthrow of the last Somoza, the FSLN Military-Political Platform of 1977 proclaimed *sandinista* goals to be 'inseparably linked to the Marxist-Leninist cause'. On September 17, 1979, exactly two months after the *sandinistas* came to power, a first order of diplomatic business was to hold an immense public rally in adulation of visiting Vietnam Premier Pham Van Dang. On September 1 and October 1 of the same year, the new revolutionary régime sent the first plane-loads of teenagers to study in Cuba; and on November 22, the first of many contingents of Cuban teachers arrived in Nicaragua. In March, 1980, leaders of the *sandinista* Directorate (ruling committee of the FSLN, a sort of politburo) visited Moscow to enter into an agreement calling for close collaboration between the Communist Party of the U.S.S.R. and the Sandinista Front.[15]

Now, of course, after a decade of *sandinista* rule in Nicaragua, the rest is history. The background is understandable and the consequences probably inevitable.

Soviet Involvement

Of course the U.S.S.R. was not the first outside power to involve itself in Central America. The British and French were active in Central America and Panama during the nineteenth century, much to the annoyance of the United States; and indeed, the Monroe Doctrine of 1823 addressed itself precisely to the perceived menace of European intrusion into the affairs of any part of Latin America.

There is little point in debating the chicken-egg question of which came first, negative U.S. reaction to the *sandinista* revolution or *sandinista* determination to gravitate into the Soviet orbit. Chronologically, the *sandinista* pro-Soviet moves began almost immediately after the overthrow of Anastasio Somoza Debayle on July 17, 1979, and continued without interruption at the same time that the Carter administration was offering friendly overtures and economic aid to the new régime; but it can be argued that the past Nicaraguan experiences with the United States induced the *sandinistas* to seek out other friends around the world.

Nor is it necessary to determine whether the Nicaraguan revolution was instigated by the Soviets, which apparently it was not.

Regardless of these chronological questions, which are still debated uselessly in some quarters, it should be easy to understand that régimes tend to gravitate toward others that share their own perspectives. Governments founded on Judeo-Christian and Western values tend to associate with each other. Moslem nations find it easy to ally with others of similar orientation. Among the Moslems, Shiites collaborate with Shiites more easily than with Sunnis, and vice versa; and Unitarians tend to mingle more with Unitarians than with holy rollers. Simply put, birds of a feather hang together. Nations and people with similar cultures, languages, political or religious values tend to hobnob with each other.

Therefore, it should be no mystery that (at least before Gorbachëv), Marxist-Leninist régimes found more in common with other Marxist-Leninist regimes than with 'reactionary imperialist' capitalist ones; and the Marxist-Leninist *sandinistas* of Nicaragua were no exception. Whatever the friendly or obnoxious behavior of the United States, the *sandinistas* would have followed this universal rule, and as quickly as possible climbed into the Cuban-Soviet orbit — though as has been pointed out above, the *previous behaviour* of the U.S. probably helped to instigate Marxist radicalism in Nicaragua.

From the standpoint of U.S. national interest, the results were considered in many American circles to be intolerable, and led to a closing of the circle from which there seemed to be no escape.

The Negative U.S. Reaction

Stripped down to these fundamental considerations, the negative U.S. reaction to the *sandinista* régime does not defy explanation. Any part of Central America is closer to New Orleans (1350 miles from Costa Rica, 1200 from Nicaragua) than Philadelphia is to Oklahoma City (1368 miles) or to San Antonio, Texas (1692 miles). Soviet-Cuban military emplacements, including airfields for long-range bombers and potential missile bases, could not be viewed by the United States without concern. Anyone who does not understand this should reflect on the Cuban missile crisis of October, 1962. Also, there is the question of control over critical sea lines of communication throughout the whole Caribbean area, with a pro-Soviet régime already in place in Cuba.[16]

The Monroe Doctrine may or may not be regarded as a daily guide to contemporary American foreign policy; but it conveyed a central theme that in this semi-anarchic world is a part of the conceived national interest of any nation anywhere: '... the American continents are henceforth not to be considered as subjects for future colonization by European powers.' Though in excessively brutal forms, the pre-Gorbachëv U.S.S.R. understood this when the Hungarian revolutionaries of 1956 appealed for help from the West, and when the Czechs attempted their 'spring revolution' in 1968. Now, of course, new conditions prevail in Eastern Europe; but, it is doubtful that the Soviet Union would stand idly by while some powerful opponent took over its neighbors.

Thus, awful socio-political conditions combined with irreversible historical clashes between the United States and Central America to set the stage for entrance upon it by Marxism-Leninism. Since this development led inevitably to intervention in Central America by members of the Cuban-Soviet bloc, the United States perceived that its national security, if not its ultimate survival, required that it halt the march of communism in the region, by doing what it could to turn back the governments and movements that espoused it.

Of course there were other factors, including economic interest, that prompted the United States to react negatively to the forward march of Marxism-Leninism in Central America; but in the realm of foreign policy, considerations of national security are and should be controlling. Therefore, there is no point in taking space to reflect on considerations of economic interest or other factors behind the anti-Marxist reaction of the United States insofar as Central America is concerned.

Is There No Way Out?

Thus, Central Americans have been entrapped by their seemingly endless social, economic and political travails on the one hand, and stereotyped ideological responses as well as foreign intrusions on the other — none of which have offered anything but intensifications of their adversities and suffering.

Now, however, dramatic events in the U.S.S.R. and Central Europe, Nicaragua, and undoubtedly more to come in Cuba, are dissolving the deceptive lures of Marxism-Leninism. Its mask removed, the doctrine that cried for 'ownership and operation of the means of production and distribution' by the 'workers and peasants' is more clearly seen as a program for a most extraordinary concentration of all power in the hands of self-appointed ideologues.

So, the hypnotic appeal of Marxism-Leninism may diminish, and for that reason the foreign interventions in Central America may recede. If these things come to pass, Central America may be granted an era of respite that she has not known in recent years; but by itself that will offer little relief from the endemic poverty and authoritarianism that have afflicted her people since the days of the 16th century when the *conquista* brought land monopoly, class domination and rule by force into the region.

Indeed, these negative factors have contributed to underdevelopment, national weakness and foreign interventionism, and can do so in the future. This period of ideological disillusionment, and hopefully of some recession in foreign entanglement, would seem to provide an opportune moment for advocates of an alternative Georgism-physiocracy (which I choose to abbreviate as 'geocracy') to get their views onto the Central American stage. Socialism, in the words of Fred Harrison a 'Millenarian Dream', is ready for replacement, in Central America as elsewhere. If as Richard Noyes contends, Henry George could provide the synthesis in the present dialectic, the oncoming Central American interregnum may provide the ideal time for its propagation.[17]

Physiocracy played a significant rôle in Spain and early Latin American thought before Henry George existed. Indeed, the subject of land reform has long been uppermost in the social concerns of Latin America, including specifically Central America. Essentially all movements of social reform in that part of the world have included some reference, often a leading or dominant one, to the need for land reform.[18] Therefore, it may seem reasonable to suppose that geocratic concepts may emerge to fill the gap left by the recession of Marxism-Leninism from Latin American public support. This also assumes that enough Latin Americans with geocratic convictions will come forth to inform their people of the existence of the alternative message. Nothing of this sort, including Marxism-Leninism, ever came forth automatically without human assistance.

Obstacles to the Emergence of Geocracy

Tax Systems. From the standpoint of a geocratic system, Central American tax patterns present a baffling hurdle. Even in an advanced country such as Costa Rica, direct taxes (on income and property, including cultivated land and lands benefiting from road improvements), take in only about 25 per cent of public revenue.

Remaining government revenue derives from indirect taxes, which bear with special ferocity on the poor. These include customs duties (both import and export!), which provide the most revenue; and food processing taxes, sales taxes, and a multitude of special taxes applied to all sorts of commercial activities. Of course these are paid to tax collectors by business and commercial elements, but are 'indirect' in the sense that they ultimately derive from higher costs which must be paid by the general population.

With the only partial exception of Costa Rica, evasion of all kinds of taxes — especially of such direct taxes as exist — combine with widespread corruption to make such things as income and property taxes, even where they legally exist on paper, largely unknown to most sectors of the population. Especially among the wealthy and powerful segments of Central American societies, such things as property or income taxes impose no burden — except where payments must be made to officials to evade them.

Under such circumstances, the success of a geocratic program would require a monumental transformation in both the tax systems and public attitudes about them.

Land Reform vs. Agrarian Reform. Unfortunately, in Central America as throughout the Spanish (or Portuguese) speaking world, the phrase 'land reform' (*reforma de la tierra*, or *reforma territorial*) cannot include the concept of a tax shift from productive labor and capital to unearned land values. The Spanish equivalents of 'land reform' refer to improvement of agricultural land — better fertilization, rotation of crops, prevention of erosion, and so on. For social transformations involving land — e.g., shifts of taxation, divisions of big estates, collectivization, etc. — the phrase is *reforma agraria* — agrarian reform.[19]

Land (Spanish, *terra*; Portuguese, *terra*), insofar as reform or social change is concerned, is in Hispanic thinking, *agrarian* land only.

Argentina, though not in Central America, illustrates this problem. According to urban architect Juan Carlos Zuccotti of Buenos Aires, two major Argentine agricultural cöoperatives favor the taxation of land values aside from improvements; but he writes, 'There is never a word about urban land'.[20]

Ironically, this may be partly the fault of eighteenth-century physiocracy, which as a counterpoise to dominant mercantilist theories played such a significant rôle in later French and Spanish thinking. The tax that the physiocrats would have substituted for other impositions of the time (such as customs duties) was to be strictly a tax on *agricultural* land and on mines, on the grounds that these were the ultimate source of all wealth — as to a large extent they were, in those times. No other kind of land value taxation was ever mentioned by physiocratic theorists.

Corruption. In connection with Central American tax systems as discussed above, mention has been made of corruption; but a special point has to be made of its pervasion of all society at all levels.

As with systems of land tenure, rule by military force, and domination by privileged classes, this is a system inherited from the Spanish (and Portuguese) colonial systems. In no way does this imply that the Spanish were or are especially corrupt, which they were not and are not. Rather, the Latin American patterns of paying off officials for accomplishment of all sorts of services, arose from entirely different factors.

The Spanish ruled their distant empire through the Council of the Indies, located not in the Americas, but in Sevilla, Spain. To try to effectuate decent treatment of the Indians, controls over commerce, proper conduct of local authorities, and a myriad of other requirements for civilized life as they conceived it, the Council issued multitudinous rules and regulations that were supposed to be applied by their viceroys, captain-generals, and lesser officials.

Many of the rules, well-intended though they undoubtedly were, were so detailed that they could not be applied in fact to particular circumstances in the Americas. Some, in promotion of the mercantilist doctrines of the time, were absurdly restrictive of trade and commerce, but not out of line with what the Council conceived to be for the welfare of the Empire.

Thus, it transpired that the only way to get a lot of needed things done was to slip payments to officials who were supposed to enforce the decrees of the Crown, which had been enunciated by the Council of the Indies. Thus, a non-Spanish ship could not unload its cargo without paying off the *oficiales aduanales* (customs officials); or, it is reported, even a builder could not construct a house with local materials without paying an inspector whose rules required he must use certain types of cement or wood or fittings found only in Spain.

The transformation of such practices from provision for the essential needs of life to out-and-out corruption for personal gain was imperceptible and understandable, and has become a way of life in Central America as in most of the rest of Latin America.

In the face of this obstacle, how can a tax reform be put into effect which would provide for (1) fair and equitable assessment, (2) tax collection proportionate to such assessment, and (3) utilization of funds collected, in accordance with the word and intent of the law?

Workers, Peasants and Intellectual Elites. Finally, if geocracy in Central America is to be put into effect and implemented, this will be accomplished by intellectual élites, not by workers and peasants. It is an unfortunate fact of life, in Central America and in most other parts of the world, that workers and peasants are likely to be poorly educated if educated at all; and in any event, they are too ground down by work and misery to have time or inclination for such foolishness. Even the Russian revolution for the 'liberation of the toilers from exploitation' was led by representatives of the élite, such as Lenin, Trotsky, Zinoviev, Kamenev, Kirov, Radek and many others including Stalin (a theological student preparing for the priesthood).

The Castro revolt in Cuba was led by young students from the University of Havana, fired with radical ideas picked up from books and professors. Even the murderous *Sendero Luminoso* (Shining Path) of Peru is led by ex-teacher Abimael Guzmán and élitist, middle- and upper-class radicalized students. Almost all the founders and leaders of the *sandinista* movement of Nicaragua were ex-students from the University of Nicaragua or other institutions of higher education, whose origins lay among the leading élite families of the republic.[21] Thus, the Chamorro family produced not only conservative opponents of the Somoza dynasty as well as of the *sandinista* regime, but also radical young supporters of the Marxist government.[22]

Reformist as well as revolutionary leadership in much of Central America, as in most of Latin America and the world, is in the hands of young people, idealistic students, almost all of them from economically privileged sectors of their societies. Therefore, inconsistent though it may seem, if geocracy is to be put into effect in Central America, these are the people who must know how to do it.

If history is as much on the side of the emergence of geocracy around the world as many of its advocates think it is, these obstacles to the application of it in Latin America may be overcome; but realism requires that its proponents understand the difficulties their proposed reforms are likely to undergo.

Concluding Note

In a recent article, Michael J. Mazarr, an authority on Cuba who has published a book (*Semper Fidel*) and several articles on the subject, wrote that José Martí, the great Cuban liberator, 'believed firmly in freedom and democracy, and his economic ideal was an enlightened development of classical liberalism, drawing from Henry George's analysis of liberalism and the utopian, democratic system of Edward Bellamy'.[23]

Is there a chance that despite all the obstacles in its path, an enlightened development of classical liberalism, inspired by utopian idealism and illuminated by the thinking of Henry George and physiocracy, might still play a rôle in the future of Central America?

As we have seen, there is a substantial background of physiocratic thought, drawn from pre-Georgist French and Iberian philosophy (see n. 3). The idea of land reform, even though associated only with agrarian land, plays a prominent rôle in Latin American reform movements. As anyone familiar with Central America knows, the monopoly of the earth is central to its endemic human travail, and a vivid consciousness of this fact is widespread.

Today, with the collapse of Marxist ideology around the world, a vacuum, a virtual mental chaos, must prevail in the minds of idealists who were captivated by the simplistic Marxist analysis of class struggle, workers' revolution and dictatorship of the proletariat.

The geocratic conception rejects all Marxist proposals for ownership and operation by the political state of the means of production and distribution, and insists that most of these must remain in private hands. It perceives human liberty and justice to be central to the advancement of the human condition. Yet, while utterly rejecting almost all the ten planks of the Communist Manifesto — most of them brutal intrusions by the state into human life — it does join with Marx and Engels in at least a part of the first one: '... application of all rents of land to public purposes.'

This concept is central to geocracy; and it provides a possibility that young idealists, until recently enamored of Marxist doctrine, may find at least some reason to learn more about the geocratic idea that the earth is rightfully the home of all humankind, and that none may be rejected from it.

In Latin America today, bitter experience with bungling and corrupt state interventionism is driving people into the arms of unbridled market economics and privatization of every conceivable type of state-run enterprise, all to be run solely on the basis of profit and personal gain.

The idea of the special, nature-created rôle of land, or of any kind of tax impositions on unearned land rents, is in no way a part of the 'free market' scheme of things. Using the tool of unbridled private gain as a device to straighten out their state-wrecked economies, administrations in Argentina, Brazil, Peru and Uruguay are trying desperately to save their nations from utter chaos and ruin.

In this scheme of things, it is not inconceivable that geocracy, which already has its old French-Iberian philosophical traditions in parts of Latin America, and its contemporary advocates in Argentina, Colombia, the Dominican Republic and perhaps Costa Rica, could exercise influence on the thinking of both the right and the left.

Almost nothing of a generalized sort can be said about all of Latin America. There are common characteristics and problems, but these differ in degree from country to country. Though in this paper much has been said about obstacles to the adoption of geocratic concepts — current tax systems, stress on agrarian land reform to the exclusion of urban, corruption, obstacles posed by dominant élites whether of the right or the left — these things are not so true in some Latin American republics as in others.

One can conceive, for example, that geocratic policies might be more effectively adopted in Chile, Venezuela or Uruguay than in Colombia, Peru or Argentina (where they are most desperately needed). By the same token, there is little question that Costa Rica's socio-political system would adapt itself more readily to geocracy than would that of Guatemala; and it is likely that the Dominican Republic could do so far better than Haiti; or, even Ecuador more readily than Paraguay.

Because of rather similar cultural backgrounds, languages (Spanish; Portuguese in Brazil; French-Creole in Haiti), histories, economic and social problems, and geographic propinquity though admittedly over vast distances, the people of Latin America are much itnerested in events that occur in all parts of their world — whether in South America, Central America, Mexico or the Caribbean. Social policies and political events in one country exert much influence on the thinking of others. Thus, at present, a wave of enthusiasm for unbridled market economies is sweeping much of the region.

In the same manner, a successful experiment with geocracy in one country could stimulate opinion and policies in others. For example, such an event in Uruguay or closer by in Venezuela, could influence the adoption of similar policies in Costa Rica; or, within Central America itself, the impact of a Costa Rican success with geocracy could influence events among her neighbors, including especially Nicaragua.

Until now, no doubt in large part because of historic animosity between the two neighbors, Nicaragua has not borrowed much if anything from her neighbor, Costa Rica; but finally, Nicaraguans are talking about replacing their armed forces with a civilian guard, 'as in Costa Rica'. It is reasonable to speculate that the open democracy, free press and other media, and better material conditions of Costa Rica, may have contributed to the recent Nicaraguan rejection of *sandinista* Marxism-Leninism.

So, let us assume for a moment that Costa Rica, which for various historical reasons already enjoys a wider distribution of landed proprietorship on her central plateau than is characteristic in other Central American countries, would adopt geocratic legislation.

What would happen? She would abolish her import and export taxes, and her international trade would be greatly stimulated. She would lift her internal excise taxes on business and commerce, and her entrepreneurs would feel, as Henry George put it, that 'an immense weight' had been lifted from their shoulders. In brief, to quote George again, 'Imbued with fresh energy, production would start into new life, and trade would receive a stimulus which would be felt to the remotest arteries' (*Progress and Poverty,* p.434).

Income taxes, with all their encouragement to fraud, would be removed; and workers and capitalists would put their increased earnings into savings, improvement, construction, and productive investment.

Costa Rica already levies low taxes on uncultivated agricultural land and lands benefiting from road improvements; to these, it would add, as a measure of compensatory revenue and economic stimulation, the taxation of all unearned land values, urban as well as rural. Urban speculators and slum owners (to be found in Costa Rica — especially San José — as elsewhere in the world), would either improve their properties, or turn them over to new owners who would.

Parts of some of the big plantations on the Caribbean and Pacific costs, and of the large ranch holdings on the Guanacaste Peninsula, would be sold to other owners, who would use them for effective production and to take care of the new burst of commerce.

With this new prosperity, and the new income from unearned land values, Costa Rica's immense external debt — as of 1990, some $4.6 billion, or $15,000 for every adult and child in the country! — would be reduced; and the republic would no longer be dependent on handouts from abroad to compensate for no longer needed social welfare and public infrastructure maintenance and development.

Can one assume that Nicaragua would in no way be influenced by such events in her neighbor republic? Or even, if such a thing were to occur as far away as Venezuela or even Uruguay or Chile, that it would have no effect in Central America or Mexico?

I hope and think it possible this may be something like the way the present dialectic is resolved, including in Central America. But the resolutions of dialectics, 'battles for the minds of men', if you will, have no automatic or pre-ordained outcomes. In Central America or elsewhere, that is decided by the active rôles that are played by determined and dedicated human beings.

Then, and then only, do 'syntheses' emerge.

NOTES

1. Georg Wilhelm Friedrich Hegel, 1770-1831, author of several philosophic works, including *The Phenomenology of Mind*, 1807; *The Science of Logic*, 1812; *Encyclopedia of the Philosophical Sciences*, 1821; *Lectures on the History of Philosophy*, 1831-36; and *Lectures on the Philosophy of History*, 1837.
2. Karl Marx and Friedrich Engels, *The Communist Manifesto*, 1848 (New York: International Publishers Co., Inc., 100th Anniversary Edition, 1948, p.9. Note: International Publishers was, and as far as I know still is, the publishing arm of the Communist Party, USA, so this is about as official a version as one can get.
3. Founder of the physiocratic school, a reaction to the restrictive mercantilist theories of the time, was François Quesnay (1694-1774) of France; its most prominent advocate was Robert Turgot (1727-1781), minister of finance under Louis XVI. The physiocrats advocated the freeing of trade from all the usual mercantilist restrictions and levies, and the raising of public revenue from a tax to be placed on agricultural and mining land, which they considered to be the source of all wealth — in contrast to the mercantilist notion that in order to have great wealth, nations should store up great quantities of precious metals. Partly as a consequence of the Napoleonic invasion of the Iberian Peninsula in the early 19th century, Spain and Portugal were influenced by physiocratic ideas; but even before that, similar ideas had been propagated in Spain by Juan Luis Vives in the sixteenth century, Pedro de Valencia and Father Juan de Mariana in the seventeenth, Miguel de Caxa de Leruela and the Counts of Floridablanca and Campomanes in the eighteenth and Alvaro Florez Estrada and Canon Francisco Martinez y Mariana in the nineteenth. Several Argentine scholars of the early nineteenth century studied in Spain, where they fell under the influence of French-Spanish physiocracy. The most famous of these would be Bernardino Rivadavia, first president of Argentina (1826-1827), who tried to put the physiocratic land tax into effect; but in those tumultuous times, he was overthrown by land monopolists led by the powerful landlord and *caudillo*, Juan Manuel de Rosas, who was later (1835-53) to become the most ruthless and implacable tyrant in the history of the Argentine republic. T. Lynn Smith, ed., *Agrarian Reform in Latin America* (Alfred A. Knopf, 1965, pp. 67-69), included three essays by

Antônio P. Figueiredo, Brazilian editor of a reformist Recife newspaper of the 1840s, whose articles bristled with protest against the landed monopoly of northeast Brazil (still a plague to this day), and offered physiocratic solutions to the problem. Today in Spain, physiocratic-Georgist movements are in progress, and there is a persistant geocratic theme in Andalusian movements for autonomy. Geocratic movements are active in Argentina and the Dominican Republic today; and individuals such as Hernán Echavarría Olózaga, ambassador to the United States during 1967-1968, write in support of geocratic proposals.

4. Selected background sources on Central American political, social and economic conditions: Thomas P. Anderson, *Politics in Central America* (Stanford: Hoover Institution Press, 1982); Anderson, *The War of the Dispossessed* (Lincoln: University of Nebraska Press, 1981; Charles T. Brockett, *Land, Power and Poverty* (Winchester, Mass.: Allen & Unwin, 1989); Victor Bulmer-Thomas, *The Political Economy of Central America Since 1920* (Cambridge: Press Syndicate of University of Cambridge, 1987); William H. Durham, *Scarcity and Survival in Central America: Ecological Origins of the Soccer War* (Stanford University Press, 1979); Henry A. Kissinger, Chairman, *The Report of the President's Bipartisan Commission for Central America* (N.Y.: Macmillan, 1984); Dana G. Munro, *The Five Republics of Central America* (N.Y.; Oxford University Press, 1918) — now a classic history; Franklin D. Parker, *Travels in Central America, 1821-1840* (University of Florida Press, 1971); Steve C. Ropp and James A. Morris, eds., *Central America : Crisis and Adaptation* (Albuquerque: University of New Mexico Press, 1984); Mark B. Rosenberg and Philip L. Shepherd, *Honduras Confronts Its Future* (Boulder, Colorado: Lynne Rienner Publishers, Inc., 1986); John L. Stephens, *Incidents of Travel in Central America, Chiapas and Yucatán* (New Brunswick, N.J.: Rutgers University Press, 1949) — a great classic, from the 1840s; William S. Stokes, *Honduras: An Area Study in Government* (Madison: University of Wisconsin Press, 1950 + later edition in 1970s); Robert C. West and John P. Augelle, *Middle America: Its Lands and Peoples* (Princeton, N.J.: Prentice-Hall, 1966); Alastair White, *El Salvador* (N.Y.: Praeger, 1973; Miles L. Wortman, *Government and Society in Central America. 1680-1840* (N.Y.: Columbia University Press, 1982).

5. It would go far beyond the scope of the present summary to attempt to describe or explain the unusual political-economic conditions of Costa Rica, which include a very long experience in constitutional democracy (since at least 1889); and somewhat higher levels of economic opportunity than are to be found in other Central American republics. Some sources in English, in addition to several in Spanish, I can provide on

request: Charles D. Ameringer, *Democracy in Costa Rica* (New York: Praeger; & Stanford: Hoover Institution Press, 1982); John and Mavis Biesanz, *Costa Rican Life* (N.Y.: Columbia University Press, 1944); — a pioneer sociological study, still significant for an understanding of the Costa Rican exception; Leonard Bird, *Costa Rica: The Unarmed Democracy* (London: Sheppard Press, 1984); Howard L. Blutstein, et al, *Area Handbook for Costa Rica* (Washington, D.C.: US. Government Printing Office, 1970); James L. Busey, *Notes on Costa Rican Democracy* (Boulder: University of Colorado Press, 1962, 1963, 1967); Lowell Gudmundson, *Costa Rica Before Coffee* (Baton Rouge: Louisiana University Press, 1986); Carolyn Hall, *Costa Rica: A Geographical Interpretation in Historical Perspective* (Boulder, Colorado: Westview Press, 1985; Chester L. Jones, *Costa Rica and Civilization in the Caribbean* (Madison: University of Wisconsin Press, 1933) — a classic study, famous among Central Americans; and Sol W. Sanders, *The Costa Rican Laboratory* (Winchester, Mass.: Allen & Unwin, 1985).

6. Among Latin Americanists, Central America is usually regarded as including five republics: Guatemala, El Salvador, Honduras, Nicaragua and Costa Rica. Panamá, which was set adrift from the South American republic of Colombia in 1903 to facilitate U.S. plans to excavate the canal, is not usually thought of as being a part of Central America. Because it was a part of Colombia, it was never a member of the five-nation United Provinces of Central America (later called Federal Republic of Central America), 1823-1838, which was formed after independence from Spain (1821) and Mexico (1823). If anything, Panamá forms an isthmian bridge between South and North America (of which Central America is a part).
7. Annual per capita income varies from $700 in El Salvador to $1,000 in Guatemala (Costa Rica, $1,350); life expectancy at birth from 55 years in Guatemala to 64 in El Salvador (Costa Rica, 69); infant mortality per 1,000 births from 73 in Honduras to 37 in Nicaragua (Costa Rica, 15); daily newspaper circulation per 1,000 population, 30 in Guatemala to 71 (?) in El Salvador (Costa Rica, 71); and adult literacy, 48% in Guatemala to 66% in Nicaragua (Costa Rica, 90%). *World Almanac and Book of Facts, 1989* (N.Y.: Pharos Books, Scripps Howard Co., 1989), pp.666, 672, 679, 681, 702-3. *Note*: All such figures, no matter where published, almost invariably come originally from official sources, so must be evaluated in that light insofar as their dependability is concerned. One may also consult the more detailed *Statistical Abstract of Latin America*, published annually by UCLA Latin American Center, University of California, Los Angeles.
8. Studies on the whole range of colonial Spanish impacts on Latin America are too numerous to cite here. It is only feasible to list a few

dependable histories: Thomas E. Alba, *Spain and the Loss of America* (Lincoln: University of Nebraska Press, 1983); John Francis Bannon, *History of the Americas* (N.Y.: McGraw-Hill, 2nd ed., 1963); E. Bradford Burns, *Latin America: A Concise Interpretive History* (N.Y.: Prentice-Hall, 1986); Simon Collier, *From Cortés to Castro: An Introduction to the History of Latin America, 1492-1973* (N.Y.: Macmillan, 1974); John A. Crow, *The Epic of Latin America* (Berkeley: University of California Press, 1980); William M. Deneven, ed., *Hispanic Lands and Peoples: Selected Writings of James J. Parsons* (Boulder, Colorado: Westview Press, 1988) — Parsons, an eloquent writer; Russell Fitzgibbon and Julio Fernández, *Latin America: Political Culture and Development* (N.Y.: Prentice-Hall, 1981); Lewis Hanke, *History of Latin American Civilization* (Boston: Little-Brown, 2nd ed., 1973); Hubert Herring, *A History of Latin America: From the Beginnings to the present* (N.Y.: Knopf, 3rd ed., 1968) Alexander von Humboldt, *Political Essay on the Kingdom of New Spain* (Norman, Oklahoma: University of Oklahoma Press, 1988) — reprint of a great 19th century classic; Benjamin Keen, ed., *Latin American Civilization: History and Society, 1492 to the Present* (Boulder, Colorado: Westview Press, 4th ed., 1986); Benjamin Keen and Mark Wasserman, eds., *A Short History of Latin America* (N.Y.: Oxford University Press, 2nd ed., 1984); Sakari Sariola, *Power and Resistance: The Colonial Heritage in Latin America* (Ithaca, N.Y.: Cornell University Press, 1972); Claudio Véliz, *The Centralist Tradition in Latin America* (Princeton University Press, 1979).

9. See Solon Barraclough, ed., *Agrarian Structure in Latin America* (Lexington, Mass.: D.C. Heath, 1973; Charles D. Brockett, *Land, Power and Poverty* (N.Y.: Unwin Hyman, 1988); Merilee S. Grindle, *State and Countryside: Development Policy and Agrarian Politics in Latin America* (Boston: Johns Hopkins Press, 1985); Alistair Hennessy, *The Frontier in Latin American History* (Albuquerque: University of New Mexico Press, 1978); Jacques Lambert, *Latin America: Social Structures and Political Institutions* (Berkeley: University of California Press, 1968); Smith, *Agrarian Reform, op.cit.*, n.1; William C. Thiesenhusen, ed., *Searching for Agrarian Reform in Latin America* (N.Y.: Unwin Hyman, 1988).

10. José M. Aybar, *Dependency and Intervention: The Case of Guatemala in 1954* (Boulder, Colorado: Westview Press, 1982); Peter Calvert, *Guatemala: A Nation in Turmoil* (Boulder, Colorado: Westview Press, 1985): Richard H. Immerman, *The CIA in Guatemala: The Foreign Policy of Intervention* (Austin: University of Texas Press, 1982); Stephen Schlessinger and Stephen Kinzer, *Bitter Fruit: The Untold Story of the American Coup in Guatemala* (N.Y.: Doubleday, 1982);

Ronald M. Schneider, *Communism in Guatemala, 1944-1954* (N.Y.: Praeger, 1959) — an excellent, thoroughly researched study; Kalman H. Silvert, *A Study in Government: Guatemala* (N.Y.: ISHI, 1977) — reprint of a 1954 study; Jean Marie Simon, *Guatermala: Eternal Spring, Eternal Tyranny* (N.Y.: Norton, 1988).

11. According to journalist Martha Honey, a resident of San José, Costa Rica, who is completing a book to be published by University Presses of Florida, the United States was (during *sandinista* rule in Nicaragua) undermining the foundations of Costa Rican democracy by using the country as a base for anti-*sandinista* activities. U.S. actions, according to Honey, included sending in hordes of CIA agents, contributing $400,000 for election of conservative candidates, setting up training camps for paramilitary units in the country, pressuring the government to install a rightwing Minister of Security in 1984, supporting establishment of a private university in competition with the national University of Costa Rica, and trying to get the government to build a secret airbase near the Nicaraguan border. — *Times of the Americas*, Vol. 33, No. 15 (December 13, 1989).

12. Sources on U.S.-Central American relations are far too numerous to begin to cite here, with many becoming outdated overnight by the onrush of Central American events. For such titles, useless though they become by the time this is published, consult author.

13. Despite dramatically changing events in Nicaragua, a few of the following sources may be of lasting importance: Eduardo Crawley, *Dictators Never Die: A Portrait of Nicaragua and the Somozas* (N.Y.: Simon & Schuster, 1985); Bernard Diedrich, *Somoza and the Legacy of U.S. Involvement in Central America* (N.Y.: E.P. Dutton, 1981); Lawrence Green, *The Filibusterer: The Career of William Walker* (Indianapolis: Bobbs-Merrill, 1937); Lindley Miller Keasebey, *The Nicaragua Canal and the Monroe Doctrine* (N.Y., 1896; available from R&D Books, P.O. Box 6952, Washington, D.C. 20032); Neill Macauley, *The Sandino Affair* (1971; reprint, Durham, N.C.: Duke University Press, 1985); Robert E. May, *The Dream of a Southern Empire, 1854-1861* (Baton Rouge: Louisiana State University Press, 1973); Richard Millett, *Guardians of the Dynasty* (N.Y.: Orbis Books, 1977); Robert A. Pastor, *Condemned to Repetition* (Princeton, N.J.: Princeton University Press, 1987) — about U.S. policy in Nicaragua; William O. Scroggs, *Filibusterers and Financiers* (N.Y.: Russell & Russell, 1916; Macmillan, 1969); William Walker, *The War in Nicaragua* (originally published, 1860; reprint, Tucson, Arizona: University of Arizona Press, 1985).

14. On Augustín Farabundo Martí, namesake of the FMLN, see Thomas P. Anderson, *Matanza: El Salvador's Communist Revolt of 1932*

(Lincoln: University of Nebraska Press, 1971). On FSLN leaders, see David Nolan, *FSLN: The Ideology of the Sandinistas and the Nicaraguan Revolution* (Coral Gables, Fla.: Institute of Inter-American Studies, Graduate School of International Studies, University of Miami, 1984).

15. Obviously, all this took place before the epoch of Mikhail Gorbachëv, who took power in 1985. The literature on the early attachment of the *sandinistas* to the Marxist-Leninist cause is authoritative, thoroughly documented, and — except among committee ideologues — completely persuasive. Dramatically changing events in Nicaragua now require that the list of such sources be reduced, perhaps only to the following: Shirley Christian, *Nicaragua: Revolution in the Family* (N.Y.: Random House, 1985); Eduardo Crawley, *Nicaragua in Perspective* (N.Y.: St. Martin's Press, 1984); Arturo J. Cruz, *Nicaragua's Continuing Struggle* (Lanham, Md.: University Press of America, 1988); John Norton Moore, *The Secret War in Central America* (Frederick, Md.: University Publications of America, 1987); Nolan, *op. cit.*, n. 14; Douglas W. Payne, *The Democratic Mask: The Consolidation of the Sandinista Revolution* (N.Y.: Freedom House, 1985; Robert Wesson, ed., *Communism in Central America and the Caribbean* (Stanford: Hoover Institution Press, 1982).

16. See Michael Desch, 'Latin America and U.S. National Security', *Journal of Inter-American Studies*, 31, 4 (Winter, 1989), pp. 209-219, where the author (a Fellow in National Security at the Center for International Affairs, Harvard University) places special emphasis on (1) the rôle of security in foreign policy considerations, and (2) the vital importance to U.S. security of the Caribbean sea lanes.

17. See Richard Noyes, 'Henry George's Place in the Dialogue', and Fred Harrison, 'Socialism: The End of a Millenarian Dream', conference papers, Henry George Sesquicentennial International Conference, Philadelphia, July 29-August 6, 1989; and appropriate chapters in this book.

18. On land reform issues in Central America, see fn. 4, above, and also Thomas L. Karnes, *Tropical Enterprise: The Standard Fruit and Steamship Company in Latin America* (Baton Rouge: Louisiana State University Press, 1979). On land reform in the broader context of Latin America, see n. 9 above. The most devastating study of third-world attempts at agrarian reform is John Powelson, Richard Stock et al, *The Peasant Betrayed: Agriculture and Land Reform in the Third World* (Lincoln Institute of Land Study, 1987). The Powelson-Stock study includes sections on Latin America, including special treatment of Nicaragua.

19. Smith, *op cit.*, n. 1, above.

20. Letter from Arq. Juan Carlos Zuccotti, November 29, 1989.
21. See 'Biographical Sketches', pp. 137-154 in Nolan, *op. cit.*, n. 14. These include not only *sandinista* leaders, but also other figures in Nicaraguan political life, mostly contemporary. Of the *sandinista* leaders, who constitute well over half the some 100 individual names, one is struck by the large numbers who came from wealthy families, or business careers, or high-paying professions, to join the FSLN. Those who originated in working, peasant or servant families are few and far between.
22. Pedro Joaquín Chamorro, Conservative, courageous editor of *La Prensa* and bitter opponent of the Somozas; his assassination, January 10, 1978, was widely assumed to have been the work of the régime, and so inflamed the Nicaraguan population that it lit the explosion of fury that brought the *sandinistas* to revolutionary victory on July 17, 1979. Violeta Barrios de Chamorro, his widow, of the National Opposition Union, elected President February 25, 1900, and inaugurated April 25; Xavier Chamorro Cardenal, Pedro Joaquín's brother, editor of pro-*sandinista* daily, *Nuevo Diaro*; Jaime Chamorro Cardenal, another brother of Pedro Joaquín, who edited the anti-*sandinista* daily *La Prensa* during most of the 1980s. Children of Pedro Joaquín and Violeta: Pedro Joaquín, Jr., in early 1980s a vigorous anti-*sandinista* editorialist in *La Prensa*; Carlos Fernando, editor of the official *sandinista* newspaper, *La Barricada* (The Barricades); Claudia Lucía, *sandinista* diplomat and writer; and Cristiana, a journalist, who writes in columns of *La Prensa*.
23. Michael J. Mazaar, 'Prospects for Revolution in Post-Castro Cuba', *Journal of Interamerican Studies*, 31, 4 (Winter, 1989), p. 25.

6

Land Policy and the Economics of Colonial Exploitation

JEROME F. HEAVEY

FROM THE time that David Ricardo introduced the concept of comparative advantage into international trade there has been strong support for the theory that nations can derive mutual benefit from specializing their production in those goods which they can produce at the lowest opportunity cost. In practice, however, international trade seems very often to have benefited some nations while impoverishing others. The major thesis of this paper is that this failure to derive mutual benefit has occurred, not because the theory of comparative advantage is invalid, but because in many cases it was inoperative. International trade based on comparative advantage will be mutually beneficial to the trading countries when the goods are traded at prices to which both countries freely consent. But under colonialism prices are effectively distorted so that the gains of specialization are captured by the metropolitan power.

The mechanism by which prices are distorted involves the limitation of the native population's access to land, often through the creation of private property rights in the land of the colonized country. Title to large portions of land is given to the citizens of the metropolitan power, and the native inhabitants then become rent paying tenants. The real price that the native population then receives for the product of its labor is the nominal price less the rent they must pay for the use of the land. In the extreme case the net income received by the tenant is a bare subsistence. This is the mechanism as it existed in Ireland. A variant of this method was used in parts of Africa, where the native population, instead of being tenants, were employed as hired laborers on the land that had been given to the

European settlers. The nominal wage was then reduced by taxes that were imposed on the native population, taxes for which the native population received no benefits. In either case the native population was compelled to work on land that they did not own, and the surplus created by their labor was expatriated to the metropolitan power.

The next two sections of this paper provide a brief review of the theory of comparative advantage and a discussion of the price boundaries that must be observed as a necessary condition for mutually beneficial free trade. After this we will discuss colonialism as a violation of these boundaries and examine the colonial experience in Ireland and in Africa.

The Theory of Comparative Advantage

The increases in production that could be gained from the specialization of labor were described by Adam Smith, and his tribute to a pin factory is one of the most often quoted passages from *The Wealth of Nations*. David Ricardo extended the analysis of specialization into the international sphere with his recognition of the importance of the comparative advantage that different nations might have in the production of different goods.

> It is quite important to the happiness of mankind that our own enjoyment should be increased by the better distribution of labor, by each country producing those commodities for which by its situation, its climate and its natural or artificial advantages, it is adapted, and by their exchanging them for the commodities of other countries ...[1]

The theory of comparative advantage is based upon one of the most fundamental concepts in economics, the concept of opportunity cost. The relationship between opportunity cost, comparative advantage, and total output is readily illustrated by an example of the sort that commonly appears in textbooks of economics. Suppose that two countries, let us call them England and Ireland, are each capable of producing food and manufactured goods. England, if it produces only food, can produce 75 million tons of food per year; while, if it produces only manufactured goods, it can produce 150 million tons of manufactured goods per year. For simplicity of calculation we will make the tradeoff in production constant within England, so that whenever England produces one ton less of food it releases resources that can be used to produce two more tons of manufactured goods.

For Ireland the maximum possible amount of food production is 50 million tons per year, and the maximum possible amount of manufactured goods production is also 50 million tons per year. We will make the same assumption regarding a constant rate of tradeoff in internal production in Ireland, so that whenever Ireland produces one ton less of food it releases resources that can be used to produce one more ton of manufactured goods.

These countries have a choice between autarky and international trade. More precisely, if there are only these two countries, then they can engage in trade only if both countries agree to trade, but if one country chooses autarky then the other country must also be autarkic.

In the autarkic situation each country can consume only what it produces internally. Suppose that the preferences of the population in each country are such that they wish to consume food and manufactured goods in equal amounts, that is, one ton of food with each one ton of manufactured goods. Then England will produce and consume 50 million tons of each good per year, and Ireland will produce and consume 25 million tons of each good per year. The total output is 75 million tons of each good per year.

Now let the two countries abandon autarky and engage in trade. The possibilities for production will be expanded. With the same preferred consumption pattern, one ton of food for each ton of manufactured goods, total production can be as large as $83\frac{1}{3}$ million tons of each good per year, an increase of $8\frac{1}{3}$ million tons per year in the production and consumption of each good. Ireland will have become specialized in the production of food, producing 50 million tons of food per year. In England the resources will become more specialized toward the production of manufactured goods, so that English production will be $83\frac{1}{3}$ tons of manufactured goods and $33\frac{1}{3}$ tons of food.

This increase in production was made possible by a more efficient use of available resources. Although England is the superior producer of both food and clothing, being able to produce a larger amount of each good than can Ireland, the latter has a *comparative advantage* in the production of food. In England the opportunity cost of producing a ton of food is two tons of manufactured goods, while in Ireland the opportunity cost of producing a ton of food is only one ton of manufactured goods. Whatever amount of food the two countries wish to produce, it is most efficient to have it produced at the lowest possible opportunity cost, and this is accomplished by having Ireland specialize in the production of food.

Prices and the Distribution of Output

The preceding argument for the advantages of specialization and trade requires only the reasonable assumption that the opportunity cost of producing a good is not the same in every country. (There is, of course, also the condition that the gains in production resulting from specialization must be greater than the transaction and transportation costs of trade.) However, although this argument demonstrates the increase of production that will result from the use of comparative advantage, it does not say how that increase in production will be divided between the two countries.

Each country's share in the gains from specialization will be determined by the prices at which the goods are traded. But the price at which the marginal unit of a good is traded will be the price at which all the units of that good are traded. Hence, the introduction of trade not only makes specialization possible, it also introduces a mechanism that determines the shares of the two countries in their *total* output.

To continue with our example, if Ireland could buy manufactured goods from England at a price of one-half ton of food for a ton of manufactured goods, then it could consume $33\frac{1}{3}$ million tons of each good, clearly better off than it had been under autarky. But, by selling manufactured goods to Ireland at this price, and therefore buying food from Ireland at the price of two tons of manufactured goods per ton of food, England emerges from the trading with 50 million tons of each good, no better off than she had been under autarky. Hence, there would be no reason for England to engage in trade, and without a trading partner Ireland must remain autarkic. To induce England to trade Ireland must be willing to pay a price for manufactured goods higher than one-half ton of food for a ton of manufactured goods.

Conversely, if England could buy food from Ireland at a price of one ton of manufactured goods for one ton of food, then England could expand its annual consumption to $58\frac{1}{3}$ million tons of each good. But in trading at this price Ireland would be buying manufactured goods from England at a price of one ton of food per ton of manufactured goods, the opportunity cost of producing the goods herself. At this price Ireland would be no better off than under autarky, and would have no incentive to engage in trade.

For both countries to engage freely in trade each must gain from trade. In our example this would require that the price of food be within the boundaries just described:

1 ton of manufactured goods < Price per ton of food < 2 tons of manufactured goods

which is the same as:

$\frac{1}{2}$ ton of food < Price per ton of manufactured goods < 1 ton of food

Any prices within these boundaries will assure that both parties will gain from trade, for each party will be buying its imported good at a price below the opportunity cost of producing that good itself, and each party will be selling its export at a price higher than it could get for the good in its own domestic market.

To illustrate what would happen if these boundaries were to be violated, let us imagine a situation where England is able to impose on Ireland's export a price of one-half ton of manufactured goods per ton of food. This price would have to be imposed on Ireland because, as we have seen, Ireland would never freely consent to trade at such a low price for its produce. At this low price England would purchase $33\frac{1}{3}$ million tons of food, paying for it with $16\frac{2}{3}$ million tons of manufactured goods. As a consequence, Ireland would be left with $16\frac{2}{3}$ million tons of each good, an income one-third less than it had enjoyed under autarky.

The Essence of Colonialism

The mechanism that will guarantee that prices will be within the boundaries for mutual benefit is the ability of each country to refuse to engage in trade unless the price of its import is below the opportunity cost of producing that good domestically (and the price of its export is above the price of that good in its domestic market). Suppose, however, that one country can impose upon the other's export a price that is below the second country's internal price. Then the first country will capture all the gains from specialization. Beyond this, the first country will capture some of the output that the second country would have produced under autarky. For the second country, then, specialization and trade become not a way to increase the amount of goods available for its own consumption, but a way to lose some of the goods it would have had if it had never engaged in trade at all. The second country will find that instead of being enriched by trade, it is impoverished by trade.

No country would freely consent to engage in trade that impoverishes it. Yet in a very large number of cases of international trade one country was able to impose a price structure that benefited itself and impoverished the other country. This is the essence of colonialism, and the imposition of such a price structure invariably involves the use of physical force.

Some writers have made a distinction between imperialism and colonialism. Walter Rodney states that 'Imperialism is essentially an economic phenomenon, and it does not necessarily lead to direct political contact or colonization.'[2] Imperialism is the establishment of a metropolitan-peripheral relationship, where production in the peripheral country is structured so as to serve the interests of and enrich the metropolitan country. All the examples of imperialism discussed in this paper were also cases of colonialism, and 'Colonialism was first and foremost a political phenomenon.'[3] Direct political, and military, contact was the indispensable condition for restructuring property rights in land, so that there are few examples of an imperial relationship that did not involve direct political contact. As Rodney himself continues, 'Africa was the victim of colonization.'[4]

It is worthwhile to distinguish further between two types of colonialism. In the first type the imperial power encountered an indigenous hunter-gatherer culture which it either exterminated or pushed aside, as in the North American colonies of England and France. In this type of colonization the now vacant land was given to settler-colonists from the imperial power. These settler-colonists were given *title* to the land, which they worked themselves, without imported slaves. Hence they could work it as they would; and all the produce of the land and their labor was theirs to do with as they wished.

In colonization of the second type the imperial or metropolitan power encountered an indigenous *agricultural* population. In these cases the major economic consequence was often the substitution of the imperial power's system of real property law for the property law system of the native population and the transfer of land titles to citizens of the metropolitan power. Raymond Crotty has called this second type 'capitalist colonialism,' the forceful imposition of a capitalist culture on an indigenous, collectivist non-capitalist society of food producers, and has pointed out that '. . . every one of the 138 or so countries that were colonies of the capitalist system has failed to develop economically.'[5]

The first type of colonialism results in the establishment of a generally prosperous population of colonists who are citizens of the imperial country. The prosperity and strength that follows from the land ownership under the first type of colonialism is evidenced by the later history of this type of colony. In Canada, the United States, New Zealand, and Australia the descendants of the original colonists, having control of their economic affairs, soon gained political independence as well, frequently without recourse to war, as in three of the four countries just mentioned, and then continued to develop economically.

In the second type of colonialism, Crotty's capitalist colonialism, there is an enclave of colonists from the metropolitan power who are given title to the best land, as in Northern Ireland and in Kenya, and who are subsidized by the imperial power and allowed to keep the profit from the land. But the indigenous population, having been pushed on to the inferior land, is then compelled to export the surplus produce of that land and the produce of their labor for the benefit of the imperial power.

To secure over the long run a share of the produce of the

conquered nation, the metropolitan power must establish a system that encourages production in the conquered nation, and which causes the export of a significant share of that production to the metropolitan country. The colonial land system was extremely effective in accomplishing this. In Ireland the native population became tenants of the new landlords. Rent payment was the mechanism used to impose a price structure that allowed the metropolitan power, England, to expropriate all the gains from trade and some of the 'pre-trade' level of output as well. An alternative mechanism to rent payments, but one which has very much the same results, was alienation of the land coupled with the employment of native labor compelled by taxation to work the alienated land for virtually no payment. With the 'development' of international markets the control of import and export prices could be further assured by monopoly over trade.

We shall review the mechanism of rents as it functioned in eighteenth and nineteenth century Ireland. Then we shall review the alternative but equivalent mechanisms as they were used in Africa in the twentieth century. In all cases the result was the same, the distortion of effective prices so that the metropolitan power gained not only all the benefits of trade, but captured enough of an additional portion of the output of the peripheral country, so that the latter became impoverished and underdeveloped.

Colonialism in Ireland

Ireland was the first of England's colonies. The substitution of English land law for Irish land law took place over the four and a quarter centuries that were required to subdue Ireland.[6] The confiscations of land in the seventeenth century left less than five percent of the land of Ireland in the hands of the Catholic natives who comprised ninety percent of the population. The result of these confiscations was an almost complete separation between those who owned the land and those who tilled it, a separation of race, religion, language, traditions, and national loyalties. The enactment of the Penal Laws in the 1690s outlawed Catholicism, making it illegal for a Catholic to own land.

In the first chapter of *The Land Question* Henry George argued the 'unpalatable truth' that the land system of Ireland was essentially the same as that which prevailed in most other places.[7] In the early chapters of the same work he pointed out the frequency of famine in other countries and the distress of the laboring classes even in the United States.[8]

The way in which the land system in Ireland *did* differ from that in the United States and England was not in the system of laws establishing private property in land, but in the nature of the gulf that separated landlord and tenant; and this gulf contributed to the distress in Ireland as it did in every other colonized country. Judge Mountifort Longfield described the relation of landlord and tenant in Ireland:

> In both countries (England and Ireland) the law is based on the feudal system, which gave the landlord a certain superiority over his tenants. But the feudal relation, with its reciprocal rights and duties, never existed in Ireland. Here the landlord never led his tenants into battle; if they fought on the same field, it was on different sides. They had no tradition of common victories or common defeats. The relation that existed between them was hostile.[9]

There was as well very often a geographical separation of landlord and tenant. Richard Barry O'Brien wrote that, 'The Anglo-Irish landlord was an absentee then (in the reign of Elizabeth). He is, in the main, an absentee today (in the reign of Victoria).'[10] Regarding absenteeism, George had argued in *The Land Question*,

> And it is further to be remarked that too much stress is laid upon absenteeism, and that it might be prevented without much of the evil often attributed to it being cured. That is to say, that to his tenantry and neighborhood the owner of land in Galway or Kilkenny would be as much an absentee if he lived in Dublin as if he lived in London, and that, if Irish landlords were compelled to live in Ireland, all that the Irish people would gain would be, metaphorically speaking, the crumbs that fell from the landlords' tables. For if the butter and eggs, the pigs and the poultry, of the Irish peasant must be taken from him and exported to pay for his landlord's wine and cigars, what difference does it make to him where the wine is drunk or the cigars are smoked?[11]

This is the point exactly. Although it does not matter where the wine and cigars are consumed, it might matter where they are *produced*, whether the expenditures on those products return to

Ireland as income for native producers. This is the sense in which national boundaries affect the definition of the problem. George argued rightly that we should not limit our observations to national units, but should look inside national boundaries as well, where we will find some portions of the population in as great a distress as is the majority of the population of any colonized country, and from the same cause. That cause is the expropriation of the fruits of the laborer through monopolization of land and control of the prices of the products of the land and labor.

The problem addressed in this paper is the identification of the mechanism by which the metropolitan power uses the colonial land system to capture excessive gains from trade with the colonized nation. If our units of analysis are two separate countries, then the fact that the inhabitants of the one country are tenants on their own native land, paying rent that is exported to landlords in the second country, makes absenteeism a matter of importance.

A further consequence of the gulf between landlord and tenant was rack renting. Largely because of that gulf the Irish tenant had little security of tenure (in contrast to the status of Protestant tenants in Northern Ireland, where the commonality of religion and nationality among landlord and tenant afforded the tenant the set of protections known as 'The Ulster Custom').[12] As a consequence of the lack of security of tenure among the rapidly growing Catholic population the competition for land in the early nineteenth century bid rents up to levels where only a subsistence income was left for large numbers of the tenants. The rent had to be paid in money, and the only way to obtain such an amount of money was by producing goods for the export market. Thus, rack renting functioned as a mechanism effectively to adjust the prices of the goods that the Irish sold. No matter what the price of Irish exports might be in trade, rent could adjust so that exports were worth little more than the amount of the rent. In a bad year, the value of output would be less than the amount of the rent, and the arrears of rent would hang over a tenant's head, threatening him with instant eviction at the landlord's whim.

With rent functioning in this way, England could allow the prices of the goods that it traded with Ireland to be established on a world market. The rent payments to the metropolitan power, for which the colony received nothing in return, had the effect of causing Ireland to sell its goods for less than their internal opportunity cost.

The argument might be made that the competition for land had the beneficial effect of insuring that only those tenants who would cultivate the land most intensively would be able to acquire the use of it. But the competition bid rents to such a level that however hard the tenant might work he himself would realize little benefit from his labors. The rents were captured by a small group of landowners and were exported out of the country.

Colonialism in Africa

At the beginning of the twentieth century the British completed construction of a rail line from Mombasa, on the coast of Africa, to Lake Victoria. The line ran through large expanses of highlands that were the collective domain of several tribes that used the lands as seasonal pastures for their herds. After completion of the railroad the colonial administration 'alienated' these lands to European settlers. That is, the lands were declared 'Crown Lands' and then sold to European settlers at nominal prices. 'Lord Delamere,' for example, 'purchased 100,000 acres of the best land for a penny per acre,'[13] and there were other estates of several times that size. (Nor were such bargains in land unique to Kenya or to British administration. In 1926, the Firestone Rubber Company acquired one million acres of supposedly independent Liberia for six cents an acre and one percent of the value of the exported rubber.

It was not only that so much of the best land was alienated to the European settlers, but the productivity of the European held land was enhanced by access to capital, placement of roads (largely paid for by taxes on the native population), favorable tax treatment, and monopoly of the most profitable commercial crops. The result was that the land the Europeans held was capable of being farmed profitably, while the Africans' land, even if it had better soil or more reliable rainfall, was not.[14]

But these plantations, even when they were not the size of Lord Delamere's, were useless to the European unless he could get the native to work for him. The African, of course, had no reason to work for the Europeans,

> ... unless the Europeans had been willing to pay in wages more than the Africans could earn from farming on their own account. But such wages would have meant little or no profit for the Europeans. Therefore Africans had to be compelled to work, partly by force, partly by taxation, and *partly by preventing them from having access to enough land for profitable crops to enable them to pay taxes without working for wages.*[15] [emphasis added]

What was meant by the phrase, 'partly by force,' was described graphically by Leonard Woolf as a system of forced labor not far removed from slavery.[16] In brief, it consisted of allowing to remain on the reserved (for Africans) lands only that part of the labor force in excess of what was required to work the European plantations. Those workers who were selected to work on the European plantations were assigned a legal status that made their situation worse than that of a serf.

Very shortly, however, a rapid population growth, similar to that which had occurred in Ireland in the early nineteenth century, occurred in Kenya in the early twentieth century, so that it became less necessary to use direct force. Population pressure and taxation were sufficient to assure an adequate supply of African labor on the European lands.

The movement of the population into paid labor and the level of taxation were such, Colin Leys reports, that, 'by the mid-1920s more than half the able-bodied men in the two largest tribes were estimated to be working for Europeans. Within the space of a generation they had effectively been converted from independent peasants producing cash crops for the new markets, into peasants dependent on agricultural wage-labour.'[17]

By Leys' estimates, these laborers were paying seventy-five percent of their wages in taxes. And the tax structure was one that was clearly designed both to enhance the economic condition of the European plantation owner and to further the exploitation of the native population. The only property tax in Kenya at this time was the hut tax, to which Africans were liable whether or not they worked for money wages. There was no property tax at all for the European plantation owners. The latter were subject to the poll tax at the insignificant rate of £1 per year. Likewise, import duties were negligible on consumer goods for the luxury end of the European market, but were a significant part of the price of the few import goods that the Africans could buy. 'Africans paid the bulk of taxation, while the Europeans received virtually the entire benefit of government services — railways, roads, schools, hospitals, extension services, and so forth.'[18] Roads in the European areas were financed by central government grants, while in the African areas they were financed by taxes on local produce.

What had occurred in Kenya had its counterpart in Ghana, on the other side of the African continent. The colonial era saw the transformation of the Ghanaian economy from production for the benefit of the native population to production for the benefit of the metropolitan powers. 'Ghana's peripheral status during the colonial period was characterized specifically by its heavy reliance on the import-export trade.'[19] As it had in Kenya, colonialism brought increased integration into the international economy but underdevelopment in the domestic economy. Ghanaian cloth was replaced by British cloth. 'By the 1890s gold mining in Ghana was an exclusively expatriate enterprise.'[20] Before the First World War cocoa for export had become the predominant agricultural crop, its production often involving the destruction of plants that might have been used for domestic consumption. Since cocoa is a consumer good, and not a necessity, Ghana's economy became highly dependent on fluctuations in the world market for cocoa, which was, moreover, dominated by a few large buyers.

In Ghana, as in Kenya, the African peasant was allowed to own land. But as in Kenya, taxation and the control of trade allowed the imperial power to expatriate the surplus of the African worker.

The mechanisms that were a part of colonialism in Kenya or in Ghana operated in other countries as well. 'Good examples of Africans literally being forced to grow cash crops by gun and whip were to be found in Tanganyika under German rule, in Portugese colonies, and in French Equatorial Africa and the French Sudan in the 1930s.'[21] But even where, as in Kenya, the African peasant was allowed to own his land in the reserved areas, the surplus which his labor produced on that land was expatriated.

> Cash-crop peasants never had any capital of their own. They existed from one crop to another, depending on good harvests and good prices. Any bad harvest or fall of prices caused the peasants to borrow in order to

pay taxes and buy certain necessities. As security they mortgaged their future crops to moneylenders in the middleman category. Non-payment of debts could and did lead to their farms' being taken away by the moneylenders. The rate of interest on loans was always fantastically high ...[22]

Replace the word 'taxes' by the word 'rent', and this passage might be describing Ireland in the nineteenth century rather than Africa in the twentieth. These moneylenders were only one link in the long chain of individuals and organizations that in concert expatriated the surplus of the African peasant. Perhaps the largest share of the surplus was taken by the European trading companies. By controlling exports and imports these companies controlled both the price which the African peasant received for his product and the price which he paid for imports. Where physical force was not used, the presence of taxation assured that the African peasant would continue to produce for export.

This expatriation of the African peasant's surplus is not far removed from the actual trade in slavery that preceded it. Thus, again from Walter Rodney,

In Britain, the notorious slave trading port of Liverpool was the first to switch to palm oil early in the nineteenth century when the trade in slaves became difficult or impossible. This meant that Liverpool firms were no longer exploiting Africa by removing its labor physically to another part of the world. Instead, they were exploiting the labor and raw materials of Africa *inside* Africa.'[23]

That the colonial powers thought this an improvement is indicated by a speech given by Joseph Chamberlain in the British House of Commons in 1903, as reported by Leonard Woolf.

He said that the capitalists in Africa who asked for taxation to compel the native to work for them at a wage were very much hurt at its being said that they wanted forced labour. Mr. Chamberlain sympathized with them. He explained that it was wrong to call this "forced labour." Forced labour was labour forced to work by physical means; but if you compelled a native to work by taxing him so much that he was compelled to work for the European and the wage offered by the European, this was not forced labour, but moral suasion.[24]

There is a striking similarity between this method of taxation and the rent paid by Irish tenants in the 18th and 19th centuries. The similarity becomes more apparent, when one reviews the requests made by European settlers for increases in taxes on Africans in order to increase the supply of labor to the plantations. Chamberlain may have been semantically correct in saying that African workers were not forced to work on European plantations. They were merely forced to pay taxes, and they could obtain the money to pay taxes only by working on the European plantations. Likewise in Ireland, the native population was not forced to work on the land. Force had to be used only to enforce the property rights of the landlord. This was done through eviction of tenants who did not pay the rent. Of course an evicted tenant faced the very real prospect of starvation.

The Aftermath of Colonialism

The purpose of this paper was to describe how the mechanisms of rents and taxation could be used to turn the promise of gains from comparative advantage into the reality of impoverishment for one of the countries engaged in trade. But this impoverishment would last long after direct political and military contact had ceased. Even after gaining political independence, countries that were the victims of capitalist colonialism remain impoverished and fail to develop economically. The failure to develop that Crotty described in the countries that had been colonies is a direct result of the expatriation of wealth that occurred in the colonial period. With so much of their domestic product being exported in the form of rents, the specialization in agriculture in the peripheral countries became exaggerated. With little or no income available for investment in the colonial economy other forms of industry withered away. Likewise, there was an enormous destruction of human capital in Africa. As the African population was separated from its traditional methods of production, the knowledge required for those methods was not passed on. Within one or two generations that knowledge is lost. The end of the colonial era saw the countries less developed, relative to the metropolitan powers, than they had been at the beginning of the period, and their rôle as peripheral members of the international economy continued.

NOTES

1. David Ricardo, *On the Principles of Political Economy and Taxation*, p. 132, in *Works and Correspondence of David Ricardo*, edited by Pierro Saffra, Cambridge, 1962.
2. Walter Rodney, *How Europe Underdeveloped Africa*, Washington, D.C.: Howard University Press, 1974, p. 137.
3. J. Forbes Munro, *Africa and the International Economy 1800-1960*, London: J. M. Dent & Sons, Ltd., 1968, p. 89.
4. Rodney, loc. cit.
5. Raymond Crotty, *Ireland in Crisis*. Dingle, Co. Kerry, Ireland: Brandon Book Publishers, Ltd., 1986, p. 16.
6. C. F. Kolbert and T. O'Brien, *Land Reform in Ireland*, University of Cambridge, Department of Land Economy, Occasional Paper No. 3, 1975, chapter 3.
7. Henry George, *The Land Question*, New York: Robert Schalkenbach Foundation, 1965, p.8.
8. George, pp. 18-20.
9. Quoted in Kolbert and O'Brien, p.12.
10. ibid., page 28.
11. George, pp. 13-14.
12. 'The Ulster Custom' guaranteed the tenant a fair rent, fixity of tenure as long as the rent was paid, and free sale of his improvements to the land. The Ulster Custom was a form of dual ownership.
13. Rodney, p. 154.
14. Colin Leys, *Underdevelopment in Kenya*, Berkeley: Univ. of California Press, 1974, p. 34.
15. Leys, pp. 29-30.
16. Leonard Woolf, *Empire and Commerce in Africa*, London: George Allen & Unwin, Ltd., pp. 345-347.
17. Leys, p. 31.
18. ibid.
19. Howard Rhoda, *Colonialism and Underdevelopment in Ghana*, New York: Africana Publishing Company, p. 59.
20. ibid.
21. Rodney, p. 157.
22. Rodney, p. 155.
23. Rodney, p. 156.
24. Woolf, p. 350.

IV

ECOLOGY AND ECO-POLITICS

7

The Greens and the Tax on Rent

DAVID RICHARDS

I

WE HUMANS are worried about the damage we are doing to our environment. This concern has now been formalised by Green political parties in many countries, or by more loosely-based movements, as in the United States and Australia. But on present evidence it seems that politically active ecologists are, on the whole, failing to articulate policies that systematically alter the fundamental relationship between our species and its habitat.

Our habitat is classed in the study of economics as natural resources, or 'land'. Though it is basic to all economic activity it has yet to be accorded much room in economic discourse. The value of natural resources has yet to be adequately reflected in economic decision-making (Dasgupta 1990; Brundtland 1987). Though Green politicians emphasise this shortcoming, they tend to recognise it only where natural resources are being rapidly depleted, and to overlook it where renewable land uses are taking place. In other words, they do not have a systematic view of the place of land in economic calculations.

It is our claim that a systematic view that appropriately relates ecology and economics was expounded over a century ago by the outspoken economist Henry George. In Part II we shall review the economic policies that are deemed on this view to be needed to meet the ecological challenge. In Part III we shall offer some remarks on the general acceptability of these policies. Then in Part IV we shall look more closely at the Green parties and movements to see to what extent they incorporate Henry George's message. Finally, in Parts V and VI we shall focus on two policy areas to illustrate general themes.

II

The message of Henry George as it relates to environmental problems is threefold. Firstly, efficient and sustainable exploitation of natural resources depends upon the proper functioning of unimpeded markets. Secondly, equitable distribution of the benefits of natural resource exploitation depends upon the recognition that these resources are the common heritage of mankind, through all generations. Thirdly, efficiency and equity depend upon each other.

The proper functioning of unimpeded markets means that either free market clearing prices should rule where markets already exist, or that markets should be created where they are absent.

Interference with already existing markets and its baleful consequences for the environment are abundantly documented. Government price support for agricultural products in the United Kingdom, for example, leads to over-use of the countryside by farmers (Bowers and Cheshire 1983: 138; and see Body, in Chapter 9). Give away prices obtained by public landowners for leases of timber rights, or by public irrigation works for water supplied, lead to over-use, and wasteful use, of forest and water resources (UNEP 1988: 206, 209). Governments not only give away the public domain, they add to the value of the gift by subsidising more intensive uses than the land can economically or ecologically support (UNEP 1988: 209). Brazilian governments, for example, have not only given away land for resettlement of overspill population in the Amazon rainforest, but have created tax incentives for cutting down more forest to make room for cattle ranching. 'Too often,' observes a recent United Nations Environment Program report, 'governments underestimate the economic and environmental viability of alternative uses' (UNEP 1988: 211).

Lack of markets, rather than impediments to their functioning, is the problem in the case of the 'commons' — the atmosphere, the oceans, rivers and streams, public spaces, and wildlife species. Because they belong to no-one, or to an uncaring public sector, no-one charges for their use. Their services are 'free'; and so there is a temptation to over-use them. The costs are born externally — by society as a whole, or by future generations. In erstwhile Communist countries, where land was until recently 'common property', all land was explicitly regarded by the planners as 'free' because no labor had gone into producing it. These countries were not known for their environmental sensitivity.

The solutions are in the first case for governments 'to remove inappropriate subsidies and incentives', as the UNEP report notes on page 212, and in the second case for governments to create exclusive rights of access to the commons and auction them to the highest bidder, as the Pearce Report to the United Kingdom government in 1989 has indicated (Pearce, Markandya, Barbier 1989: 161-166). Europe is beginning to scale down farm subsidies, and Brazil has removed direct tax incentives for deforestation. The American Environmental Protection Agency has experimented with tradeable air-pollution permits, and successfully used tradeable lead quotas to facilitate oil refineries' reduction of the lead content of petrol. Such solutions are undoubtedly Georgist. But they do not by themselves contain the full substance of the Georgist proposal.

'What is probably the deepest truth we can grasp? That alone is wise which is just; that alone is enduring which is right,' wrote George in *Progress and Poverty* (1879):

> In justice is the highest and truest expediency . . . Unless its foundations be laid in justice the social structure cannot stand. Our primary social adjustment is a denial of justice. In allowing one man to own the land on which and from which other men may live, we have made them bondsmen in a degree that increases as material progress goes on . . . Let the landholders have, if you please, all that the possession of the land would give them in the absence of the rest of the community. But rent, the creation of the whole community, necessarily belongs to the community.

For Henry George, equity and efficiency formed a seamless garment. He was an ardent advocate of free markets on both grounds, but, in the case of land, he observed that it was not desirable on either ground, nor even necessary, for the owner of the land, unless it be society as a whole, to receive direct financial benefit merely on account of ownership. The only legitimate demand for land is either to use it productively, or for its natural services. Land (including the commons) is a *sine qua non* of human interaction and production, and also yields direct services, such as satisfying the desire for wilderness, absorbing pollution or, in the case of the tropical rainforests, providing global air-conditioning. Any interest in land as a mere financial investment interferes with the performance of these functions. It also makes the distribution of the financial surplus accruing to land unequal among people. George's most controversial prescription, therefore, was that the community should recover all the land rents that the creation of freehold tenancies had alienated into private ownership.

The rules by which land is occupied dictate the way people relate to each other and determine the success with which they interact. The system of land tenure may be used to divide people, or to integrate them into healthy communities. Examples of the former case are the *apartheid* laws of South Africa, which created the Bantustans to segregate races, and the large rural estates of Latin America which also vouchsafe the best land to a few. An example of the latter case may be found in Denmark, where the Viking tradition that the land belongs to all the people has underpinned specific tenurial measures, such as taxes on land value and on the imputed rent of owner-occupied housing, which have allowed the development of a relatively equal society.

Another Georgist prescription we have already mentioned: the users of land and natural resources already in the public domain should be charged the full market rent. Not to do so would be to alienate the rent.

A third prescription would be to ensure that any new types of property rights in natural resources that are created by government decree are designed to return the resource's rent to the community. As Professor Dales has put it, for example, in the case of rights (marketable permits) to emit waste into rivers: 'The rights should be for one year only, the price of one right for one year representing the annual rental value of the water for waste disposal purposes' (Dales 1968). It is not sufficient for governments simply to create new land markets. They must do so by extending the public domain and charging full rent for its use.

III

That every person in every generation has an equal right to the use of land was Henry George's basic moral axiom. It is one with which few people would disagree, and it is certainly common ground in the

Green movement. Collection of land rent by the community is not commonly perceived as its necessary logical outcome, however. Socialists see the connection, but go on to make the fatal mistake of proscribing private ownership of land altogether, thereby missing another connection — between private decision-making and prosperity.

Perhaps J. S. Mill diagnosed the most important reason for missing the connection when he described the law of rent as the *pons asinorum* of political economy. *The Concise Oxford Dictionary*'s entry for *pons asinorum* runs 'bridge of asses, i.e. 5th proposition of the 1st book of Euclid, hence, anything found difficult by beginners.' As the concept of economic rent has still to be widely grasped, the possibility of a political movement for appropriate land reform would seem to be as remote as ever.

Henry George's message appears destined to fall between political stools. To Greens it offers equitable sharing of the world's natural resources; to non-Greens, economic efficiency and, hence, growth. Within both groups, it offers thoroughgoing private ownership of producible goods and services to those of Rightward persuasion, and untrammelled social ownership of natural resources to those of Leftward persuasion. But it cannot satisfy all of these four corners of the political boxing ring at the same time, or any of them all of the time.

The compensation of landowners, to which Henry George objected, is also one which prevents all but the more devout Greens or Reds considering a thoroughgoing application of Henry George's main proposal. Tideman notes (see Chapter 2) that in the USA only a popular movement embracing most landowners as well as non-landowners would enable the constitutional change necessary to allow major curtailment of owners' rights to income from land without compensation. And without such popular support the task of designing politically feasible compensation procedures, even in the form of a phased introduction over a long period, is a daunting one.

This combination of unfamiliarity of terms, awkwardness of political fit, and high popularity threshold requirements explains why George's message often meets with the response: 'If it's so good, why hasn't it been tried?'

IV

The Message and Deep Ecology

The United Kingdom Green Party The Green movement is strong on goals but weak on practical policies for achieving those goals. It is therefore host to many nostrums claiming to show how things really work and how to put them right. Land value taxation is seen by many Greens as one such nostrum, propagated by cult followers of an American frontiersman who intone incessantly about land rents. Although it has found its way into the rolling Manifesto of the UK Green Party, it occupies a cobwebbed compartment of its own ('Land Tenure') and is not seen as an important part of economic policy.

The case of the UK Green Party is instructive, as it is one of the few Green parties that has been faced with the message of Henry George. In 1981 it devoted both its Party Conferences to land tenure policy, but despite intense and exhausting debate it failed to reach agreement and has been wary of broaching the subject ever since.

The aims of land tenure policy were quickly established. They were to

(a) re-establish land as a common heritage and community asset, no longer subject to monopoly or speculative pressures;
(b) establish for all equal right to occupy land, so providing a proper framework for the ecological use of land in small units;
(c) guarantee security of tenure to occupiers of land on this new basis;
(d) ensure that returns from land which are in no way due to the efforts of individuals shall accrue to the community (Ecology Party 1981: 9).

This is a perfect statement of the Georgist position. Controversy raged, however, over whether these aims could be better achieved by 'positive' land redistribution or by instituting a self-regulating mechanism in the form of a land value tax, to be called, more appropriately, Community Ground Rent (CGR). The argument was conducted by a few enthusiasts on either side whilst the majority of those present struggled to understand 'the complex issues involved' (Oubridge 1986).

Those against CGR (who preferred to call it Land Tax) were of the opinion that it was a flat rate tax per acre of farmland, such as was supposedly used under colonialism to drive the indigenous population off the land into cities. It was seen therefore as an instrument for concentrating land in the hands of rich farmers, or at least forcing farmers to over-use land. They also thought it would be unworkably complex to implement. Their own proposals of stripping the public sector of its surplus acres, putting statutory limits on the size of holdings, vesting surplus land in a National Land Bank or in local authorities, and selling or letting it to individuals and collectives appeared to them to be more practical.

Community Ground Rent found its way into the Party Manifesto after the first conference despite time running out before the alternative proposals could be put. It was then rejected in favor of statutory limits at the second conference, but the 'Great Land Debate' ('the greatest controversy the Party has ever known') was not formally concluded, and the Manifesto was not amended (Oubridge 1986). Massive procedural failure determined the outcome, but it took much of the rest of the decade for the wound to heal and for the subject to be re-opened at party conferences.

The presence of CGR in the Green Party's *Manifesto for A Sustainable Society* was, therefore, for many years an accident of history. Its roots were too strong, however, for that accident to be reversed. Opponents softened their attitude considerably, but the Party's Land Working Group was informed that they were still awaiting a 'two sentence explanation' of why, in particular, CGR would be good for small farmers. Nevertheless, with room left for 'positive measures' to redistribute land if necessary, CGR finally found a *bona fide* place in the Green Manifesto in 1988 (Green Party 1988: 74-76).

There is also a wide feeling that CGR is 'potentially unpopular because it would be seen as a new tax bearing largely on owner-occupiers' (Wilmore 1989). Two-thirds of UK homes are owner-occupied. Moves are afoot to tie CGR to the Party's Basic Income Scheme, which would be a form of visible compensation, and which itself faces potential unpopularity. Funding by CGR would take some of the pressure off income tax (*Land & Liberty* 1987: 53), and would also be a way of using 'inherently unearned income' rather than transfers from the working population to provide for those who choose not to work (Wilmore 1989).

Some opponents of this position, however, regard income from investing in land titles as no more 'inherently unearned' than income derived from investing in other assets. They therefore regard CGR — as opposed to a comprehensive wealth tax — as inherently discriminatory. Nevertheless, they advocate a J. S. Mill style 100 per cent tax on increments in land rent to prevent land speculation (Chapman 1990).

This diffidence regarding CGR, and the increase in tax revenue envisaged as well as CGR revenue, shows that the Green Party pays no heed to one of George's less controversial prescriptions — the need to reduce government distortion of markets. Suffice it to say that the Green Party is a high tax party.

It is not surprising therefore that there is no doubting the Party's commitment to the other less controversial Georgist prescription. It does not hold back from advocating resources taxes and pollution taxes. Both are attempts to share the 'commons' equitably and efficiently. The former tackle the 'temporal commons' of non-renewable resources, which if underpriced are over-consumed by earlier generations who thus deny rights of access to later generations. The latter are the 'spatial commons' referred to earlier.

Resources taxes designed to raise the costs of non-renewable resources to consumers and encourage re-use and recycling are known in America as severance taxes. Robert Andelson comments:

> Although the taxation of land rent is, of course, the method characteristically emphasised by Georgism, a severance tax is simply a different technical application of the same philosophy, adapted to different circumstances but equally amenable to determination by the market (Andelson 1991).

One caveat might be that the issue of rights to consume certain tonnages of raw materials (like Daly's Depletion Quotas — Ekins 1986: 231), along the lines of rights to dump certain tonnages of waste, would be a more thoroughgoing market proposal. Rates of consumption would be more strictly controlled, and the market would accurately determine the resource rents which flow from them. Tax levels on the other hand would be less easy to determine;

for the effects on consumption rates would not be known. The same reservation applies to pollution taxes *vis-à-vis* pollution permits. The Green Party, however, does not like the terminology of 'permitting' pollution, as opposed to 'taxing' it. Nor is it quite happy with the idea of creating new markets.

Deep Greens the world over share with the Left (Reds) their antipathy towards markets. From the evidence of history they do not believe that markets work, except in favor of the rich, and do not believe that they can be made to work. A summary quote from an 'eco-socialist' active in the UK Green Party may serve to show how far the message of Henry George is from penetrating this corner of economic thinking:

> ... while Green rhetoric often implies a wholesale rejection of the economic status quo, few of the concrete proposals envisage basic structural change, tending rather to suggest piecemeal ecological or social reforms. There is no advocacy of changes in the ownership of large companies, for example; and although the 1987 Green Party manifesto carries a marginal note pointing out that '52% of the UK's land is owned by a mere 1% of the population', the policy on land tenure — the levying of Community Ground Rent — stops short of envisaging any expropriation of that rich 1 per cent (Ryle 1988: 41).

Other Green Parties The first of all the Green parties, the Values Party of New Zealand, understood the connection between common rights in land and the public collection of land rents because of its Maori connections (Noble 1979). But the Party barely survives.

The most famous Green Party, *Die Grünen* of West Germany, has not been introduced to the connection. Apart from its Marxist elements, it is known to be slow in its development of thinking on economic policy. Its economic spokesman in 1985 regarded the existence of vacant houses in German cities as 'a political problem, not necessarily a problem of property,' which could be solved by having the will to enforce already existing laws 'prohibiting this kind of abuse' (Spretnak and Capra 1986: 94). Five years later, the analysis had not deepened.

The Green movement developed rapidly towards the end of the 1980s in the Soviet Union, where environmental problems now come second only to food shortages as an electoral issue. Green parties have been formed in each of the Baltic republics, where they have been influential in the separatist movements (Peel 1990). In the Soviet Union, green policy is at present simple to formulate; abandon each new investment mega-project, because it has been planned with total disregard to the environment in line with anthropocentric communist ideology; 31 out of 34 scheduled nuclear power stations had already been abandoned by early 1990, according to a Soviet government representative at a *Die Grünen* conference. The prospect of undoing the damage that has already been done is, however, more daunting.

In the shadow of such clear-cut environmental imperatives it is less clear how much importance will be accorded by Greens to the more subtle issues of land tenure. The Land Law approved by the Supreme Soviet in February 1990 (Peel 1990) moved towards private ownership of land in agriculture by introducing tenancies and leases and the right to bequeath land to one's children, but stopped short of allowing the right to buy and sell land. It is possible, therefore, that, in this particular area, communist ideology may yet bestow a valuable legacy, by retaining land rent for government revenue. The Soviet Union would, however, still have to devise a method for measuring the full market rental value of land (see Harrison, Chapter ?).

The Other Economic Summit Two alternative economic summits were held, in London in 1984 and in Bonn in 1985, in conscious opposition to the economic summits of western world leaders in those years. Their aim was to bring together the ideas of those who oppose current economic orthodoxies from a Green perspective, and develop what was claimed to be a New Economics. The work continues, and is now organised by The Living Economy Network (LEN). The book of the conferences, *The Living Economy* (Ekins 1986), contains two expositions on land reform, from a microeconomic and a macroeconomic point of view, both of which are Georgist. But, as in the UK Green Party, the confidence to relate the position to other economic issues, apart from the possibility of funding a national income scheme, does not exist.

Scepticism over the benefits of current market institutions is also strong, but market solutions to problems are willingly embraced. A Universal Stock Ownership Plan to spread share ownership, and marketable Depletion Quotas to conserve non-renewable resources, are two examples.

The Green Movement in the USA The Green Movement in the United States is still at grass roots level. Gradually a Green Politics is emerging, but at the beginning of the 1990s a national Green Party had yet to appear. The features distinguishing it from its European counterparts seem to be the political system within which it operates, and its geographical spread, rather than any innate characteristics. The same tensions exist between realists and fundamentalists, socialists and conservationists, materialists and spiritualists. But US politics is the arena of the two-party system *par excellence*, and huge geographical area also militates against the development of a unified third party.

However, the US has produced Henry George, the strongest allegiance to the market system, and much of the theory of environmental economics; so one might expect American Greens to be relatively strong on economic policy issues. But they are not (see page 167). As in Europe, emphasis on democratic control of the future still tends to be thought of in terms of political institutions rather than market institutions.

Nevertheless, 'the serious end of the USA's Green movement accepts the need for land value taxation,' Paul Ekins, coordinator of The Living Economy Network, assures the present author. He cites the monthly publication *New Options*, edited by Mark Satin. It has an impressive list of well-known Greens on its Board of Advisers. The February 1989 article, 'Affordable Housing: Laying the Groundwork' assessed what the land value tax offers and concluded

> with a bit of luck, 'Lower Taxes to the Ground' (or 'Own Production, Not Creation') will be a rallying cry of activists in the 1990s . . . Someday soon, most Americans are going to get tired of listening to Jack Kemp and Jesse Jackson argue about how to throw money at the housing problem. Will Common Ground [the Georgist movement] and the U.S. Greens then be ready to roll?

A Green quarterly which is directly descended from the Georgist movement is *Green Revolution*. It is published by the School of Living, which currently sponsors the Fourth World Assembly, and is strongly decentralist. Elsewhere, a statement from the Catholic bishops of the Heartland (Midwest) addresses ecological use of land and 'calls for small-is-beautiful *land reform* as the only sustainable course for rural America,' according to Charlene Spretnak (Spretnak and Capra 1986: 252). This involves 'taxation of agricultural land "according to its productive value rather than its speculative value", "taxing land progressively at a higher rate according to increases in the size and quality of holdings" (a proposal in the Jeffersonian tradition),' amongst other measures. The reservations of some UK Green Party activists about the effect of land value taxation on small farmers are clearly absent here.

It is difficult to assess the degree of penetration of the Georgist message through such a decentralised movement, but it is there, and undoubtedly has strong advocates where the Green political platform is being constructed.

The Message and Shallow Ecology

The emergence of 'shallow ecology' in recent years — the mainstream response to the international issues of acid rain, the greenhouse effect and the hole in the ozone layer — may hold out more promise for the spread of land value taxation than the earlier emergence of the Greens, or 'deep ecology'. This is partly because market solutions to problems are more intelligible to Rightward-leaning non-Greens, and partly because such solutions involve creating new types of property which have not yet been converted into private vested interests and thus do not present compensation problems.

The former UK Prime Minister, Mrs Margaret Thatcher, signalled the acceptance in the inner sanctums of the Establishment of the importance of Green issues during her set-piece speech at the annual Conservative Party Conference in 1988. And she did so in distinctly Georgist terms:

> No generation has a freehold on this earth.
> All we have is a life tenancy — with a full repairing lease.

The European elections of 1989 provided further evidence of the upswing in the political fortunes of the Green movement. Massive gains were made by the Green Parties throughout the Community (except in West Germany where their already significant vote merely held up). In the UK their proportion of the vote surged from 0.5 per cent to nearly 15 per cent. This is less surprising if it is borne in mind that the environment is one of the areas where policy is increasingly being set at the Community level.

A 'carbon tax' on fossil fuel burning, to reduce emissions of the 'greenhouse gas' carbon dioxide, was already being considered by the Community, and is also being looked at sympathetically by the UK Government. Putting a price on the environment and allowing the market to allocate its use, rather than increasing government controls, is the preferred Conservative Party opinion, according to recent Environment Secretaries (e.g. Ridley 1989: 15-16). An academic environmental economist, Professor David Pearce, was appointed special adviser to the Environment Secretary; and in an officially commissioned report he rehearsed the arguments for pollution taxes and marketable pollution 'permits'.

As argued earlier, both measures are essentially Georgist ways of sharing scarce resources. The first has the tactical advantage, however, from a Georgist perspective, that it may not be alienated from the public sector (though it may be less efficient). Given the Conservative Government's propensity to 'privatize' public assets, it is likely that any pollution permits created will be sold 'freehold', as it were, rather than leased annually to the highest bidder.

In the United States, deep ecologists (Greens) are actually standing in the way of practical action on the environment, whilst shallow ecologists (economists) are pressing for it. Politicians might have been more committed but for the 'litigious' Greens. Frances Cairncross writes in *The Economist*:

> In spite of the hostility of environmentalists, who see them as a way of making money from dirt, economic measures to tackle pollution might increase. Regulations work best when they can be applied to a few large polluters ... governments will increasingly have to turn to taxes and charges ... As monitoring improves and the costs of additional clean-up increase, marketable permits will also look more attractive. In June President Bush announced a scheme to cut sulphur-dioxide emissions with a scheme of tradeable permits for electricity utilities. The Environmental Protection Agency is considering using marketable permits to phase out chlorofluorocarbons (CFCs). Indeed, some in the administration would like to see CFC permits auctioned, so that the windfall

profits from its diminishing supply accrue to the government, not the chemical companies (Cairncross 1989: 10).

In view of the revenue that sufficiently onerous taxes or permits might raise, it is possible to envisage a big shift away from current forms of public revenue to 'green revenue'. President Bush's 'no new taxes' platform could not limit the scope of tax reform indefinitely, for environmental improvement by regulation alone would be too costly to the economy (*The Economist* 1990). Given the educational impact that raising public revenue from natural assets (land) would have, it is possible that the Green Revolution could spill over into more Georgist views on existing land ownership.

Even arch-conservatives are able to concede that Georgist land tenure is the most effective way of occupying previously unowned territories. Dr Donald Denman, Professor Emeritus of Land Economy at Cambridge University, regards the seabed as 'a rare opportunity for the land value taxers to start again at the beginning ... to pursue a 100% rent tax policy without upsetting entrenched interests' (Denman 1984).

V

Other virgin territories spring to mind as untrammelled by western-style private vested interests (though not tribal interests): Antarctica and the tropical rainforests. The Amazon basin, for example, presents an opportunity for the application of sound principles of land tenure to resolve environmental and economic conflicts simultaneously.

The Brazilian Government needs $15 billion each year to service its foreign debts, which it will have to realize by imposing austerity programs on the already poor — rather than by the 1989-90 expedients of freezing or capping payments. This process commenced on the day of President Collor's inauguration in early 1990, though, remarkably, it began by aiming at the rich who had benefited from years of four-figure inflation.

Brazil has within its sovereignty a vast renewable natural resource of great value to the rest of the world — the rainforest, which combats global warming significantly, and accounts for a large fraction of the world's gene pool. If it were to lease this resource as a nature reserve (with sustainable uses) to the rest of the world at a rent that would supersede all possible gains or savings from allowing the forest to succumb to settlers, cowboys and gold diggers, it would not only be free to settle its debts rapidly, release constraints on its own people, and safeguard tribal territories, it would also be acting in the best interests of all other nations, by putting capitalist doctrine into practice, and showing that markets can be for the equal benefit of all. Meanwhile, because the rental value to the highest bidder of conserved rainforests has not been tested, rich, capitalist-orientated nations are agonising over, not just debts that are due, but how to give aid to poorer nations in order to reduce their impact on the world's climate.

'Debt-for-nature' swaps, in which mainly voluntary organisations buy debt from countries at discounted rates provided that the money is used for conserving forests, are a free enterprise recognition of the principle. But the matter should not be debt-related, and should be the concern of governments and the United Nations, as should all global environmental problems that may be tackled by correct assignment of property rights. The Green Movement, which has highlighted the issue, has been slow to see the solution — though Nicholas Guppy, of Survival International, and Dr Norman Myers, a leading conservation scientist, were within sight of it a decade ago (Guppy 1980: 5; Myers 1979: 248, 269).

However, Brian Johnson, a forestry consultant to the Worldwide Fund for Nature and the European Commission, observes

> The era of international bargaining over ecological rent, however organised and paid, has already begun. A start on bargaining with the government of the Amazon and the Congo Basin (together they contain almost half of all remaining rainforest) cannot be long delayed .. If the forests perform such vital functions for us all, are not their owners — the people of their 'host' countries — entitled to some form of 'rent' for the benefit we get from them? (Johnson 1989).

He cites a calculation putting 'the capital value of the giant cooling plant we call Amazonia at about £450 trillion' (sterling). An annual yield on that value of 0.2 per cent would account for Brazil's debt service. A carbon tax, adding less than 1 per cent to electricity bills in the European Community to provide $56 billion annually, is suggested as a possible source of revenue. But the effect on the already rich in Brazil, who would undoubtedly benefit the most through land value appreciation and repayment of internal debt, is not considered. It is in such a context that the more complete approach of Henry George shows its strength. If land rent as a whole were the source of the funds, then the distributional issue would also be confronted.

The traditional Georgist proposal of returning to all the people the rental value of already occupied land forms the other blade of the scissors which must be forged to cut through the problem. As Cairncross notes (1989: 22), World Bank studies have documented part of the cause:

> Brazil's tax system (like that of many other countries, developed and developing) virtually exempts agriculture and turns it into a tax shelter. That adds to the demand for land and drives up its price, making it harder for the poor (who pay no income tax, so get no tax breaks) to buy. That in turn has helped to drive the landless north towards the Amazon.

One need only observe that the *latifundia* of South America would exist and the landless peasants be herded around even without tax breaks for agriculture making it *harder* for the poor, to show that the fundamental need is for land reform. But can the Greens be expected to lead the way on such an all-embracing issue?

The West German Greens are considering advocating a world climate fund, but its funding is seen in welfarist terms rather than as an opportunity for market reform. Draft foreign economic policy guidelines discussed at a *Die Grünen* conference in March 1990 proposed that the fund should receive one per cent of the GNP of each industrialized country. This is justified 'on the basis of the benefit the industrial countries have derived thus far from the exploitation of natural resources and from the free transfer of pollutant materials to the Third World countries,' according to a working paper. The concept of rich countries paying back 'historical debts' clearly is not a market reform concept; for bygones are bygones in the market place. 'Fairer prices reflecting social and ecological costs for raw materials, semi-finished and finished goods' are therefore seen as a separate reform of the world economic order.

In the Georgist framework, however, common development funds and fairer market prices are integrally related. The inclusion of full resource costs in the prices of Third World exports, and equal distribution of the proceeds, would have eliminated much of the exploitation that has occurred in international trade, as Jerome Heavey demonstrates in Chapter 6. An ideal framework for international financial payments would be organised by the United Nations and would level the global playing field for economic competition. In the absence of the necessary international cooperation, however, unilateral rent-claiming action by countries monopolising resources of global value might be the next best alternative.

VI

Another area where land rent is not being realized, both in the public and private sectors, and the environment is being damaged as a consequence, is in the inner cities. Vacant urban wasteland not only blights neighborhoods but pushes settlement further out into the countryside. But this is an area where the Georgist analysis is beginning to be heard amongst conservationists. In Britain, the Civic Trust, a major charity dedicated to protecting and improving the urban environment, recognises that land speculation is the most important cause of the problem and recommends that 'an urgent study of taxation on vacant land be commissioned by the government ...' (Civic Trust 1988: 37).

Two research organisations that promote the market economy — The Adam Smith Institute and the Institute of Economic Affairs — have found their contributors advocating the same solution to the problem, and doing so more positively (Loveless 1987: 29; Chisholm and Kivell 1987: 63). However, the IEA contributors limit their recommendation to vacant land alone: '... it does not follow that Henry George's ideas must be applied to the taxation of all land,' they write. They are also concerned, as is the Civic Trust, that the tax rate should be 'not so high as to encourage ill-conceived schemes.' In contrast, the Adam Smith Institute's contributor expresses no such reservations; he sees the tax as applying to all land.

The Green movement and Henry George's philosophy grow from the same ground: the finiteness of the Earth and the need to share her fairly. But George did not quarrel with mainstream economics' search for efficiency. His position forms the natural meeting place between orthodox economics and the 'other economics'. As the need actually to implement environmental policies becomes more pressing, many from both sides may yet find themselves attracted to it.

REFERENCES

Andelson R. V. (1991), 'Commons Without Tragedy', in Andelson R. V. ed. *Commons Without Tragedy,* London, Shepheard-Walwyn.

Bowers J. K. and Cheshire P. (1983), *Agriculture, the Countryside and Land Use,* Methuen, London and New York.

Brundtland, Gro Harlem (1987), 'Environment and Development: A Creative Challenge', the inaugural *Sir Peter Scott Lecture,* World Goodwill Occasional Paper, World Goodwill, London.

Cairncross F. (1989), *Costing the Earth: A Survey of the Environment*, Supplement in *The Economist*, 2-8 September, London.

Chapman D. (1990), 'Community Ground Rent Policy: What it is, and why we should amend it', Paper for the Economics Working Group, Green Party, January, London.

Chisholm M. and Kivell P. (1987), *Inner City Waste Land*, Hobart Paper 108, The Institute of Economic Affairs, London.

Civic Trust (1988), *Urban Wasteland Now*, London.

Dales J.H. (1968), 'Land, Water and Ownership', in *Canadian Journal of Economics*, November, Toronto.

Dasgupta P. (1990), 'The Environment as a Commodity', in *Oxford Review of Economic Policy*, Spring, Oxford.

Denman D. (1984), 'Land Value Taxation in Deep Water', in *Land & Liberty*, Nov.-Dec., London.

Ecology Party (1981), *Ecobulletin No. 7*, July/August, London.

Economist, The, (1990), 'Cleaning the air can foul up the economy,' 10-16 February, London.

Ekins P. ed. (1986), *The Living Economy: A New Economics in the Making*, Routledge & Kegan Paul, London.

Green Party (1988), *Manifesto for a Sustainable Society*, London.

Guppy N. (1980), 'Some Crucial Issues of Our Time', in *Environmental Conservation*, Vol. 7, No. 1, Foundation for Environmental Conservation, Geneva.

Johnson B. (1989), 'Why we must pay rent for our rainforest air-conditioning,' in *The Independent*, 14 September, London.

Land & Liberty (1987), 'Greens' Land Tax Gusto', July-August, London.

Loveless J. (1987), *Why Wasteland?*, Adam Smith Institute, London.

Myers N. (1979), *The Sinking Ark*, Pergamon Press, London and New York.

Noble E. (1979), 'Turangawaewae', in *Land & Liberty*, Nov.-Dec., London.

Oubridge B. (1986), 'Reopening the Great Land Debate', Paper for the Land Working Group, Green Party, October, London.
Pearce D., Markandya A., and Barbier E.A. (1989), *Blueprint for a Green Economy*, Earthscan Publications Ltd, London.
Peel Q., (1990), 'Rescuing the poisoned earth', and 'Farmers' woes', in *The Soviet Union*, a Financial Times Survey, 12 March, London.
Ridley N. (1989), *Policies against Pollution: the Conservative Record – and Principles*, Policy Study No. 107, Centre for Policy Studies, London.
Ryle M. (1988), *Ecology and Socialism*, Radius Books, London.
Spretnak C. and Capra F. (1986), *Green Politics, Palladin*, London.
United Nations Environment Programme (1988), *World Resources 1988-89*, Report by The World Resources Institute and The International Institute for Environment and Development, Basic Books, Inc., New York.
Wilmore P.L. (1989), 'Community Ground Rent and Basic Income', Draft Voting Paper in Autumn Conference supplement to *Econews*, Green Party, London.

8

Incentive Taxation and the Environment: complex — yet feasible

JÜRGEN BACKHAUS AND JACOB JAN KRABBE

MOST PEOPLE associate Henry George with his proposal for a single tax on land. Although this association is correct, since George tied his name to the single tax proposal for which he campaigned during his bid for mayor of New York City in 1886, it would be wrong to consider George either a political utopian or the author of a very limited scheme of real estate taxation. As we shall argue, his classic *Progress and Poverty* (1879) contains the blueprint of a comprehensive policy towards the environment and the prudent use of natural resources. The policy relies on essentially one instrument. The so-called land tax is a confiscatory tax of the rents drawn from owning all kinds of natural resources, not just land. Although the Georgist program of environmental policy employs just one instrument, it is carefully designed to be far reaching in its effects.

This chapter offers a general characterization of George's economics in section I, considers the rôle of nature in George's theory in more detail in section II, relates his vision to modern economic theory in section III, and discusses the price system with respect to regulating the scarce resources of nature in more detail in section IV. Section V develops a scenario for the reversal of natural resource use in a Georgist world, and section VI gives a practical example by way of illustration.

The bulk of this study is literally based on Henry George's *Progress and Poverty*. In trying to demonstrate the logic of the Georgist system with examples such as those addressed by the

American 'Super Fund' legislation, we move slightly beyond a literal interpretation of George while remaining true to his principles. We show that Henry George's basic approach to economic thinking is timely in the light of some pressing problems currently experienced by industrialized nations. This study makes essentially two contributions. The first three sections show what Henry George's contribution consisted in and how it stands up in the light of contemporary economic thinking. Ultimately, our claim of Henry George's timeliness can only be tested by trying to show what it can accomplish in dealing with a contemporary problem. We take the current clean up efforts in the context of the American Superfund program as our point of departure and suggest how a Georgist approach to industrial siting might result in a more economical use of natural resources, rendering efforts such as the Superfund superfluous in the future. Obviously, before implementing a Georgist system, a phase of transition would be necessary, depending on the different institutional circumstances, and designed to clean up past and present pollution.

I. Henry George's Economics: A General Characterization

As the title of his famous book suggests, Henry George was concerned with explaining the sources of economic growth in order to overcome poverty. George wanted to show why — under current institutional arrangements — *progress* had not eliminated poverty. His is a thoroughly development oriented or evolutionary approach, emphasizing the institutional causes and barriers to economic development, and remaining critical towards the classical doctrine on which he otherwise relies. To George a perfect example of an oversimplistic approach seems to be the Malthusian doctrine. As George sees it: 'For poverty, want, and starvation are by this theory not chargeable either to individual greed or to social maladjustments; they are the inevitable results of universal laws. . . .' (George 1979: 99).

For George, who wanted economics to be a science that could be used to solve social prolems, a good economic theory would identify a specific cause for a societal problem which could be corrected by appropriate political or social action. This pragmatic attitude emerges from the prose of this practical man, whose ambitions were not primarily those of scholarship but of social progress. He was not shy in registering his disagreement with economic writers who were trying to make economics a professional scholarly discipline. In emphasizing such differences, George rendered himself a disservice in that he never became part of a scholarly tradition, nor did he found an academic school of his own.[1] Consequently, many economists today would not even consider him as one of their own. The reasons for contemporary economists' scepticism *vis-à-vis* Henry George have little to do with his competence as an economist. As Schumpeter (1954: 865) points out:

> He was a self-taught economist, but he *was* an economist. In the course of his life, he acquired most of the knowledge and of the ability to handle an economic argument that he could have acquired by academic training as it then was. In this he differed to his advantage from most men who proffered panaceas. Barring his panacea (the Single Tax) and the phraseology connected with it, he was a very orthodox economist and extremely conservative as to methods.

Even about the Single Tax, Schumpeter has some kind words to say:

> The proposal itself, one of the many descendants of Quesnay's *impôt unique,* though vitiated by association with the untenable theory that the phenomenon of poverty is entirely due to the absorption of all surpluses by the rent of land, is not *economically* unsound, except in that it involves an unwarranted optimism concerning the yield of such a tax. In any case, it should not be put down as nonsense. If Ricardo's vision of economic evolution had been correct, it would even have been obvious wisdom. And obvious wisdom is in fact what George said in *Progress and Poverty* (Chapter I, Book IX) about the economic effects to be expected from a removal of fiscal burdens if such a removal were feasible.[2]

One has to agree with Schumpeter that the Single Tax issue may have stood in the way of a proper appreciation of George's contribution to economics. Most economists conversant with Henry George's writings would probably agree that the Single Tax on land proposal should not be considered his main contribution to economic analysis. We disagree. It was the central part and cornerstone of his political program, and he failed politically — for instance in his bid for the mayorship in New York City. Stripping his contribution of the language that befits programmatic literature, we feel that his writings contain a thorough contribution to natural resource economics. It is this aspect of his work that we try to set out on the following pages.

As Schumpeter remarks, despite the oratory, George was a fairly thorough economist. His basic contention is that there are institutions in society which hold back economic progress, bringing about unnecessary poverty of the many in the interests of a few. If these impediments to human ingenuity and industry were removed, poverty could be overcome and progress attained. As we shall explain later, his evolutionary theory could take on organic traits, society being considered like an organism. In that, he anticipates some more recent developments in systems theory. An organic approach is not surprising insofar as 'living nature' takes the central place in George's exposition. Only as he confronts nature and draws upon her riches, is man, in his ingenuity, able to produce wealth. While animals and plants, by virtue of their existence and proliferation, press against the limits of their subsistence, man, if given access to natural resources, is able to extend those limits for himself. He can play the laws of nature, as George puts it, ever more effectively using natural resources and thus create a surplus over what had previously been available.

The underlying notion is optimistic indeed, since George opined that as long as man can function in ecosystems in a creative way and remains unhindered by social institutions, the rate of progress would by far exceed the rate of growth in the population. The more men there are, the further division of labor can develop and the more ingenuity will be displayed in using nature's riches to man's advantages. In this sense, nature is the most important factor of production, and George would speak of land, labor and capital in that order. However, 'land' is a shorthand for all natural resources. As he himself points out, 'the term land includes all natural opportunities or forces' (1979: 162). This is an important terminological matter, since many misunderstandings of George's economics derive from too narrow a conception of what he understood by land. Even the much criticized concept of the Single Tax appears in a rather different light if we consider it as concerning the rent of all natural resources, not just land.

George distinguishes between the three standard factors of

production, as opposed to the two original factors, land and labor. Labor includes 'all human exertion' and hence land denotes all the natural resources which man finds at his disposal. Since the Georgist concept of land is of central importance for our discussion, and since he is explicit about it, let us quote *verbatim*:

> Land, labor, and capital are the three factors of production. If we remember that capital is thus a term used in contradistinction to land and labor, we at once see that nothing properly included under either one of these terms can be properly classed as capital. The term land includes, not merely the surface of the earth as distinguished from the water and the air, but the whole natural universe outside of man himself, for it is only by having access to land, from which his very body is drawn, that man can come in contact with or use nature. The term land embraces, in short, all natural materials, forces, and opportunities, and, therefore, nothing that is freely supplied by nature can be properly classed as capital. A fertile field, a rich vein of ore, a falling stream which supplies power, may give to the possessor advantages equivalent to the possession of capital, but to class such things as capital would be to put an end to the distinction between land and capital, and, as far as they relate to each other, to make the two terms meaningless (George 1979: 38).

As Schumpeter had pointed out, the starting point for George's economics is Ricardo. George pushed the Ricardian approach to an extreme by adding a special twist. Since property in land — and natural resources in general — establishes singular rights in those resources, George felt justified in saying that: 'Rent, in short, is the price of monopoly, arising from the reduction to individual ownership of natural elements which human exertion can neither produce nor increase' (1979: 167). He did not suggest, however, that land owners acted in a co-ordinated way so as to avoid competition among each other. By way of explanation, he adds that: 'The law of rent is, in fact, but a deduction from the law of competition, and amounts simply to the assertion that as wages and interests tend to a common level, all that part of the general production of wealth which exceeds what the labor and capital employed could have secured for themselves, if applied to the poorest natural agent in use, will go to the landowners in the shape of rent' (1979: 170). Hence, 'rent' is 'the share in the wealth produced which the exclusive right to the use of natural capabilities gives to the owner' (1979: 166). Consequently the private ownership in natural resources creates a claim on income that would otherwise have accrued in the form of wages or interest payments.

It is noteworthy that George's theory even extends into a macroeconomic dimension. An almost 'Keynesian' optimism shines through when he elaborates on how effective demand stimulates the creation of wealth. 'Just as the subsistence of the laborers who built the Pyramids was drawn not from a previously hoarded stock, but from the constantly recurring crops of the Nile Valley; just as a modern government when it undertakes a great work of years does not appropriate to it wealth already produced, but wealth yet to be produced, which is taken from producers in taxes as the work progresses; so it is that the subsistence of the laborers engaged in production which does not directly yield subsistence comes from the production of subsistence in which others are simultaneously engaged' (George 1979: 76).

Inhibiting forces to economic development are thus not to be found in the economic process as such; they are social, namely to be found in exclusive claims on natural resources.

In the course of time, as all the marginal land was to be claimed and the western frontier pushed all the way to the Pacific Ocean, George expected that the claim on the social product laid by the private ownership of land in the form of the land rent would steadily increase. As a matter of fact, this is not quite what we have observed even in densely populated western countries. While the actual development might have surprised Henry George, it is not in conflict with his economic theory. Indeed, his own theory, as he so aptly explained, would have suggested what really happened. Since man is able to play the games of nature, agricultural productivity has increased way beyond expectations, and this has reduced the relative scarcity of land. On the other hand, uses other than agriculture have assumed increasing importance. Yet, one would be wrong in focussing on land only. Henry George is talking about natural resources in general. And here it is true that the share of the social product claimed by the need to keep up commonly owned natural resources is steadily increasing. Of course, there is no element of proprietal rent here, rather we witness the opposite: an ever increasing scarcity due to overuse of commonly owned resources.

This development can be analysed in terms of George's crucial distinction between dysfunctional and functional land rent. The distinction refers, on the one hand, to income derived from the property of the resource as such, for instance to income derived from unworked land. Such income, according to George, has no productive purpose or function in the economic system. On the other hand, people may receive income from whatever work they have done to a natural resource in order to improve it. Improvements that have been made on a natural resource should generate income, the function of which is to stimulate such improvements.

The guarantee of private property rights in improvements to natural resources is not stipulated in an *a priori* fashion. George adopts a functionalist legitimization of private property titles. 'What is necessary for the use of land is not its private ownership, but the security of improvements' (George 1979: 398). Hence a functional distinction between private property rights in improvements and common property in the natural resources. The distinction is actually carried further. Since the productive use of natural resources may generate positive externalities, not every improvement can be privately appropriated. The externalities belong to the common property domain, too. 'The law of society is, each for all, as well as all for each. No one can keep to himself the good he may do, any more than he can keep the bad. Every productive enterprise, besides its return to those who undertake it, yields collateral advantages to others. If a man plant a fruit tree, his gain is that he gathers the fruit in its time and season. But in addition to his gain, there is a gain to the whole community. Others than the owner are benefited by the increased supply of fruit; the birds which it shelters by far and wide; the rain which it helps to attract falls not alone on his field; and, even to the eye which rests upon it from a distance, it brings a sense of beauty. And so with everything else' (George 1979: 435).

This telling passage implies that in addition to the rents from natural resources, the accumulated unappropriable improvements in these resources are part of the common property domain. This includes the entire cultural heritage of a country, landscape, the architectural harmony of historic cities and villages, and so on. Realizing that these common resources, to the extent that they are privately used, can potentially generate a stream of tax income up to 100% of the value of their rent, we wonder whether Schumpeter in his pessimistic assessment of the overall yield of the Georgist tax fully appreciated the extent of the tax base. However, in addition to the full rent from natural resources and the full rent from common property improvements, there is a further Georgist stream of tax revenue stemming from the obverse of those improvements guaranteed to their improvers.

It is perfectly in keeping with George's approach also to look at the impairments to natural resources. For instance, an industry that spoils the land by contaminating the groundwater or pouring poisonous substances into it reduces the value of this natural resource. Hence, such an industry should derive a negative stream of income for damaging the land. The principle is certainly applicable beyond land use. Consider an oil field beneath the sea. Applying George's reasoning, the developer should receive an income from exploring and developing the oil field, but not from the resource as such, upon which the owner state should levy a royalty. Likewise, fishermen should derive income from going out to sea and fishing, but not from the presence of the fish as such, unless they were fish farming and increasing the fish supply. Hence, in a Georgist world, fishermen would be expected to pay a fee for their use of the unimproved waters wherein they fish.

Now consider the case where an oil rig spills oil into the sea, destroying the fish. Although the fishermen do not own the resource, the operators of the oil rig have impaired the natural resource owned by the community, and for that impairment a negative income stream should be derived; or, to put it in less stilted language, the community should derive an income compensating for the abuse of the commonly owned natural resource. As Schumpeter sensed, this is perfectly in keeping with conservative economics. Broadening the scope of what natural resources comprise, however, also broadens the base of the Single Tax, and thus might sway those who are pessimistic about its fecundity. In addition, it should be pointed out that the Georgist tax, from the point of view of allocative efficiency, is fairly neutral. The Single Tax on natural resource use is a tax as close to the allocational neutrality of the textbook tax as one can get. It neither impedes productive economic activity, nor does it distort the price structure. And thirdly, it conforms to the benefit principle. Yet, it tends to economize on natural resources and to encourage sound economic growth, which in turn has a tax base broadening effect.

The last important element which we want to highlight is technology or, as George preferred to call it, 'mental power'. 'Mental power', he said, is 'the motor of progress' (1979: 507). This he meant with respect to three different aspects: mental power might be devoted to the extension of knowledge, or the improvement of methods, or else the betterment of social conditions. Just as did his contemporaries Gustav Schmoller and Lujo Brentano, he emphasized the latter by way of pointing out that: 'It has the same effect as increased skill or industry' (1979: 308).

There is a special reason why he felt that way. Without calling it by this name, George had a theory of rent seeking behaviour, and he was thus interested in making the distinction between human effort devoted to upholding the institutions which led to mere rent seeking, thus hindering progress, and that effort which led to genuine wealth creation. Obviously, the extension of effort on 'non-progressive purposes' should be minimalized in the interest of society. 'These non-progressive purposes in which mental power is consumed may be classified as maintenance and conflict. By maintenance I mean, not only the support of existence, but the keeping up of the social condition and the holding of advances already gained. By conflict I mean not merely warfare and preparation for warfare, but all the expenditure of mental power in seeking the gratification of desire at the expense of others, and in resistance to such aggression' (George 1979: 507).

II. Nature: A Central Focus of George's Theory

Wealth is said, by George, to consist of natural products, due to their having been secured, moved, combined, separated or in other ways modified by human desires (1979: 41). Natural resources are 'the storehouse upon which [man] must draw for all his needs, the material to which his labour must be applied for the supply of all his desires' (1979: 295). Labor is defined as the factor of production 'which gives value to material things' (1979: 42). Production is then adequately defined as a process of value creation. It is the creation of value, not reaping its fruits, which is considered production. Accordingly, in agriculture, production does not take place during harvest time 'but step by step during the whole process' (1979: 68). Here, as in various other respects, George's strongly resembles physiocratic theory. The resemblance is, however, not perfect. While for the physiocrats production is necessarily tied to biological processes that take place in nature, George considers production as the interaction between man and nature. Biological and non-biological forms of production may substitute for each other.

Today, we can look upon George's theory of production as a forerunner of an ecologically oriented economics such as the 'materials balance' approach of such economists as Kneese, Ayres and d'Arge (Kneese 1970), but this approach remains more in a mechanistic systems theoretic context. Consider the following: 'Life does not use up the forces that maintain life.' And he adds: 'The human being, physically considered, is but a transient form of matter, a changing mode of motion. The matter remains and the force persists' (George 1979: 133-134). George postulated that an increase in population density will always cause an increase in welfare. Schmoller was more cautious in suggesting that in his time and place, that is Germany at the end of the 19th century, as a consequence of technical innovation and institutional change, there was room for growth in the population. Both George and Schmoller thought of economies that develop; their point of view was dynamic.

From today's point of view, we are surprised by George's optimism. Will industrial production not use up natural resources? George wrote for a time when the frontier was still moving west and he did not consider the destruction of natural resources through the industry of men. However, although he may have underestimated the importance of raw materials, his theory contains the germs that enable us to adequately deal with such a use of natural resources, as we point out in sections 4-6.

In discussing nature, George focussed on what he considered to be the shortcomings of classical thought. In particular, he was critical of Malthus, Ricardo and John Stuart Mill in as much as they asserted that an increase in population would result in a decrease of the average welfare of the populace. Based on this criticism, he formulated an alternative philosophy of development, which, according to him, does not suffer from shortcomings similar to those of classical theory. Yet, sometimes one gets the impression that in his critical zeal he was pushing too far.

Biological processes take a central place in George's scheme of thought. We may even recognize in his writings the modern ideas of an ecological equilibrium and an ecologically sustainable process of production. George speaks of a 'natural balance' between 'the reproductive and destructive forces of nature' (1979: 196). In his vision, the remuneration of the factors of production depends on regularities by which the living organisms of nature abide. His theory of distribution is certainly consistent. The incomes of all three factors of production are all determined in terms of the same reasoning. This consistency has a price. George's theory of distribution renders but a partial view. His notion of production contains much more than just reaping the fruits of nature. Yet, beyond agriculture, the theory of distribution remains incomplete — although certainly amendable.

Production, says George, 'does not merely mean the making of things, but includes the increase of value gained by transporting or exchanging things' (1979: 155). He distinguishes three 'modes' of production, namely: '*Adapting*, or changing natural products either in form or in place so as to fit them for the satisfaction of human desires. *Growing*, or utilising the vital forces of nature, as by raising vegetables or animals. *Exchanging*, or utilising, so as to add to the general sum of wealth, the higher powers of those natural forces which vary with locality, or of those human forces which vary with situation, occupation, or character' (George 1979: 186).

Only one 'mode', namely 'growing', determines the prices of the factors of production. In other words, 'the reproductive or vital force of nature' (1979: 182) determines the prices of the factors of production. While the other two modes are well considered important in the process of production, they play no rôle in his theory of price formation. Still, George talks about the 'productive power in men' (1979: 184), and these powers fall mainly within the mode of production characterized as 'adapting natural products'.

George was certainly right in saying that institutional changes in economy and society can result in such an increase in welfare on earth that many more people could live on it than up to now, when

Georgist reforms have taken place on only a very modest scale. Where such reforms have taken place, they have actually been very successful. George emphasizes economies of scale that a country can reap as its population grows. He also pin-points a fair number of inefficient uses of the means of production. Yet we think that he went too far in asserting that an unlimited number of people might be able to live a decent life on earth.

A brief look at his method may help us illuminate his thinking. George worked empirically. He drew conclusions from observations, and California served him as a special testing ground. The growth in California's population, which allowed for a deeper division of labor, is considered not only a condition but even the cause of an increase in her welfare. In this respect as in others, his approach parallels that of the historical school and notably Schmoller (Schmoller 1900: 182 [1]; 184 [2], who talked of the *Verdichtung der Bevölkerung*, a term which not only means an increasing population density but likewise an increase in opportunities of productive interaction among men. But George went further than Schmoller.

Classical thought, on the contrary, was a search for defining general equilibria. George did not appreciate this aspect of the classical approach, and consequently he did not accept the classical conclusions. Equally noteworthy in George's thought is his use of biological ideas. We find a similar approach with Roscher (see Krabbe 1987). Statements such as life 'does not use up the forces that maintain life' make him a comfortable neighbor to such ecology economists as Nicholas Georgescu-Roegen who also use organic models (Georgescu-Roegen 1976).

As far as George is concerned, population growth can for our practical purposes continue uninhibited, as long as men have enough 'elbow room' (1979: 134). We feel that assertions such as these, motivated by his desire to disprove Malthus, not only go too far but are also in discord with the basic structure of his thinking. George does not need these extreme statements. On the contrary: his theory allows one to develop remedies against the overuse of natural resources that might put the subsistence of men at peril.

III. George's Vision in Terms of Economic Theory

George's approach to reality may be described in the following way. His method was an integration of the approach discussed in the previous section and classical thought. Hence, one might say that he combined a dynamic theory of an organistic type with classical equilibrium theory. The Ricardian rent theory, which he so vigorously opposed when discussing the sources of economic welfare, is nevertheless the basis for his theory of distribution. As he said himself, his integration took place 'in an original and subtle way.' Let us explain.

When George tried to describe how income is being distributed among the factors of production (land, labor and capital, identified and named in this order), he was dealing with an equilibrium model that could not be more classical. Yet in this model we can distinguish a macro level and a micro level. George suggested that the factors of production and the income accruing to them have to be defined in a consistent way (1979: 160). The distinction must be based on logical reasoning, and the attribution of income to the factors of production must be possible without leaving a residual. His basic macroeconomic equation (1979: 171) is this:

$$\text{Produce} = \text{Rent} + \text{Wages} + \text{Interest}$$

Produce is the national income minus depreciation. Rent is the net income from the land. Wages are the sum of all incomes from labor, including the wages of the entrepreneurs. Interest is the price for using capital. According to George, the net land rent is an improper part of income, and the implication of that assumption is revealed when the equation is rewritten as:

$$\text{Produce} - \text{Rent} = \text{Wages} + \text{Interest}$$

The larger the dysfunctional land rent, other things being equal, the less of national income can be distributed as wages and interest.

On the micro level, the factors of production and the income they derive are defined in such a way that nature becomes the focal point again. The land rent is discussed in classical terms: 'The rent of land is determined by the excess of its produce over that which the same application can secure from the least productive land in use' (George 1979: 168). His notion of the interest rate again reminds us of the physiocrats. The amount needed to compensate the capital owners for the use of the capital, according to George, equals the increase in the 'vital forces of nature' (1979: 182) accomplished with the investment. The interest rate is thus based upon 'the active power of nature; the principle of growth, of reproduction', this being due to the fact that there is life on earth (1979: 181). Ultimately, interest depends upon the reproductive powers of nature. While capital itself is sterile, the average power of increase which attaches to capital stems from its use in 'reproductive modes'.

Likewise, trade occurs because nature is so varied in different places and trade makes more effective use of the fruits of nature. By 'interchangeability' the creation of value with raw materials is related to biological processes of production (George 1979: 182). Labor income is defined in similar terms. 'Wages depend upon ... the produce which labor can obtain at the highest point of natural productiveness open to it without the payment of rent' (1979: 213) or similarly, on p. 205: 'what a given amount of labor will yield will vary with the powers of the natural opportunities to which it is applied.' The microeconomic framework in which the factors of production operate is perfect competition in all markets, and the price of a factor of production depends on both the average and the marginal productivity, or else the average and marginal income from that factor. The model which is basically static is being dynamized with George's organic theory of development based on nature, which we discuss in the next section.

In the static model, the net land rent is considered an improper income and thus an improper cost component. In the ideal world of things which the writer aimed at, the land rent as defined above will be claimed by government and will be its main source of revenue. We noticed earlier that this idea has been often ridiculed as reflecting a gross overestimation of the possible revenue. Not unlike many modern welfare theorists, George was indeed optimistic about the likely behavior of those in public office. Government will not act so as to maximize the rent revenue, that is as a monopolist, but instead in order to maximize social welfare. Government will levy a user charge on land, reflecting the 'shadow price' of its use, whereby the shadow price would be calculated under the assumption of perfect competition.

Yet Henry George was clearly not quite as naive about the courses of action in which governments are likely to engage as we might think at first glance. Interspersed throughout the book are critical remarks about the dangers of government bureaucracy and their proclivity to supporting monopolized industry. Yet George did more than just issue warnings. Properly interpreted, George proposed an intricate tax constitution with the most parsimonious means. The tax constitution was designed to harness the taxing government in the interest of economic prosperity, forcing the public authority to make the most prudent use of available natural resources taking into account the long term perspective. How can this claim be sustained? Let us look at the different features of the Georgist system and how they fit together.

The first feature is the obvious simplicity of the tax system, of which George was very proud. There is just one tax, the tax on natural resources broadly conceived, and the tax rate can be set at up to 100% without risking disincentive effects. This important feature of minimizing the excess burden of taxation is achieved by splitting the property rights in the functional way described above. The truly appropriable improvements form private property rights, and the remainder stays in the public domain. Whoever wants to use any aspects of the public domain for his private purposes is expected to compensate the community for this use. This implies that it becomes increasingly costly to put common property resources to a sub-optimal use. George minces no words about this feature of his system: 'If land were taxed to anything near its rental value,' as he suggested it should be, 'no one could afford to hold land that he was not using, and consequently, land not in use would be thrown open to those who would use it. Settlement would be closer, and, consequently, labor and capital would be enabled to produce much more with the same exertion' (1979: 413-414).

A constant intensification of resource use, apart from stimulating economic processes in general and undermining the entry barriers created by mere priority in resource use, broadens the tax base and thereby allows the public sector to grow. The public sector can, however, only grow as long as it stimulates this search for an ever more efficient use of natural resources. This implies that the fiscal condition for government growth is only met [if the government constantly disappoints traditional elements] in society, bringing about dislocation by forcing new and more efficient resource use upon conceivably reluctant traditional resource users. In the Georgist system, the tax state does have a redistributive function. But it does not redistribute from productive to non productive members in society. On the contrary, it redistributes from less efficient producers to more efficient producers, from established lines of production to new entrants, with the intention to relieve poverty by stimulating progress. The Georgist tax constitution shares some of the features discussed in the modern literature on constitutional public finance, notably the restriction of the tax base and the incentives presented to government to make the restricted tax base more productive.[3]

In the form it was presented, somehow George's vision does not seem to fit the picture of contemporary highly developed western economies. While he does consider nature in the physical sense as a supplier of 'raw materials,' he may have underestimated the extent to which industrial development is based on such supplies. Consider the following statement on technological development:

> 'So, every improvement or invention, no matter what it be, which gives to labor the power of producing more wealth, causes an increased demand for land and its direct products, and thus tends to force down the margin of cultivation' (1979: 249).

This forcing down of the margin of cultivation, George considers in purely organic terms. In developed western economies one might expect technological development to take the form of depleting and exhausting the stock of natural resources. A different view emerges if we follow George's own definition and interpret his notion of land more broadly in order to include all manner of natural resources. George does so himself, as when he was trying to refine his model (1979: 258) in order, for instance, to include 'mineral lands.'

The exhaustion of a mine is clearly different from the exploitation of a waterfall. George includes both in his definition of land. While the waterfall continues to fall and will, under normal circumstances, not be exhausted by the sheer tapping of the power of the falling water, a mine will generally be depleted. As we recall, only improvements in natural resource use are protected by private property rights, but impairments, such as the depletion of a mine, are clearly not. In a Georgist system of natural resource use, the depletion of a mine has to be compensated for, with the community receiving the rental value from the site as well as the rental value from the extracted materials according to the valuation of the most productive user. This more comprehensive system of compensation will certainly check the exhaustion of natural resources which many environmental economists rightly fear. On the other hand, George did not want to prevent the exhaustion of natural resources, when this was in the interest of progress. He clearly did not want to leave the ore in the mind or the coal in the ground. Yet the Georgist system requires compensation for the impairment on the basis of the rental value of the natural resource.

Economic growth in western societies has not really led to a drastic increase in the demand for agricultural land. The opposite is almost true. It has, however, led to a dramatic increase in the extent and manifold ways in which claims are laid on the most multifarious aspects of nature, such as the water, the air, vegetation and climate, soil and animal organisms, to name but a few.

There is one basic difference between land, on which most of George's attention was centered, and other natural resources of which he speaks only occasionally. The (surface of) land can be surveyed and parcelled out, fenced and defended against intruders and in this way made a private property. For most of the other natural resources, such a privatization process would be much more difficult and it is often inconceivable. Take air as an example, and let us invoke standard collective goods theory. Air is clearly indivisible. It moves about and cannot be contained. Fresh and good air is scarce, yet it must be a collective good, since nobody can be excluded from breathing it. Still, alternative uses are clearly rivalrous. If a brewery ejects its fumes, the sweet smell is laid over the entire city and nobody in the city can really escape breathing it: surely there will be some who may object? This is even more so in cases where paper mills, crude oil refineries or combustion in dense traffic are concerned. Note that the brewery may have been in the city for many centuries, and claiming a traditional right to operate in its existing location.

The same would apply to groundwater. A difficulty with establishing property rights for individuals or localities over groundwater reservoirs is that the location may not be completely known and may even be subject to change. Normally, rights of use will be established that can be monitored by some common authority.[4] Yet, the common property can be impaired. If someone contaminates the groundwater, all the wells in an entire region may have to be sealed. Similarly, the healthiness of the soil affects everybody, by way of vegetation, wildlife and climate. Yet, it can be readily contaminated and such contamination may be almost impossible to reverse.

Vegetation and wildlife form an ecological system with the environment. While man has, as George puts it, the gift of playing nature, he also has the gift of misreading the rules. The introduction of one particular specie can upset the entire system, with inescapable consequences for everyone. So one would say that the entire natural environment is a common property resource, and the conservation of it a task from which everybody can profit, and which may be spoiled by very few. Finally, it is not only the natural environment that has this feature; the historical and cultural heritage, a particularly designed landscape, and the historic architecture of a city have common property features.

IV. Scarcity and the Price System

In chapter five of the 7th book, Henry George describes how property in land had made it scarce and unavailable for farming and ranching, when, in fact, plenty of it was still unranched and unfarmed but held in anticipation of increased future value. Only a superficial reading of *Progress and Poverty* would nourish the impression that, in George's opinion, it was the institution of private property and the market system that had created this scarcity. Let us look at his rendition in detail. 'The republic has entered upon a new era,' he says, because the frontier has been pushed all the way to the Pacific Ocean and there is no free land to be claimed anymore.

> The public domain is almost gone — a very few years will end its influence, already rapidly failing. I do not mean to say that there will be

> no public domain. For a long time to come there will be millions of acres of public lands carried on the books of the Land Department. But it must be remembered that the best part of the continent for agricultural purposes is already *overrun*, and that it is the poorest land that is left. It must be remembered that what remains comprises the great mountain ranges, the sterile deserts, the high plains fit only for grazing. And it must be remembered that much of this land which figures in the reports as open to settlement is unsurveyed land, which has been *appropriated by possessory* claims or locations which do not appear until the land is returned as surveyed. California figures on the books of the Land Department as the greatest land state of the Union, containing nearly one hundred million acres of public land — something like one-twelfth of the whole public domain. Yet so much of this is covered by railroad grants or held in the way of which I have spoken ... (George 1979: 391 — our italics).

The land, then, has been taken, claims have been staked, railroad companies have built lines and hence were able to claim the land surrounding it, and the first credible use determines what happens with the resource in the future. It is only after private property has been established that a market can begin to function.

George does not describe market forces as allocating the land initially; the allocation of land is decidedly a nonmarket one. The claims need to be officially sanctioned and the new land must be surveyed before a trade in it can begin. Hence, the land will be held in reserve until that time when the title is secure and thus tradable. We notice, of course, that it is not only the institution of property that is necessary for a market in land to develop. A transfer of title requires a contract and thus a legal environment in which contracts can be drawn up, executed and guarded against breach. Thirdly, both property and contract cannot exist as institutions without the third legal institution, liability, to protect the other two. There is no property in anything without a liability on whoever trespasses.

In fact the phenomenon George was describing involves not an orderly transfer of private property in land, but a rather less orderly 'run' to stake private claims on common property. His remedy, as is well-known, calls for taxing the rent derived from the ownership title, while not taxing the improvements made by people to the land.

This remedy neutralizes the negative economic effects of a speculative 'run' on natural resources. By claiming a resource, one incurs a tax liability. Improving the resource remains the only lucrative course of action, which benefits both the private owner of the improvements and the taxing authority.

Setting up private property arrangements to allow markets to determine the use of aspects of common property resources is extremely difficult. As Hahn and Hester (1986) described in their analysis of the Emissions Trading Program adopted by the American Environmental Protection Agency, most of these markets have to be set up within particular corporations, since the ways in which various polluters affect the common property resource (the air) are diverse. In one particular location, there may not be many polluters competing with each other. However, one polluter may have several technologies or processes which bear upon the same common resource. Hence, most of these programs involve policies directed at one particular polluter, employing emission reduction credits with the specific techniques of 'bubbles', 'netting' and 'banking' all designed at (arbitrarily) restricting the common property used by the polluter, but allowing him to make the most efficient use of his various polluting activities.

The standard setting itself is arbitrary in the sense that it does not allow an optimal overall use of the common property in question. It will invariably start from the current level of polluting activities and accept the current distribution of polluting activities among various polluters. This acknowledges the grandfather rights of the traditional polluters and restricts access to new ones. The process is identical to the one described by George with respect to land. The traditional users of common resources did not acquire a right to pollute; they took it and continue to use it in an environment which changes the value of such rights.

The grandfathering of rights to natural resources (at the expense of potential new uses) is not only central to Henry George's concern and approach to economic policy; it is also at the heart of contemporary environmental policy debates. Wallace Oates, in his discussion of the rôle of economic incentives in environmental policy, notes the opposition to incentive-based environmental policies 'from pollutors themselves'. With respect to tradable permits, he notes that they have traditionally 'not been distributed by auction. Instead they have been distributed free of charge to existing pollutors. Such a grandfathering of pollution rights greatly reduces the opposition of existing sources to the program' (Oates 1988: 6-7). And Edmund H. Mantell, in a paper dealing with the economics and the politics of environmental protection, makes grandfathering traditional resource use the central feature of his proposal. We quote the central passage from his paper:

> The Gordian Knot of conflicting special interests might be cut by legislative action to assign property rights on the basis of the pre-existence of the challenged economic activity. To explain, when firms are determined to enjoy property rights which permit pollution, there should be no legal obstacle and no objections to paying firms which curtail their production or even leave the industry (or the site) as a result of corrective policy. It is the assignment to these firms of enforceable property rights which legitimizes the selective enforcement/subsidy policy.
>
> However, firms which have never produced pollutants have not exercized a property right and the denial to them of the right to pollute *de novo* does not exact from them a benefit which they previously enjoyed. This means, for example, that new entrants into the industry would not be eligible for subsidy payments, and, moreover, they could not expect selective enforcement of pollution abatement regulation to be imposed on them (Mantell 1985: 444).

The proposal is strikingly at variance with a Georgist approach to regulating natural resource use. By selective enforcement Mantell means that existing industries, if they are particularly opposed to environmental regulations and if they can muster sufficient political support, should be spared application of these standards. Such politically well heeled industries are, of course, the monopolies Henry George tried to politically neutralize with his system of dynamic taxation driven by the process of technical innovation. New technologies make the use of natural resources more valuable and therefore, by virtue of the rental tax, tend to drive the traditional users out of the resource use, unless they improve their productivity. Selective enforcement of environmental regulations would render the Georgist process inoperative.

Grandfathering traditional uses, on the other hand, with tradable permits, although bestowing an unearned windfall gain on them which George feels belongs to society, at least does not undercut the process of technical change. The traditional users relinquish the traditional use, in their own interest, by selling the tradable permits to a bidder whose bid exceeds the value of the permit to the traditional user with his obsolescent process of production. Hence, issuing tradable permits to current users, as done by the Environmental Protection Agency in the United States right now, at least lets the opportunity costs of alternative resource use enter the economic decisions of traditional users.

Henry George's solution is attractive because nature becomes an increasingly scarce input into industrial production. As described by George, this scarcity is exacerbated by the fact that old uses are already imposing their claims on natural resources, and with population density increasing and possible uses multiplying as well as standards of living increasing, many new uses of natural resources are denied because of the existing ones. Even areas of hitherto worthless but unimpaired natural resources become valuable and command a premium. A contemporary example in the spirit of George may underline the point.

The Black Hills are a mountainous area located at the end of the big plains and extending through the Dakotas, Nebraska, Wyoming and Montana. After many protracted conflicts and after the Sioux-Indians had been pushed all the way to the mountains, in 1851 the government recognized the Sioux-Indians' title to some sixteen million acres and agreed to provide food rations for ten years.[5] In return, the Sioux allowed wagon trails to be built through their territory. Conflicts continued and after the battle at Little Big Horn in 1876, Congress cut off the food rations. The conflict ended when the Indians ceded seven million acres of the Black Hills to the United States in return for assistance. In 1923, the Sioux filed a claim for $500m in compensation for the Black Hills. The claim was dismissed in various courts, but continued to be refiled until 1980, when the Supreme Court awarded $600m to the Sioux for the Black Hills. By then, however, the tribe tried to dismiss its attorney for having taken the wrong legal strategy, refusing to accept the money and insisting on receiving the Black Hills back. What was essentially worthless a century ago — except for the soon disappointed hope of finding gold — what had been given away in exchange for temporary assistance in rations, through the intense process of industrialization on the private land and the continued protection of the unceded

Indian lands in the public domain, had become a most valuable resource. It was finally valued higher than the compensation payment which, at the time, was the highest ever recorded in such claims.

Technological progress and the intensified use of natural resources results in an increasing value placed on unimpaired natural resources. Traditional users of natural resources derive an ever increasing rent without paying compensation, and their grandfather rights become obstacles to competing uses of natural resources. This serves to impede technical progress.

V. Reversal of Use

An important aspect of Henry George's approach is that he separates natural resources from the improvements that may have been made upon them (which he calls capital). The first remains in social ownership, while investment in the second is attributed to whichever private agent made the change. Those changes are always positive in George's context. This split between the natural resource and the alterations made upon it is an important ingredient for an optimal repartitioning of property rights to enhance an economy's ability to grow and progress (Furubotn 1981). The split establishes a criterion on the basis of which renewable natural resources, once dedicated to a particular use, can be automatically reclaimed when the purpose no longer exists or ceases to be as pressing as it used to be. The issue turns on a very simple consideration. Natural resources are limited, while the potential uses are unlimited, changing over time with technical progress: hence the need to reclaim natural resources according to present valuations.

The basic idea can be discussed with reference to the attempt to clean up hazardous waste.[6] In the United States, as in many other industrialized countries over the last hundred years, hazardous waste has been placed in many thousands of locations. An exact number of such sites is not yet known, but there are tens of thousands of them. This waste poses serious threats to human health and the environment. While it may sometimes be possible to determine who deposited the waste, the common law (torts) approach of invoking liability and claiming compensation has clearly proven inadequate.

There are several reasons for this inadequacy. Firstly, evidence as to responsibility for depositing hazardous waste is difficult to collect and sustain in court, particularly if the waste was deposited long ago. Secondly, cause and effect relationships are difficult to establish in environmental cases, since the ecological system interacts in itself and multiple causations occur routinely. Thirdly, even if a tort-feasor can be identified and the tort (i.e. damage) be proven, there may not be a party that has standing and that could, consequently, claim compensations. This is the case if the damage has not yet occurred. It is also the case if the damage has occurred but has affected a large number of people diversely, so a class cannot be formed. Fourthly this points to weaknesses in using the tort system as a discovery procedure for such waste. As a matter of fact, the tort system has a number of built-in incentives for concealing the extent of the waste and its perils, while establishing few countervailing incentives to expose the threat. Fifthly, if the first four reasons have not proven to be enough of a hindrance, the tort system normally can handle only the relatively smaller cases, since the damage inflicted upon a community by a hazardous waste catastrophe would routinely exceed the net asset value of the tort-feasor.

The Comprehensive Environmental Response, Compensation and Liability Act, commonly known as Superfund, along with similar State legislation, has effectively supplanted the tort system with a complex mixture of regulation, public works and litigation. While the Superfund project has supplanted the tort system, the Fund has not discontinued but strengthened it. This has to do with the financial arrangements of the Superfund program. The Environmental Protection Agency which administers the Superfund may identify potentially responsible parties that are strictly, retroactively, jointly and severally liable. In principle, the government may collect from any single party the entire costs of clean up of a site to which hundreds have contributed. Yet the difficulty of carrying out the program, which is largely financed out of a tax on petroleum and feed-stocks, has led, during the first six years, to very little waste being removed or made safe.

To illustrate how George's economics contributes to a policy oriented analysis of these problems, we discuss the problem of hazardous waste as if it had occurred in a Georgist type world. In George's world, the ownership of land entitled you to the value of the improvements only, not to the value of the land. If hazardous waste is deposited on land, that activity can, of course, hardly be called an improvement. It is the opposite. Someone who disimproves or impairs the land would have to compensate the community for this land abuse and, finally, to revert the land back to its original state. This would apply irrespective of whether someone impairs his 'own' land or that of another party. Hence, specific uses will give rise to a tax liability. Three problems need to be addressed in turn. (1) How can such a scheme be administered? (2) How can the reconvertibility of a common property resource be assured, and (3) when should reversal occur?

The administration of his scheme is a point George addresses at length. He was anxious not to create a new bureaucracy in charge of overseeing land use. Instead, his scheme uses the assessment that are routinely carried out for property tax purposes — i.e. the rental value of land in its unimproved state. The process would operate fairly similarly if impairments had to be assessed. Firstly, the common property would be assessed in terms of its natural pristine state, yielding the (resource) rent that had to be paid. Secondly, the user would owe the respective tax authority the value of the impairments imposed upon the property. Where there is a market for the properties, the figure can be readily obtained from the market. A different question arises when the common property cannot be marketed. This question will be addressed in the next section.

One of the reasons for the tort system to fail is the likely inadequacy of net assets owned by the tort-feasor to cover the damage. A similar problem arises in our context, if we want to make sure that the abused common property can be recoverted to its original state. Normally, such a reconversion will be very costly. This problem, in the Georgist world, does have a straightforward solution. The user of the common property can be asked to file three valid bids from competent contractors with a demonstrable track record outlining the clean up operation needed and the price required. These bids, one might assume, would be valid for a limited period of time, such as a year. The user could then either deposit a bank guarantee covering the average amount of the three bids; or carry insurance to the same extent. This *bonding* would obviously have to be revised continuously, depending on the expiration of the bids, and this continuous revision would reflect probable costs in the clean up operation as they occur over time.[7]

There is, then, a dynamic element built into the proposal. Old users, instead of being grandfathered, are continuously confronted with the true opportunity costs to the community of their particular use of the resource. There is a strong incentive to think about production processes that spare the environment. Conversion will occur when either the impairment charge, reflecting the willingness to pay off competing users, notably potential new users, increases to the point where the old use of the common property resource has become uneconomical to the user; or when the alternative benefits to the community from competing uses grow beyond the benefits hitherto received.

The vexing difficulties with hazardous waste clean up that the Superfund operation is saddled with would not have occurred in George's world. Most of these difficulties stem from a strong desire on the part of the potentially responsible parties to conceal the true extent and nature of the waste deposited. These difficulties explain why the American environmental protection agency, having spent $3 billion and committed another $1.5 billion on Superfund projects, by the end of 1989 had not cleaned up more than 40 out of 12,024 sites on the Superfund priority list of the nation's worst poison dumps. Instead, the money was spent on gathering information, identifying waste dumps and establishing responsibilities and reliable clean up techniques (Hobbs Sheibla 1989).

The Georgist proposal outlined here generates opposite incentives. The bid requirement for the clean up operation necessitates a continuous analysis of all the relevant implications of the use of the common property that eventually has to be reversed. The fiscal incentives work their way through the organization of the (corporate) user to safeguard the quality of the environment. The American Superfund experience allows us a glimpse at the extent of those fiscal incentives in a Georgist world. Cleaning up just the toxic sites for which the Superfund has been created is estimated to require $500 billion, according to the Congressional Office of Technology Assessment (Hobbs Sheibla 1989: 18). In a Georgist world, this amount would have been remitted into the state coffers, together with compensation for all those impairments of natural resources which are not toxic for which estimates are not available. In a Georgist world, these expenditures, instead of being financed out of tax revenues (with their accompanying disincentive effects), would have constituted public revenue. In addition, public regulators would have been free to determine the most appropriate treatment of impaired sites. The information, instead of having to be collected through an extremely costly procedure, would already have been available due to the bid requirement described above.

VI. An Example in Practice

George was a thoroughly practical man and he saw no difficulty in administering his proposal, the 'remedy'. Assessing the rent of land and the value of the improvements could be done with reasonable accuracy, since there was a market in land to check against. However he noted that many of the resources that cannot but be held in common property for that reason have no market, and hence, no ready and undisputable way of assessing their value. This lack of accuracy does not imply the absence of even a rough idea of what a particular resource may be worth to a particular community, even if a precise and monetizable price tag is nowhere to be found.

Again, the Georgist solution is reasonably straightforward. Consider the case of a county that has a precious forest, with a lake nearby that serves as its water reservoir. Hunting, fishing and other recreational activities take place here.[8] A paper mill applies for permission to operate on the margin of the forest, drawing on the raw wood produced in both this forest and the neighboring communities. The paper mill approaches the county with the prospect of creating a certain number of jobs and additional tax revenues. Under current circumstances, the county will normally be glad to grant the permit if it is short of job opportunities or tax revenues. Let us assume the pollution from the mill is reversible and not externalized beyond the jurisdiction of the community. The paper mill would change the environment, however. It emits an unmistakable smell, it uses large amounts of water, the forest will change its composition of trees, which will change the vegetation in general and wildlife in particular. The constant noise and smell affect the recreational value of the area. Under current tax and tenure arrangements, should the paper industry fall upon hard times in the future, the new jobs may likely be lost. But if the paper mill remains, the recreational area also is lost. With the paper mill in place, a new venture would be hard to attract into the formerly recreational area. A Georgist approach would lead to a different outcome.

Since there is no apparent way of assessing the value of the permit to the county, other than by saying that the paper mill will bring jobs and tax revenues, let us assume that we go by these two figures, a certain number of jobs (L) and a certain amount of tax revenues (T). To the treasurer of the county, one figure translates into the other, since a job with the paper mill on average carries a certain additional net revenue to the county. The permit could then be granted provided the mill yields what it promised: the approximate number of new jobs and the approximate additional net tax revenue. The permit would be conditional upon fulfilling that promise, being automatically revoked if one or the other of the criteria were not met. In addition, as outlined in the preceding section, should the firm — for instance due to the termination of the permit — cease operations, the area which it had affected would have to be reconverted to its original pristine state. This reconversion would have been ensured by the bonding procedure outlined in the preceding section.

Such an arrangement should provide for both parties to the transaction, the mill and the county, to be able to discontinue the exchange of jobs and tax revenues against the use of natural resources after proper notice has been given. The extent of that notice would have to depend upon the time horizon needed for a businesslike investment decision.

This proposal is one of a number of possible variations on George's framework (Backhaus 1988). It splits property into two parts, the natural resource which remains with the community, and the improvements (the plant of the paper mill) which is private. This is extended into the area where there is no market for natural resources. A collective valuation procedure must substitute for a market evaluation. It takes into account the possibility that a particular use, instead of making improvements on the natural resource, impairs its usability for alternative future uses. Compensation is required for such impairments.

VII. Conclusions

A substantial number of natural resources are inefficiently used. We refer not only to the overuse of common resources, but also to the disincentive effects entailed in the acquisition of property rights by means of the grandfathering of established uses. Grandfathering can serve as an effective entry barrier to new industry. To develop a remedy, we have sketched out an alternative system in the spirit of Henry George. This paper stays true to Henry George, however, in systematically covering all natural resources, and in suggesting that damage to natural resources can be effectively dealt with along the lines of Henry George's fiscal policy. And we have shown how industrial development can be approached to ensure an efficient use of natural resources that satisfies the criteria set out before and promotes progress to overcome poverty.

NOTES

1. In the latter part of his life, after *Progress and Poverty* had become an international best seller, George spent most of his time as a public lecturer. This may be the reason why, all over the world, there are (sometimes small) political groups claiming to propagate his ideas. Interestingly, the ideas of these groups differ substantially one from the other, occupying the entire political spectrum from left to right.
2. While there is still disagreement about the yield of a Georgist land tax, some recent estimates approach 25% of GNP. See Cord (1985), and Banks (1989).
3. For this literature, see for instance the seminal work by Geoffrey Brennan and James M. Buchanan, 1979.
4. With respect to water use, see Victor Brager and W.E. Marten (1989).
5. This account is based on the report in the *National Law Journal*, Vol. 9, nr. 47 (1987), pp. 20-25.
6. The following discussion is based on an internal and preliminary account, that Peter Reuter of the Rand Corporation was kind enough to show. The material we are discussing here is public knowledge.
7. This bonding requirement is similar to the one required under the US Surface Mining Control and Reclamation Act of 1977 (P.L. 95-87). This law calls for bonding and specifies landscape contours, vegetation, *etc.*
8. For a further description of this procedure, see: Jürgen Backhaus, 1988.

REFERENCES

Backhaus, J. G. 'Justiziable Bedarfsprüfung im Genehmigungsverfahren: ein Lüneburger Vorschlag', in: Jörg Finsinger and Jürgen Simon (eds.) *Recht und Risiko,* Munich: VVF, 1988, pp. 94-112.

Banks, Ronald. *Costing the Earth,* London: Shepheard Walwyn, 1989.

Brager, V. and Marten, W. E. 'Allocating a "Scarce" Resource, Water in the West: More Marketlike Incentives Can Extend Supply but Constraints Demand Acquitable Policies'. *American Journal of Economics and Sociology,* Vol. 48.3, July 1989, pp. 259-271.

Brennan, G. and Buchanan, J. M. *The Power to Tax,* Cambridge: Cambridge University Press, 1980.

Cord, S. 'How Much Revenue Would a Full Land Value Tax Yield?', *The American Journal of Economics and Sociology,* Vol. 44, no. 3, 1985, pp. 279-294.

Furubotn, E. G. 'Co-Determination and the Efficient Partitioning of Ownership Rights in the Firm', *Journal of Institutional and Theoretic Economics,* Vol. 137 (1981), pp. 702-709.

George, H. *Progress and Poverty,* New York: Schalkenbach Foundation, 1979.

Georgescu-Roegen, N. 'Dynamic Models and Economic Growth' (1974), in: N. G-R, *Energy and Economic Myths: Institutional and Analytical Economic Essays,* New York: Pergamon, 1976.

Hahn, R. W. and Hester, G. L. 'Where do All the Markets Go? An Analysis of EPA's Emission's Trading Program'. Paper read at the Annual Meetings of the American Economic Association, New Orleans Louisiana, December 1986.

Hobbs Scheibla, S. 'Messy Clean Up: Superfund Turns into a Super Flop', *Barron's,* December 18, 1989, pp. 18, 19, 34.

Krabbe, J. J. 'Organistic Theory in Economics: The Contribution of the Historical School', *International Journal of Social Economics,* Vol. 14 (Number 3/4/5) (1987), pp. 105-117.

Kneese, A. V., Ayres, R. U. and d'Arge, R. C. *Economics and the Environment: A Materials Balance Approach,* Washington D.C.: Resources for the Future, 1970.

Mantell, E. H. 'On the Economics and the Politics of Environmental Protection: Policy Conflicts can be mitigated by Selective Enforcement and Tax-Finance Subsidies'. *American Journal of Economics and Sociology 44.4, October 1985, pp. 435-447.*
44.4, October 1985, pp. 435-447.

Oates, W. 'The Role of Economic Incentives in Environmental Policy'. Paper presented at the annual meetings of the American Economic

Association, New York, December 1988 in a session on 'Economics and the Environment'.

Schmoller, G. *Grundriss der allgemeinen Volkswirtschaftslehre* I, Leipzig: Duncker & Humblot, 1900 (1), 1923 (2).

Schumpeter, J. A. *History of Economic Analysis,* New York: Oxford University Press, 1954.

V
INTERNATIONAL TRADE

9

Protectionism, Rent and the Dynamics of Agricultural Degradation

RICHARD BODY

HENRY GEORGE never used the word ecology, for which he is not to be blamed for the word was yet to be uttered in his lifetime. Were he with us today, I suspect the word would often be on his lips. He would tell us, I believe, that the ecological argument for free trade was no less strong than either the moral or economic one. That is my theme. Let me see if I can persuade you of its truth.

The protectionist barriers to industrial trade, whether in the form of tariffs or otherwise, are a shadow of what they were and, though they are inherently pernicious, I put them outside the argument. It is agricultural protectionism that is rampant and doing vast and incalculable damage to the economies of every country in the world, with Hong Kong, devoid of any farmers, the one exception. This is the protectionism that is ecologically damaging. There is a parallel between the economic and ecological cost of agricultural protection; as one rises, so does the other.

In Scotland there are many rugged mountains, though they call them hills, and nothing is grown upon them. They are the habitat of the wild red deer that gain some sustenance on the lower ground below the barren rocks. Of all these bleak points, Ben Nevis may be the bleakest, where snow settles most of the year and the cold winds blow in all seasons. Yet even on Ben Nevis, the people of Scotland could grow thousands of bananas, and even export them to Jamaica and Ecuador or any other corner of the world where there is a surplus of cheap bananas that cannot be sold.

Allow agricultural protectionism to divert enough money from efficient industries by way of taxation, and hand it over to inefficient banana growers on Ben Nevis, then any difficulty in either growing or selling them can be overcome.

Of course, it is absurd, but let me spell out the absurdity to show what I mean. First, you collect great quantities of earth and carry it to the slopes of Ben Nevis; next you construct elaborate glass houses; then install central heating and, finally, plant your bananas. All this might cost many millions of dollars; never mind, the taxpayers have been coerced and the money is there. Eventually a crop is grown; perhaps no more than fifty or a hundred are fit to eat; again never mind, the economic cost may be a million dollars a banana, but the money is there to subsidise their sales, and over in Jamaica where a banana costs a dime, we can sell them at just a little less with a generous enough export subsidy.

Absurdity is only a matter of degree. In England we could buy wheat from the world market at £50 a tonne or thereabouts. The Common Agricultural Policy prevents us from doing so; instead we have ploughed up a quarter of the North Yorkshire moors where once not even sheep were kept, and only the grouse were to be seen; and having drained and fertilised the ground at vast expense and built new roads to carry the farm machinery up to the moorland heights, we are growing wheat on some of this land. It sells for over twice the price of wheat of far better quality that can be imported at £50 a tonne. The difference between the two prices exists because the wheat that costs £50 a tonne is grown on a farm that is naturally suited for the purpose and the wheat costing over £100 a tonne is extracted from a soil and climate that manifestly is not naturally suited to the growing of wheat.

To any Georgist this is painfully obvious. Wheat should be grown where nature has indicated that it should be. Monetary cost is the indicator.

Let us see how this monetary cost is made up. The first requirement of a farmer is land, and the cheaper he can buy it or rent it the better for him; but only in conditions of universal free trade will the monetary cost of the land be governed exclusively by its quality. Once protectionism creeps in the price becomes distorted: it goes up in value if protectionism begins in the country where it is, and its value goes down in a country exporting without protectionism.

What has happened in the United Kingdom would have interested Henry George. It is not very difficult to calculate the total sum of money that has been given to agriculture either directly in subsidies by the Government and EEC or indirectly by artificially high food prices paid by the consumer for each of the years since a system of guaranteed prices began after World War II. Each year's figure ought to be adjusted to allow for inflation. Adding up the figures we have a total of £70,000 millions.

Now let us see what has happened to the price of farmland in the same period. We have five grades of land and in respect of each we can look up the record for farm sales just before the system began. Again, we must make adjustments for inflation so we express them in the current value of the £. That done, we look at the value of the land today. We next take the number of acres that exist for each of the five grades of land and multiply by the value of each acre. A simple subtraction of one total from the other gives us the sum of money by which the value of farmland has risen over and above the value of inflation. Can you guess the answer? Were Henry George here now, he could raise his hand and say the answer was £70,000 millions. Indeed, it is.

Now when some time ago I did these sums, I shouted 'Alleluyah!' I thought I would become famous, having discovered some new economic truth which would be called Body's Law. It was not to be. David Ricardo long ago had said it all in his *Theory of Rent.* It comes to this: if the state artificially raises the price of a product, the value of the asset that produces it will rise to a level that nullifies the advantage gained by the producer.

Ricardo was writing about the Corn Laws in the first decade of the 19th Century England. He showed that if you tax imported wheat to raise its price to protect the farmer, the price of land — i.e. rent — will go up and continue to go up until it wipes out the benefit to the farmer of taxation. The beneficiary is a man who owns the land.

Monetary cost, as I said, is the indicator of where nature decrees something should be grown. It follows that protectionism will foul up the cost. By artificially raising the value of farmland, it puts up the rent that has to be paid. The more protection that is given, the more rents go up, and the more rents go up, the more the farmer must persuade his acres to yield a larger crop.

In days gone by this could not be done. At best, only a marginal increase could be gained because we did not know how to increase yields. The sciences related to agriculture have changed all that; amazing advances have been made, and today yields may be two, three or four times more than they were. Thus if rising rents or mortgage costs force farmers to try to increase their production, means are there to enable them to do it. These means have an economic cost measured in monetary terms, but they also have an ecological cost which is not so easily quantifiable.

Soil erosion is measurable however; and when farmers are forced by unfair competition or goaded by subsidies to increase their yield, soil is invariably lost to a degree that cannot be replaced naturally. In recent years Australian wheat growers have seen their price driven down to £45 a tonne as a result of the EEC dumping wheat on to the world market at a price even lower than that. So they have flogged their land to such an extent that to grow one tonne of wheat they may lose up to thirteen tonnes of soil. Yet there are great areas of Australia capable of growing wheat at the lowest economic cost and because land is cheap there, the farmer need grow no more than half a tonne to the acre to earn a good livelihood; but that supposes he faces fair competition. With land at only a few dollars an acre, such an Australian farmer has his first requirement for the production of food or fibre at so favourable a cost that he has no or little need for nitrates and pesticides, both of which can do great ecological damage. He can afford a low input to low output system. The more he has to raise his output, the greater will be the need for additional inputs. These are primarily artificial fertilisers and pesticides. Thus the higher the input to output ratio the greater the danger of ecological harm being done by those two inputs.

High levels of output also require the farmer to make more economic use of his land. Some people may see no harm in that. What, then, do you think of the farmer who fells all his trees and rips up all his hedgerows because they take up space which could be used for growing a crop? In making more economic use of his land he is also tearing away the habitat of the wildlife and changing the scenery of the landscape for the worse — unless one thinks trees are ugly things.

If the world's population can be fed on a universal low input to low output ration, it would be economically sensible to do so because the cost of production would obviously be lower, as would be the cost to the consumer. We would also be growing our food and fibres in those areas where it was most economical to do so, for the elements of nature — the soil, climate and terrain — had decreed that those areas were naturally the most suitable for the purpose. This ideal requires a policy of total free trade throughout the world. It means, of course, that nature is on the side of free trade. Such a low input to low output system prevailing in the world ensures that our supply of food and fibres comes in a way which make the least demand upon our land — and here I use the word 'land' as Henry George would, in its wider sense, in other words, upon our natural environment.

Once we start to produce our food or fibres in areas that are not of the lowest economic cost, we artificially raise the input to output ratio so that we begin to use inputs that would otherwise be unnecessary. Their purpose is to induce the land to yield more than it does naturally. And what is against nature, we can be sure, is ecologically damaging.

With manufacturing or any other industry, except fishing, which is comparable to farming, we can increase production by raising the input to output ratio without necessarily doing any harm ecologically. This cannot be the case where we increase the production of food or fibres because the increase in the inputs needed to raise output act as agents to direct the course of nature.

In conditions of complete free trade food and fibres are grown at the lowest economic cost; and this means at the lowest input to output ratio that is necessary to enable supply to match demand. The greater the degree of agricultural protectionism, the more the economic cost of production rises, and with it the input to output ratio.

Every time the input to output ratio is stepped up artificially by agricultural protectionism there is a change of venue for some form of production; and the diversion must be from a natural to a less natural venue. The consequent change in the level of inputs must with agricultural protectionism be always upwards. This diversion will take two forms: fewer inputs will be used where they can be made most effective and used instead where they are less effective; secondly, a greater use of inputs will be required, and more of them will therefore be extracted from nature. The latter is of major importance. Many of them are natural resources which are finite. Thus agricultural protectionism goads us to use up finite resources more quickly than would otherwise be the case. This is a cause for concern unknown to Henry George; for in his day the inputs used by agriculture were replaceable and infinite. Let us spell them out.

Energy came from human labour and equine effort. Man and horse did the work, and most farm machinery was simple and replaceable without damage to our natural resources. The horse has gone and man's muscle is almost incidental. Oil has taken over. Total energy consumption for the United Kingdom is, in round figures, 200 million tonnes of oil or oil equivalent annually. Sir Kenneth Blaxton of the Rowett Research Institute has calculated that the production and processing of our food uses 26% of that figure. It represents about one tonne of oil to one acre of our cultivated land. It also represents a sixteen fold increase since the days of the tractor. It does not mean that we should scrap all our tractors and combines and breed a million horses to take their place; but, as agricultural protectionism always has the effect of inducing us to grow more than we need and in the wrong places, the consumption of this finite resource is made greater than it should be.

Then there are the artificial fertilisers. The more we are induced by protectionism to produce food in less suitable places, the greater the need for these inputs. Nitrates come from oil and we in the UK have quadrupled our use for them and thus added to the depletion of a natural resource. They are not used, and need not be used, by hundreds of thousands of farmers who have the soil, climate and terrain to grow food with a low input to low output ratio — that is, if the rest of the world would allow it. Phosphates, also used as artificial fertiliser, are being extracted from the earth at a rate so fast that this precious finite resource will be exhausted in the area where we know they exist. What happens then? There may be a case for using these artificial fertilisers that stimulate production in countries where hunger prevails, and they are the poorest countries of the Third World. How can they afford to pay for them when the comparatively rich farmers in the protectionist countries of the West outbid them? Free trade would have the effect of naturally restricting their use to where they would be most cost-effective. Then there is that other weapon of modern agriculture — the pesticide. The modern farmer in the protectionist economies has got himself hooked upon this form of poisoning. And pesticides are nothing unless poisonous. By definition a pesticide kills pests.

The pests killed are of thousands of species, mainly of course insects and those herbs that farmers may call weeds. Yet they all have a place in ecology. What is a pest to the farmer is — not may be — a food for another creature in nature's world. Since that great American writer, Rachel Carson gave us *The Silent Spring*, there has been no serious dispute about the danger of pesticides. Birds by the million have died from their use. The otter in England has become virtually extinct; for we now know that man's poison sprayed upon the crops has percolated into the rivers to enter the fish and the poison has passed into the otter. Nature's world is in balance. Every single part of it has either life within it or is a source of life for a living creature. It is one vast predatory system; and even every atom of the human body will have a predator at some stage. Predators, even the imperceptible microbe, keep nature's world in balance; and given the chance make it ecologically infinite.

Today's man rushes in with his pesticides, incapable of comprehending the endless catalogue of consequences. Of course, he does it on this scale for one reason only. The accusing finger must be pointed at agricultural protectionism. By now it must be clear that in conditions of universal free trade, the minimum input to output ratio would exist, and therefore the fewest number of pesticides would be used to poison the earth.

I have said nothing about the destruction of the rain forests, and only hinted at the loss of ancient woodlands and thousands of miles of hedgerows, as has been the case in England. Nor have I told of food processed from our animals. This brings us to the use of hormones and antibiotics, both necessary in modern animal mass production. Surely there is no need for me to overegg the pudding? The argument must be irrefutable.

Protectionism distorts the natural flow of trade — that is its purpose. Production is increased where it would not be if nature had her way; and it is increased where it would not be, also if she had her own way. The factors of production are forced to change with protectionism; and of the four that economists speak about, land, capital, labor, and enterprise, the ecologist says land is the most precious. And who dares contradict him? Because it is precious, we should use it carefully — and that means ecologically. To use a word sadly out of fashion, we ought to be good husbandmen. As land includes all our natural resources, we should husband them by using them, particularly those that are finite, to the most effect. That implies matching the supply of food with its demand by a ratio of input to output as low as we can make it. That can only be achieved by free trade among all nations. True, that may be an impossible dream for some years to come. But at least we can strive to attain it, and in so doing set an example for those who fail to understand it.

Free trade makes sure that production, whether of food or of anything else, takes place where the four factors of production blend effectively with the maximum cost. In any form of production where land — in its widest sense — is an important factor, regard must be had for its right use. As it can not be ecologically right to use land wrongly, it must follow that in agricultural production, which is more dependent upon land than any other, its right use is of the greatest concern. The more a farmer is goaded to take more from his land than it can yield naturally or is prevented from taking as much as it can do so naturally (and both are the consequences of agricultural protectionism) the more land is wrongly used. Nature's resources are accordingly diverted artificially by state coercion.

Thus the more the natural flows of international trade are messed up by agents of state control, the more nature herself is messed up. Messing up nature is my term for the gratuitous and unnecessary damage to our ecology.

10

Trade and Investment: preserving the fruits of liberty

C. LOWELL HARRISS

ONE MAJOR theme of Henry George's life work was that international free trade serves human welfare. 'Protection' — man-made restrictions — must do needless harm.

He wrote brilliantly in condemning the use of the coercive power of government to restrict opportunity to buy and sell across national boundaries. For another occasion, I gathered a few selections from his *Protection or Free Trade.*[1]

'Free' and 'freedom' are terms whose general sense we understand. At the margins of application they do have elements that can be subject to debate. For present purposes, however, we can think of freedom as being limited by governmentally (politically) created restrictions on what human beings may do. The limitations imposed by government, one must recognize, may provide support for private actions (monopolistic) that also limit what others can do. For example, 'voluntary' restrictions on the steel and autos and textiles that may be exported to the United States from other countries embody, in fact, governmental actions. Moreover, they burden American consumers without yielding revenue to government, as would a tariff.

Buying, selling, and investing across national boundaries are not as free from governmental restrictions as George would have wished. But the mammoth volume — and it is mammoth — of transactions today must testify to both opportunity and its successful use.

There has been a huge growth of foreign trade and investment. Measurement of the increase from decade to decade presents problems. For example, the creation of two or more countries where there was once one has sometimes turned what would have been domestic trade into international — East-West Germany before reunification, for instance.

There are many other reasons why it is difficult to measure changes in foreign trade. New products and services are not readily compared with those of the past. Inflation and the use of many new currencies greatly complicate the use of money figures for comparisons over time. The numbers collected have errors from many sources — various kinds of services, as well as smuggled goods, escape counting; and record keeping is incomplete. Many final products consist of assemblages of parts fabricated in several different countries, frequently by the same multinational company.

Yet one conclusion must stand out from the best data available: the growth of international trade, of both goods and services, has been very great indeed. The same applies to flows of both short- and long-term investment capital.

This growth of international trade and investment has been part of the striking economic progress which is evident when we compare economic conditions five decades ago with those of today. (I suggest 50 years because it was then that the United States was embarking on its campaign for the reciprocal reduction of tariffs. Secretary of State Cordell Hull had succeeded in getting authority to use the treaty power, as against Congressional determination of specific tariff rates.)

The U.S. population today is 248 million (115 million, or 90 percent, more than in 1939). The increased numbers of people have also raised their levels of economic well-being. Adjusting for inflation, one finds that personal consumption expenditures per capita have risen by around 150 percent. Since World War II the populations of many other, but not all, lands have likewise achieved a remarkable improvement in levels of living.

One cause of what has been the substantial human accomplishment of higher living standards for more persons has been the opportunity to deal more freely across national boundaries — buying and selling goods, the provision and receipt of services, and the investment of capital. The US Gross National Product in today's dollars is nearly 20 times that of 1950 (well after World War II). Foreign trade increased, relatively, even more. Exports from this country are around 25 times, and imports 30 times, as high as in 1950. (These figures show orders of magnitude, not precise amounts.)

When foreign trade grows from year to year, people must not only expect to benefit, but also succeed in doing so. The buying and selling result from choices made voluntarily. Some of the reasons for, and sources of, benefits from exchange deserve note, even though space limitations restrict us.

Nature did not distribute resources equally over the world. Climate and topography vary significantly. Denver cannot accommodate ocean liners. Copenhagen does not offer good conditions for skiing. Fortunately, exchange can overcome obstacles that inhere in nature. Residents of Denver drink coffee, and Danes ski. In short, we can overcome the effects of obstacles growing out of the way the world was created. Doing so often requires movement across national boundaries.

It is not only natural resources that are distributed unequally. The historical accumulations of capital equipment and of human skills differ widely from one place to another over the world. Trade permits consumers and producers, even those in lands not yet developed, to draw upon facilities in other countries.

People in one area (nation) can benefit by specializing and utilizing intensively those resources that are relatively plentiful at home, and importing goods and services that are relatively more plentiful elsewhere. The division of labor — specialization — permits human beings to develop skills. Goods and services that would otherwise be utterly unobtainable can be had when people specialize and exchange. Intricate and expensive equipment can be used when enough customers can be served to permit the costs to be recovered. Consumers who could not possibly afford such production facilities can reap the fruits by exchange, not only the exchange that is possible within the boundaries of their own country but over the world.

For many reasons, larger volume of operations often permits lower cost per unit. There are economies of scale — the larger the scale of output, the lower the cost per item. The lowest cost per unit, benefiting all customers, may require volumes of output for which markets in just one country are too small.

Another benefit from freedom of international trade deserves emphasis. The freer that trade is over the world, the greater the forces of competition. Tendencies toward monopoly and the restrictions it produces are weakened by competition: the larger the area of effective competition — many economies are distinguished from one or a few — the smaller the burdens of monopoly. The reduction of governmentally created obstacles to exchange must enlarge the opportunity for more and more human beings — and in ways beyond the obvious.

Despite the benefits of freedom and the burdens from restrictions, governments continue to impose obstacles — man-made impediments to the achievement of higher levels of living. But, through painstaking effort, changes that Henry George would have praised have been achieved.

Old and New Man-made Barriers

The period since World War II has seen a drastic reduction in tariffs and the freeing of currency movements and of capital for investment. Agreements among governments to resist pressures to erect obstacles have undoubtedly headed off moves to create new barriers and to raise old ones. No one can know what would have come about in the absence of the General Agreement on Tariffs and Trade (GATT), with its buttressing of forces of freedom. In the USA and many other countries political leadership continues generally to endorse support for encouraging trade. (Lip service is not always matched by action.) The articulation of intellectual support for freedom may have had inspiration in Henry George's work. Although any direct connection in forming opinion will have been rather long ago, 'ideas have consequences,' even though delayed.

Today, however, there are still all too many restrictions on foreign trade, and pressures to create new ones, chiefly non-tariff barriers. There are quotas and other quantitative restrictions, such as 'voluntary' agreements, orderly marketing arrangements, anti-dumping rules, sanitary codes, and so on.

Henry George's world did not know many of the kinds of restrictions that are imposed today. Human ingenuity finds new ways to use, or propose to use, the compulsion of government to impair freedom of trade and investment, devices to create a 'new protectionism.' Rationalizations for doing so challenge those of us who advocate freedom. For example, policies to regulate agriculture for domestic reasons have led to costly impediments to world trade. For a time, but perhaps less so today, persons trying to plan the development of poor economies often believed that trade restrictions could be used to advance progress, e.g., import substitution policies that not only raise costs to consumers but impair the ability to compete in world markets.

Mercantilist-type considerations account for some government export subsidies that lead other governments to complain of unfairness and to counter with new obstacles. Actual or alleged dumping, for example, selling abroad at prices below those at home, may lead governments elsewhere to impose burdens such as U.S. countervailing duties. 'Buy American' laws for Federal, state, and local procurement give domestic sellers preference while burdening the taxpayer. Some governments impose domestic-content requirements, for example 50 percent of the final value of a product must consist of domestic input (labor and components).

Protection or Free Trade,[2] written more than a century ago, could not discuss some of today's realities. Yet George's reasoning stands. The case for freedom, for opportunity, remains overwhelmingly valid. The dangers from the use of government coercion are unending.

Today, just as a century ago when Henry George presented the case for free trade, there are advocates for restriction. (The term 'restriction' seems preferable to 'protection,' with the latter's connotations of something good.) Some arguments are the same. But there are elements that are modern.

Let us note a general reality of great significance: there will always be opportunities to do 'good things' by concentrating benefits on a relatively small group, taking a little from each of a vastly larger number. The benefits are not 'for free.' The restrictive action, such as a tariff or a quota, imposes costs. They may be completely or largely hidden. Typically they impose small burdens on many to provide relatively large benefits for the few.

This type of imbalance exists often. For example, as an economist I know that U.S. trade restrictions keep sugar prices in this country at a multiple of the free world market price. As I drafted this paper I heard the broadcaster tell me and millions of other listeners that sugar makes up only a small fraction of the price of a candy bar. His message: 'You get a bargain.' But you can be sure that those persons who impose the burdens expect not pennies but great fortunes.

Sometimes 'discrepancies' — much for a few taken from millions in small amounts — result from free choice, such as mass patronage of professional athletics that permits stars to receive 40 or more times the earnings of the average American; in such cases one can approve (without necessarily applauding) the choices of others. But when the coercive power of government is used to force us to pay others without any assurance, any presumption, or perhaps even any pretense, of informed consent, must we not condemn the process?

I cannot vouch for, but I can believe, reports that restrictions on steel imports have destroyed many more jobs in U.S. companies using steel (some in export production) than have been saved in steel production. Such restrictions permit U.S. steel companies to charge prices higher than in a free market. The limits on the import of autos from Japan made American consumers pay more for cars than they would have if the market had been free; the presumed beneficiaries, employees of auto companies, generally get higher compensation relative to effort and skill than most Americans. The program of quota restriction was advanced and put into effect with talk about the benefits, which are to a relative few; only minuscule attention was given to the costs forced on the far larger numbers of consumers who must suffer.

The few who expect relatively much have incentive to devote concentrated effort. The many have so little at stake individually that they cannot afford to organize and press their interests.

The infant industry argument does have appeal — shield an industry until it can get established. Much evidence confirms the reality of the learning curve — unit costs decline as producers gain experience. Getting into such positions does provide strength for expansion and competition in the world. But converting a theoretical possibility into practical, real-life achievement does not work out. Infants may grow but will not admit to being grown up enough to stand without the continuation of shielding and the power to charge consumers more than free market prices.

The use of tariffs and other restrictions as instruments for bargaining in international arenas has received support in Congress. The usual case says to foreign governments, in effect, 'We shall impose burdens on American consumers to induce you to reduce barriers that restrict exports from the U.S. (and burden your consumers).' Or: 'Your companies are selling to American consumers for less than to your domestic consumers — dumping; we shall therefore impose burdens at home that reduce this unfair competition for American producers.' Perhaps such bargaining can bring more good results than bad.

I am skeptical. Let us keep our eyes open to see whether results can be determined and evaluated. The retaliation to be expected can start a series of responses that lead to deplorable results.

Another consideration may differ from anything in Henry George's day — consideration for the balance of international payments. The United States has had a deficit for several years, and it continues. (Presumably the deficit is to be condemned, not an obvious conclusion.) Will not putting quotas, tariffs, and other restrictions on imports help to reduce imports and thus cut the deficit in the balance of payments? Probably not much, if any, and at excessive cost. But on these matters, in a world of flexible exchange rates, one encounters complexities and uncertainties. Experts believe that trade restrictions lead not to reductions in balance of payments deficits so much as to the lowering of real income.

National defense looms larger in American life today than in Henry George's time, and it deserves respect in the formulation of economic policy. But what, really, will serve national defense? This question requires far more than the testimony of parties directly interested in specific industries or activities. I would be reluctant to pass judgments on real-world situations but am inclined to be skeptical, especially as to the effectiveness and efficiency of trade restrictions as a means of serving the national defense.

Foreign Policy

Complications arise from the use of international trade and finance to try to help implement foreign policy. Policy makers see many and varied specific objectives in a complex and changing world. In matters of foreign policy and trade, economic results do not include all that will be taken into account. Evaluation cannot rest on reasons that would be adequate in a straightforward world. One thinks of prohibitions applying to trade with South Africa, Nicaragua, North Korea, Communist China, Iran, and the Soviet Union, and, in contrast, special trade provisions for Israel and Caribbean countries.

In trying to judge such policies and proposals for others, one must recognize, first, a set of considerations that involve the desirability of the noneconomic foreign policy goals. Are they highly meritorious? Or of dubious merit? Or definitely wrong?

Then there will be consideration of the effectiveness of the trade provisions in achieving the goal(s). Will what is actually done really help? Predicting what is likely to come will involve questions. What retaliations may be imposed? Evaluating what seems to have resulted in somewhat similar cases, if any, will be difficult.

Then one must ask about the cost relative to the probable benefit. Will countries generally friendly to us cooperate? Or will they (their businesses) try to take advantage of new opportunities to fill gaps left by the U.S. withdrawal? No good answer may be available. The future reactions of others are unknowable, although one may draw upon some past experience for guidance. Will domestic producers freed of some competition from abroad raise prices? While reason and available evidence may lead to likely conclusions, most often one deals with unique situations and no comparable precedents.

The domestic industries affected may, or may not, be able to supply useful information about what to expect. Can biases be adequately measured? What will be the economic and political reactions? Some American farmers did not welcome embargoes on export of grain to Russia. Interrelations among parts of the economy and of the society as a whole cannot be adequately taken into account.

I wish that in good conscience I could endorse general principles about the use of restrictions on foreign trade and investment for varied noneconomic goals of foreign policy. But such presumption would not be responsible. Conditions differ. What is clear is the need for the best analysis possible, kept up to date. There is also need for keeping open the opportunities for revision or abandonment of policies when conditions warrant. Beware of creating new special interests resting upon the trade restrictions!

The temptation to misuse potentially positive arguments for trade restrictions to help achieve foreign policy goals can be strong. This whole range of considerations presents disturbing aspects. And one must also recognize that foreign policy goals can be hampered by trade restrictions growing out of domestic politics. U.S. sugar regulations hurt the Philippines and some Caribbean and Central American countries that the United States would like to see in a better economic condition.

International trade and finance are subjects of wide concern. Every country faces current issues of significance. The daily news touches on matters of trade barriers, currency exchange rates, international loans, and conditions for competition. The further reduction of barriers to exchange in Europe scheduled for 1992, along with the recent Canadian-United States treaty and the continuing negotiations under GATT, will keep the issues alive. There are matters for decision at frequent intervals. Action will be required; even a decision to do nothing requires the act of decision. Large amounts, both financial and real, can be involved in trade actions that may hinge on small differences between two sides. Tipping the balance one way or the other can result from just a little more or less effort and pressure by the public.

The public must be provided with the kind of statement of principles that Henry George articulated. His language is so vivid that it can serve today. It is timeless. Does the fact that his words have existed for more than a century mean there is no need to repeat the message? By no means. No more than a handful of persons active today will have read Henry George on free trade. Whatever public opinion seems to be, the depth of conviction as to the principle of economic freedom can certainly use support. Where it is weak, additional effort by the advocates of free trade could contribute to constructive action.

The two great themes of Henry George's work — free trade and reform of the property tax — are elements of a set of principles for enlarging human welfare, for enabling men and women to utilize their potential for a better life.

NOTES

1. C. Lowell Harriss, 'Guidance from an Economics Classic,' *The American Journal of Economics and Sociology*, Vol. 48, No. 3, July 1989, pp. 351-356. Views expressed there and in this chapter are the author's and not necessarily those of any organization with which he is associated.
2. Henry George, *Protection or Free Trade*, New York, 1886. Current edition published by Robert Schalkenbach Foundation, New York, 1980.

APPENDIX

Open Letter to Mikhail Gorbachev

Three Nobel prize-winning economists — Franco Modigliani, James Tobin and Robert Solow — are among a distinguished list of scholars who signed an open letter to Mikhail Gorbachev. Their letter urged the Soviet President to retain land in public ownership, and to raise government revenue by charging market rents for the use of land.

Mr Gorbachev believed that land — unlike capital — was unique, and ought to remain in social ownership. Under public pressure to privatise land, during the summer of 1990, he declared that a union-wide referendum ought to be held, first, to determine the will of the people. On December 24, 1990, the Congress of People's Deputies agreed to stage that referendum.

The proposal to fund government expenditure out of the rent of land — rather than from taxation on labor or capital — is a policy most clearly associated with Henry George, who articulated the social benefits of this fiscal strategy in *Progress and Poverty* (1879).

Mr Mikhail Gorbachev,
President, Union of Soviet Socialist Republics.

Dear Mr Gorbachev:

The movement of the Soviet Union to a market economy will greatly enhance the prosperity of your citizens. Your economists have learned much from the experience of nations with economies based in varying degrees on free markets. Your plans for freely convertible currency, free trade, and enterprises undertaken and managed by individuals who receive the profit or bear the losses that result from their decisions are all highly commendable. But there is a danger that you will adopt features of our economies that keep us from being as prosperous as we might be. In particular, there is a danger that you may follow us in allowing most of the rent of land to be collected privately.

It is important that the rent of land be retained as a source of government revenue. While the governments of developed nations with market economies collect some of the rent of land in taxes, they do not collect nearly as much as they could, and they therefore make unnecessarily great use of taxes that impede their economies — taxes on such things as incomes, sales and the value of capital.

Social collection of the rent of land and natural resources serves three purposes. First, it guarantees that no one dispossesses fellow citizens by obtaining a disproportionate share of what nature provides for humanity. Second, it provides revenue with which governments can pay for socially valuable activities without discouraging capital formation or work effort, or interfering in other ways with the efficient allocation of resources. Third, the resulting revenue permits utility and other services that have marked economies of scale or density to be priced at levels conducive to their efficient use.

The rental value of land arises from three sources. The first is the inherent natural productivity of land, combined with the fact that land is limited. The second source of land value is the growth of communities; the third is the provision of public services. All citizens have equal claims on the component of land value that arises from nature. The component of land value that arises from community growth and provision of services is the most sensible source of revenue for financing public services that raise the rental value of surrounding land. These services include roads, urban transit networks, parks, and public utility networks for such services as electricity, telephones, water and sewers. A public revenue system should strive to collect as much of the rent of land as possible, allocating the part of rent derived from nature to all citizens equally, and the part derived from public services to the governmental units that provide those services. When governments collect the increase in land value that results from the provision of services, they are able to offer services at prices that represent the marginal social cost of these services, promoting efficient use of the services and enhancing the rental value of the land where the services are available. Government agencies that use land should be charged the same rentals as others for the land they use, or services will not be adequately financed and agencies will not have adequate incentive or guidance for economizing on their use of land.

Some economists might be tempted to suggest that the rent can be collected publicly simply by selling land outright at auction. There are a number of reasons why this is not a good idea. First, there is so much land to be turned over to private management that any effort to dispose of all of it in a short period would result in an extreme depression in prices offered. Second, some persons who could make excellent use of land would be unable to raise money for the purchase price. Collecting rent annually provides access to land for persons with limited access to credit. Third, subsequent resale of land would enable speculators to make large profits unrelated to any productive services they offer, resulting in needless inequity and dissatisfaction. Fourth, concern about future political conditions would tend to depress offers. Collecting rent annually permits the citizens of future years to capture the benefits of good future public policies. Fifth, because investors tend to be averse to risk, general uncertainty about the future will tend to depress offers. This risk aversion is sidestepped by allowing future rental payments to be determined by future conditions. Finally, the future rent of land can more justly be claimed by future generations than by today's citizens. Requiring annual payments from the users of land allows each year's population to claim that year's rent. While the proceeds of sales could be invested for the benefit of future generations, not collecting the money in advance guarantees the heritage of the future against political excesses.

The attached Appendix provides a brief technical discussion of issues of the duration of rights to use land, the transfer of land, the assessment of land, social protection against the abuse and subsequent abandonment of run-down property, and redistribution among localities to adjust for differences in natural per capita endowments. While these issues need to be addressed, none of them present insoluble problems.

A balance should be kept between allowing the managers of property to retain value derived from their own efforts to maintain and improve property, and securing for public use the naturally inherent and socially created value of land. Users of land should not be allowed to acquire rights of indefinite duration for single payments. For efficiency, for adequate revenue and for justice, every user of land should be required to make an annual payment to the local government, equal to the current rental value of the land that he or she prevents others from using.

Sincerely,

NICOLAUS TIDEMAN, Professor of Economics,
Virginia Polytechnic Institute and State University.
WILLIAM VICKREY, President for 1992,
American Economic Association.
MASON GAFFNEY, Professor of Economics,
University of California, Riverside.
LOWELL HARRISS, Professor Emeritus of Economics,
Columbia University.
JACQUES THISSE, Professor of Economics,
Center for Operations Research and Econometrics,
Université Catholique de Louvain, Belgium.
CHARLES GOETZ, Joseph M. Hartfield Professor of Law,
University of Virginia School of Law.
GENE WUNDERLICH, Senior Agricultural Economist,
Economic Research Service, U.S. Department of Agriculture.
DANIEL R. FUSFELD, Professor Emeritus of Economics,
University of Michigan.
ELIZABETH CLAYTON, Professor of Economics,
University of Missouri at St. Louis.
ROBERT DORFMAN, Professor Emeritus of Political Economy,
Harvard University.
CARL KAYSEN, Professor of Economics,
Massachusetts Institute of Technology.
TIBOR SCITOVSKY, Emeritus Eberle Professor of Economics,
Stanford University.
RICHARD GOODE,
Washington, D.C.
SUSAN ROSE-ACKERMAN, Eli Professor of Law and Political
Economy, Yale Law School.
JAMES TOBIN, Sterling Professor Emeritus of Economics,
Yale University.
RICHARD MUSGRAVE, Professor Emeritus of Political Economy,
Harvard University.

FRANCO MODIGLIANI, Professor Emeritus of Economics,
Massachusetts Institute of Technology.
WARREN J. SAMUELS, Professor of Economics,
Michigan State University.
GUY ORCUTT, Professor Emeritus of Economics,
Yale University.
EUGENE SMOLENSKY, Dean of the School of Public Policy,
University of California, Berkeley.
TED GWARTNEY, Real Estate Appraiser and Assessor,
Anaheim, California.
OLIVER OLDMAN, Learned Hand Professor of Law,
Harvard University.
ZVI GRILICHES, Professor of Economics,
Harvard University.
WILLIAM BAUMOL, Professor of Economics,
Princeton University.
GUSTAV RANIS, Frank Altschul Professor of International Economics,
Yale University.
JOHN HELLIWELL, Professor of Economics,
University of British Columbia.
GIULIO PONTECORVO, Professor of Economics and Banking,
Graduate School of Business, Columbia University.
ROBERT SOLOW, Institute Professor of Economics,
Massachusetts Institute of Technology.
ALFRED KAHN,
Ithaca, New York.
HARVEY LEVIN, Augustus B. Weller Professor of Economics,
Hofstra University.

Appendix on Technical Issues

All individuals and enterprises should have the right to continue using the land they have been using, for as long as they are prepared to pay the rent of that land. The amount of rent to be paid will vary as the economy evolves. As is traditional in countries with market economies, if land is needed for some public purpose such as a highway, the judicial process should guarantee the user fair compensation for any improvements that have been made in good faith. Every user of land should also have the right to transfer ownership of the improvements on the land, together with the right to continue using the land upon payment of rent, to any buyer on any terms upon which they mutually agree.

For the rent of land to be collected publicly, land must be assessed, and then reassessed regularly. The assessment process is simplified by the fact that land rental values tend to change smoothly with location. Initially, a map of the value of land can be made by auctioning scattered sites on a rental basis, and then interpolating for the value of other sites, based on the experience of Western appraisers and assessors regarding the manner in which the value of land varies systematically. To update assessments in future years, the assessment office would auction sites that had been relinquished by their users, or sites with improvements that were almost fully depreciated, that had been acquired in voluntary transactions. Interpolation would again be used to estimate the rent of sites that had not been transferred.

With all or nearly all of the rent of land collected publicly, it would be necessary to guard against the possibility that users of land with fully depreciated improvements would abandon their property, leaving the State to demolish the improvements in preparation for the next use of the site. This potential problem can be avoided by requiring every user of land to post a government bond as a 'security deposit' that the land will not be abandoned in a run-down condition. Interest on the bond would be applied to the annual rent.

Collection of the rent of land is best managed by local governments, but justice, as well as efficiency in migration incentives, requires that the part of rent that is attributable to nature rather than community development be shared on an equal per capita basis. Thus there is need of clearinghouse mechanism, into which all localities would deposit collections of rent from nature in excess of the average per capita amount, and from which other localities would receive compensation for their deficiencies of rent from nature, relative to the average per capita amount.

About the Authors

Jürgen Backhaus (JSD 1976, PhD 1985, The University of Constance) has served as the Professor of Public Economics at the University of Limburg in the Netherlands since 1986. His publications and research cover most areas of public finance.

Sir Richard Body, a member of Britain's parliament since 1966, operates a farm in Berkshire, England. He is a former Chairman of the House of Commons Select Committee on Agriculture. He is the author of three books on agriculture, and a vigorous critic of political measures which distort the market in the food-producing sector.

James L. Busey (Ph.D., Ohio State University) became Professor Emeritus of Political Science at the University of Colorado in 1980, having taught there since 1952. He has published five books and monographs on Latin American political systems, and has written articles, chapters and book reviews about Latin American and Canadian political systems. He has lectured in Mexico, New Zealand, Great Britain, Brazil and Canada, and has done research in Mexico, Central America, South America, the Caribbean, Portugal and Spain.

Fred Harrison (B.A., Oxford, M.Sc. University of London) is an investigative journalist who has been, since 1987, Director of the Centre for Incentive Taxation. He writes the Centre's newsletter, *Economic Intelligence* and is editor of the 96-year-old bi-monthly journal, *Land and Liberty.* He is a co-author of *Critics of Henry George: A Centennial Appraisal* (Fairleigh Dickinson University Press, 1979) and the author of *The Power in the Land* (Shepheard-Walwyn, 1983).

C. Lowell Harriss (Ph.D., Columbia University) is Professor Emeritus in economics at Columbia University and Senior Advisor of the Academy of Political Science. He is President of the Robert Schalkenbach Foundation. He taught economics at Columbia from 1938 until 1981, when he became Executive Director of the Academy of Policy Science. He was awarded the 1990 Distinguished Service Award in Economic Education by the Joint Council on Economic Education and the National Association of Economic Educators.

Jerome F. Heavey (Ph.D., Pennsylvania State University) teaches economics at Lafayette College, is a member of the editorial board of the *American Journal of Economics and Sociology*, and is at work on a history of the pre-independence Irish land reform. He sees himself as 'one of the larger winners from state lotteries,' having written his doctoral dissertation on the subject.

Jacob Jan Krabbe studied economics at the NEH in Rotterdam, now Erasmus University. After graduating, he was appointed to the staff of Wageningen Agricultural University, where he now serves as associate professor [*universitair hoofddocent*]. He teaches economic theory, environmental economics and history of economic thought.

Richard Noyes has been editor and publisher of weekly newspapers in New Hampshire communities (*Monadnock Ledger, Salem Observer)* since 1956. He was an elected delegate to two Constitutional Conventions in that state (16th, 1974, and 17th, 1984). He is President of the International Union for Land Value Taxation and Free Trade. He wrote *At The Edge of Megalopolis: A history of Salem, N.H., 1900-1974.*

David Richards (M.A., Oxford) is senior researcher with the Economic and Social Science Research Association, London. He supervised a major portion of the research for *Costing the Earth* (London: Shepheard-Walwyn, 1989), and is engaged in a major research project applying Georgist economics to environmental issues.

Francis M. Smith (Ph.D.), now a business consultant, made his career as a colour chemist. He was technical director in a multi-national chemical company and President of both the Paint Research Association and the Oil and Colour Chemists' Association. As a consultant, he assists in the search for new inventions for long-term investment, and runs nursery workshops for the unemployed in down-town East Manchester.

T. Nicolaus Tideman (Ph.D., University of Chicago, 1969) is Professor of Economics at Virginia Polytechnic Institute and State University, where he has taught since 1975. He was visiting professor of economics at the University of Buckingham, England, 1985-86. He taught economics at Harvard 1969 to 1973, during which time he was a senior staff economist on the President's Council of Economic Advisors.

Index

Abalkin, Leonid, 79, 85
acid rain, 166
Ackerman, Bruce, 55
Adam Smith Institute, 171
Adams, John, 17, 40
Africa
  colonialism, 146-150
  land policy, 136
Aganbegyan, Abel, 83-84
Agis, 16
agrarian policy
  Soviet Union, 85-88
agrarian reform
  Central America, 122
agricultural protectionism, 8-9, 207-214
agriculture
  China, 88-90
Amazon basin, 168-169
Andelson, Robert, 162
Antarctica, 168
apartheid, 158
Arbenz, Jacobo, 115
Armas, Carlos Castillo, 115
Ayres, R. U., 183

Bain, Alexander, 18
bankruptcy, 20
Bantustans, 158
Baumol, William, 229
betterment, 63
Blaxton, Sir Kenneth, 212
Brazil
  rainforest, 168-170
  taxation system, 170
Breitel, Judge
  Penn Central Transportation Co vs City of New York case 5-6
Brentano, Lujo, 182
Bush, George, 9, 168

Cairncross, Frances, 167, 170
Camden Borough Council, 64
Canadian-United States treaty, 223
Canary Wharf, 64
capitalism, *see also* market economics
  failure, 13, 15, 20, 39
carbon dioxide, 167
carbon tax, 167, 169
Carson, Rachel, 213
Catholicism
  outlawed in Ireland in the 1690s, 143
Central America
  corruption, 122, 123-124
  geocracy, 121-129
  land reform, 121, 122-123
  Marxism, 116-121
  relations with the United States, 115-120
  socio-political adversity, 113-114
  taxation, 122
Chamberlain, Joseph, 149-150
Chamorro family, 124
China
  agricultural reform, 88-90
chlorofluorocarbons, 50
Churchill, Winston, 103
Civic Trust, 171
Clayton, Elizabeth, 228
Collor, President, 168
colonialism, 141-150
  Africa, 146-150
  Central America, 113-114, 123-124
  exploitation, 136, 141-150
  Ireland, 142-146
  vs imperialism, 141-142
Columbia Law Review, 23
Common Agricultural Policy, 208
commons, 101, 156
  auction, 157
  resources and pollution taxes, 162

communism, 13, 39, 41, *see also* Marxism; socialism
comparative advantage, 136-140
compensation, 63
  property rights, 47-58, 159
conceptual severance, 51-53
Condorcet, 24
confiscation
  property rights, 47-58
Cord, Steven, 21
Corn Laws, 209
corruption
  Central America, 122, 123-124
Costa Rica, 113-114
  effect of adoption of geocratic legislation, 127-128
  relations with United States, 115
  taxation, 122
Crossman, Richard H., 41
Crotty, Raymond, 142, 150
Czechoslovakia
  International Monetary Fund loan, 79, 98

Dales, J.H., 158
d'Arge, R.C., 183
Darwin, Charles, 17
Debayle, Anastasio Somoza, 118
debt-for-nature swaps, 169
defence, 221
deficits, 20
definitions
  betterment, 63
  planning gain, 62-63
deforestation, 156-157
Denman, Donald, 168
Denmark
  land tenure, 158
Department of the Environment
  Circular on Planning Gain, 62-63
Department of Health Services
  costing of services, 69
development land tax, 63
Dewey, John, 19
dialectics
  George Hegel, 14, 15-16, 112
Dickinson, John, 25
Dorfman, Robert, 228
Durant, Will, 16

East Germany
  socialism, 80-81
Eastern Europe
  post-Marxist reform 3-4, 103-104
  taxation post-socialism, 79-81
ecology, 155, *see also* environment; The Greens; natural resources
  land value taxation, 98
economic rent, 33, 101, 159
The Economist 19-20, 167-168
Edwards, Jonathan, 21, 36-37
  Freedom of Will, 40
efficient market system, 100-101
Ekins, Paul, 165
El Salvador
  Marxist leadership, 117
  relations with United States, 115
Elson, Professor Martin, 7
employees
  redeployment in the Soviet Union, 96
energy, 212
Engels, Friedrich, 15, 25
environment *see also* The Greens; natural resources
  land value taxation, 98, 174
  preservation, 155-158
  urban, 171
Epstein, Richard, 50
Europe
  1992, 223
European Economic Community
  Green movement, 166-167
  protectionism accorded to farmers, 8-9, 209
Evans, George, 31

farmland
  price, 9, 209
  Soviet Union, 86-88
fertilisers, 210, 212
Fichte, 16
financial exaction, 61
The Financial Times, 4, 70-71
Firestone Rubber Company, 146
food
  European Economic Community dumping, 8-9, 210
  Soviet Union, 85-88

foreign policy
  and international trade, 221-223
foreign trade
  and foreign policy, 221-223
  growth, 215-218
Fourth World Assembly, 165
free trade
  Henry George's theme, 223-224
  threat to 8-9, 218-223
Friedman, Milton, 94
Fusfeld, Daniel R., 228

Gaffney, Mason, 228
Garrison, William Lloyd, 21
General Agreement on Tariffs and Trade (GATT), 218, 223
  break down of talks in December 1990, 8-9
geocracy, 113, 126-127
  Central America, 121-129
  Costa Rica, 127-128
George, Henry, 2-3, 9
  birth, 17
  economic theory, 175-191
  The Land Question, 143-144
  on free trade, 223-224
  on property rights, 26-27
  on socialism, 103
  on technology, 182, 189
  Progress and Poverty, 4, 6, 16, 157, 174
  Protection or Free Trade, 215, 219
  The Science of Political Economy, 16
  Single Tax on the rental value of land, 4, 20-21, 33, 174, 176, 181, 188
  Social Problems, 7
George, Lloyd, 103
Georgescu-Roegen, Nicholas, 185
Ghana
  colonialism, 148-149
Gide, André, 41
Gilder, George, 18
Giles, Benjamin, 40
glasnost, 79, 84
Goetz, Charles, 228
Goldsmith, Oliver, 36
Goode, Richard, 228
Gorbachev, Mikhail, 3
  land ownership issue, 4-5, 104
  open letter to, 225-230
  post-Socialism, 77-79, 82-86
Gracchus, Tiberius, 16, 22, 23, 27
Greeley, Horace, 31
Green Party
  Community Ground Rent (CGR), 98, 160-162
  land tenure policy, 160
Green Revolution, 165
greenhouse effect, 166, 167
The Greens, 24, 155
  acceptability of Henry George's message, 159
  Green political parties, 160-164, 166-167
  land value taxation, 159-172
  Soviet Union, 163-164
  United States, 165-166, 167-168
Griliches, Zvi, 229
Grosvenor, Gerald (Sixth Duke of Westminster), 72
Die Grünen, 163, 170
The Guardian, 39
Guatemala
  Marxist leadership, 117
Guppy, Nicholas, 169
Guzmän, Abimael, 124
Gwartney, Ted, 229

Hahn, R. W., 193
Harris, Laurence, 39
Harriss, Lowell, 228
Harvard Law Review, 48
Haskins, Charles, 37
hazardous waste, 196-199
Hegel, George
  dialectics, 14, 15-16, 112
Heimert, Alan, 40
Helliwell, John, 229
Henry Stewart Conference Studies, 73-74
Hester, G. L., 193
homelessness, 20, 27
Honduras
  Marxist leadership, 117
  relations with United States, 115
Hull, Cordell, 216

Hungary
International Monetary Fund
loan, 79, 98

imperialism
vs colonialism, 141-142
incentives
consequences for the environment, 156-157
income tax
Poland, 80
infrastructure
Soviet Union, 97
inner cities, 171
Institute of Economic Affairs, 171
International Monetary Fund
loans to Warsaw Pact countries, 79, 98
international trade
and foreign policy, 221-223
growth, 216
investment
growth, 215-218
Iraq, 9
Ireland
colonialism, 142-146
land policy, 136
landlord and tenant relationship, 143-145

James, William, 19
Japan
land tax, 93
Meiji Revolution, 92-93
Jefferson, Thomas, 17, 31, 40
Johnson, Brian, 169
Julian, George Washington, 31

Kahn, Alfred, 229
Kaysen, Carl, 228
Kenya
colonialism, 142, 146-148
Kneese, A. V., 183
Knight, Thomas S., 18-19
Kulaks, 93
Kuwait, 9

Labour Party, 103

land *see also* natural resources
Georgist concept, 177-182, 189-196
land ownership
Soviet Union, 4-5, 104, 164
United Kingdom, 71-72
land prices, 9, 33-34, 58, 209
land redistribution
Soviet Union, 87-88
land reform
Central America, 121, 122-123
land speculation
United States, 36-38
land tenure
Denmark, 158
South Africa, 158
UK Green Party, 160
land value taxation, 33
100%, 47, 53, 55, 57-58
application, 225-230
environmentally friendly, 98, 174
Henry George's Single Tax, 4, 20-21, 33, 174, 176, 181, 188
property rights, 47-58
solution for post-socialist reform in the Soviet Union, 94, 96-104, 225-230
urged during Louis XVI's reign, 22
land values
as company assets, 70-71
change of land use increases, 68
disparity, 67-68
increase by granting of planning permission, 60-61
Latin America
geocracy, 121-129
land reform, 121
land tenure, 158
market economics, 126
privatisation, 126
Lenin, Vladimir Ilyich, 38
Levin, Harvey, 229
Leys, Colin, 147
Liberal Party, 103
liberty, 32, 41
Licinius, 36
The Living Economy Network (LEN), 164, 165

local authorities
  planning gain, 60-70
Locke, John, 15, 23
  on money, 28, 29
  Second Treatise on Civil Government, 25-30
London Borough of Newnham, 64
London Docklands Development Corporation (LDDC), 63-64
London Underground
  example in planning gain, 74
Longfield, Mountifort, 144
Louis XV, 22
Louis XVI, 22
Lycurgus, 36

MacPherson, C. B., 29-30
Madison, James, 30-32, 55
Malthus, 183, 185
Mantell, Edmund H., 194
market economics, 100-101, *see also* capitalism
  Latin America, 126
Marti, José, 125
Marx, Karl, 15, 23, 25
  on property, 26
  ridicule of Henry George, 102
Marxism, 24-25, 28, 80-81, 112-113, *see also* communism; socialism
  Central America, 116-121
Mazarr, Michael, J., 125
Michelman, Frank, 48, 53
Mill, John Stuart, 159, 162, 183
Miller, Perry, 37, 39
Modigliani, Franco, 225, 229
money
  John Locke's thesis, 28, 29
Monroe Doctrine, 118, 119
Moses, 36
Musgrave, Richard, 228
Myers, Norman, 169

natural resources
  economics, 177-191
  efficient exploitation, 155-158
  regulating use, 194
  reversal of impairment 196-202
  wasteful use by the Soviet Union 82-84, 86
New Options, 165
New Zealand
  Values Party, 163
Nicaragua
  Marxist leadership, 117-118
  Soviet involvement, 118-119
  United States intervention, 115-120
nitrates, 210, 212
Nock, Albert Jay, 35

Oates, Wallace, 193
O'Brien, Richard Barry, 144
oil, 212
Oldman, Oliver, 229
Oppenheimer, Franz, 35
opportunity cost, 136, 137-140
Orcutt, Guy, 229
ozone depletion, 50, 166

Paine, 15
Pearce, David, 167
Pearce Report, 157
Peirce, Charles Sanders, 17-19, 21-22, 42
  birth, 17
  Chance, Love and Logic 18
  on greed, 38
Penn Central Transportation Company
  Grand Central Station case 5-6
perestroika, 78, 79, 84, 86, 103
pesticides, 210, 213
Pham Van Dang, 118
phosphates, 212
physiocrats, 22, 113, 183
Pilkington family, 72
planning gain, 60-74
  definition, 62-63
  Department of Environment Circular, 62-63
  examples, 63-68, 74
  government support, 73-74
Podhoretz, Norman, 41
Poland
  International Monetary Fund loan, 79, 98
  taxation, 80
pollution permits, 163, 167
pollution taxes, 162-163, 167
Pontecorvo, Giulio, 229

population growth, 183, 185
poverty, 28-29
pragmaticism, 19, 22
pragmatism 18-19, 22
prices
and distribution of output, 139-140
and taxation, 94-96
land, 9, 33-34, 58, 209
pricing mechanism, 101
privatisation, 90-92
Latin America, 126
Water Boards of England and Wales, 71
production
and comparative advantage, 137-140
Henry George's definition, 182-183, 184
Progress and Poverty, 4, 6, 16, 157, 174
proletariat, 27, 28, 30, 39
property development
planning gain, 60-74
property rights
confiscation and compensation, 47-58, 159
Henry George's view, 26-27
John Locke's thesis, 26-27, 29-30
Karl Marx on, 26
Keystone Bituminous Coal Association vs DeBenedictus case 52-53
Penn Central Transportation Co vs City of New York case 5-6
Soviet Union, 104
United States, 30-32
protectionism, 215, 219
farmers in the European Economic Community, 8-9, 209

Quesnay, François, 23
quotas, 218, 220, 221

rack renting, 145
rainforests, 168
Ranis, Gustav, 229
Reagan, Ronald, 78
rent
theory of, 94-96
resources taxes, 162
Ricardo, David, 3, 33, 178, 183
comparative advantage, 136, 137
Principles of Political Economy and Taxation, 83
Theory of Rent, 209
Ridley, Nicholas, 68
roads
Soviet Union, 97
Rodney, Walter, 141, 149
Rogers, Will, 27
Roosevelt, Franklin D.
Wealth and Poverty, 32
Roscher, 185
Rose-Ackerman, Susan, 228
Rowett Research Institute, 212
The Royal Opera House, 65-66
Ryzkov, Nikolai, 79
St Columbia Hospice, 64
Samuels, Warren J, 229
Sandino, Augusto César, 116
Satin, Mark, 165
Schilling, 16
Schmoller, Gustav, 182, 183, 185
School of Living, 165
Schumpeter, J. A., 176-177, 178, 180
Scitovsky, Tibor, 228
severance taxes, 162
slave trade, 149
slavery, 56
Smith, Adam, 3, 15, 23, 101-102
Wealth of Nations, 25, 34-35, 137
Smolensky, Eugene, 229
Social Problems, 7
socialism, 28, 41, 103, *see also* communism; Marxism and Henry George, 103
and Mikhail Gorbachev, 77, 103
collapse, 16, 20, 25, 125
soil erosion, 210
Solon, 36
Solow, Robert, 225, 229
Somoza dynasty, 124
Somoza, Anastasio, 116
South Africa
land tenure, 158
Soviet Union
agrarian policy, 85-88
food, 85-88
Green parties, 163-164

Soviet Union – *contd.*
involvement in Nicaragua, 118-119
Land Law 1990, 164
land ownership, 4-5, 104, 164
post-Marxist reform, 3-4, 77-110
Property Law 1990, 104
wasteful use of natural resources, 82-84, 86
Sowell, Thomas, 20
Spain
Central American colonies, 113-114, 123-124
Spretnak, Charlene, 166
Stalin, 93
Stoddard, John, 37
subsidies
consequences for the environment 156-157, 210
Sun Yat-sen, 3, 89
Survival International, 169

takings, 48-58
tax evasion
Central America, 122
taxation *see also* land value taxation
and prices 94-96
Central America, 122
colonial Africa, 147-148
Costa Rica, 122
post-socialist Eastern Europe, 79-81
technology
Henry George's views, 182, 189
Thatcher, Margaret, 3, 78, 166
Third World, 8
Thisse, Jacques, 228
Tideman, Nicolaus, 23, 228
Tobin, James, 225, 228
Tolstoy, Leo, 3, 78
Tower Hamlets Borough Council, 64
Town and Country Planning Acts, 60, 62
trade restrictions, 218-221
Turgot, Jacques, 22
Turner, Frederick Jackson, 31-32
Turner, James, 40-41

United Kingdom
planning gain, 60-74
United States
constitutions, 25, 40
Green movement, 165-166, 167-168
land ownership, 30-32
land speculation, 36-38
relations with Central America 115-120
Super Fund legislation, 175, 197, 199
takings, 48-58
urban environment, 171

value added tax
Poland, 80
Values Party, 163
Vanderbilt, William, 115
Vaughn, Karen I., 29-30
Vickrey, William, 228

wages
command economy, 81
Walker, William, 115
Wallace, Alfred Russel, 17
Water Boards of England and Wales
privatisation, 71
welfare state
United States, 27, 32
West Germany
Die Grünen, 163, 170
Westminster City Council, 65, 69
Westminster, Sixth Duke of, 72
Whelan, Thomas, 116
Winthrop, John, 39-40
Woolf, Leonard, 147, 149
Worldwide Fund for Nature, 169
Wright, Richard, 41
Wunderlich, Gene, 228

Yeltsin, Boris
on land ownership, 4

Zuccotti, Juan Carlos, 123